THE 'HITLER MYTH'

The 'Hitler Myth'

Image and Reality in
the Third Reich

IAN KERSHAW

Oxford   New York

OXFORD UNIVERSITY PRESS

Oxford University Press, Walton Street, Oxford OX2 6DP

Oxford New York
Athens Auckland Bangkok Bombay
Calcutta Cape Town Dar es Salaam Delhi
Florence Hong Kong Istanbul Karachi
Kuala Lumpur Madras Madrid Melbourne
Mexico City Nairobi Paris Singapore
Taipei Tokyo Toronto

and associated companies in
Berlin Ibadan

Oxford is a trade mark of Oxford University Press

First published 1987 by Oxford University Press
First issued as an Oxford University Press paperback 1989

British Library Cataloguing in Publication Data

Data available

Library of Congress Cataloging in Publication Data
Kershaw, Ian.
The 'Hitler myth'.
Translation of: 'Der Hitler-Mythos'.
Bibliography: p.
Includes index.
1. Germany—Politics and government—1933–1945.
2. Hitler, Adolf, 1889–1945. 3. Public opinion—
Germany. 4. Propaganda, German—History—20th
century. I. Title.
DD256.5K46513 1987 943.086 86-28583
ISBN 0-19-282234-9

13 15 17 19 20 18 16 14 12

Printed in Great Britain by
Biddles Ltd
Guildford and King's Lynn

FOR TRAUDE

PREFACE

THIS is a completely refashioned and extended version of a book which I originally wrote in German, and which was published under the title *Der Hitler-Mythos. Volksmeinung und Propaganda im Dritten Reich* (Stuttgart, 1980). The original German version arose directly from my involvement in the major research project run by Professor Martin Broszat and his team in Munich, *Widerstand und Verfolgung in Bayern 1933–1945*, and the work duly concentrated exclusively on exploring Hitler's image among the population of Bavaria. While the Bavarian weighting is still present, and is left more or less intact in the case-study Chapters 3 and 4, I thought it essential for the English version not only to remove the topographical emphasis which prevailed in parts of the original, but also to extend the analysis to the whole of Germany and to incorporate sources from other areas of the Reich. This involved a considerable amount of new research and a good deal of rewriting as extensive *Sopade* and SD, Gestapo, and other police and government reports relating to regions other than Bavaria were explored and the results included in the text. I wanted, too, to take the opportunity of revising the previous version in the light of relevant subsequent publications. And in addition to the many alterations and the inclusion of much non-Bavarian material, I have provided for this version a completely new Introduction and Conclusion, and also an entirely new Chapter 9 on 'Hitler's Popular Image and the "Jewish Question" '—an area which I had deliberately, but mistakenly (I later felt), omitted from the German text.

Aware from the outset of all the changes which would have to be made, I was initially reluctant to prepare an English-language version. I was persuaded to do so after the publication of *Popular Opinion and Political Dissent in the Third Reich* (Oxford 1983). I had always seen the two works—based as they are on substantially the same body of material, but exploring different aspects of opinion formation and political attitudes and behaviour under the Nazi regime—as closely interrelated studies. I was most grateful, therefore, that Oxford University Press could provide me with the opportunity to make both works available in the same language, and that the Institut für Zeitgeschichte in Munich was prepared to grant me the rights to bring out an English version of *Der Hitler-Mythos*, which had originally appeared in the Institut's *Schriftenreihe*.

All in all, then, the present volume amounts in many respects practically to a new book rather than a straightforward translation of the German text. My personal debts of gratitude remain, however, unchanged and it gives me great pleasure to repeat them here. Tim Mason, Jeremy Noakes, Alan Milward, John Breuilly, Peter Hüttenberger, Falk Wiesemann, and Elke Fröhlich all made important contributions to the creation of the German version. More recently, Bill Carr, Dick Geary, Hans Mommsen and Otto Dov Kulka have also greatly influenced my thinking in many respects and provided stimulus and encouragement. Above all, my lasting and most sincere thanks go to Martin Broszat, who, quite apart from the original inducement to examine the 'Hitler myth', invested time and effort in the project beyond any call of duty, down to the stylistic refinement of my German text, and in addition generously contributed an Introduction to the German version, placing the work in the context of recent writing on the 'Hitler phenomenon'.

At the time of the original research in Bavaria, I had the most helpful co-operation from archivists in all the Bavarian State Archives, and in the extension of the research I have benefited greatly through the kind assistance of archivists in other record repositories, especially the Bundesarchiv, Koblenz, the Archiv der sozialen Demokratie, Bonn, the Zentrales Staatsarchiv, Potsdam, and the Institut für Marxismus-Leninismus, Zentrales Parteiarchiv, in East Berlin. I would especially like to record my grateful thanks to the staff of the Institut für Zeitgeschichte for encouragement, help, and expert advice at the time I was beginning this work, and ever since.

The research for the German version was generously funded by the Deutscher Akademischer Austauschdienst, the British Academy, the Twenty-Seven Foundation, the Nuffield Foundation, and the Area Studies Grants of Manchester University; subsequent research by the British Academy exchange arrangement with the Akademie der Wissenschaften der DDR and the Leverhulme Foundation. All these institutions have my unbounded thanks. Most of all, however, I would like to express once more my major debt of gratitude to the Alexander von Humboldt-Stiftung, which most generously supported lengthy stays in Germany in 1976–7 and again in 1985, and without whose backing this work could not have been commenced, let alone completed.

The last debts are the greatest of all. My family have had to bear the brunt of absences entailed in the research and writing of this book, and I thank them most sincerely for the sacrifices they have made in my cause.

Finally, the German version, *Der Hitler-Mythos*, would not have been written at all without the encouragement of Traude Spät. The dedication, at least, should remain unchanged in this version.

I.K.

Manchester
May 1986

CONTENTS

INTRODUCTION

FEW, if any, twentieth-century political leaders have enjoyed greater popularity among their own people than Hitler in the decade or so following his assumption of power on 30 January 1933. It has been suggested that at the peak of his popularity nine Germans in ten were 'Hitler supporters, Führer believers'.[1] Whatever qualification may be needed for such a bald assertion, it can be claimed with certainty that support for the Nazi Party never approached such a level, as Nazi leaders themselves well recognized.[2] Acclaim for Hitler went way beyond those who thought of themselves as Nazis, embracing many who were critical of the institutions, policies, and ideology of the regime. This was a factor of fundamental importance in the functioning of the Third Reich. The adulation of Hitler by millions of Germans who might otherwise have been only marginally committed to Nazism meant that the person of the Führer, as the focal point of basic consensus, formed a crucial integratory force in the Nazi system of rule. Without Hitler's massive personal popularity, the high level of plebiscitary acclamation which the regime could repeatedly call upon—legitimating its actions at home and abroad, defusing opposition, boosting the autonomy of the leadership from the traditional national-conservative élites who had imagined they would keep Hitler in check, and sustaining the frenetic and increasingly dangerous momentum of Nazi rule—is unthinkable. Most important of all, Hitler's huge platform of popularity made his own power position ever more unassailable, providing the foundation for the selective radicalization process in the Third Reich by which his personal ideological obsessions became translated into attainable reality.

Biographical concern with the details of Hitler's life and his bizarre personality—fully explored in numerous publications[3]—falls some

---

[1] S. Haffner, *Anmerkungen zu Hitler*, Munich, 1978, p. 46.
[2] See ch. 3 below.
[3] e.g. A. Bullock, *Hitler. A Study in Tyranny*, rev. edn., London, 1964; J. C. Fest, *Hitler. Eine Biographie*, Frankfurt a.M., 1973; J. Toland, *Adolf Hitler*, New York, 1976; R. Binion, *Hitler among the Germans*, New York, 1976; R. G. L. Waite, *The Psychopathic God—Adolf Hitler*, New York, 1977. For doubts about the virtue of biographical approaches to Hitler, see H. Graml 'Probleme einer Hitler-Biographie. Kritische Bemerkungen zu Joachim C. Fest', *VfZ*, xxii (1974), 76–92.

way short of explaining the extraordinary magnetism of his popular appeal. Nor can Hitler's obsessive ideological fixations, also well known, satisfactorily account for his remarkable popularity. It would, for example, be easy to exaggerate the drawing power of anti-Semitism as the determining element in winning support for the Nazi Movement[4] (though its functional importance as a unifying idea *within* the Movement is scarcely disputable). And for a population concerned with improving material conditions from the depths of the slump and overwhelmingly frightened of the prospect of another war, the idea of a coming war for *Lebensraum* was unlikely to have a dominant appeal.[5] It has been plausibly suggested, therefore, that deep into the dictatorship itself Hitler's own ideological obsessions had more of a symbolic than concrete meaning for even most Nazi supporters.[6]

What seems necessary is to add to the extensive knowledge of Hitler as a person by turning the focus on to the *image* of Hitler as Führer. The sources of Hitler's immense popularity have to be sought, it has rightly been claimed, 'in those who adored him, rather than in the leader himself'.[7] This book tries to take a step in that direction. It is not, in fact, primarily concerned with Hitler himself, but with the propaganda image-building process, and above all with the reception of this image by the German people—how they viewed Hitler before and during the Third Reich; or, expressing it slightly differently, less what Hitler actually was than what he seemed to be to millions of Germans. Within this context, as a study in political imagery, it aims to demonstrate how the 'Hitler myth'—by which I mean a 'heroic' image and popular conception of Hitler imputing to him characteristics and motives for the most part at crass variance with reality—served its vitally important integratory function in providing the

---

[4] See S. Gordon, *Hitler, Germans, and the 'Jewish Question'*, Princeton, 1984, ch. 2, for a recent summary of the evidence.

[5] For the subordinate part played by foreign policy as a topic at Nazi meetings in Northeim before 1933, see W. S. Allen, *The Nazi Seizure of Power. The Experience of a Single German town, 1922—1945*, 2nd edn., New York, 1984, p. 322. Nazi propaganda in this period tended to speak of the future only in the vague sense that a united Germany would once more become a world power to reckon with, or that Germany would once again gain overseas colonies. For a suggestive survey of the 'main ideological themes' of rank-and-file Nazi members in the early 1930s, see P. Merkl, *Political Violence under the Swastika*, Princeton, 1975, pp. 450ff.

[6] See M. Broszat, 'Soziale Motivation und Führer-Bindung des Nationalsozialismus', *VfZ*, xviii (1970), 392–409.

[7] T. W. Mason, 'Open Questions on Nazism', in R. Samuel (ed.), *People's History and Socialist Theory*, London, 1981, p. 207.

regime with its mass base of support.[8] It seeks to ascertain the central foundations of the 'Hitler myth'; on what basis it was erected, and how it was maintained. In so doing, it attempts to establish the main elements of consensus which the 'Hitler myth' embodied, and, finally, to suggest the implications of the 'Hitler myth' for the implementation of Nazi ideological aims.

The dual concerns of image-building and image-reception are closely intermeshed. There is not the slightest doubt that the 'Hitler myth' was consciously devised as an integrating force by a regime acutely aware of the need to manufacture consensus. Hitler himself, as is well known, paid the greatest attention to the building of his public image. He gave great care to style and posture during speeches and other public engagements. And he was keen to avoid any hint of human failings, as in his refusal to be seen wearing spectacles or participating in any form of sport or other activity in which he might not excel and which might make him an object of amusement rather than admiration. His celibacy, which Goebbels portrayed as the sacrifice of personal happiness for the welfare of the nation, was also regarded by Hitler as a functional necessity directed at avoiding any loss of popularity among German women, whose support he saw as vital to his electoral success.[9] All this was closely related to Hitler's known views on the 'psychology of the masses', already expounded in *Mein Kampf* and taking a line similar to that in Gustave le Bon's writings on the almost boundless manipulability of the masses.[10] And during the Third Reich itself, Hitler was evidently aware how important his 'omnipotent' image was to his leadership position and to the strength of the regime. To this extent, it has been aptly stated that 'Hitler well understood his own function, the role which he *had* to act out as "Leader" of the Third Reich', that he 'transformed himself into a function, the *function of Führer*'.[11]

The manipulative purpose behind the 'Hitler myth' was, therefore, present from the outset. It was also welcomed and furthered in quite

[8] For Georges Sorel's perceptive presage of the importance of myth to modern mass movements, see the comment of Noel O'Sullivan in his *Fascism*, London, 1983, pp. 119–23.

[9] *'Es spricht der Führer'. 7 exemplarische Hitler-Reden*, ed. H. von Kotze and H. Krausnick, Gütersloh, 1966 (henceforth cited as von Kotze), p. 42.

[10] See ibid., pp. 31 ff.

[11] T. W. Mason, 'Intention and Explanation: A Current Controversy about the Interpretation of National Socialism', in G. Hirschfeld and L. Kettenacker (eds.), *Der 'Führerstaat'. Mythos und Realität*, Stuttgart, 1981, p. 35.

cynical terms, for the 'stupefying of the masses'[12] and their weaning away from the lure of socialism towards an anti-socialist, counter-revolutionary mass movement, by those members of the ruling classes prepared to give active backing to the Nazi Party—though it would be easy to exaggerate the extent to which the 'Hitler myth' was either built to serve, or objectively did ultimately serve, the interests of monopoly capitalism.[13] What does seem indisputable is that the constructed 'Hitler myth' was indispensable in its integrative function, firstly as a counter to the strong centrifugal forces within the Nazi Movement itself, and secondly in establishing a massive basis of consensus among the German people for those aims and policies identifiable with the Führer. And the more the objective contradictions in the social aspirations of Nazism's mass base became apparent, the greater was the functional necessity for the reification and ritualization of the 'Hitler myth' in order to provide a firm base of affective integration.[14]

Towards the end of 1941, at the height of Nazi power and domination in Europe, Goebbels claimed the creation of the 'Führer myth' as his greatest propaganda achievement.[15] He had some justification for his claim, and we will indeed be partially preoccupied in subsequent chapters with examining the 'Hitler myth' as an achievement of 'image-building' by masters of the new techniques of propaganda. However, it has been rightly pointed out that the 'heroic' Hitler image was 'as much an image created by the masses as it was imposed on them'.[16] Propaganda was above all effective where it was building upon, not countering, already existing values and mentalities. The ready-made terrain of pre-existing beliefs, prejudices, and phobias forming an important stratum of the German political culture on to which the 'Hitler myth' could easily be imprinted, provides, therefore, an equally essential element in explaining how the propaganda image

[12] M. Weißbecker, 'Zur Herausbildung des Führerkults in der NSDAP', in K. Drechsler *et al.* (eds.), *Monopole und Staat in Deutschland 1917–1945*, East Berlin, 1966, p. 122.

[13] An exemplary statement of such an interpretation can be found in E. Gottschling, 'Der faschistische Staat', in D. Eichholtz and K. Gossweiler (eds.), *Faschismusforschung. Positionen, Probleme, Polemik*, East Berlin, 1980, pp. 95–8.

[14] The functional purpose of ritual in the Nazi State has recently been well emphasized by S. Taylor, *Prelude to Genocide*, London, 1985, ch. 7.

[15] R. Semmler, *Goebbels. The Man Next to Hitler*, London, 1947, pp. 56–7.

[16] J. P. Stern, *Hitler. The Führer and the People*, London, 1975, p. 111.

of Hitler as a 'representative individual' upholding the 'true sense of propriety of the German people' could take hold and flourish.[17]

Necessarily, therefore, we start with the roots of the leadership cult, which long pre-dated the rise of Nazism, and with its early gestation within the Nazi Movement before its extension to the mass electorate between 1930 and 1933. As is well known, in the March election of 1933—held in a climate of national euphoria on the Right and extreme terroristic repression of the Left—less than one voter in two supported Hitler's Party. Most Germans were still either hostile to or unconvinced by their new Chancellor. Yet in the course of the next three years or so, against the backcloth of an apparently total revitalization of German society, Hitler won over that 'majority of the majority'[18] which had not voted for him in 1933. The Führer cult was now firmly established as a mass phenomenon, providing the Nazi regime with the legitimation of an adored leader enjoying an unprecedented degree of adulation and subservience from his people. Even at the time of Hitler's appointment to the Chancellorship at the end of January 1933, that had scarcely seemed conceivable. The transition from the image of Party leader to that of supreme national leader forms the theme of the second chapter. A number of important elements in the build-up of the 'Hitler myth' are examined more closely in subsequent chapters. The extraordinary reflection of Hitler's popular image in reactions to the massacre of the SA's leadership in the 'Night of the Long Knives' of 30 June 1934, the detachment of Hitler in popular consciousness from the Nazi Party itself and from the misdeeds and sullied repute of local Party bosses, and the way in which, thanks not least to public professions of support from hierarchy and clergy, Hitler's prestige was able to ride the dangers of the 'Church struggle' largely unscathed, are given detailed consideration. The last theme in the manufacture of the 'Hitler myth' which we explore is the way in which first a series of unimaginable successes in foreign policy, then the very heights of tension, and eventually the outbreak of war affected the shaping of the legendary Führer image. By the time of the German victories in the west in 1940, the main components of the 'Führer myth', culminating in that of the great military genius though at the same time the representative of the

---

[17] The term 'representative individual' appears to have been coined by Stern. See ibid., pp. 9ff, and also L. Kettenacker, 'Sozialpsychologische Aspekte der Führer-Herrschaft', in Hirschfeld and Kettenacker, pp. 103, 110, 119ff, 132.

[18] Haffner, p. 43.

ordinary 'Front soldier', had been assembled. The later chapters deal with its initial resilience amid slow decline but then total collapse as the Third Reich fell into ruins. The final chapter departs from the chronological sequence in order to tackle a last complex and important theme: the role and significance of the 'Jewish Question' in Hitler's public image.

The sources for the investigation fall into two main categories: firstly, innumerable internal confidential reports on opinion and morale compiled on a regular basis by German government officials, by the police and justice administrations, by Nazi Party agencies, and by the security service (SD); and, secondly, down to the early years of the war, the rich reports filtering out of Germany to the exiled opponents of the Nazi regime, above all those fed to and circulated by the leadership of the exiled SPD (now calling itself the *Sopade*) in Prague, then Paris, and finally London. I have discussed the merits and pitfalls of this material elsewhere.[19] It will suffice here, therefore, to point to additional problems of these sources in relation to a reconstruction of popular conceptions of Hitler.

Obviously, we cannot quantify Hitler's popularity at any given time during the Third Reich. The reports of the regime's own agents provide us with a large number of varied subjective comments, qualitative judgements on the state of popular opinion. Naturally, people were particularly cautious about making disparaging comments about the Führer, whatever criticism might be risked about other aspects of Nazi rule. And the citizen's fear of criticizing Hitler was compounded by the anxiety of those compiling opinion reports not to offend their superiors. We have to face up to the possibility, therefore, that eulogies of praise in the reports might reflect the opinion—genuine or forced—of the reporter rather than the public.

---

[19] I. Kershaw, *Popular Opinion and Political Dissent in the Third Reich*, Oxford, 1983, pp. 6 ff. The character and value of internal opinion reports is explored in, e.g., the introductions to the various sections of *Bayern in der NS-Zeit*, ed. M. Broszat, E. Fröhlich, and F. Wiesemann, Munich/Vienna, 1977; A. H. Unger, *The Totalitarian Party*, Cambridge, 1974, pp. 221–62; M. G. Steinert, *Hitlers Krieg und die Deutschen*, Düsseldorf, 1970, pp. 40–8; *Meldungen aus dem Reich*, ed. H. Boberach, Neuwied, 1965, pp. ix–xxviii; and L. D. Stokes, 'The *Sicherheitsdienst* (SD) of the *Reichsführer SS* and German Public Opinion, September 1939–June 1941', Johns Hopkins University Ph.D. thesis, Baltimore, 1972, pp. 194–253. A good survey of the structure of Gestapo and SD reporting (with particular reference to the 'Jewish Question') is provided by Otto Dov Kulka, 'Die Nürnberger Rassengesetze und die deutsche Bevölkerung', *VfZ*, xxxii (1984), 584 ff. And for an evaluation of the *Sopade* material, see Michael Voges, 'Klassenkampf in der "Beitriebsgemeinschaft" ', *Archiv für Sozialgeschichte*, xxi (1981), 329–43.

Even if the reported comments faithfully reflect public attitudes, these attitudes may, of course, be themselves the expression of a more or less coerced conformity rather than of Hitler's genuine popularity. In the nature of things, it is more difficult to interpret the pro-regime comments of the reports, where scepticism about the underlying elements of fear and coercion is bound to prevail, than it is to evaluate the anti-regime comments and actions of the population, which often speak for themselves. A potential danger, therefore, is an over-estimation of oppositional attitudes and a corresponding playing-down of genuine approval and consensus. Given the type of material at our disposal, there is no objective or external criterion for solving this difficulty. However imperfect, the historian's judgement, based on patient source criticism, acquaintance with the complete mass of material available from different reporting agencies, and a readiness to read between the lines has to suffice.

The reports are not, however, beyond echoing direct criticism of Hitler. From the mid-war years on, a body of adverse comment—unmistakable even if veiled in expression—accumulates, strengthening, therefore, the argument that the positive tenor of the reports before this time had on the whole reflected genuine popularity and the absence of widespread and substantial criticism of Hitler. At the same time, there is sufficient witness—for instance, in the proceedings of the political 'Special Courts' as well as in anonymous letters and the reported activities of 'enemies of the State'—to the kinds of negative comments made about Hitler in the Third Reich, even if these seem, until the middle of the war, to have reflected the views of only a small minority of the population.

The *Sopade* reports[20] naturally contain an in-built bias diametrically opposite to that of the internal reports. *Sopade* reporters gladly seized upon expressions of anti-Nazi sentiment, which they encountered not infrequently in their main milieu of operation among the industrial work-force, and tended at times to err in judgement in the direction of an over-rosy estimation of the extent of underlying opposition to the regime. The editors of the *Deutschland-Berichte* (*Germany Reports*) are well aware of this danger, as indeed were some of

---

[20] The central digests, the *Deutschland-Berichte der Sozialdemokratischen Partei Deutschlands 1934—1940*, henceforth *DBS*, have now been published in seven volumes by Verlag Petra Nettelbeck, Zweitausendeins, Frankfurt a.M., 1980. The reports of the 'Border Secretaries', on which the central reports rest, are to be found in the Archiv der sozialen Demokratie (Friedrich-Ebert-Stiftung), Bonn.

the *Sopade*'s 'Border Secretaries' who were sending in the reports. It is all the more striking and suggestive, therefore, that even this oppositional source is on numerous occasions fully prepared to testify to the power and significance of the Hitler cult and to accept that the Führer's massive popularity even extended to working class circles which had recognizably not been won over to Nazism. Though there are some important divergences and a totally different perspective, the *Sopade* material offers for the most part convincing corroboration of the picture of the Hitler image and its impact which can be gained from the internal sources. There is sufficient evidence, then, as the following chapters try to show, to be able to point at least in an imprecise way to the pattern of development of Hitler's image, to the curve of his popularity and the reasons behind it.

In characterizing the leadership cult attached to Hitler and in assessing the nature of its impact, the theoretical insights provided by Max Weber's 'ideal type' of 'charismatic authority' still, despite doubts about their applicability to concrete historical cases, appear to me to be invaluable.[21] Max Weber conceptualized charismatic leadership, which he contrasted with 'traditional' and 'legal' (i.e. resting on impersonal, 'rational', bureaucratic rules) domination, as an extraordinary, unstable, and therefore transient form of rule, tending to arise in unusual or crisis conditions, and directed not at the solution of everyday problems of government but at the overcoming of supradimensional crises and emergencies. Charismatic authority rests on the 'heroism or exemplary character' of the leader, on the qualities by which 'he is considered extraordinary and treated as endowed with supernatural, superhuman, or at least specifically exceptional powers'.[22] Charisma, then, is a quality determined by the subjective perceptions of the followers.[23] The 'followers' of the leader are won

---

[21] Weber's model has been criticized in its application to specific political circumstances by, among others, C. J. Friedrich, 'Political Leadership and the Problem of Charismatic Power', *Journal of Politics*, xxiii (1961), and C. Ake, 'Charismatic Legitimation and Political Integration', *Comparative Studies in Society and History*, ix (1966–7). Though it does undoubtedly contain weaknesses and limitations, a convincing defence of Weber's theory and of its application to modern political rulers, not least Hitler, has recently been advanced by Arthur Schweitzer, *The Age of Charisma*, Chicago, 1984. Weber's model is also usefully deployed in another recent work by F. Weinstein, *The Dynamics of Nazism. Leadership, Ideology, and the Holocaust*, New York, 1980, pp. 81 ff.

[22] Max Weber, *Economy and Society*, ed. G. Roth and C. Wittich, Berkeley, 1978, pp. 214–15, 241.

[23] Ibid., p. 242: 'What is alone important is how the individual is actually regarded by those subject to charismatic authority, by his "followers" or "disciples".'

over and their backing derived from personal loyalty, not abstract 'rules' or positions, sustained by great deeds, resounding successes, and notable achievements, which provide the repeated 'proof' of the leader's 'calling'. The bearer of charisma 'seizes the task for which he is destined and demands that others obey and follow him by virtue of his mission. If those to whom he feels sent do not recognize him, his claim collapses; if they recognize it, he is their master as long as he "proves" himself.'[24] Failure, therefore, certainly a chain of failures, means a fatal undermining of charisma. Even without failure as such, the constant threat to charismatic rule is 'routinization'—the lapse back into stabilization, regulation, systematization, normality. Only the dynamism of recurring success can sustain charismatic authority which, therefore, is inherently unstable, forming a 'revolutionary' but 'emergency', transitory type of rule.[25]

Charismatic authority was seen by Max Weber chiefly in the context of forms of 'primitive' society, where war-lords, chieftains, prophets, and magic-men could thrive. And his analysis of the charismatic 'following' relates to the immediate bodyguard, disciples, or agents of the leader. The conceptualization has been successfully applied by a number of historians to Nazism, in particular to Hitler's relations with his 'paladins' and his standing within the Movement.[26] But the implications have seldom been extended to the wider framework of Hitler's relationship with the German people,[27] although in an age of mass communication and mass politics this seems a perfectly legitimate and potentially rewarding exercise.

One of Germany's foremost historians remarked recently that it remained a prime task for scholars 'to analyse systematically and historically the construction of the charisma which did not surround Hitler at an early date, but which he first gradually developed and maximally exploited until, as undisputed Führer, he stood at the

---

[24] Ibid., p. 242.

[25] Ibid., pp. 246, 1114–15.

[26] Notably by J. Nyomarkay, *Charisma and Factionalism within the Nazi Party*, Minneapolis, 1967; W. Horn, *Führerideologie und Parteiorganisation in der NSDAP, 1919–1933*, Düsseldorf, 1972; and M. R. Lepsius, 'From Fragmented Party Democracy to Government by Emergency Decree and National Socialist Takeover: Germany', in J. J. Linz and A. Stepan (eds.), *The Breakdown of Democratic Regimes*, Baltimore/London, 1978, pp. 61 ff.

[27] Kettenacker, 'Sozialpsychologische Aspekte', and M. H. Kater, 'Hitler in a Social Context', *Central European History*, xiv (1981), 243–72 are exceptions to this generalization.

pinnacle of Movement and State'.[28] Important aspects of this task—for example, the intellectual roots of 'charismatic authority', the political structures which favour it,[29] the pseudo-religious dimension of its appeal, comparison of the Hitler cult with leadership cults in other societies, first and foremost in Fascist Italy, and its influence upon foreign 'opinion-leaders'—need more systematic treatment than could be offered here. But the book attempts to contribute towards the task in helping to clarify the bases of Hitler's charismatic appeal and immense personal popularity, and in demonstrating the indispensability of the 'Führer myth' to the functioning of Nazi rule. And, as I hope to show, admiration for Hitler rested less on bizarre and arcane precepts of Nazi ideology than on social and political values—if often distorted or represented in extreme form—recognizable in many societies other than the Third Reich. To that extent, however strange the deification of Hitler by the people of a modern industrial nation may seem to us, its causes contain a message which is not altogether comforting.

[28] H.-U. Wehler, '30. Januar 1933—Ein halbes Jahrhundert danach', *Aus Politik und Zeitgeschichte*, 29 Jan. 1983, p. 50.

[29] In dealing comparatively with a broad typology of 'charismatic' forms of rule, Schweitzer, *The Age of Charisma*, brings out the peculiarities and novelty of the fascist charismatic type and its untypicality as the form of politics normally resulting from the breakup of democracy, thus emphasizing the need to place the emergence of 'charisma' in the context of the pre-existing political culture.

PART ONE

The Making of the 'Hitler Myth', 1920–1940

I

'Führer of the Coming Germany'
The Hitler Image in the Weimar Era

We believe that Fate has chosen him to show the way to the German people. Therefore we greet him in devotion and reverence, and can only wish that he may be preserved for us until his work is completed.

Goebbels, 1929

'HEROIC' leadership was a significant element in the ideas of the nationalist and *völkisch* Right long before Hitler's spectacular rise to prominence. It can justifiably be regarded as 'one of the central ideas of the anti-democratic movement in the Weimar Republic' and 'one of its indispensable articles of faith'.[1] Even after Hitler had momentarily stepped into the limelight during the Putsch fiasco of 1923, it was some considerable time before *völkisch* writers and politicians propagating the 'Führer idea' commonly came to associate their expectations with the leader of the NSDAP. The idea and the image of a 'Führer of the Germans' had therefore already been moulded long before it was fitted to Hitler, and for years existed side by side with the growth of Nazism without it being obvious to the protagonists of the need for 'heroic' leadership that Hitler himself was *the* leader for whom they had been waiting.

The readiness to place all hope in 'leadership', in the authority of a 'strong man', has in itself of course not been peculiar to Germany. Promotion by threatened élites and acceptance by anxious masses of strong authoritarian leadership, often personalized in one 'charismatic' figure, has been (and still is) experienced by many societies in which a weak pluralist system is incapable of resolving deep political and ideological rifts and is perceived to be in terminal crisis. Given the intensity of the crises of parliamentary systems in numerous European

---

[1] K. Sontheimer, *Antidemokratisches Denken in der Weimarer Republik*, 4th edn., Munich, 1962, p. 268.

states in the inter-war era, and in a climate where the Great War still cast its long shadow, populist and militaristic leadership cults sprang up throughout Europe as part of Fascist and quasi-Fascist counter-revolutionary movements, most prominently outside Germany of course in the 'Duce cult' of Fascist Italy.[2] Though the emergence of a leadership cult in Germany can clearly be seen in this European-wide perspective, its characteristic features and form of articulation have to be located in elements of a specifically German political culture long pre-dating Hitler.

The roots of 'heroic' leadership ideas in Germany extend deep into the nineteenth century, to the political notions and the mythical visions of Germanic leadership associated with the romantic-conservative strain of early *völkisch*-nationalist thought. Victory, valour, and heroism were all components of a growing 'cult of the nation' in such circles, in which sacral festivals of fire and light, accompanied by intermingled Germanic pagan and Christian symbolism and mystical ritual, celebrated, from the early nineteenth century onwards, the 'German' defeat of Napoleon at the 'Battle of the Peoples' at Leipzig in 1813 and the 'rebirth', strength, vitality, and hope arising from national unity. Such 'heroic' and mystical Germanic symbolism was, of course, by no means the dominant strain of German nationalism, either before or after Unification. But after 1871 the concern of the new German State to manufacture the 'nationalization of the masses' kept alive and extended such symbolism.[3] One outward manifestation was the erection in the later nineteenth century of gigantic national monuments—on a scale and of a character not found, for example, in the British political culture of the time—granite glorifications of mythical heroes, great victories, and national triumph. Militarism, heroism, and national unity, garbed in religious symbolism, were also the keynotes of the newly-instituted national feast day to celebrate the victory over the French at the battle of Sedan in 1870.

[2] See the comparative assessment by Rudolf Vierhaus, 'Faschistisches Führertum', *Historische Zeitschrift*, clxxxxviii (1964), 614–39; and specifically on the 'Duce cult', see P. Melograni, 'The Cult of the Duce in Mussolini's Italy', *Journal of Contemporary History*, xi (1976), 221–37, and J. Petersen, 'Mussolini. Wirklichkeit und Mythos eines Diktators', in K. H. Bohrer (ed.), *Mythos und Moderne*, Frankfurt a.M., 1983, pp. 242–60.

[3] For what follows, see esp. G. L. Mosse, *The Nationalization of the Masses*, New York, 1975, chs. 1–4; and also T. Nipperdey, 'Nationalidee und Nationaldenkmal in Deutschland im 19. Jahrhundert', *Historische Zeitschrift*, ccvi (1968), L. Kettenacker, 'Der Mythos vom Reich', in Bohrer, *Mythos und Moderne*, pp. 261–89, and K. Vondung, *Magie und Manipulation*, Göttingen, 1971, ch. 1.

The projected image of the Kaiser—again so different from contemporary depictions of the English monarchy—also captured the blend of military strength, national unity, heroic achievement, and pseudo-religious symbolism. A prime example was the colossal monument, erected in 1897 and largely financed by veterans' associations, of Kaiser Wilhelm I, mounted and in military uniform, on the Kyffhäuser in Thuringia, one of Germany's 'holiest' mountains where, according to the saga, Frederick Barbarossa was sleeping until the rebirth of the medieval Reich.[4] Overshadowed by Bismarck, Wilhelm I's rule had been largely depersonalized and institutionalized. A new young, ambitious, autocratic, and demagogically inclined Kaiser and the departure of Bismarck from the scene transformed the image of the Kaiser into a fully fledged, personalized Hohenzollern cult.[5] According to a leading contemporary political figure, Wilhelm II combined in his own person 'the two images of the governing statesman and the sleeping Hero-Kaiser', while a prominent evangelical theologian claimed that 'in the heart of every German there also lives a clear image of the Kaiser which is the expression and the product of our whole history'.[6]

The rapid disillusionment of the exaggerated hopes and expectations placed in the new Kaiser by the German Right promoted, however, a counter personality-cult of heroic stature in the nostalgic elevation and veneration of the deposed 'Iron Chancellor'. Pilgrimages to Bismarck's home in Friedrichsruh took place from all over the Reich; he 'became a myth in his lifetime, the political prototype of what was later called "national opposition", an opposition, which unlike that of the *Reichsfeinde*, had the country's interests very much at heart and was led by a great man. Anti-Semites, nationalists, and pan-Germans who dreamt of a great Germanic Reich climbed on to his band-wagon.'[7] A remarkable manifestation in stone of the Bismarck cult was the building between 1900 and 1910 of some 500 'Bismarck

[4] See Mosse, pp. 62–3 and Pl. 9.

[5] For the changing image of the Kaiser, see E. Fehrenbach, *Wandlungen des deutschen Kaisergedankens 1871–1918*, Munich/Vienna, 1969, and 'Images of Kaiserdom: German attitudes to Kaiser Wilhelm II', in J. C. G. Röhl and N. Sombart (eds.), *Kaiser Wilhelm II. New Interpretations*, Cambridge, 1982, pp. 269–85. On the extension of the cult of empire and monarchy, see also W. K. Blessing, 'The Cult of Monarchy, Political Loyalty, and the Workers' Movement in Imperial Germany', *Journal of Contemporary History*, xiii (1978), 357–75.

[6] Cited in Fehrenbach, 'Images', p. 276.

[7] G. Mann, *The History of Germany since 1789*, Harmondsworth, 1974, pp. 413–14.

Towers', scattered around Germany and styled after the tomb of the Gothic King Theodoric at Ravenna, to honour the memory of the creator of German unity.[8]

Growing disappointment on the populist Right in Wilhelm II promoted notions of a 'people's Kaiser' who, embodying strength and vitality, would crush Germany's internal enemies and at the expense of 'inferior peoples' would provide the new nation with the greatness it deserved and would win empire for 'a people without living space'.[9] The heroic image of a future German 'people's Kaiser' was painted in extreme form by Heinrich Class, head of the Pan-German League, in his chauvinistic polemic *Wenn ich der Kaiser wär (If I were the Kaiser)*, published under a pseudonym in 1912 and going into five editions within two years:

The need still lives on today in the best of our people to follow a strong, able leader; all who have remained unseduced by the teachings of ungerman democracy yearn for it, not because they are inclined to servility or are of weak character, but because they know that greatness can only be brought about through the concentration of individual forces, which again can only be achieved by the subordination to a leader. It would be good fortune for our people, if this leader should arise in the bearer of the crown.[10]

By the time that Class was writing, the ideas which he represented—including as an important component images of 'heroic' leadership arising from the ideological strains of German political culture which I have briefly described here—had gained considerable ground especially, though by no means only, among the Protestant middle classes and 'intelligentsia'. Romantic-nationalist leadership ideals were also finding resonance in substantial parts of the bourgeois youth movement.[11] The growing appeal already before the First

---

[8] Mosse, pp. 36–7.

[9] See Fehrenbach, *Wandel*, esp. pp. 158–83.

[10] D. Fryman (= H. Class), *Wenn ich der Kaiser wär*, 5th edn., Leipzig, 1914, p. 227.

[11] A 'Germanic' vocabulary, later incorporated into the *völkisch* Right and Nazism, including terms such as 'Führer', 'Gau', and 'Heil-Gruß', together with rituals of fire and other forms of neo-heathen cults which the Nazis took up, was already prevalent in the Youth Movement around the turn of the century. See Vondung, pp. 16–17. Despite this, it would, of course, be an over-simplification to see the pre-war bourgeois youth groups as direct precursors of the Hitler Youth. On this, see the survey of the literature by P. D. Stachura, 'German Youth, the Youth Movement, and National Socialism in the Weimar Republic', in P. D. Stachura (ed.), *The Nazi Machtergreifung*, London, 1983, pp. 68–84, and his *The German Youth Movement 1900–1945. An Interpretative and Documentary History*, London, 1981.

World War of 'heroic' leadership notions in populist-nationalist circles of the German Right—and there are parallels, if somewhat weaker in intensity, in pre-Fascist Italy, which helped to prepare the ground for the later emergence of the cult of the Duce[12]—was largely shaped by the increasing gulf between the perceived need for national integration and unity and the patent lack of integration which prevailed in reality.[13] This gulf was itself enhanced and accentuated by three interlinked factors: the social and political disruption accompanying a practically simultaneous transition to nation-state, constitutional government (if strongly authoritarian in character), and industrialized society;[14] the deep fragmentation of the political system (reflecting fundamental social cleavages);[15] and, not least, the spread of a chauvinistic-imperialist ideology clamouring for a rightful 'place in the sun' for Germany, a supposed 'have-not' nation.[16] The basic conditions for the increasing receptivity to 'heroic' leadership ideas and for the growth of exaggerated expectations in a coming leader lay above all in the combination of the aggressive, expansionist hopes placed in a grandiose *Weltpolitik* and acute perceptions of the weaknesses and dangers of bourgeois party and interest politics in the face of the growing challenge to the political and social order from the democratic forces of socialism. The deeper the internal rifts of a society, one might speculate, and the greater the gulf between high expectations from a government and an actual performance so disappointing as to undermine the legitimacy of the political system, the greater is the potential for the spread of notions of 'charismatic' or 'heroic' leadership, seeming to offer a fundamental break with the past and a new and great future.

[12] See the comments of J. Petersen in *Der italienische Faschismus. Probleme und Forschungstendenzen. Kolloquien des Instituts für Zeitgeschichte*, Munich, 1983, pp. 34ff, and M. Knox, 'Conquest, Foreign and Domestic, in Fascist Italy and Nazi Germany', *Journal of Modern History*, lvi (1984), 26ff.

[13] For the relationship between the growth of fascism and the lack of pluralist national integration in Italy and Germany (in the post-war period), see the stimulating essay by W. S. Allen, 'The Appeal of Fascism and the Problem of National Disintegration', in H. A. Turner (ed.), *Reappraisals of Fascism*, New York, 1975, pp. 44–68.

[14] See the remarks of W. Schieder, in *Totalitarismus und Faschismus. Kolloquien des Instituts für Zeitgeschichte*, Munich, 1980, p. 47.

[15] See Lepsius, pp. 61ff.

[16] On this, see G. Eley, *Reshaping the German Right*, New Haven/London, 1980, esp. ch. 5; R. Chickering, *We Men Who Feel Most German*, London, 1984, esp. ch. 4; and, from a Marxist-Leninist perspective, J. Petzold, *Die Demagogie des Hitlerfaschismus*, East Berlin, 1982, esp. pp. 32ff.

This point was, of course, far from reached in Germany in 1914, when the outbreak of war amid national euphoria appeared to overcome internal tensions and divisions and offer the promise and grandeur of new horizons. In fact, however, the war—as is well known—only served to accentuate the divisions until reaching revolutionary breaking-point in 1918. In *völkisch*-nationalist and rabidly expansionist circles, rapidly growing in size before the end of the war as the creation of the mass *Vaterlandspartei* in 1917 showed, an idealized 'trench experience' (reflected in nationalist war literature after 1918) of 'true leadership' and soldierly loyalty and cameraderie intensified, radicalized, and partially remodelled pre-existing 'heroic' leadership ideals. For those who fought on after 1918 in the *Freikorps*, personal loyalty to the heroic military leaders whose names the brigades bore became attached to practical counter-revolutionary politics.[17] And veterans' organizations, prominent among them the huge *Stahlhelm*, continued to propagate such sentiments throughout the Weimar era.[18] In fact, the trauma of 1918 for the Right—the military collapse, fall of the monarchy and old order, and the coming to power of the hated Social Democrats, earlier defamed as 'enemies of the Reich'—transformed the previously more latent than active notions of authoritarian 'heroic' leadership into a broad counter-revolutionary force, if at first a vague and divided one, posing an alternative vision to that of the Weimar party-political system.

Among the broad spectrum of political and psychological forces which contributed to the shaping of the 'heroic' leadership idea, the pseudo-religious colouring is worthy of note. Partially derived from traditional acceptance of authority, partly too from the secularization of Christian belief in salvation—particularly among German Protestants, whose attachment to the Church was dwindling, but who were traditionally brought up to accept authority, particularly that of the State, the leadership idea being propagated by the *völkisch*-nationalist Right offered a kind of secularization of belief in salvation. And within the Protestant Church itself, already being rent by theological divisions amounting to a 'crisis of faith', a wing developed in which *völkisch* political ideas were blended in an unholy mixture with

---

[17] See R. G. L. Waite, *Vanguard of Nazism. The Free Corps Movement in Postwar Germany 1918–1923*, Cambridge, Mass., 1952.

[18] See A. Klotzbücher, *Der politische Weg des Stahlhelm, Bund der Frontsoldaten, in der Weimarer Republik*, Erlangen, 1965, pp. 122, 127.

Christian revivalism.[19] The propagation of such sentiments further helped prepare the ground among ordinary Protestants for the receptivity to notions of 'political salvation' which a 'genuine' national leader could offer, and which would bring with it Christian renewal. We will encounter the strong religious aspect of the 'heroic' leadership notion on a number of occasions as we explore the development of the Hitler cult both before and after 1933.

Völkisch-nationalist leadership expectations in the Weimar era broke with traditions of a monarch–subject relationship, replacing it with partly neo-feudal, but partly pseudo-democratic notions of a relationship between leader and 'following' in which the leader represented in an authoritative way the will of the people without standing above and outside it in the fashion of a monarch or dictator.[20] Ideal leadership was now envisaged in a man from the people whose qualities would embody struggle, conflict, the values of the trenches. Hard, ruthless, resolute, uncompromising, and radical, he would destroy the old privilege- and class-ridden society and bring about a new beginning, uniting the people in an ethnically pure and socially harmonious 'national community'. It was a complete counter-vision to the image of the 'leaderless democracy'[21] of Weimar and its divisive system run by contemptible 'politicians', mere party functionaries.

The extreme fragmentation of Weimar politics and the deep political and ideological divisions which denied any hope to unity or integration within the Weimar 'system' not only kept alive such visions on the nationalist and *völkisch* Right but contributed to the growing appeal of the scathing attacks in rightist tracts on 'the obvious lack of leaders which imprints on our era, so poverty-stricken in ideas, the stamp of spiritual and political permanent crisis'.[22] 'Leadership', it was claimed, was not to be found in constitutional 'systems', but came as destiny from the inner essence of a people. As one text rather mystically put it: 'The Leader cannot be made, can in this sense also not be selected. The Leader makes himself in that he comprehends the history of his people.'[23] Salvation could only come about through a

---

[19] See J. Conway, *The Nazi Persecution of the Churches, 1933–1945*, London, 1968, pp. 9–12. The recent work by R. P. Ericksen, *Theologians under Hitler*, New Haven/London, 1985, provides a stimulating analysis of the intellectual background prompting three leading Protestant theologians to welcome Nazism.

[20] For the 'new élitism', see W. Struve, *Elites against Democracy, Leadership Ideals in Bourgeois Political Thought in Germany, 1890–1933*, Princeton, 1973, esp. pp. 11 ff.

[21] See Sontheimer, pp. 268–70; Horn, pp. 25–8; and Vierhaus, pp. 616 ff.

[22] Cited in Sontheimer, p. 270. [23] Cited in ibid., p. 273.

leader, selected and blessed by 'providence', who would rescue Germany from its plight and restore it to greatness. 'In our misery', it was said by one writer in the post-revolutionary phase, 'we long for the Leader. He should show us the way and the deed which could make our people honest again (*wieder ehrlich*).'[24] As embodiment of the people's need and longing, he would be the 'bearer of godly power of destiny and grace',[25] the 'executive organ of a power transcending him'.[26] In stark contrast to the colourless and miserable political compromisers of Weimar, the future leader would be a figure of outstanding skill and political strength, decisive and bold in resolution, to whom his 'following' could look in admiration and devotion. A text from the year 1920 specifies characteristics of the 'leader' which some fifteen years later were important attributes of the Hitler image:

The Leader does not conform to the masses, but acts in accordance with his mission. He does not flatter the masses; hard, straightforward, and ruthless, he takes the lead in good days and in bad. The Leader is radical; he is entirely that which he does, and he does entirely what he has to do. The Leader is responsible; that is, he carries out the will of God, which he embodies in himself. God grant us leaders and help us to true following.[27]

In this extreme form, the belief in 'heroic' leadership still of course occupied only a fringe position on the far Right of the political spectrum in Germany in the early 1920s, though elements of such sentiments unquestionably reached into the ranks of those who at the time gave their support to bourgeois-conservative parties and movements. By the later 1920s, and especially in the growing political as well as economic crisis of the Depression era, perceptions of the total failure of Weimar democracy and mortal crisis of the entire political system allowed the image of 'heroic' leadership to move from the wings of politics to centre stage. Many, quite apart from the Nazis, in the so-called 'patriotic' organizations of the Right, inspired by the example Mussolini had set in Italy, were calling for a national dictator to rescue Germany from its misery. The massive *Stahlhelm* war-veterans' association, for example, demanded 'the strong hand' to rid Germany

---

[24] Cited in ibid., p. 272.
[25] Cited in ibid., p. 272.
[26] Cited in ibid., p. 275.
[27] Cited in ibid., p. 272. The new style of leadership, embodying ideals which stood in extreme opposition to those of liberal bourgeois politics, and which in 'normal times' might have been subject to scorn rather than admiration, is emphasized by Vierhaus, p. 630.

of 'the plague of parliamentarism', and claimed the people needed 'a dictator, a Mussolini, who would sweep out the entire muck with an iron broom' and lead Germany to 'victory and freedom'.[28] Just how far the 'heroic' leadership idea had penetrated society by this date, and how far it was associated not merely with reactionary-romantic, quasi-religious notions, but with thoroughly materialistic considerations in an advanced industrial state, is shown by the vocabulary of contemporary analyses of the economics of the motor-car industry in the 1920s, which reached the conclusion that the misery of the industry could only be overcome by a 'superior leader personality, a man of strong action', and spoke in the context of motor-car manufacture of 'salvation or destruction', 'ways to freedom', and 'struggle for world domination'.[29]

In the early 1920s, we are still far from the point where Hitler, as yet no more than a provincial beerhall rabble-rouser, could himself be popularly associated with the 'heroic' leadership image, and be seen by the mass of the people as just that great leader sent by providence to unite Germany and restore its greatness. But within little more than a decade, a vision taken seriously at one time only on the lunatic fringe of the extreme Right had come, by the mid-1930s, to be the central, all-embracing idea in German political life. Based largely on recent analyses of the internal history and development of the Nazi Party and its growing base of support before 1933, the remainder of this chapter attempts to sketch the growth of the 'Hitler myth' within the Nazi Movement—its acceptance first of all by a hard-core of Party fanatics then by a swelling number of new members and before 1933 by the third of so of the population which voted Nazi—and also to indicate some of the contours of Hitler's image in non-Nazi sectors of the population in the years immediately preceding the 'seizure of power'.

Already in 1920–1 Hitler was occasionally referred to within the NSDAP as 'Führer', though usually only as one of the Party's leaders alongside its Chairman, Anton Drexler. Usage of the term 'our Führer' became gradually more frequent from the end of 1921 following Hitler's take-over of the Party leadership in July that year, mainly

---

[28] Klotzbücher, pp. 127, 334, and see also pp. 13, 122.
[29] Cited in H. Heimann, 'Die Entwicklung des Automobils zum Massenkonsumartikel in Deutschland', Ruhr-Universität Bochum, Magisterarbeit, Bochum, 1983, p. 24 and n. 67.

in connection with Hitler speeches at Party meetings,[30] at which he repeatedly underlined his indispensability to the Movement as its most gifted speaker. The version 'our Führer' remained at this time synonymous with the title 'Führer of the NSDAP', which appears to have been publicly employed for the first time, instead of the older and more conventional form of 'Chairman of the NSDAP', in the Party's paper, the *Völkischer Beobachter*, on 7 November 1921.[31] In its usage in 1920–1, therefore, the term 'Führer' was quite explicitly and conventionally limited to Hitler's leading position within the NSDAP. A significant shift took place, however, when, following Mussolini's so-called 'March on Rome' in October 1922, the term was for the first time extended in analogy to the Italian 'Duce'. In a meeting in the Hofbräuhaus, a huge Munich beerhall, in November 1922, Hermann Esser, one of the Party's leading lights, proclaimed Hitler to be Germany's Mussolini, and references to 'our Führer Adolf Hitler' without restriction to his Party offices multiply in the *Völkischer Beobachter* thereafter, particularly from mid-1923 onwards.[32] An article in the *Völkischer Beobachter* in December 1922 seemed, in fact, for the first time to make the explicit claim that Hitler was *the* Führer, for whom Germany was waiting. Its author spoke of 'the joyful certainty' of Hitler followers leaving a parade in Munich 'to have found something which millions are yearning for, a leader'.[33] Already that year a book dedication to Hitler styled him 'the great man of deed ... the fearless leader of Germany's resurrection', though before 1930 or so dedications to 'the upstanding German' or 'the German fighter of the present day' were more common formulations.[34]

Within the Nazi Party, then, the beginnings of a personality cult around Hitler go back to the year before the Putsch, when Hitler had already acquired a certain political standing, at least in the Munich area, where one press reporter dubbed him as 'alongside the Hofbräuhaus ... the only notable rarity in Munich'.[35] In a speech at

---

[30] A. Tyrell, *Vom 'Trommler' zum 'Führer'*, Munich, 1975, p. 225 n. 399, p. 274 n. 152.

[31] Weißbecker, p. 121.

[32] Tyrell, *'Trommler'*, pp. 274–5 nn. 151–2; Weißbecker, p. 121; C. Berning, *Vom 'Abstammungsnachweis' zum 'Zuchtwart'. Vokabular des Nationalsozialismus*, Berlin, 1964, p. 82; W. Maser, *Der Sturm auf die Republik. Frühgeschichte der NSDAP*, Stuttgart, 1973, pp. 354–7.

[33] Cited in Berning, p. 82.

[34] Cited in ibid., p. 82.

[35] *Hitler. Sämtliche Aufzeichnungen 1905–1924*, ed. E. Jäckel and A. Kuhn, Stuttgart, 1980, p. 939, no. 538 (henceforth cited as Jäckel and Kuhn).

the Circus Krone in Munich in April 1923, Göring, at that time Commandant of the SA, claimed that 'many hundred thousands' were already convinced 'that Adolf Hitler is the only man who could raise Germany up again'.[36] Letters to Hitler around this time from Bavarian right-wing circles also reflect the enthusiastic hopes placed in him, even going so far as to draw parallels between him and Napoleon.[37] New members of the NSDAP in Memmingen at the end of 1923 were sworn in 'solemnly in life and death to Hitler' and the former marching song of the *Freikorps* Ehrhardt Brigade, now with a new refrain promising loyalty 'unto death' to Hitler who 'will soon lead us from this distress', was said to be gaining increasing popularity in Nazi circles.[38]

Outside these small groups of fanatical Bavarian Nazis, Hitler's image and reputation at this time—so far as the wider German public took any notice of him at all—was little more than that of a vulgar demagogue capable of drumming up passionate opposition to the government among the Munich mob, but of little else. The image contrasted vividly with the 'salon manners' which Hitler was cultivating in order to ensure his acceptability with Munich's right-wing upper-bourgeoisie, who in turn were prepared to believe that even a somewhat eccentric stump-orator who could drum up mass support for the counter-revolutionary cause was by no means altogether without his uses.[39]

Despite the overdrawn expectations and hopes of some of his followers, Hitler's self-image at this time did not differ greatly from that of many outside observers. He accepted the fact that his role was that of the 'drummer up' of support, whose job it was to pave the way for the actual great leader who would follow and take Germany out of its misery. 'His self-awareness', it has been claimed, 'did not alter in principle from the beginning of his political career until the day of the attempted Putsch.'[40] A full survey of Hitler's speeches before the Putsch seems to suggest, however, that there was some adjustment in his concept of political leadership in 1922–3, partly no doubt in the light of his admiration for Mussolini's success in Italy. His increasing

---

[36] Cited in Tyrell, '*Trommler*', p. 274 n. 151.

[37] Ibid., pp. 161–2.

[38] Ibid., p. 274 n. 151.

[39] See H. Auerbach, 'Hitlers politische Lehrjahre und die Münchener Gesellschaft 1919–1923', *VfZ*, xxv (1977), 1–45.·

[40] Tyrell, '*Trommler*', p. 165.

preoccupation with 'heroic' personality and leadership, with unconditional obedience to a leader from the people and responsible to
the people, and with the historic nature of the 'mission' which the
leader would carry out, can be traced in his public statements in late
1922 and 1923. As late as May 1923, Hitler said he was still merely
preparing the way in order to give the dictator, when he should come,
a people ready for him.[41] Only two months after this he declared,
somewhat ambivalently, that salvation could be found not in majority
decisions of a parliament, but only in the value of personality and that
as leader of the NSDAP he saw his task 'in accepting the responsibility'.[42] In October he was prepared to leave the leadership question
unanswered until 'the weapon is created which the leader must
possess'. Only at that stage would it be necessary to 'pray to our Lord
God that he give us the right leader'.[43] And on trial before the Munich
'People's Court' in March 1924, accused of treason, he accepted
Ludendorff as the 'military leader of the coming Germany' and 'leader
of the coming great showdown', but claimed for himself the role of
'political leader'.[44] Though still uncategorical, it appears that Hitler's
concept of leadership was sharpening and becoming more 'heroic' in
1923, but that it was still unclear both who the 'great leader' was to be,
and also what precisely Hitler's role would amount to once the
'drumming up' was done. He was, it seems, in his self-image already
part-way along the transition from 'drummer up' to 'Führer'. Since
Hitler's 'heroic' image of leadership matched no single contemporary
'personality', not even Ludendorff, it needed only the failure of the
Putsch to transform the unclear conception of his role in the latter
months of 1923 into that of the heroic leader-figure himself in *Mein
Kampf*—a transition already presaged by the increased self-
confidence Hitler had shown at his trial.[45]

It was during the period of his imprisonment in Landsberg that
Hitler, in the months in which he read avidly and meditated, held
daily 'seminars' with his co-internees, received numerous visitors who
fawned on him in adulation, and wrote the first draft of *Mein Kampf*,
became convinced that he was not just destined to drum up support,

[41] Jäckel and Kuhn, p. 924, no. 525.
[42] Ibid., p. 946, no. 544.
[43] Ibid., p. 1268, no. N22.
[44] Ibid., p. 1188, no. 620. For further comments by Hitler in the years 1922–3 about
'heroic' leadership, see ibid. pp. 578, 616, 641–2, 723, 767, 811, 837, 924, 932, 973, 1268.
[45] See Tyrell, *'Trommler'*, pp. 165 ff.

but to be the Führer himself.[46] Probably the echo he encountered on the German Right in his new-found role as martyr of the 'National Movement' and the flattery and hero-worship he received from dispirited members of the Party, smashed, demoralized, and split in his absence, contributed substantially to his changing self-awareness. To some extent the expectations now being placed on Hitler were therefore helping to preform the image which he was coming to adopt for himself.[47] The 'Führer myth' was a creation of his following before Hitler himself adjusted to the role.

The 'quiet years' of the Nazi Movement between 1925 and 1928, when the NSDAP, refounded in 1925, scarcely found a mention in the non-Nazi press and achieved a miserable 2.6 per cent of the vote in the 1928 Reichstag elections, were however the years in which the Party organization was extended to the whole of the Reich, and the membership substantially increased. In this period, the Nazi Party became the political reservoir of all remaining groupings of the *völkisch* Right, and Hitler's leadership position within the Party became firmly consolidated and scarcely challengeable. Though the refounding of the Party in February 1925 had been directly initiated by Hitler and his Munich entourage, the split in the Movement following the Putsch and the 'leaderless period' of his internment meant that the consolidation of his leadership after 1925 did not take place effortlessly. Especially in north Germany, where Hitler's standing in *völkisch* circles had been far less commanding than in Bavaria, his leadership position did not initially go without challenge.[48] The successful fending-off of a challenge from northern factions at the Nazi gathering at Bamberg in February 1926[49] was, however, a major step on the way to winning over the sceptical Party leadership in the north and to establishing Hitler's outright supremacy and standing. Only a short time later, Joseph Goebbels, up to then a supporter of the more strongly pseudo-socialist faction of the NSDAP, was converted to a devoted and fanatical Hitler-believer, received the *Gau* of Berlin as the first fruits of Hitler's patronage which meant so much to him,[50] and was thereafter the most eloquent exponent of the 'Hitler myth' in

[46] Ibid., pp. 150–74.
[47] Ibid., p. 173.
[48] See e.g. J. Noakes, *The Nazi Party in Lower Saxony*, Oxford, 1971, pp. 65–78.
[49] See ibid., pp. 78–81; Horn, pp. 240ff; D. Orlow, *The History of the Nazi Party, 1919–1933*, Pittsburgh, 1969, pp. 68–70.
[50] See Nyomarkay, p. 13; Orlow, pp. 72, 92.

the Nazi Party. Later that same year, in a letter of extreme adulation, he associated Hitler directly with his vision of Germany's awaited leader. The true leader, he declared, was not elected, was not subject to the whims of the masses, was not a parliamentarian but a liberator of the massses. With obvious pseudo-religious connotations, he spoke of the Führer as 'the fulfilment of a mysterious longing', and of a man who showed them in their deepest despair the way to a faith and 'like a meteor before our astonished eyes' had 'worked a miracle of enlightenment and belief in a world of scepticism and despair'.[51]

The conscious build-up of the 'Führer myth' in the years following the refoundation of the Party had the clear function of compensating for the lack of ideological unity and clarity within the different factions of the Nazi Movement. The Führer figure provided the cement binding together the 'following' of ordinary Party members and subordinate Party leaders—establishing a point of unity which was all the more important now that the Nazi Movement had extended beyond its original Bavarian boundaries and incorporated quite heterogeneous elements from other parts of the Reich. An outward sign of the binding of the Party faithful to the figure of their leader was the introduction within the NSDAP in 1926 of a compulsory 'Heil Hitler' fascist-style salute, which had been sporadically employed since 1923.[52] The functional significance of the 'Hitler myth' as a stabilizing and an integrating element within the Movement is clearly indicated in the readiness of Grégor Strasser, head of the Party organization and in personal terms by no means close to and still rather critical of Hitler, to recognize the value of the 'Führer myth' and unhesitatingly to contribute to its establishment. In an article he published in 1927, for example, he spoke of the relationship of Party members to Hitler in Germanic neo-feudal terms as that of duke and vassal:

An utter devotion to the idea of National Socialism, a glowing faith in the victorious strength of this doctrine of liberation and deliverance, is combined with a deep love of the person of our leader who is the shining hero of the new freedom-fighters ... Duke and vassal! In this ancient German, both aristocratic and democratic, relationship of leader and follower, fully comprehensible only to the German mentality and spirit, lies the essence of the struc-

---

[51] Cited in E. K. Bramsted, *Goebbels and National Socialist Propaganda 1925–1945*, Michigan, 1965, p. 199.

[52] A. Tyrell, *Führer befiehl... Selbstzeugnisse aus der 'Kampfzeit' der NSDAP. Dokumentation und Analyse*, Düsseldorf, 1969, pp. 129–30, 163–4.

ture of the NSDAP ... Friends, raise your right arm and cry out with me proudly, eager for the struggle, and loyal unto death, 'Heil Hitler!'.[53]

Among those 'shaping' the Hitler image from an early date was also Rudolf Heß, who in a private letter written in 1927 wrote that it was above all necessary

that the Führer must be absolute in his propaganda speeches. He must not weigh up the pros and cons like an academic, he must never leave his listeners the freedom to think something else is right. ... The great popular leader is similar to the great founder of a religion: he must communicate to his listeners an apodictic faith. Only then can the mass of followers be led where they should be led. They will then also follow the leader if setbacks are encountered; but only then, if they have communicated to them unconditional belief in the absolute rightness of their own people.[54]

It does not seem to be stretching psychology too far to see in this accurate reflection of Heß's own fawning devotion, as in Goebbels's attitude towards Hitler, a search for a secular instead of a religious faith. Of course, many of the Party's most long-standing members, especially those with rank in the Movement and those far removed from the centre of Party activity in Munich, privately retained a more sober attitude towards Hitler. As long as it was not absolutely clear whether all remaining *völkisch* groups would go over to the NSDAP, Hitler remained for many leading figures in the Movement, quite apart from any personal qualities he might be seen to possess, largely a symbol of Party unity. In a private letter in 1927, for example, Karl Dincklage, Deputy *Gauleiter* of Hanover, commented that, though in his *Gau* they were loyal followers of Hitler, 'it's quite immaterial whether we think Ludendorff or Hitler is the greater. That's left to each one of us to decide.'[55]

The Führer cult was by this time, however, already gaining pace among the growing rank and file of the Party. While fully recognizing the propaganda value of the personality cult and therefore lending his encouragement to it, Hitler was nevertheless anxious to avoid the embarrassment and damage which could come from the more extreme forms of tasteless adulation of the 'god-sent leader'. The tone of a particularly banal poem—it is striking how often doggerel verse was

---

[53] Ibid., p. 163; J. Noakes and G. Pridham (eds.), *Documents on Nazism*, London, 1974, pp. 84-5.
[54] Tyrell, *Führer befiehl*, p. 173.
[55] Ibid., p. 167.

chosen by Hitler-adorers to express their adulation—published on his fortieth birthday and addressing him as 'Wayland the Smith', 'Siegfried', and 'hero of the Front'—was obviously too much even for Hitler. He claimed that the poem, which had been mercilessly parodied by the anti-Nazi sector of the press, had been written and published without his permission and against this express wishes, and withdrew for a while his weekly column in the *Illustrierter Beobachter*.[56] Clearly, however, he had no objection to Goebbel's birthday greeting on the same day in the Berlin Party newspaper, *Der Angriff*, which expressed the belief 'that Fate has chosen him to show the way to the German people. Therefore we greet him in devotion and reverence, and can only wish that he may be preserved for us until his work is completed.'[57]

Such effusive expressions of adulation were not necessarily typical of the feelings even of the majority of Party members, whose objective grounds for optimism did not appear too obvious given the minimal influence of the NSDAP on mainstream politics before 1929. And Party members in the provinces, unceasingly active despite the poor showing of the NSDAP in the 1928 Reichstag election, when it attained only 2.6 per cent of the popular vote and a mere twelve seats in the Reichstag, were too conscious of local factors influencing their prospects of success to place their hopes in Hitler alone. The situation was altered fundamentally by the result of the 1930 Reichstag election, which took place amid growing crisis not only of the economy but of the State itself, and brought the Nazis a spectacular 6.4 million votes, 18.3 per cent of votes cast, making them, with 107 seats, at one fell swoop the second largest party in the Reichstag. Little wonder the leadership was jubilant about a vote which far exceeded their wildest expectations[58] and signified the breakthrough not only to a mass following, but also to mass publicity. Already, a year earlier, the Party

[56] Ibid., p. 388 and illus. 5. Two years earlier, again presumably for fear of the scorn which political opponents were pouring on the excesses of the 'heroic' leadership cult, a massive oil-portrait of Hitler, intended to form the backcloth to the delegates' congress hall, was removed, almost certainly on Hitler's express orders, before the beginning of the Party Rally at Nuremberg—A. Tyrell, *III. Reichsparteitag der NSDAP, 19.—21. August 1927*, Filmedition G122 des Instituts für den wissenschaftlichen Film, Ser. 4, No. 4/ G122, Göttingen, 1976.

[57] Cited in Bramsted, p. 201. In his private diaries, however, Goebbels could still write critically of Hitler. See BAK, NL118/62, entries for 1 March, 29 and 30 June 1930.

[58] Goebbels entered in his diary: '107 mandates at one go. None of us expected that.'—BAK, NL118/62, entry for 16 Sept. 1930.

had managed to shed much of its 'lunatic fringe' image and, as the propaganda front-line for Hugenberg and other seriously-regarded leaders of the 'National Opposition' in the campaign against the Young Plan, to attract more media attention, and to acquire more political and social acceptability among the conservative-minded bourgeoisie. But now, following the election triumph of 14 September 1930, the NSDAP and its leader were big news—*the* media talking-point. It was the stage at which the Hitler cult ceased to be the fetish of a still small Party of fanatics and began for millions of Germans to signal the hope of a new political age.

Even after the triumph of the 1930 election, many intelligent and informed observers of the German political scene felt that the Nazi Party was bound sooner or later to collapse and break up into its component parts.[59] Its social base was diffuse—that of an out and out protest party;[60] it had no clear political programme to offer, only a contradictory amalgam of social revolutionary rhetoric and reactionary impulses; and not least it was heavily dependent on the personality cult surrounding the demagogue Hitler—seen as the mouthpiece of petty-bourgeois resentments, but ultimately a dilettante who, despite temporary success in the conditions of severe economic and political crisis, was bound in the end to succumb to the real power bastions and traditional ruling élites.

The underestimation of the Nazi Movement by many critical outside observers in 1930 was partly rooted in the underrating of the force of the personality cult, of the clamour for the strong man and 'charismatic' leader among ever-widening circles of the population in the gathering gloom of the Depression. Political 'biographies' of rank-and-file members joining the Nazi Party before 1933, several hundred of which have survived and recently been analysed, provide striking evidence of the power of the 'Führer myth' within the Movement, and of the recruiting magnetism of the personality cult. One Party member

[59] See e.g. S. Neumann, *Die Parteien der Weimarer Republik*, Stuttgart, new edn. 1965, pp. 73 ff; P. Fabry, *Mutmaßungen über Hitler. Urteile von Zeitgenossen*, Düsseldorf, 1969, pp. 40–5.

[60] For the social base of Nazi support and the character of its electoral appeal, see now the excellent analysis of T. Childers, *The Nazi Voter. The Social Foundations of Fascism in Germany, 1919–1933*, Chapel Hill/London, 1983. M. Kater, *The Nazi Party. A Social Profile of Members and Leaders, 1919–1945*, Oxford 1983, provides a statistical breakdown of the social structure of the Party membership. The literature on the social composition of Nazi support is well surveyed by M. Jamin, *Zwischen den Klassen. Zur Sozialstruktur der SA—Führerschaft*, Wuppertal, 1984, pp. 11–45.

wrote that after hearing Hitler speak for the first time 'there was only one thing for me, either to win with Adolf Hitler or to die for him. The personality of the Führer had me totally in its spell.'[61] Another described his 'conversion' to Nazism: 'I did not come to Hitler by accident. I was searching for him. My ideal was a movement which would forge national unity from all working people of the great German fatherland. . . . The realization of my ideal could happen through only one man, Adolf Hitler. The rebirth of Germany can be done only by a man born not in palaces, but in a cottage.'[62] Such unmistakable biblical allusions occur not infrequently in the auto-biographical pennings of these ordinary Nazis. Many, such as the following example, have tones redolent of a secularized faith:

A non-Nazi who has not experienced the enormous elementary power of the idea of our Führer will never understand any of this. But let me tell these people as the deepest truth; whenever I worked for the Movement and applied myself for our Führer, I always felt that there was nothing higher or nobler I could do for Adolf Hitler and thereby for Germany, our people and father-land. . . . The real content of my life is my work for and commitment to Hitler and towards a National Socialist Germany . . . Hitler is the purest embodi-ment of the German character, the purest embodiment of a National Socialist Germany.[63]

At Party rallies, young Nazis competed with each other in claims that the Führer had looked at them. For one 'Party Comrade' who, pressing through the cordon of SS men, managed to stretch out his hand and have it touched by Hitler, the experience was so over-whelming that the 'Heil' greeting stuck in his throat 'as he, looking at me for several seconds, briefly presses my hand. . . . My comrades, witnesses of my good fortune, gather round me. Each one wants to shake the hand which had rested in the right hand of the Führer.' In another case, a 'Party Comrade' who had received a small bunch of three red carnations direct from the Führer himself had to be satisfied with a few small remains, which he kept at home as a memento, after his friends had ravaged the bunch and grabbed bits of the flowers for themselves.[64] In their quasi-religious superstition, such actions and

---

[61] Cited in Merkl, p. 539, and see also p. 453.

[62] Cited in ibid., p. 540.   [63] Cited in ibid., pp. 396–7.

[64] C. Schmidt, 'Zu den Motiven "alter Kämpfer" in der NSDAP', in D. Peukert and J. Reulecke (eds.), *Die Reihen fast geschlossen*, Wuppertal, 1981, pp. 36–7. For the adula-tion of Hitler at the Party Rally of 1929, see the recollections of Otto Wagener in H. A. Turner (ed.), *Hitler aus nächster Nähe*, Frankfurt a.M. Berlin/Vienna, 1978, pp. 17–21.

sentiments are almost reminiscent of the supposed healing qualities of the touch of medieval monarchs. The contemporary Hitler image for young Party members was accurately portrayed by the comment in a recent interview of a former SA man who, at the age of eighteen, was by 1928 already a convinced Nazi: 'Naturally we saw in Herr Hitler the man who knew everything, who could do everything, who would see everything through if he once had a chance to exercise power. He was already the model for us young National Socialists. This man appeared to us as a person of integrity.'[65]

These 'old fighters' of the Nazi Party were obviously extreme cases of susceptibility to the Hitler cult. However, the rapid growth of the Party membership between 1930 and 1933 meant that an ever increasing number of Germans were beginning to be exposed to the 'Führer myth'. From 1930 Hitler had to be taken seriously as a political force in Germany. Whereas earlier the non-Nazi press had paid little attention to Hitler and the NSDAP, from 1930 onwards Hitler was scarcely out of the headlines for long—apparent corroboration of the growing feeling that, whether one was for or against him, he was a political figure who was out of the ordinary, and whom one could not ignore. The build-up of the Hitler cult was, therefore, now no longer confined largely to Nazi members, but was extending to far wider sections of the population. Outside the Party faithful and loyal Nazi voters, the Hitler image was still far removed from the later legendary figure. But Hitler was nevertheless acquiring the repute of a Party leader extraordinary, a man towards whom opinion could not remain neutral. Wherever he went he polarized political feelings. It was scarcely possible to adopt a position between ecstatic approval and bitter condemnation.

Before returning the Nazis' own image of Hitler, we need to glance briefly at the counter-images in the three rival ideological blocks of the socialist and communist Left, political Catholicism, and the nationalist bourgeois-conservative Right. In different ways, in fact, even these 'anti-images' contributed to centring increased attention— if of a largely negative kind—on the extraordinary leader of the NSDAP.

The picture of Hitler portrayed in the left-wing press, both socialist and communist, was dominated by the Marxist stereotype of the

[65] L. Steinbach, *Ein Volk, ein Reich, ein Glaube?*, Berlin/Bonn, 1983, p. 31.

lackey of right-wing imperialist forces in the pay of the captains of monopoly capital, tool of the enemies of the working class. Hitler in power, it was nevertheless prophesied with some accuracy, would inevitably mean poverty, repression, untold misery, and ultimately war. Anti-fascist theories developed on the model of Italian Fascism were more or less carried over to Hitler and the NSDAP. Dubbing him simply 'leader of the German fascists', the outright attacks on him by the socialist press—frequently conveyed through heavily-laden sarcasm, slurs casting doubt on his alleged bravery at the Front during the First World War, and libels about his corruptibility through bribes from industry or from abroad—sought to reveal the personality cult for a sham.[66] 'Germany's saviour' was duly dismissed as 'nothing more than a lance corporal: a conceited braggart'.[67] His coarse brutality was signified by headlines such as 'Assault with Rhinoceros Whip: Whip found in Hitler's Car', followed by a story that on a visit to Magdeburg, occupants of Hitler's car had badly beaten up a group of *Reichsbanner* men they had passed on the roadside.[68]

The tendency on the Left, as in a different way on the conservative Right, to underrate Hitler was strong. Even Carl von Ossietzky, writing in the *Weltbühne* with far more foresight than many other left-wing publicists, labelled Hitler a charlatan and thought the German bourgeoisie unimaginably stupid to follow such a 'half-mad deadbeat' ('*halbverrückte Schlawiner*'), a 'cowardly, effeminate, pyjama character', a mere 'creature of industry'.[69] According to Otto Braun, the SPD Prussian Minister President until July 1932, Hitler was no more than the 'prototype of the political adventurer' able on the basis of demagogy financed from murky sources to gather together despera-does, profit-seekers, and reactionaries who opposed the State—'the pied piper of Braunau', in the depiction of an SPD brochure in 1932.[70] The belittling of Hitler was, if anything, even more pronounced in KPD propaganda, where both personality and personality cult were played down, and Hitler was seen consistently in the *Rote Fahne* as the

---

[66] *Münchner Post*, 24 Mar. 1931.

[67] *Fränkische Tagespost*, 24 Oct. 1932.

[68] Ibid., 25 Oct. 1932.

[69] Fabry, pp. 57, 59; and see G. Schreiber, *Hitler. Interpretationen 1923–1983. Ergebnisse, Methoden und Probleme der Forschung*, Darmstadt, 1984, pp. 39 ff. The first part of Schreiber's book provides an excellent survey of perceptions of Hitler in contemporary publications.

[70] Fabry, pp. 162–3.

hireling of capitalists and landowners.[71] As is well known, some grotesque misjudgements led to Thälmann, the KPD leader, claiming in 1931 that 'Fascism does not begin when Hitler comes; it has long since begun', as late as autumn 1932 regarding Brüning as 'the most important figure among bourgeois politicians and the coming man', and writing off the chances of 'the clever and calculating German bourgeoisie' letting Hitler into power since it was inconceivable that a Hitler government could get capitalism out of its cul-de-sac.[72] For the KPD, which since 1928 had been fully engaged in attacking the 'social fascism' of the SPD, there was no substantial difference between the main non-communist candidates in the 1932 presidential election: a vote for Hindenburg was a vote for Hitler.[73]

None the less, the growing Hitler cult was not without its impact on the political thinking of the Left. It has been suggested, in fact, that a leadership cult, unprecedented in a German workers' party, was even being consciously developed in this period around Ernst Thälmann, now styled 'Leader of the German Proletariat'.[74] Evidently irritated by a phenomenon they could for the most part only inadequately grasp, writers on the Left were frequently content to put the Hitler cult down to mass hysteria among the Nazi followers. One attempt to offer an explanation, in the well-regarded socialist journal *Das Freie Wort*, in November 1932, looked to the sphere of female mass psychology, seeing Hitler's attractiveness lying in a feminine quasi-erotic appeal to the hysteria of the sinking 'lumpen bourgeoisie'. The author of the article, entitled 'The Woman Hitler: Psychology around a Leader', pointed to Hitler's 'prima donna character . . . his rehearsed gestures, his pathological vanity towards himself and his Movement' as being essentially feminine characteristics, and cited with approval a depiction of Hitler by the Italian Fascist Malaparte, who had apparently written that there was nothing manly about Hitler, and that 'his feminine side explains the success of Hitler, his power over the masses'.[75]

---

[71] See e.g. W. Ruge, *Das Ende von Weimar. Monopolkapital und Hitler*, East Berlin, 1983, pp. 177, 179, extracts from *Rote Fahne*, 15 July, 6 Aug., 1930.

[72] Cited in S. Bahne, 'Die Kommunistische Partei Deutschlands', in E. Matthias and R. Morsey (eds.), *Das Ende der Parteien*, Düsseldorf, 1979, pp. 658, 677 and n. 6; and see O. Flechtheim, *Die KPD in der Weimarer Republik*, Frankfurt a.M., 1969, p. 265.

[73] Ruge, pp. 236–7.

[74] Flechtheim, p. 256.

[75] In IfZ, MA 731, NSDAP-Hauptarchiv 1/13.

The negative image of Hitler portrayed in the left-wing press presumably contributed to bolstering the general deep hostility to
Nazism which prevailed among those sections of the working class
who had been brought up under the influence of socialist and communist subcultures and traditionally anchored in the ranks of
organized labour. And it continued to be part of the propaganda of the
illegal worker resistance, after the smashing of the left-wing parties,
their institutions and publicity organs, and the trade unions during the
first months of 1933 had forced negative images of Hitler underground
and into the subculture of opposition, attempting to combat the
regime's monopoly of the mass media through homespun broadsheets, factory-wall daubings, and lavatory graffiti. However, the
increasingly obvious inadequacies of the simple picture of Hitler as no
more than the agent of monopoly capital added significantly to the
disorientation of the Left after 1933 and their difficulties in providing a
realistic analysis of the power structures of the new Regime.

Apart from the organized sectors of the working class, the Nazis had
greatest difficulty, as is well known, in penetrating the Catholic sub-
culture, where the dominant image of Hitler provided by Catholic
'opinion leaders' was equally negative. The main attack was levelled at
the anti-Christian essence of the Nazi Movement and of its leader's
philosophy.[76] Publications sought to demonstrate that Hitler's ideas
stood in direct contradiction to the teaching of the Christian
catechism.[77] Especially in Bavaria, where Catholicism was dominant
and extreme anti-Marxism widespread, he and his Movement were
seen as a variant of 'godless Bolshevism'—an association which was
frequently to recur after 1933 during the 'Church struggle'.[78] Though
Catholic anti-Nazi polemics generally concentrated on attacking the
anti-religious, and especially anti-Catholic, thrust of Nazism, some
publications did offer a devastating assault on the entire Nazi
doctrine. Hitler's brutality, contempt for human rights, warmonger-

[76] For the ban imposed by some bishops on Catholics becoming Party members, and
other restrictions, see G. Lewy, *The Catholic Church and Nazi Germany*, London, 1964,
pp. 8–15.

[77] See Schreiber, pp. 88ff.

[78] See Lewy, p. 10. One provincial Bavarian newspaper, not an organ of the BVP but
nevertheless articulating the sentiments of Catholic 'white-blue' Bavaria, spoke
sarcastically of the Nazis as the 'Fatherland saviours with the red lining', taking the
view that 'the entire blurb on the posters about social advancement' was nothing more
than 'a cover-up for a socialist dictatorship of the proletariat and a red centralized state
with a disguised godless movement'—*Miesbacher Anzeiger*, 19 Apr. 1932.

ing, and elevation of force to a principle of political behaviour, were all castigated in Catholic publications of the early 1930s.[79] One Catholic weekly above all, *Der Gerade Weg*, published in Munich under the editorship of Dr Fritz Gerlich—murdered in Dachau in 1934—and Fr. Ingbert Naab, kept up a relentless assault on Hitler, describing him in September 1932, at a time when, despite his open show of solidarity with five of his SA men who had been condemned to death for the brutal murder of a communist in Potempa, the Centre Party was involved in negotiations with the Nazis, as 'the incarnation of evil'.[80]

A few months earlier, the alleged hostility of Hitler to the Church had played a key role in persuading the Catholic parties to support the Protestant, and 'pious', Hindenburg in the election for the Reich Presidency. Catholic campaigners were keen to decry the personal qualities of the 'nonentity' Hitler and his suitability for the elevated position as Head of State. Speakers of the Bavarian People's Party, the right-wing sister to the German Centre Party, and drawing on all the social prejudices of a party of the Bavarian 'establishment', poured scorn on the notion that 'Hitler, the decorator' could win respect abroad, claimed he lacked all the necessary background and educational qualities to be the Head of State, and that there was simply no comparison between Hitler, who had left Austria in 1912 to avoid his military service, and the war-hero Hindenburg.[81] They were equally concerned to attack and debunk the neo-pagan deification and mythologizing of Hitler. One speaker told of a woman who had erected an altar in her house with a picture of Hitler in place of the monstrance, and declared that he could simply not understand the German people for letting itself be led astray by such a charlatan: 'Hitler has succeeded in organizing the idiots, and only idiots, hysterics, and fools to go the NSDAP.' His election, he prophesied, would bring irreparable harm and destruction to Germany.[82]

Hitler was himself well aware of the need to counter his anti-Christian image if his Party were to break through in Catholic areas. He was keen even in the early 1920s not to antagonize unnecessarily the Catholic Church.[83] And during the rise to power the NSDAP

---

[79] Schreiber, pp. 91 ff; Lewy, pp. 17–18.

[80] Cited in Lewy, p. 21; and see Fabry, pp. 104–5.

[81] IfZ, MA 731, NSDAP-Hauptarchiv, 1/13; GS Waldsassen an das BA Tirschenreuth, 29 Feb. 1932; GS Altenschönbach an das BA Gerolzhofen, 4 Apr. 1932.

[82] Ibid., GS Plössberg an das BA Tirschenreuth, 11 Mar. 1932.

[83] Lewy, p. 7; J. Conway, 'National Socialism and the Churches during the Weimar Republic', in Stachura, *The Nazi Machtergreifung*, p. 135.

made particular efforts—largely in vain—in Catholic areas such as the
Rhineland and Bavaria to emphasize its 'positive Christianity', to deny
the slur that it was an anti-religious party, and to claim that National
Socialism alone could provide the Church with a barrier against
Marxism.[84] In 1930 Hitler felt compelled to distance himself from
Alfred Rosenberg, one of the leading Party ideologues, whose book
The Myth of the 20th Century had cemented his reputation as the
dominant representative of the 'new heathenism' and prominent 'hate
figure' of the Catholic Church.[85] And speaking before a mass
gathering in the Catholic stronghold of Bavaria in April 1932, Hitler
told his audience that while north German Protestants had labelled
him a hireling of Rome and south German Catholics a pagan
worshipper of Woden, he was merely of the opinion—here playing to
some widespread anti-clerical sentiments—that priests in Germany,
just as was the case in Italy, should end their political activities and
confine themselves to denominational matters and pastoral duties:
what the Pope had admitted in Italy, he concluded, could not be sinful
in Germany. In fact, he was at pains to stress, he himself was deeply
religious, the 'spiritual distress' of the German people even greater
than its economic misery, and the toleration of over fourteen million
anti-religious atheistic Marxists in Germany highly regrettable.[86]

Despite these disclaimers, the negative image of 'neo-heathenism',
which the NSDAP could not shake off, undoubtedly played a considerable role in bolstering the high level of relative immunity to
Nazism which prevailed before 1933 in Catholic circles. Even after the
disappearance of the Catholic press in the early years of the Third
Reich, Catholic clergy were able to sustain the image through their
own subtle 'propaganda' methods—greatly assisted by the often crude
assaults of the Nazis themselves in the 'Church struggle'—and it
remained throughout the Third Reich an important basis of the
alienation of the Catholic population from the regime and of forms of
partial opposition to Nazism in the Catholic subculture. Even so, the
notion that there might be some authoritarian, patriotic, anti-Marxist,
residual 'good' in Nazism, that 'National Socialism, notwithstanding

[84] See Lewy, p. 14; Childers, pp. 258–9; F. J. Heyen (ed.), *Nationalsozialismus im
Alltag*, Boppard a.R., 1967, p. 37; and G. Pridham, *Hitler's Rise to Power. The Nazi Movement in Bavaria 1923–1933*, London, 1973, ch. 5.

[85] See Fabry, p. 101.

[86] *Fränkischer Kurier*, 8 Apr. 1932; *Miesbacher Anzeiger*, 19 Apr. 1932; GStA, MA
102144, RPvNB/OP, 19 Oct. 1932.

everything, might succeed some day in eliminating from its programme and its activities all that which conflicted in principle and
practice with Catholicism',[87] offered the opening for the volte-face
which Catholic bishops were prepared to make following Hitler's
avowals of tolerance and support for the Church in March 1933 and
the potential, too, for driving a wedge between 'the god-fearing
statesman' Hitler and the anti-Christian Party radicals, especially
Rosenberg.[88]

The image of Hitler portrayed in the media of the remaining major
ideological block outside Nazism, that of the national-conservative
Right, was of course nothing like so negative as that of the Left and of
the Catholics. Generally, the image prevailed of Hitler as the mass
agitator, the 'drummer up', the gifted demagogue capable of firing
emotions in the national cause. The bourgeois press showed a good
deal of sympathy for the ideas which Hitler represented, and gave him
and the Nazi Movement increasing, usually at least moderately
favourable, coverage. His extreme nationalism and rabid anti-
Marxism were of course seen as very positive attributes, and his
demagogic talents were linked to hopes that he might wean the masses
from socialism. At the same time, there were anxious worries about the
'socialism' of the NSDAP—fears which intensified in the campaign
for the November election of 1932 in the wake of the Nazi participation in the Berlin transport strike just prior to it.[89] There was some
ambivalence about the level of Nazi violence, which was partly seen as
a matter for concern, but more usually as valiant self-defence against
communist outrages. It was obviously felt, however, that Hitler
himself should not be directly associated with the violence, as the
sharp criticism of his support for the Potempa murderers demonstrated.[90] The most negative appraisal of Hitler in the national-
conservative bourgeois press was voiced during the presidential
election campaigns of March and April 1932, when the unimpeachable
qualities of the ageing Field Marshal Hindenburg, again prepared
selflessly to do his duty for the nation and epitomizing German

[87] Cited in Lewy, p. 17.
[88] Ibid., p. 23, and ch. 2 *passim* for the 'adjustment' of the Catholic hierarchy's
position in early 1933.
[89] See Schreiber, pp. 69–71; Childers, p. 204; R. Hamilton, *Who voted for Hitler?*,
Princeton, 1982, pp. 95, 127, 142, 166–7, 178, 186, 192–3, 196–7, 208–9; Noakes and
Pridham, p. 139.
[90] See Hamilton, pp. 95, 142.

national values, were compared with the qualities of his opponent—social upstart, mouthpiece of the ill-informed, ill-educated, hysterical masses, head of a movement containing wild extremists and un-savoury elements, and not least a 'party man' as opposed to Hindenburg, the national leader.[91] In particular Hitler's rejection of the post of Vice Chancellor in August 1932 gave the bourgeois-national press a new opportunity to attack Hitler's lust for power and to warn against a man who would only be satisfied with the sole rule of his party. During the course of 1932, however, the attitude of the right-wing non-Nazi press became on the whole more favourably inclined towards Hitler. At any rate, if disinclined to further the Hitler personality cult or provide shows of open enthusiasm, and if publicly voicing some concern about the prospect of a Hitler-led government, conservative German-National orientated newspapers like the Berlin *Deutsche Tageszeitung* were by the end of 1932 coming to 'see no other solution now than to charge Hitler with the solution of the crisis'.[92]

During the five election campaigns of 1932, as the frenetic energy of the Nazi Movement put Germany in a ferment, the Führer cult reached new heights in the rapidly expanding Nazi press.[93] In the *Völkischer Beobachter*, which had increased its circulation almost five-fold between 1929 and 1932,[94] and in other Nazi organs, the impression was reinforced from day to day of the unstoppable march to power of a mass movement united behind its leader, a man with a mission to save Germany, and a man who was going his way irrespective of temporary setbacks. While the non-Party press prosaically referred to 'Herr Hitler' or 'the leader of the NSDAP', in the Nazi press he was 'Adolf Hitler' (never just 'Hitler'), 'our Leader', or simply 'the Leader'.[95] Increasingly—a designation which seemed to express the inevitability of the historical process which would bring Hitler to power and create

[91] See R. Morsey, 'Die Deutsche Zentrumspartei', in: Matthias and Morsey, pp. 303–4, for the portrayal of a 'heroic' Hindenburg image at this time.

[92] Cited in Hamilton, p. 95.

[93] Though still dwarfed by the bourgeois, Catholic, and socialist press, the number of Nazi-owned newspapers had increased from 6 dailies and 43 weeklies in 1930 to a total of 127 publications, with a circulation of well over a million, by 1932—Z. Zeman, *Nazi Propaganda*, Oxford, 1964, pp. 20, 28–9.

[94] Ibid., p. 28.

[95] See Noakes and Pridham, p. 104, where Louise Solmitz, a Hamburg school-teacher, commenting on a Hitler meeting in April 1932 noted: 'Nobody spoke of "Hitler", always just "the Führer".'

a new Germany—he was being portrayed as 'the Leader of the coming Germany'.[96]

Among fanatics, the Führer cult now knew no bounds, and its more outlandish expressions provided some useful ammunition for the ideological enemies of the Nazis. The socialist journal *Das Freie Wort*, for example, cited an article entitled 'The House Altar of National Socialists' in order to pour scorn on the ludicrous extremes Hitler-worship had reached among some of his women followers:

Hitler is the alpha and omega of our world philosophy. Every National Socialist house must have a place in which the Führer is near at hand. Generous hands and hearts must offer him small tributes every day at such a place in the form of flowers and plants.[97]

And wholly counter-productive in propaganda terms were the occasional 'enthusiasms' of local Party speakers who, even in outright Catholic strongholds, went so far as to claim that the only historical parallel with Hitler, who had begun with seven men and now attracted a huge mass following, was that of Jesus Christ, who had started with twelve companions and created a religious movement of millions.[98] Though the pseudo-religious motivation which obviously lay for many behind the Hitler cult produced such extraordinary and embarrassing expressions of adulation, the more routine products of Nazi propaganda generally found more effective ways of tapping it, as in a report in the *Stürmer* about the unexpected arrival of Hitler at a conference of Party functionaries from Streicher's *Gau* of Franconia at Nuremberg in September 1932:

Immense joy expresses thanks to the Führer. He has poured tremendous strength into the hearts of the many hundreds who were present. They are proud to have such a man as their Leader. None of the participants will ever forget this conference. For each one of them it has become a sacred experience, which means to him the joyful fight for Hitler, for Germany.[99]

---

[96] *Flamme*, 3 July 1931, in: IfZ, MA 731, NSDAP-Hauptarchiv, 1/13; *Völkischer Beobachter*, 28 July 1931, 25 Nov. 1932.

[97] In: IfZ, MA 731, NSDAP-Hauptarchiv, 1/13.

[98] GStA, MA 102138, RPvOB, 22 Feb. 1932. The speaker reportedly added that Hitler had been exposed to similar persecution and character assassination as Christ. Another Nazi speaker, mentioned in the same report, declared that Hitler had been 'chosen by a higher Being for his mission'.

[99] *Der Stürmer*, No. 36, Sept. 1932, in: IfZ, MA 731, NSDAP-Hauptarchiv, 1/13.

Such a 'love-affair' with Hitler, when not merely conscious
propaganda stylization, was even now by no means shared by the
vastly increased army of Nazi followers. Recent research has amply
demonstrated the complexity of interpreting the variety of motives
which brought people to give their support to Nazism.[1] The elements
in the mix, in which hard material self-interest intermingled with
more 'irrational' forms of motivation, will never be known precisely in
the absence of contemporary opinion surveys, and speculation is
inevitable. It would clearly be mistaken, in focusing on the Hitler cult,
to play down other central aspects of the Nazi appeal. Yet its importance as the fulcrum of Nazi propaganda appeal cannot be doubted,
and its function in integrating and personalizing in the Führer figure
the disparate motivation of Nazi supporters, drawn from vague
ideological precepts and social promises, was absolutely fundamental.
As the 'mouthpiece' of, in particular, lower middle-class resentments
and aspirations—the 'incarnation of the petty bourgeois mentality'[2]—
Hitler articulated and legitimized individual grievances, demands,
and self-interest, while the personal bonds of loyalty to the Führer
sharpened the point of identification in a Movement whose centrifugal tendencies were always threatening to tear it apart.[3] And for the
'established' bourgeoisie who, at least in the big cities, were in
increasing numbers finding Nazism a not unattractive proposition,[4]
Hitler offered—for all his apparent lack of 'statesmanlike' qualities—a
counter to the widespread doubts about the NSDAP's capabilities of
providing a responsible governing Party.[5] By 1932 the 'idea' of
National Socialism had, for Nazi supporters at least, long since been
fused into the figure of the Führer. And for the Nazis' opponents, too,
the personalization of ideology and organization was symbolized by
the fact that the NSDAP was now commonly dubbed 'the Hitler
Movement' and local Party activists as 'the Hitlers'.

Wide propagation of important components of the 'Hitler myth'
occurred during the contest for the Reich Presidency in March and

---

[1] I have attempted to summarize the findings of some of this research in 'Ideology,
Propaganda, and the Rise of the Nazi Party', in Stachura, *The Nazi Machtergreifung*,
pp. 162–81.

[2] L. Kettenacker, 'Hitler's Impact on the Lower Middle Class', in D. Welch (ed.),
Nazi Propaganda: The Power and the Limitations, London, 1983, p. 11; Kettenacker,
'Sozialpsychologische Aspekte der Führer-Herrschaft', pp. 103, 119.

[3] See esp. Broszat, 'Soziale Motivation', and Orlow, pp. 217–20 and 299–302.

[4] This is the main finding of Hamilton, *Who voted for Hitler?*

[5] See Louise Solmitz's comments in Noakes and Pridham, pp. 110, 139.

April 1932, especially during the second run-off ballot in which Hitler challenged Hindenburg directly. In this, the leader of the NSDAP, before 1929–30 still a relative unknown in the framework of national politics, was able to garner over thirteen million votes—well over a third of the total cast—and emerge as a candidate of comparable stature to the winner, the revered Field Marshal of the First World War who had enjoyed the backing of all the major parties apart from the NSDAP and KPD. The visual impact of Nazi propaganda was striking. All over Germany in the last days before the election and in conscious contrast to coloured election posters, a poster depicting Hitler's head on a completely black background appeared. Stark slogans hammered home the message that a vote for Hitler was a vote for change; a vote for Hindenburg was a vote for the status quo.[6] The election was portrayed as a contest between the representative figure of the Weimar 'system', and the Leader of the new, young Germany, 'the Führer, the Prophet, the Fighter ... the last hope of the masses, the shining symbol of the German will to freedom', in Goebbels's rhetoric.[7]

The second presidential campaign, squeezed into a week before the election on 10 April, was made spectacular through new advances in the manufacture of the 'Hitler myth'. The advertised 'great propaganda journey of the Führer through Germany'[8] was for the first time in election history carried out largely by aeroplane, which Hitler had charted to transport him around the country to campaign meetings. In the first campaign, when he still journeyed by road, he had held speeches in twelve cities in an eleven-day tour. By taking to the skies in his well-publicized *Deutschlandflug*, accompanied by the slogan of 'the Führer over Germany', Hitler was now able to address major rallies in twenty different cities within a spell of only six days. In his four airborne campaigns between April and November 1932, Hitler addressed in all 148 mass rallies, averaging some three major meetings a day, often speaking before crowds 20,000 to 30,000 strong in the big cities, and being seen in person and heard in this one year by literally millions of Germans.[9] It was by any measure a remarkable

---

[6] Ibid., p. 103.

[7] Cited in Bramsted, p. 201. For a good survey of the election propaganda, see Childers, pp. 196–8.

[8] Noakes and Pridham, p. 104.

[9] E. Deuerlein (ed.), *Der Aufstieg der NSDAP in Augenzeugenberichten*, Düsseldorf, 1968, pp. 382, 385, 394, 402; M. Domarus (ed.), *Hitler. Reden und Proklamationen 1932–1945*, Wiesbaden, 1973, pp. 101–3, 117–20, 138–42.

performance of campaign speaking, in which Hitler reached the
masses as no German politician had done before him.

Though undoubtedly a chief function of the mass rallies, conducted
with the passion of revivalist meetings and with Hitler adopting a tone
of political 'missionary' and prophet, was to stir the already committed
and preach to the converted,[10] the 'Germany Flights' unquestionably
also helped to popularize the Hitler cult way beyond the ranks of
existing Nazi members and convinced supporters. Hitler owed his
unfailing appeal as a speaker in the depths of the economic crisis, in
which high emotions swung like a pendulum from fear and despair to
euphoria and utopian hopes for the future, to his ability to tailor his
speeches exactly to the crisis mentality and mood of untrammelled
aggression and hatred for the 'system' of his predominantly middle-
class audiences.

The flavour of one such rally was captured in the notes of a
Hamburg schoolteacher, Louise Solmitz:

The hours passed, the sun shone, expectations rose. . . . It was nearly 3 p.m.
'The Führer is coming!' A ripple went through the crowds. . . . There stood
Hitler in a simple black coat and looked over the crowd, waiting—a forest of
swastika pennants swished up, the jubilation of this moment was given vent in
a roaring salute. Main theme: Out of parties shall grow a nation, the German
nation. . . . His voice was hoarse after all his speaking during the previous
days. When the speech was over, there was roaring enthusiasm and applause.
Hitler saluted, gave his thanks, the Horst Wessel song sounded out across the
course. Hitler was helped into his coat. Then he went. How many look up to
him with touching faith as their helper, their saviour, their deliverer from
unbearable distress—to him who rescues the Prussian prince, the scholar, the
clergyman, the farmer, the worker, the unemployed, who rescues them from
the parties back into the nation.[11]

Hitler deliberately took his campaigns during the 'Germany
Flights' not only to the big cities, but also deep into the provinces,
where the propaganda impact was if anything even more striking.
Reports of Hitler's progress through Bavaria provide some indication
of this. In the sleepy small towns of provincial Bavaria, the Hitler
meeetings were a phenomenon never previously experienced by the
local population. The *Miesbacher Anzeiger* for instance, a local news-

---

[10] This aspect of Nazi propaganda is heavily emphasized by R. Bessel, 'The Rise of
the NSDAP and the Myth of Nazi Propaganda', *Wiener Library Bulletin*, xxxiii (1980),
20–9.
[11] Noakes and Pridham, p. 104.

paper with Bavarian 'white-blue' political colouring, spoke of Hitler's
speech in the small Upper Bavarian town on 17 April in the Bavaria
Landtag election campaign, for which thousands had waited for hours
in pouring rain, as 'an unprecedented sensation' for Miesbach.[12] Of
course, Hitler had always had considerable drawing-power as a
speaker.[13] But there was little comparison between the attendances in
earlier campaigns and those in 1932. In Günzburg, for example, Hitler
had attracted about 1,200 persons—a number matched in some SPD
meetings—to a speech in 1930. When he returned there in October
1932 to hold 'a programmatic election speech', the meeting was
attended by an estimated 7,000–8,000, large numbers coming from way
outside the district, and had to be held in the great halls of the
Mengele factory not, as earlier, in the town's gymnasium.[14] The
atmosphere of the meeting and the adulation of Hitler, heightened as
was normally the case at Hitler rallies by expectations driven to fever
pitch in the lengthy wait for his arrival, were played upon in the
stylized reportage of the *Völkischer Beobachter*:

In the afternoon hours the great migration begins. On foot, on cycle and
motorcycle, on waggons and in cars, people stream in from all sides. . . . Long
before the start, both great halls are packed. . . . Thousands have to stand
outside. . . . Then the Führer comes. The SA can hardly keep a path open for
him through the masses. Joyful 'Heil' greetings salute him. The three-year-
old little daughter of Sturmführer Schmalzgruber of Burgau presents him
with a large bouquet of flowers, the six-year-old small son of SA-man Linder a
picture. And again I see, as so often before, that joyful sparkle in the Führer's
eyes as he lays his hand on the head of the children . . .[15]

This Hitler meeting, greeted with 'almost hysterical enthusiasm' by
the Führer's supporters, may well—whatever the hyperbole of the
report—have tipped the balance in the election campaign in this
district where, in contrast with the pattern in the Reich as a whole, the
NSDAP managed to increase its vote in the November election of
1932.[16]

[12] *Miesbacher Anzeiger*, 19 Apr. 1932.

[13] A report of an election campaign meeting held at Markt Grafing in August 1930, for
instance, estimated a total attendance of about 4,000 and mentioned that a parallel
meeting had to be held in another hall—GStA, MA 102138, RPvOB, 19 Aug. 1930.

[14] Z. Zofka, *Die Ausbreitung des Nationalsozialismus auf dem Lande*, Munich, 1979, pp. 41,
78, 89; *Völkischer Beobachter*, 13 Oct. 1932 (where the attendance figure was given as a
richly inflated 30,000); GStA, MA 102149, RPvS, 19 Oct. 1932.

[15] *Völkischer Beobachter*, 13 Oct. 1932.

[16] Zofka, p. 41.

The reports in the *Völkischer Beobachter*, under banner headlines such as 'Grandiose Progress of the Hitler Days' or 'The Führer's Victory March through Bavaria's *Gaue*', naturally constructed an image of Hitler which could provide the most diametrical contrast to the vilification of Germany's current rulers. The 'people's Führer' with his massive army of support was compared with von Papen, no more than head of a government devoid of any popular legitimacy and reliant 'merely on a small circle of reactionaries' for its backing.[17] Hitler took up the line of attack in his speeches, exploiting popular stereotypes of the fat salaries and comfortable living of cabinet ministers to scourge von Papen, allegedly owner of property worth five million marks but still drawing his Chancellor's salary, whereas he rejected such a salary for all time and had interest in nothing but selfless work for his people.[18]

The Nazi press eulogizing of Hitler's campaign trail could not, of course, hide the fact that down to the end of 1932 the NSDAP had failed to make any serious inroads into the blocks of support for the worker and Catholic parties. Even within the Nazi Party itself, Hitler's 'charisma' was by no means unlimited.[19] According to one report in March 1932, some National Socialists were adding their voices to those claiming that Hitler did not possess the necessary qualities and abilities for the position of Reich President, saying: 'Hitler has so far acted only as a political agitator; but you can't imagine him as Reich President.'[20] Nor did Hitler's mass rallies always match expectations. The sober, if not unbiased, accounts of the State authorities frequently contrast vividly with the ecstatic reporting of the Nazi press. Hitler's speech to a meeting of 4,000 in Würzburg on 6 April 1932, for example, was said not to have met the 'exaggerated expectations' of the audience and to have been 'a disappointment even for Party supporters', while the 7,000 to 8,000 persons attending a rally in the

[17] *Völkischer Beobachter*, 14 Oct. 1932.

[18] IfZ, MA 731, NSDAP-Hauptarchiv, 1/13, Pd Hof, 15 Oct. 1932.

[19] 'Opposition' to Hitler had manifested itself in serious fashion in the 'Stennes Revolt' of the eastern SA in spring 1931, and there was, of course, considerable disenchantment with Hitler's tactics during the growing crisis within the Party in the autumn of 1932, culminating in the resignation of Gregor Strasser. See Orlow, pp. 216ff; P. D. Stachura, *Gregor Strasser and the Rise of Nazism*, London, 1983, ch. 6. What seems nevertheless significant is that in the Stennes crisis Hitler was able successfully to deploy his 'charisma' in appealing for personal loyalty and defusing the situation, and that in late 1932 Strasser's resignation took place without any attempt to pose a challenge to Hitler's leadership position.

[20] GStA, MA 102151, RPvUF, 4 Mar. 1932.

village of Pocking in Lower Bavaria in October 1932, which the *Völkischer Beobachter* had described as 'A Mighty Show of Confidence in National Socialism on the part of Lower Bavarian Peasants', were said to have been mainly Party members from the region along with some who had come out of mere curiosity.[21]

Above all, the election weariness and the internal difficulties within the NSDAP provided a testing time for Hitler's 'charismatic' appeal in the autumn of 1932. Goebbels had feared earlier in the year that the Party was in danger of 'winning itself to death' in elections,[22] but by the time the propaganda machine had slotted into gear for the fifth major campaign of the year, control of the State seemed as distant as ever. Impatient in the seemingly endless struggle for power, especially after Hitler had refused the President's offer of the Vice Chancellorship but nothing more in a meeting on 13 August 1932, Party members were beginning to say they had had enough of 'a Party whose Leader does not know what he wants and has no programme'.[23] And some Protestants supporters were reacting in dismay to talk of coalition negotiations with the Catholic Centre Party the same month.[24] By October 1932, Hitler had the rare experience of speaking in a half-empty auditorium during a visit to Nuremberg, centre of the Nazi Franconian heartland.[25] This critical period for Hitler indicates how dependent the manufactured Hitler 'charisma' was on conjunctural factors, how fragile it could be, and how only recurring success could guarantee its vitality.

Nevertheless, there seems little doubt that already before the 'seizure of power' more than thirteen million Germans were at least potential 'Hitler believers', won over in principle to the 'leadership principle' and the personality cult which had been built up around Hitler. Opinion about Hitler in the remaining majority of the population varied largely along the ideological lines which we have surveyed: implacable hatred in the ranks of organized labour, deep suspicion among Catholics, but, in the national-conservative middle classes

---

[21] Ibid., 19 Apr. 1932; GStA, MA 102144, RPvNB/OP, 19 Oct. 1932, where it was added that Hitler's campaign tours would do little to affect the expected drop in Nazi votes at the coming election.

[22] Orlow, p. 254.

[23] GStA, MA 102151, RPvUF, 21 Sept. 1932.

[24] Morsey, pp. 315 ff.

[25] IfZ, MA 731, NSDAP-Hauptarchiv, 1/13, Pd Nürnberg-Fürth, 14 Oct. 1932; GStA, MA 101241/2, Pd Nürnberg-Fürth, 31 Oct. 1932; GStA, MA 102154, RPvMF, 19 Oct. 1932.

above all, the feeling that despite his lack of social standing and the 'socialist' tendencies of his Movement the man might have his uses for a time.

At least three general factors have to be taken into account in explaining how, despite these varied and often heatedly negative attitudes towards Hitler, the Führer cult could within a strikingly short time after January 1933 extend its hold to wide sections of the population, and eventually in some degree to the great majority of Germans.

Of crucial significance was the widespread feeling that the Weimar political system and leadership was utterly bankrupt. New 'leadership' was 'in the air'. Vain attempts had been made to associate the attributes of this 'leadership' even with such unlikely contenders for 'charisma' as Brüning and Hugenberg, and during the presidential elections, Hindenburg too had been seen as a 'heroic figure' and described as 'leader of the German nation'.[26] In 1932, press reports from all sides conveyed a strong impression of almost complete governmental paralysis and of an utterly divided nation tearing itself apart in a succession of the most bitter election campaigns. In such conditions, the image of a dynamic, energetic, 'youthful' leader offering a decisive change of direction and backed by an army of fanatical followers was by no means unattractive. Many with grave doubts were prepared to give Hitler a chance. And compared with the pathetic helplessness of his immediate predecessors as Chancellor, the apparent drive and tempo of Hitler's government in the months after he took office seemed impressive.

Secondly, the gross underestimation of Hitler before 1933 again paved the way for at first reluctant or condescending, and then often wholehearted enthusiasm for the way he apparently mastered within such a short time the internal political situation which had seemed beyond the capabilities of an upstart rabble-rouser.

Thirdly, and most importantly, Hitler embodied an already well-established, extensive, ideological consensus which also embraced most of those, except the Left, who had previously not belonged in the Nazi camp. Its chief elements were virulent anti-Marxism and the perceived need for a powerful counter to the forces of the Left; deep hostility towards the failed democratic system and a belief that strong, authoritarian leadership was necessary for any recovery; and a wide-

[26] See Morsey, pp. 292, 294, 303–4; Childers, p. 207.

spread feeling, even extending to parts of the Left, that Germany had been badly wronged at Versailles, and was threatened by enemies on all sides. This pre-existing, wide consensus offered the potential for strong support for a national leader who could appear to offer absolute commitment, personal sacrifice, and selfless striving in the cause of inner unity and outward strength.

A leading article on 31 January 1933 in a conservative newspaper, the *Münchner Neueste Nachrichten*, which had the fifth largest circulation in Germany and had taken a line more hostile to the Nazis than practically any other organ of the bourgeois press, suggests amid tones of continued scepticism the conditions in which Hitler could make rapid gains in popularity with the prestige of the Chancellorship behind him. It was written by Erwein Freiherr von Aretin, a monarchist who had frequently crossed swords with the Nazis and was to be promptly taken into 'protective custody' in March 1933:

We have seen an unprecedented collapse of State order in the last months. . . . We have . . . such an extent of power intrigue behind us that we would be deceiving ourselves if we did not honestly express the hope that this change will be a lasting one, and that the magnitude of the task will not tear the new men away from the narrowness and deadness of the parties into a world in which there are only Germans and their enemies. . . . The greatest economic problem of our days, unemployment, lies before the new government like a huge mountain to be climbed. None of its predecessors was able to tackle it effectively. The Hitler cabinet will be aware that nothing could bring it so much trust as success here. Here no one can refuse it active assistance. In the struggle against need and hunger there can be no parties. Here the critic of so many years must show that he can do better. Then no German will deny the new cabinet the thanks which it should be its first endeavour to earn.[27]

The sentiments seem clear: success in the pursuit of national goals and banning the divisiveness of party politics could bring Hitler new stature as a national, not party, leader and with it the potential for the conversion of former lukewarm supporters, waverers, or even opponents into admirers of the Führer and thereby at least partial adherents of the Nazi State. It was the task of Nazi propaganda, now rapidly gaining a near monopoly of media control, to bring about that conversion.

[27] *Münchner Neueste Nachrichten*, 31 Mar. 1933. For von Aretin, see his autobiography: E. von Aretin, *Krone und Ketten. Erinnerungen eines bayerischen Edelmannes*, Munich, 1955.

2

'Symbol of the Nation'
The Propaganda Profile of Hitler,
1933–1936

> You don't get round to talking any longer out of pure wonder and
> amazement at everything our Hitler is doing. . . . Since the man
> has taken history into his hands, things work.
>
> *Schwäbisches Volksblatt,* 9 Sept. 1933

> We see in . . . him the symbol of the indestructible life-force of
> the German nation, which has taken living shape in Adolf Hitler.
>
> Otto Dietrich, euology on Hitler's birthday, 1935

THE seemingly unending torchlight procession, staged by Berlin
Gauleiter Goebbels, which wound its way past Hitler and Hindenburg
as they watched from the balcony of the Reich Chancellery on the
evening of 30 January 1933, was meant to signify that Hitler's appointment to the Chancellorship was no normal change of government.
The spectacular celebration of Hitler's personal triumph and the
'victory' of his Movement was intended to suggest to the German
people that they were witnessing a historic break with the past, the
dawn of a new era. And already voices could be heard saying that
Hitler would never relinquish the power he had won.[1]

Outside the Nazi Party and its supporters, however, Hitler's elevation to the Chancellorship did nothing overnight to alter existing
perceptions. Among those still holding to the Catholic parties, many
doubtless shared the sentiments expressed in a leading article on
31 January 1933 in the *Regensburger Anzeiger*, a newspaper aligned to the
Bavarian People's Party, that a Hitler Chancellorship marked a 'leap
into the dark'. On the Left, especially, the view prevailed that Hitler
would be no more than the 'front-man' for a cabinet of reactionaries

---

[1] See e.g. GStA, MA 106682, RPvS. 6 Feb. 1933, 21 Feb. 1933.

dominated by Hugenberg, von Papen, and their friends, the direct representatives of Germany's ruling classes. And it was widely presumed that the heterogeneous nature of the catch-all Nazi programme promising all things to all men would quickly result in a far-reaching disillusionment of the NSDAP's mass base and a rapid drop in Hitler's popularity.[2] Away from the clamour of the big city celebrations of the 'seizure of power', Hitler's appointment to the Chancellorship initially did nothing, in those parts of provincial Germany which the Nazis had far from won over by 1933, to break through the wall of profound apathy and scepticism created by the miseries of the Depression and apparently ceaseless and fruitless electioneering and party-political wrangling. Pessimism generally prevailed here: many thought that there was little chance of Hitler bringing about any improvement, some 'that Hitler would not even be as long in office as his predecessor General von Schleicher'.[3]

Attitudes towards Hitler and the new government were already, however, becoming more positive in such areas during the course of February 1933. If many remained unconvinced, they were at least prepared to give Hitler a chance to see what he could do: things could scarcely get worse. In Lower Bavaria and the Upper Palatinate, for example, where reports at the beginning of February had pointed out the lack of enthusiasm of the overwhelmingly Catholic peasantry in the region for the change of government, it was being suggested towards the end of the month that Hitler's take-over of the government had been 'not unfavourably received' in farming circles and that opinion was gaining ground, especially among former supporters of the Bavarian Peasant League, 'that Hitler's the right man'.[4] From Upper Bavaria, too, it was reported 'that the new Reich government is encountering little rejection among the peasantry' who were prepared to wait and see, then judge it on results. And already the increased import duty on cattle and the slight improvement in wood- and

[2] See GStA, MA 106670, RPvOB, 6 Feb. 1933.
[3] GStA, MA 106672, RPvNB/OP, 3 Feb. 1933; and see also StAM LRA 76887, GS Landsham, Markt Schwaben, Anzing, Ebersberg, Markt Grafing, and Aßling, reports from 11 and 12 Feb. 1933.
[4] GStA, MA 106672, RPvNB/OP, 20 Feb. 1933. The Bavarian Peasants' League indeed lost 41,000 votes (29% of its electoral support) between November 1932 and March 1933. In Lower Bavaria, where at the 1928 Reichstag election it had won 35.3% of the vote, it sank from 16.9% in November 1932 to a mere 9.5% in March 1933— M. Hagmann, *Der Weg ins Verhängnis*, Munich, 1946, pp. 15*, 17*.

cattle-prices were being put down as successes of the government, raising hopes among farmers of better things to come.[5]

From the beginning the Hitler government seemed to possess a dynamism and force which contrasted sharply with the paralysis of previous administrations. The vitality of the regime was reflected in the reporting style even of newspapers not particularly well-disposed towards Nazism, contributing to a growing feeling stretching beyond existing Nazi support, that the turning-point had been reached, that something at least was now being done. And at the centre of these expectations stood the new Reich Chancellor.

It was not simply that Hitler now had the prestige of the Chancellorship behind him. Already Nazi propaganda was working to create the impression that Hitler was a new and different kind of Reich Chancellor. And the campaign for the Reichstag election on 5 March provided ample opportunity to bestow fresh attributes on the Chancellor of the 'national uprising', and to emphasize his personal leadership 'genius'. In the 'revised' campaign conditions of early 1933, with the Nazis rampant and their ideological enemies subjected to brutal repression, the 'rally' style of the big city was now extended to the countryside in greater measure than ever before. Hitler's Chancellorship was trumpeted as no mere change of government, but as a 'world-historical event'. Nazi speakers did not tire of portraying Hitler as the last bulwark against the threat of communism, the final hope of peasants and workers, the protector of the Christian religion. Above all, Nazi propaganda appealed to voters to give the new Chancellor a chance: 'Hitler has not betrayed us up to now. We must first give the man time to work.'[6]

Whereas the non-Nazi press, in these weeks following the 'take-over of power', usually spoke simply of 'Reich Chancellor Hitler', the *Völkischer Beobachter* coined the appellation 'People's Chancellor'— suggesting new pseudo-democratic bonds between the people and the 'man from the people' who was now their leader. 'A true People's Chancellor passes through the ranks of his followers', ran the heading of a report of a Hitler mass meeting in Nuremberg in late February.[7]

    [5] GStA, MA 106670, RPvOB, 20 Feb. 1933, 4 Apr. 1933; StAM, LRA 76887, GS Markt Grafing, 12 Feb. 1933.
    [6] I have directly drawn for this paragraph on reports of propaganda meetings held in the Starnberg district of Upper Bavaria. See StAM, LRA, 28340, GS Gauting, 4 Feb. 1933, 13 Feb. 1933; GS Aufkirchen, 9 Feb. 1933, 10 Feb. 1933. The tone is wholly typical for the 1933 campaign.
    [7] *Völkischer Beobachter*, 27 Feb. 1933.

Non-Nazi newspapers remained, however, less than impressed. 'Again the same accusations and promises', commented a Catholic newspaper, reporting sarcastically on 'Nuremberg's Great Day' on which the 'People's Chancellor' was coming and on the massive efforts of the Nazi propaganda machine to drum up the masses to provide the 'Führer' with the adulation he expected. 'The critical spectator', concluded the report, 'left the hall disappointed with the speech of the "People's Chancellor".'[8] At least among the Press and political 'opinion leaders', views about Hitler remained down to March 1933 divided along party-political lines. Hitler was at best granted the general respect accorded to the holder of the office of Chancellor. He was the Head of Government, but in the eyes of at least two-thirds of the German people not yet 'the Führer'.

In the election of the 5 March 1933, the parties of the Left—despite severe repression—and the parties of political Catholicism retained a remarkably high proportion of their traditional electoral support. Outside the ranks of the Left, however, the potential support for the new government's policies, and in particular for the person of the Chancellor, was certainly greater than the extent of the Nazi vote in the election. Not every vote cast for non-Nazi parties in March 1933 was a vote against everything Hitler stood for: some at least of what Nazism seemed to offer appealed to far more than hardened Nazi supporters. One factor was the slight improvement in the economic position which was already noticeable in the first weeks of 1933 after the Depression had bottomed out during the winter. More important, however, was the increased prestige accruing to Hitler among considerable sections of the middle classes and in conservative circles from the ruthless repression of the Left, especially the communists, which the Nazi-assisted police in Prussia under Göring's control had been carrying out. Exploitation of the long-standing hatred of socialism and communism (scarcely distinguished as brands of Marxism and thus the enemy of the existing social order, of religion, and of Germany itself) by the selective wave of terror unleashed against the Left undoubtedly brought Hitler early popularity, extending even into the ranks of Catholic voters. A report from a Catholic rural district of Upper Bavaria illustrates the positive echo of the 'purge' of the Left in Prussia, already before the boost to anti-Left prejudice which the Reichstag Fire created:

[8] *Bayerische Volkszeitung*, 27 Feb. 1933.

Hitler's clearing up nicely in Prussia. He's throwing the parasites and spongers on the people straight out on their ear. He should follow it up in Bavaria, too, especially in Munich, and carry out a similar purge. . . . If Hitler carries on the work as he has done so far, he'll have the trust of the great proportion of the German people at the coming Reichstag election . . .[9]

Already here there are clear signs of what became apparent, at least to some foreign observers, immediately following the Reichstag Fire: that the draconian measures adopted by the government—suspension at one fell swoop of the most basic civil rights of the Reich Constitution through the promulgation of an 'Emergency Decree for the Protection of People and State' against 'communist acts of force', and massive police raids rounding up thousands of communists in Prussia in the night of 28 February—encountered little criticism and no small degree of favour among the majority of ordinary, middle-class Germans and among the rural population. The attack on the communists was seen, according to one fairly typical report as 'a long-necessary act of liberation'.[10] The far-reaching significance of the Reichstag Fire 'Emergency Decree' was recognized only by few. Rather, the welcome it received gave Hitler's popularity a new boost on the eve of the election.[11]

Although there were already not a few, even apart from the Left, who were prepared to believe that the Nazis had themselves set fire to the Reichstag, the majority of the population undoubtedly supported the police actions against the KPD, which now seemed to be tackling 'in the national interest' the problem of the proclaimed 'red danger' at its root.[12] Clearly Hitler stood to gain massively from the degree of anti-communist paranoia which extended way beyond the ranks of the Nazi Movement and, while not created, was doubtless furthered by the openly propagated pro-Moscow stance of the KPD. Hitler had said in opposition that heads would roll in the event of a Nazi take-over of power. Now, in acting with utter ruthlessness, he could be portrayed as the eliminator of a national danger. It was not the last

[9] StAM, LRA 76887, GS Anzing, 25 Feb. 1933.
[10] GStA, MA 106677, RPvOF/MF, 5 Mar. 1933; see also GStA, MA 106682, RPvS, 4 Mar. 1933.
[11] See GStA, MA 106672, RPvNB/OP, 5 Mar. 1933, where it was expressly claimed that 'the drastic action against the troublemakers' had satisfied the 'alarmed population' and resulted in a rise in the Nazi vote at the election.
[12] For a graphic indication of the fever-pitch anti-communism after the Reichstag Fire, see the editorial of the *Miesbacher Anzeiger* of 2 Mar. 1933, cited in Kershaw, *Popular Opinion*, pp. 117–18. See also Noakes and Pridham, pp. 174–5.

time that brutality and repression in the interests of 'peace and order' would increase Hitler's popularity and function as an important component of the 'Führer myth'.

Nevertheless, in the March election of 1933, held against the back-cloth of the assault on the Left and in the heady atmosphere of what Nazi propaganda styled as the 'national uprising', fewer than half of the voters cast their ballot for the NSDAP. The Nazis had still been unable to make a decisive breakthrough in the electoral blocks of the Left and of political Catholicism. At the same time, however, assisted by a record turn-out, they had garnered a higher proportion of the vote than any other party had ever managed during the Weimar era. And notable gains were recorded especially in rural Catholic areas, such as in Lower Bavaria, where the increase in the Nazi vote compared with the July election of 1932 amounted to 22.9 per cent.[13] Particularly the poorer sections of the population, who had never been wholly integrated into political Catholicism, now showed themselves open to the appeal of the growing 'Hitler myth'. It seems certain that at the time of the election, Hitler's personal popularity was already far greater than the attractiveness of the NSDAP. But it was only after the election that the graph of Hitler's popular standing turned sharply upwards as Germany's political landscape was fundamentally trans-formed and the shift in his image from party leader to national leader began to be accomplished.

Hitler-euphoria now burgeoned in unrestrained fashion. The author of one small book, for instance, wrote of these weeks as 'The German Hitler Springtime' and prefaced his heroic story of the 'seizure of power' with a 'poem' of pseudo-religious piety:

> Now has us the Godhead a saviour sent,
> Distress its end has passed.
> To gladness and joy the land gives vent:
> Springtime is here at last.[14]

If such 'verses'—and this is no isolated example—were still nauseating to most who were not outright Nazi devotees, the dramatic changes taking place in Germany during these weeks in early 1933 provided the propaganda machine with full and unbridled opportunity to centre on Hitler not as the Party leader or Head of Government, but as the focal

[13] Hagmann, p. 23.
[14] W. Beuth, *Der deutsche Hitler-Frühling. Die Wiederaufrichtung Deutschlands durch den Volkskanzler des Deutschen Reiches Adolf Hitler*, Frankfurt a.M, 1933, pp. 9, 50ff.

point of the 'national rebirth'. The feeling that dynamic and fundamental change was taking place in the interest of the whole nation and
of national unity, that an end was being made to the old policies which
pandered to particular interests and thereby perpetuated social and
political divisions, was not confined to Nazi enthusiasts.[15] The
grandiose theatrical coup of the festive opening of the Reichstag at the
Potsdam Garrison Church on 21 March—symbolically, as newspapers
were quick to point out, the first day of spring and the dawn of a new
season—not only heightened the sense of the 'national awakening',
but was also an important step on the way to establishing Hitler's
prestige as a national leader. This was further enhanced two days later
in his Reichstag speech advocating the introduction of an Enabling
Act, in which he poured vitriolic scorn on the socialists—communist
deputies had, of course, already been arrested or had taken flight—but
was careful not to offend the religious sensitivities of members of the
Catholic parties, and promised solemnly to uphold the position of the
Churches in the State.[16]

   The great flood of opportunists now wanting to join the Nazi
Party—the 'March Fallen', as the 'Old Fighters' of the Party dubbed
them—had been under way since the election. Now, following the
opening of the Reichstag in Potsdam, massive displays of loyalty to the
new government were staged in nearly every German town and city.
Reports noted that the enthusiasm of the great majority of the population 'found expression in absolutely elemental fashion'.[17] The
Bavarian provincial newspaper, the *Miesbacher Anzeiger*, which we
have already cited, reflected the extraordinary atmosphere of 'renewal'
which permeated the heady nationalist expectations of late March in
its reportage on 'The Day of the German People':

What is taking place in Germany today is the struggle not only for the renewal
of the idea of the State, but also for the reshaping of the German soul. . . . The
German people has liberated itself from the nightmare which bore down on it
for so many years, and has started out on the way to a new and, one hopes,
blessed era. . . . May the 21 March be the day of the beginning of a united and
indivisible free German people's community embracing all well-meaning

---

[15] See e.g. the reactions of Louise Solmitz, a national-conservative rather than Nazi
supporter, in Noakes and Pridham, pp. 160–2.
[16] See ibid., pp. 190–5.
[17] GStA, MA 106677, RPvOF/MF, 7 Mar. 1933; and see GStA, MA 106672, RPvNB/
OP, 5 Apr. 1933.

sections of the people and based on a Christian, national, and social foundation.[18]

Within days, 'Hitler-Oaks' and 'Hitler-Lindens'—trees, which as ancient pagan symbols had long been incorporated in nationalist liturgies in Germany—were planted in hundreds of towns and villages. Communities competed in the effusiveness of their laudations as they rushed to make Hitler an honorary citizen, as at Bochum in the Ruhr where the petition declared that 'a Prince Bismarck forged together the Reich, an Adolf Hitler is forging together the nation into a united people'.[19] The conferring of honorary citizenship on Hitler and also on Hindenburg, a phenomenon occurring the length and breadth of the country, was meant to symbolize the unity between the old and new Germany which had been emphasized at Potsdam. The need to decide between Hitler and Hindenburg which had faced the voters in Spring 1932 had now dissolved into harmonious unity. The stage management of the 'Day of Potsdam' succeeded brilliantly in exploiting the authority and charisma of the revered Reich President in the interests of the new Nazi rulers. Especially during the first months of the regime, the mutual respect and admiration of Chancellor and Reich President were constantly emphasized. Already during the election campaign the NSDAP had produced posters showing the venerable Reich President and the 'youthful', dynamic Chancellor standing together beneath the slogan: 'The Marshal and the Corporal: Fight with Us for Peace and Equal Rights.'[20]

The intended association of old and new, of the traditional authority of Hindenburg with the plebiscitary mandate of Hitler, was obvious. Such propaganda doubtless helped in transposing to Hitler some of the trust in Hindenburg as the embodiment of German national values. Hitler's exaggeratedly humble obeisance before the aged Field Marshal and his 'blessing' of the 'new Germany' embodied by the Chancellor in the Potsdam Garrison Church above the tomb of Frederick the Great, given massive coverage in press and newsreel, was in this respect a masterpiece of suggestive propaganda. But although Hindenburg continued to be incorporated into Nazi imagery until his death in 1934, there could be no doubt that the

[18] *Miesbacher Anzeiger*, 22 Mar. 1933.

[19] Cited in J. V. Wagner, *Hakenkreuz über Bochum*, Bochum, 1983, pp. 219–20.

[20] See H. Huber and A. Müller (eds.), *Das Dritte Reich. Seine Geschichte in Texten, Bildern und Dokumenten*, 2 vols., Munich/Vienna/Basle, 1964, i. 125; and F. V. Grunfeld, *The Hitler File*, London, 1974, p. 158.

intended hero of the image-builders was not the old Reich President, who for more than seven years had represented the hated Republic, but the 'People's Chancellor', Hitler, whose star was clearly in the ascendant. And following the promulgation of the Enabling Act on 24 March 1933, his dominance as Chancellor, now no longer reliant on the President's 'emergency decree' powers, was also institutionally secured.

For the majority of the population, the national euphoria of the weeks following the March election which focused on Hitler (and to a much lesser extent on Hindenburg) was unclouded by concern over the simultaneous wave of repression and terror directed at those who did not wish to belong to the new 'people's community'. The mass arrests of communists and other 'enemies of the State' which took place in March throughout Germany met with the same popular approval as the earlier assault on the Left in Prussia and the draconian measures following the Reichstag Fire. There is no reason to doubt that a report from Lower Bavaria was accurately reflecting the opinion of a majority of the population, not only in that region, when it recorded the satisfaction of the people 'that the communist agitators have for the most part been rendered harmless'.[21] Though in Bavaria the new state administration felt obliged to quell rumours of arbitrary mass arrests and point out that it was only ex-functionaries of the KPD or *Reichsbanner* who had been taken into 'protective custody', it extended the coercive net through an appeal to 'self-policing' by requiring—with reference to the 'Malicious Practices Act' of 21 March 1933—'every nationally-minded People's Comrade ... to report to the Gendarmerie responsible on any insulting of the Reich government or any degradation of the national revolution'.[22] This open invitation was eagerly taken up in a wave of denunciations—criticized in its extent even by the police authorities themselves—made by many ordinary citizens, often arising from a personal grudge towards a neighbour or workmate.[23]

[21]GStA, MA 106672, RPvNB/OP, 5 Apr. 1933; see also GStA, MA 106682, RPvS, 22 Mar. 1933.

[22] *Miesbacher Anzeiger*, 24 Mar. 1933.

[23] See GStA, MA 106682, RPvS, 6 Apr. 1933; GStA,MA 106680, RPvUF, 20 Apr. 1933. On the social and political significance of denunciation, see M. Broszat, 'Politische Denunziationen in der NS-Zeit', *Archivalische Zeitschrift*, lxxiii (1977), 221–38; and R. Mann, 'Politische Penetration und gesellschaftliche Reaktion. Anzeigen zur Gestapo im nationalsozialistischen Deutschland', in R. Mackensen and F. Sagebiel (eds.), *Soziologische Analysen. Referate aus den Veranstaltungen der Sektionen der Deutschen*

An atmosphere of intimidation and vigilance against a careless remark which prying ears might seize upon naturally contributed greatly towards a drastic reduction in negative comments about Hitler, which were now punished with particular severity by the new 'Special Courts' set up to deal speedily with political offences. Press censorship and the threat of coercion facing open expression of dissenting opinion meant effectively that from now on the only public image of Hitler remaining was that put out by Goebbels, Dietrich, and other purveyors of official propaganda. Anti-Hitler comments were now forced underground, able to find expression for the most part only in illegal pamphlets of the anti-Nazi opposition, in hurriedly-scribbled graffiti, and in the incautious comments of tongues loosened by alcohol.

Just how far the personality cult had developed within such a short time was shown by the celebrations for Hitler's forty-fourth birthday on 20 April 1933, already going far beyond any 'normal' honouring of a Head of Government. The streets and squares of practically every German town and city were festooned with the outward signs of adulation and public acclamation of the 'People's Chancellor'. Though the propaganda machine had excelled itself, it was evidently able to build upon an already existent extensive propensity in wide sections of the population to accept at least some elements of the expanding Hitler cult. Goebbels did not stop short of drawing parallels with Bismarck. Other birthday well-wishers went even further. And since his achievements were those of one formerly denigrated as a mere 'drummer' and agitator who was 'no statesman', they were all the greater for having been attained 'only through the full commitment of his personality'.[24]

The wave of acclamation for Hitler was infectious. And it served not only to reinforce the devotion of the already converted, but to isolate the reluctant and hesitant by making them feel outsiders from a society in which the adulation expressed by millions was the norm. The reporting in the newspapers—not yet fully 'co-ordinated' in their treatment—conveyed the same impression. The *Völkischer Beobachter*,

Gesellschaft für Soziologie beim 19. Deutschen Soziologentag, Berlin, 1979, pp. 965–85. Denunciation is also a central concern of a forthcoming study by Prof. Robert Gellately, Huron College, London, Ontario.

[24] *Völkischer Beobachter*, north German edn., 21 Apr. 1933; and see Bramsted, pp. 204–6.

now with its rapidly increasing readership, trumpeted: 'The Nation Pays Tribute to the Führer. The entire German people celebrates the birthday of Adolf Hitler in dignified, unpretentious ceremonies. All towns and villages in unprecedented displays of bunting, religious services, torchlight processions, and parades. Countless shows of loyalty to the People's Chancellor . . .'[25] The bourgeois *Münchner Neueste Nachrichten*, now naturally far more sympathetic to National Socialism than it had been before 1933, also interpreted the size of the demonstrations as open proof of how much Hitler was entitled to the 'name of honour' of the 'People's Chancellor'. It required no great deeds of propaganda or organization, claimed the newspaper, to stir the people in all parts of the Reich to such massive participation, and concluded:

In a unison of hearts scarcely imaginable a few weeks ago, the people declared its allegiance to Adolf Hitler as Leader of the new Germany. . . . In short: the enthusiastic participation on the personal day of honour of the Chancellor has provided the proof that Adolf Hitler is recognized as Führer in the consciousness of the entire people, and that the heart of Germany belongs to him.[26]

The 'Hitler Day' had proceeded in Bavaria much as in the rest of Germany, as a 'joyful celebration of the people'. Flags and greenery adorned the houses even in small villages. In the city centre of Munich, shop windows displayed pictures and busts of Hitler garlanded with flowers and laurel wreaths, houses were richly decorated, trams carried festive bunting, and large crowds gathered expectantly wherever they thought they could catch a glimpse of Hitler who, however, in a show of pseudo-modesty spent the day in his private apartment. The extraordinary rhetoric, already stretching the limits of superlatives, used by Nazi speakers when eulogizing Hitler, as in the following extract from a speech of the Bavarian Minister of Education Hans Schemm, could only have fulfilled its propaganda function by appealing to sentiments already present among the recipients of the message amounting practically to an expression of 'secular faith' invested in the person of Hitler:

Only if we set contemporary historical events in parallel with the whole of German history will we know what the name Hitler signifies. Looking now at

[25] *Völkischer Beobachter*, north German edn., 21 Apr. 1933.
[26] *Münchner Neueste Nachrichten*, 21 Apr. 1933. The next paragraph and quotation are also based upon the same reportage.

the face of Germany, we see that another master builder is behind it, who has extracted what is most beautiful from the German soul. . . . He has created a new face of Germany as the artist and master builder whom the Lord God has given to us. If we encompass the events of two thousand years, then we must come to the conclusion that the final shape has only now been found. To be allowed to be Adolf Hitler's mason, carpenter, and lowliest day labourer is a gift of heaven. In the personality of Hitler, a million-fold longing of the German people has become reality.

It was recognized by the manufacturers of the Führer cult that the heavy emphasis on Hitler's many-sided 'genius' in public addresses and press reportage—he was also being styled in April 1933 as the 'greatest expert' on stage and theatre as well as 'the greatest master builder and architect in Germany'[27]—had the danger of playing down the 'human qualities' of the 'People's Chancellor'. Compensation was provided in the image of loyalty and compassion shown in the pathos of a reported visit to the bedside of a dying 'Old Fighter' of the Movement, to whom the Führer spoke 'full of fatherly gentleness and goodness', departing with 'a long, heartfelt handshake'.[28] Goebbels took up the incident in his birthday address, emphasizing how familiar Hitler's 'human qualities' were to his close comrades, even if they were as yet less well-known to the millions of his new devotees. He was not only the symbol of their future hopes; his true greatness lay in the simplicity of his personality. Goebbels ended in the sickly sentimental tone appealing to a banal sense of intimate identity of leader and led which was to be the hallmark of his birthday eulogy in future years: 'We give you our hands and vow that you will ever be for us what you are today: "Our Hitler!" '[29]

Hitler still had far to go before he won over the majority of those who had not supported him in March 1933. But the birthday celebrations of April 1933 were a step on the way. In the six weeks since the election, Hitler's image had already been significantly transformed. He was no longer the Party leader opposing the State and polarizing opinion, but rather—according to the now more or less uniform Party propaganda—the symbol of unity of the German people, even for many who continued to see in the NSDAP a Party of particularist interests.

[27] Ibid., 21 Apr. 1933.
[28] *Völkischer Beobachter*, north German edn., 21 Apr. 1933.
[29] Cited in Bramsted, p. 206.

During the next few months further important steps were taken in the process of eliminating all possible alternative sources of political allegiance which might counter loyalty to Hitler. The disbanding of the remaining parties removed any lingering possibility of open organizational counter-loyalty. This found its symbolic expression in the extension of the Nazi Party's 'Hitler Greeting' into, increasingly, the standard greeting for all Germans. The simple but constantly employed 'Heil Hitler' became the outward profession of support for the regime—whether given freely, resignedly, or under pressure—while its refusal was a clear sign of political nonconformity. The 'German Greeting', as it was now styled, was both propaganda and coercion: anyone not wishing to be seen as a political outsider, with all the consequences which might follow, was ready to offer at least a half-hearted 'Heil Hitler'; and the sea of outstretched arms at every big rally provided an impressive outward witness to the professed unity of Leader and People.

The compulsory use of the 'German Greeting' for all public employees followed a directive issued by Reich Minister of the Interior Frick on 13 July 1933, one day before the ban on all non-Nazi parties, and was designed to express 'outwardly the solidarity of the entire German people with its Leader'. The accompanying decree, which imposed the 'Hitler Salute' also on non-Party-members during the singing of the national anthem and the Horst-Wessel Song, carried the scarcely veiled threat that 'anyone not wishing to come under suspicion of behaving in a consciously negative fashion will therefore render the Hitler Greeting'. Even physical disability was no excuse. A rider to the decree, added a fortnight later, stipulated that if physical disability prevented raising the right arm, 'then it is correct to carry out the Greeting with the left arm'![30]

Another outward indication of the growing 'Hitler myth' was the constant stream of 'pilgrims' heading for the Berghof near Berchtesgaden, hoping to catch a mere glimpse of the Führer. 'The Obersalzberg has become a sort of pilgrimage place', noted one report. 'The area around Wachenfeld House is constantly occupied by men and women admirers. Even on walks in isolated spots the Reich Chancellor is pursued by a throng of intrusive admirers and inquisitive persons.'[31]

---

[30] BAK, R43II/1263, Fos. 93, 164.
[31] GStA, MA 106670, RPvOB, 19 Aug. 1933. According to reports reaching the *Sopade* in mid-1934, pieces of wood from the garden fence of Hitler's house on the Obersalz-

The reports of the Bavarian Government Presidents—in their continuity and extent unmatched for this period by any other part of the Reich—are unanimous in their indication that the months between April and September 1933 saw notable gains in support for Hitler and the Nazi Regime, even among those who had previously been hostile or at best lukewarm in their backing. In September, the first Party Rally since the 'seizure of power' gave Hitler full opportunity to laud the achievements of National Socialism—especially his own achievements.[32] But neither rhetoric nor coercion would have been very effective in building up the Hitler image had it not been for what appeared to be already notable successes of the Reich government. The feeling that the government was energetically combating the great problems of unemployment, rural indebtedness, and poverty, and the first noticeable signs of improvement in these areas, gave rise to new hopes and won Hitler and his government growing stature and prestige.[33] It was the newly acquired and increasing confidence about the economy rather than the actual—initially rather modest— improvements which contributed to the shaping of the 'Hitler myth' in this period. The 'homely' language used by Nazi editors of little provincial newspapers played its part, too, in attributing—with legendary over-simplification—any sign of improvement and change in the locality to the greatness of Hitler, as in the following extract published in a small Swabian newspaper in early September 1933:

You don't get round to talking any longer out of pure wonder and amazement at everything our Hitler is doing. . . . Since the man has taken history into his hands, things work. . . . And there's work since Hitler has been at it. At last things are happening. But the best of it is that everybody's helping to create work. That's how it has to be. Then we'll get the cart out of the mire. Just take a look at our Adolf-Hitler-Square. There's such a building, hammering, and knocking there that it's a joy. I'll say it again and again. I can only be amazed. Who would have thought it, that Günzburg would get a Danube harbour? Not

berg were being taken away 'as relics', and one woman had even scratched up the earth which Hitler had trodden on while walking to his house—*DBS*, i. 101, 26 June 1934.

[32] Domarus, pp. 296–9.

[33] e.g. GStA, MA 106670, RPvOB, 20 Apr. 1933, 4 May 1933, 5 Aug. 1933; MA 106672, RPvNB/OP, 5 Apr. 1933, 6 June 1933, 5 July 1933, 7 Aug. 1933; MA 106677, RPvOF/MF, 20 Apr. 1933, 20 Sept. 1933, 6 Oct. 1933; MA 106680, RPvUF, 20 Apr. 1933, 6 May 1933, 21 July 1933, 18 Aug. 1933, 6 Sept. 1933; MA 106682, RPvS, 6 Apr. 1933, 22 Apr. 1933, 7 June 1933, 3 Aug. 1933, 19 Aug. 1933.

a soul, I'll tell you. Ha! Just look down at the new railway bridge. That's what I
call a people's economy . . .[34]

That the railway brige had already been started in 1932 before
Hitler came to power was not mentioned. That the town of Günzburg
despite the talk of it in 1933 would not get its Danube harbour, the
good townsfolk could not know. The most important thing was the
feeling that things were improving again. And popular mentality
matched the aims of propaganda in personalizing the change of
atmosphere and attributing it all to Hitler.

The withdrawal of Germany from the League of Nations in October
1933 and the subsequent referendum and first plebiscitary Reichstag
election set for 12 November marked a further stage in the build-up of
Hitler's prestige. The NSDAP was now, of course, the sole party
campaigning, with a single list of candidates ('The List of the Führer').
Though the 'election' aimed at the approval and legitimation of the
policies and achievements of the government as a whole, the tenor of
the accompanying propaganda campaign was almost exclusively
directed at ensuring the required show of loyalty to the person of
Hitler. Even the non-Nazi press now referred increasingly and
regularly to him as 'the Führer', whereas the appellation 'People's
Chancellor' now occurred much less frequently.

The Nazi press found ever new ways of lauding Hitler's achievements, incomplete though they yet were. Hitler himself set the tone in
his speech in Weimar on 1 November, in which he said that he had
demanded four years to rid Germany of six million unemployed and
had already in a brief nine months provided 'work and bread' for two
and a half million jobless.[35] An alleged audience of 15,000 farmers
constantly interrupted Reich Farmers' Leader Darré with 'thunder-
ous applause' when, in a speech in Munich, he compared the miserable state of agriculture at the time of the 'take-over of power' with the
Führer's subsequent mighty achievements. The lesson for every
farmer, pointed out Darré, was clearly 'that he stands and falls with
Adolf Hitler'. The public works and employment creation
programmes were at this time the most effective Nazi propaganda
themes, and here too all credit in the first instance went to Hitler, 'who
has set the mighty work programme in the Reich underway'.[36]

---

[34] *Schwäbisches Volksblatt*, 9 Sept. 1933. I am grateful to Dr Zdenek Zofka for this
reference.   [35] *Münchner Neueste Nachrichten*, 3 Nov.1933.
[36] Ibid., 6 Nov. 1933.

Despite the obvious lack of freedom accompanying the 'election', which offered no alternative to Nazi policy and no certainty of secrecy at the ballot box, the result—90 per cent in the plebiscite, 87.8 per cent in the 'Reichstag election'[37]—was an undeniable success for Hitler. For the outside world, too, it provided a public demonstration of the broad support which he enjoyed in Germany. Opponents and doubters who had dared to stay away from the poll or to vote 'Nein' were exposed as a tiny minority. Just how authentic the results really were is shown by the fact that the inmates of the concentration camp at Dachau—not generally known as a bastion of Nazi support—produced a 'Ja'-vote of 99.5 per cent in the plebiscite![38] However, despite the meaningless nature of the official voting figures, it is difficult to doubt that by November 1933—and especially in issues of defence and foreign policy which were primarily at stake in the plebiscite—Hitler enjoyed an unforced support extending way beyond the level of support he had received in the March election earlier in the year. If the majority of Germans found the extremes of the Hitler cult laughable or nauseating, they were now ready to accept that he was no ordinary politician: above all, it was difficult to ignore his 'achievements'.

The old Reich President himself, no less, confirmed this on the anniversary of Hitler's appointment to the Chancellorship in a published letter expressing his 'sincere recognition' of Hitler's 'devoted work' and 'great achievement':

Much has happened in the past year with regard to the removal of economic distress and the reconstitution of the Fatherland, and great progress has been made. . . . I am confident that in the coming year you and your fellow workers will successfully continue, and with God's help complete, the great work of German reconstruction which you have so energetically begun, on the basis of the new happily attained national unity of the German people.[39]

During the summer and autumn, Hitler had also shown himself ready to halt the 'revolutionary fervour' and wild, arbitrary actions of the Party activists and storm-troopers which had characterized the 'seizure of power' phase, and to direct the energies of the Movement

[37] See BAK, R18/5350, Fo. 83, and, for investigations into complaints of electoral irregularities, Fos. 95–104, 107–22. See also M. Broszat, *The Hitler State*, London, 1981, pp. 91–2. A detailed anlaysis is provided in K. D. Bracher, G. Schulz, and W. Sauer, *Die nationalsozialistische Machtergreifung*, Ullstein edn., Frankfurt a.M. 1974, i. 480ff.

[38] *Münchner Neueste Nachrichten*, 13 Nov. 1933.

[39] Ibid., 30 Jan. 1934.

into 'evolutionary' channels.[40] This removed the reservations of many who were increasingly ready to accept the Führer's authority while retaining a critical stance towards the Party and its affiliations and to refuse to identify Hitler with the misdemeanours of the Party activists.

By the time of the second recurrence of Hitler's birthday celebrations since the 'take-over of power', the Führer cult was relatively firmly established. The atmosphere of popular celebration in 1933 had given way by 1934, however, to the ritual incantation to a totem idol. Newspapers carried the eulogy of the Reich Press Chief, Dr Otto Dietrich. But Dietrich's paean of praise was stereotype and cliché-ridden: the creation of 'work and bread' and the 'turn of fate of the German people' were attributed solely to Hitler, who 'had risen from out of the people, and still stands today among the people'.[41]

The eulogy had a hollow ring to it for the many who had yet to see anything of the great benefits of the Third Reich which Nazi propaganda was daily trumpeting. It had become obvious to broad sections of the population during the winter of 1933–4 that the social and economic improvements which had actually taken place scarcely matched the grand claims the Nazis were making. The progress of the Nazi 'economic miracle' was still extremely limited, a fact which was bound up for many with the first disappointments about unfulfilled promises made before the 'seizure of power'. The enthusiasm of summer 1933 about the prospects for the economy had faded. Among the peasantry, sections of the lower middle class, and not least among industrial workers and the millions still unemployed, the feeling grew that the economic reality of the Third Reich bore scant relation to its propaganda.

Reports from all parts of the Reich testify to a significant deterioration in mood—no doubt contributing to the more restrained tone of the celebrations for the Führer's birthday—during the first half of 1934.[42] This was not without effect on attitudes towards Hitler himself. A *Sopade* report from south-west Germany in late spring 1934 claimed that 'criticism was no longer stopping at Hitler'; one from Saxony declared that the mood was also directed against 'the Führer, the

[40] See Broszat, *The Hitler State*, pp. 204 ff.

[41] *Völkischer Beobachter*, north German edn., 20 Apr. 1934.

[42] See the reports, particularly the sections dealing with the economy, for February and April 1934 from Gestapo offices throughout Prussia in ZStA Potsdam, RMdI 25721, 26060. And for Bavaria, see Kershaw, *Popular Opinion*, pp. 46 ff, 75 ff, 120 ff. See also *DBS*, i. 9–14, 99–122, reports from 17 May 1934 and 26 June 1934.

unnatural glorification of whom is declining'; and the Berlin agent concurred that while criticism up to around four weeks earlier had been along the lines that Hitler meant well but had bad counsellors, he was now also coming under attack, and that was the case too in the Labour Service camps and within the SA, where it was gradually being realized 'that Hitler does not want any socialism'.[43] The *Sopade* analysts acknowledged, nevertheless, that their reports did not speak in unison. Other accounts they received still pointed to extraordinary popular adulation of Hitler, extending into the working class.[44] According to a Berlin reporter, Hitler was credited with honest intentions, and it was said he could do nothing for the maladministration of his underlings. This same account accepted that this attitude was only in part a result of the 'systematic Führer propaganda'; it had also to be attributed to the undoubted impact of Hitler's personality on 'ordinary people', 'and Hitler still possesses a great deal of personal trust in particular among the workers'.[45]

As such comments suggest, continuing discontent about social and economic conditions—much of it presumably expressed, not least in the working class, by those who had never wholly been won over to Nazism—was perfectly compatible with recognition of other 'achievements' of the regime, in particular those attributed to Hitler himself. Everyday grievances based on material dissatisfaction, important though they were in forming popular attitudes, by no means necessarily signified total rejection of Nazism or of the Führer, who stood in a sense above and outside the 'system', detached from the 'everyday' sphere of dismal 'normality'.[46] Though by no means unscathed in the light of gathering economic discontent, it seems clear that the 'Hitler myth' could transcend daily material worries and function as a compensatory mechanism. While the euphoria unleashed by a Hitler speech or by a major foreign policy success was of short duration before giving way again to the greyness of everyday life, there was a lasting residual feeling, evidently shared by many, that, whatever the temporary hardships and cares, the Führer was in

[43] *DBS*, i. 101–2, 26 June 1934.

[44] Ibid., i. 100–1, 26 June 1934.

[45] Ibid., i. 10–11, 17 May 1934. See also L. Eiber, *Arbeiter unter der NS-Herrschaft. Textil- und Porzellanarbeiter im nordöstlichen Oberfranken 1933–1939*, Munich, 1979, p. 110; and T. W. Mason, *Arbeiterklasse und Volksgemeinschaft*, Opladen, 1975, pp. 123, 149 n. 233.

[46] I have argued this point at greater length in my essay 'Alltägliches und Außeralltägliches: ihre Bedeutung für die Volksmeinung 1933–1939', in Peukert and Reulecke, pp. 273–92.

control and knew the way forward to better times. Unquestionably, therefore, the 'Hitler myth' had a crucial stabilizing and integrating function within the Nazi system in defusing discontent and offering a sphere of 'national' policy and 'national' interest lying outside the normality of 'daily life' which drew even critics of the Regime to support of major aspects of Nazi rule.

Especially among the politically naïve and economically deprived, the 'legendary' quality of the Hitler image was clearly apparent in the frequent simple attribution to the Führer personally of whatever social benefits it was felt the regime had provided. A characteristic expression of this can be seen in the report in autumn 1935 of a Nazi Block Leader from Mühldorf am Inn in Upper Bavaria about the distribution of Winter Aid among the poor inhabitants of his block.[47] He was, he wrote, surprised and encouraged by the completely unexpected response he had encountered among the 'poorest of the poor' in his locality, mainly the unemployed, pensioners, and widows. The comments of one elderly pensioner particularly impressed him:

He had been well provided in the previous winter from the Winter Aid and sang the praises of the Winter Aid as the greatest deed of the Führer. The old man lives in a very shabby room, but the picture of the Führer looks down from the smoke-blackened walls which have not seen a coat of paint in a long time.

A woman told him how grateful she was that the State now really cared for the poor. Asked whether she received Winter Aid, another woman answered: 'What *are* you thinking of? Since Hitler has been in charge, my husband has had work in winter too. So we can make ends meet. Of course, things used to be different.' The wife of a former communist added:

At first things were tough, because you know yourself that we were branded communists. But when you're unemployed for four years you become radical. For two years my husband has been working in Töging. Look here, there's the picture of the Führer hanging in our one-time communist hovel, and beneath the picture I've taught my girl the Our Father. I, who left the Church in 1932. Every day my girl has to say an Our Father for the Führer, because he has given us back our daily bread.

---

[47] The following is taken from StAM, NSDAP 494. I referred to this report in a different context in *Popular Opinion*, pp. 128–9.

Whatever the embellishments—both of the Block Leader, and of those he had visited—there is an authentic ring about such comments, reflecting again a tendency not uncommon in politically 'unsophisticated' sections of the population to personalize their feelings of gratitude by attributing whatever social benefits the Third Reich had brought them directly to Hitler as their author and instigator. For the politically 'unschooled', the distribution of Winter Aid and other forms of 'social welfare' carried out by the Party as 'propaganda of the deed', all personalized as the 'social achievement of the Führer', was often sufficient to persuade them of the myth 'that the Führer in contrast to the former Marxist government, cares for the poor'.[48]

Two events in summer 1934 contributed decisively to the further development of the Führer image: the suppression of the so-called 'Röhm Putsch'; and the merging of the offices of Chancellor and Reich President following the death of Hindenburg on 2 August 1934. The remarkable popular reactions to the bloody massacre, ordered by Hitler himself, of the SA leadership on 30 June 1934, which far from damaging his prestige brought a sharp increase in his popularity, will be dealt with in the next chapter. The second major impetus to the development of Hitler's image came from Hindenburg's death, which provided the propaganda machine with a further opportunity to exploit the great prestige of the deceased in the interests of the Nazi regime. Press reportage of Hindenburg's death and funeral spoke of him as the 'national myth of the German people', the 'true Ekkehart', the 'monumental memorial from the distant past', whose greatest service had been to pave the way on 30 January 1933 for the 'young National Socialist Movement'.[49]

Hitler could afford to be generous. The only person who, on the basis of his constitutional position, might have offered conservative élites any potential of a countervailing force to the Nazi leadership, had joined the Valhalla of national heroes and would pose no further threat. The speedy abolition which followed of the office of Reich President—'indivisibly bound to the name of the great deceased'[50]— and the swearing of a personal oath of loyalty to Hitler by civil servants and soldiers of the Reichswehr, were acts of power politics which

---

[48] IML/ZPA, St.3/44/1, Fo. 180, LB of Stapo Breslau, 4 Mar. 1936.
[49] *Münchner Neueste Nachrichten*, 3 Aug. 1934; J. C. Fest, *Hitler, Eine Biographie*, Ullstein edn., Frankfurt a.M., 1976, p. 651.
[50] *Münchner Neueste Nachrichten*, 3 Aug. 1934.

carried deep symbolic significance. On 4 August headlines could proclaim: 'Today Hitler is the Whole of Germany'.[51]

The plebiscite of 19 August, called to legitimate the changes since Hindenburg's death, was little more than a ritual act of acclamation for Hitler's now constitutionally unlimited Führer authority. It was the only one of the four national plebiscites in the Third Reich—unlike those of 1933, 1936, and 1938—which was not called to acclaim a major foreign policy triumph. In this case, it amounted solely to a show of confidence in Hitler. The propaganda campaign preceding the plebiscite was—again unusually in this case—a short and relatively low-key affair, in which Hitler himself did not take part. The theme was the need 'to provide anew and more emphatically than ever proof to ourselves and the world of the unity of Leader and people'. Hitler had, it was claimed, united a divided people and opened the way to freedom. It was now the duty of every German to demonstrate this unity in the struggle with the Führer for the Reich. The slogan was: 'Hitler for Germany—the whole of Germany for Hitler'.[52]

The result of the plebiscite showed that the unity of Leader and people was less complete than the Nazis had hoped. According to the official figures, 84.6 per cent had voted 'Ja', but in some parts of Germany—particularly in heavily working-class areas—up to a third had refused to give Hitler their vote.[53] The decline in the 'Ja' vote compared with November 1933, which so disappointed the Nazis, was undoubtedly a reflection of the widespread economic discontent in 1934, coupled with the growing disenchantment with the Nazi Party and its representatives. A report from Aachen noted before the plebiscite that some voters had reservations about casting their ballot for the Führer 'because it could be seen as a vote of confidence in the Reich government and Party'. And one ballot paper in Potsdam had scrawled across it: 'For Hitler, Yes, for his Big-Shots, No'.[54] Such

[51] Ibid., 4 Aug. 1934.

[52] Ibid., 19 Aug. 1934.

[53] For the drop in the 'yes' vote in comparison with November 1933, see BAK, R18/5355, 'Die Volksabstimmungen am 12. November 1933 und 19. August 1934'. A regional analysis of the plebiscite can be seen in Bracher et al., *Die nat. soz. Machtergreifung*, i. 486–98.

[54] *Volksopposition im Polizeistaat*, ed. B. Vollmer, Stuttgart, 1957, p. 74; IML/ZPA, St.3/936, Fo. 17, RP Potsdam, 5 Sept. 1934. A similar mood had been observed somewhat earlier in the year by the *Sopade* among the inhabitants of rural areas of Brandenburg, who had reportedly stated that in the event of another plebiscite they would write on the ballot sheet: 'For Adolf Hitler, yes, but a thousand times no for the brown big-shots.'—*DBS*, i. 11, report of 17 May 1934.

sentiments indicated the tendency to separate Hitler from the sullied image of his underlings—a phenomenon we shall explore in the following chapter.

Despite the relatively unsatisfactory outcome of the plebiscite from a Nazi perspective, there is no doubt that the removal of the troublesome SA leadership and the new power accruing to Hitler following Hindenburg's death provided a new impetus to the Führer cult. With the traumatic events of the summer behind him, Hitler could give open expression to his feeling of satisfaction, even triumph, at the Nuremberg Party Rally in September 1934.

The great Party celebration at Nuremberg in 1934 was above all a vehicle for the transmission of the Führer cult. The Führer had, of course, been the focal point of the proceedings at earlier rallies. But now he towered over the Party, which had come to pay him homage. The supra-dimensional Hitler image was now consciously built up. On Hitler's express orders, and working to a title, 'The Triumph of the Will', which he himself had devised, the talented young film director Leni Riefenstahl, whose adulation of the Führer never brought her to apply for Nazi Party membership, was commissioned to film the Reich Party Rally. From beginning to end, her film concentrated so exclusively on Hitler, that even his closest paladins stood completely in his shadow, reduced to the level of film extras. After the troubled summer, the film aimed to demonstrate strength and unity— strength of determined will in overcoming all obstacles and ultimately triumphing; unity of Party and people in their bond of loyalty to the Führer. The symbolism was replete from the very beginning, as Hitler's aeroplane descended through the clouds over Nuremberg, casting a cruciform shape over the marching storm-troopers and the thousands awaiting him in ecstatic expectation in the streets below. What has been called 'the tone of insistent messianism' which pervades the film,[55] continues to the climactic end of the Rally in which the unity of Leader, Party, and People was mystically proclaimed by Rudolf Heß: 'The Party is Hitler. But Hitler is Germany, just as Germany is Hitler. Hitler! Sieg Heil!'[56] The film

[55] D. J. Diephouse, 'The Triumph of Hitler's Will', in J. Held (ed.), *The Cult of Power. Dictators in the Twentieth Century*, New York, 1983, p. 51.
[56] Cited in D. Welch, *Propaganda and the German Cinema, 1933–1945*, Oxford, 1983, p. 157. For a good analysis of the film, see ibid.. pp. 147–59. The Hitler cult dominated *Triumph des Willens* to a far greater extent than it had done the film which Leni Riefenstahl had made of the previous Party Rally of 1933 under the title of *Sieg des Glaubens*. This earlier film, which formed in many respects a 'dummy run' for *Triumph des Willens*,

played to packed houses when it was released.[57] The accompanying programme produced by the Reich Propaganda Ministry clearly stated the message the film was to convey. In emphasizing the Führer's 'heartfelt kindness' as he greeted the peasant women who had come to Nuremberg in their traditional costumes, and his 'manly earnestness' as he reviewed the line of standard-bearers, the film was showing 'how very much this nation belongs to the Führer, how very much the Führer belongs to it! In every glance, in every handshake, there is expressed the confession and the vow: "We belong together, in eternal loyalty together".'[58] Those seeing the film were clearly witnessing not a documentary on the Reich Party Rally, but a celluloid exposition of the Führer cult.

In 1934–5 the Führer cult also began increasingly to determine the constitutional doctrine of the Third Reich. Leading experts on constitutional law such as Huber, Forsthoff, and Koellreuther now formulated their contrived doctrines of the 'Führer State', legitimizing through mystical notions of the incarnation of the will of the people in the person of Hitler the omnipotence of the Führer and reducing the government to his mere advisory body.[59] As Hans Frank, head of the Nazi Lawyers' Association, put it a few years later: 'Constitutional Law in the Third Reich is the legal formulation of the historic will of the Führer, but the historic will of the Führer is not the fulfilment of legal preconditions for his activity.'[60] The 'Hitler myth', the personality cult surrounding the Führer, had by this time long since caught hold of prominent sections of the bourgeois intelligentsia and social élites, whose contribution to its legitimation—drawing on social standing and supposed intellectual 'gravitas'—was considerable.

---

still allowed Hitler's paladins a share of the limelight in contrast with the 1934 film. Ernst Röhm, in particular, featured prominently, which, it is suggested, was the reason why Hitler allegedly ordered copies of the film to be destroyed following the 'Night of the Long Knives' in 1934. It was, in fact, presumed until recently that not a single copy of the film had survived—H. Hoffmann, ' "Victory of Faith" (1933) by Leni Riefenstahl', unpubl. paper, pp. 5, 15–16.

[57] Though according to a report from Berchtesgaden, the cinema visitors to see *Triumph des Willens*, when it ran in Bad Reichenhall for the first three Sundays in October 1936, were almost exclusively Austrians who streamed over the newly-opened borders in cars and on their bicycles—StAM, LRA 29655, BA Berchtesgaden, 3 Nov. 1936.

[58] Cited in Welch, p. 151.

[59] See ibid., p. 146; *Der Nationalsozialismus. Dokumente 1933–1945*, ed. W. Hofer, Frankfurt a.M. 1957, pp. 82–3; *DBS*, v. 525–31.

[60] Noakes and Pridham, p. 254.

The ebbing morale of 1934, the product in good measure of social and economic grievances and undoubtedly contributing to the 'meagre' result of the August plebiscite, was combated in the first months of 1935 by two great 'national' successes: the Saar Plebiscite in January, with its unexpectedly good result for the Nazi regime—90 per cent of the Saar population voting for integration into the Reich; and the reintroduction of universal military service—a clear snub to the western allies in its breach of the provisions of Versailles—in March 1935, celebrated with a spectacular parade as the birth of a new German 'Wehrmacht'. Reports reaching the *Sopade* pointed out pessimistically the impact of the Saar plebiscite on the popular mood within Germany, and how much more difficult it made the work of the socialist resistance to Hitler.[61] The integrative effect of the re-introduction of military conscription, announced without prior warning as a spectacular coup, was also depressingly obvious to *Sopade* observers:

Enthusiasm on 17 March enormous. The whole of Munich was on its feet. People can be forced to sing, but they can't be forced to sing with such enthusiasm. I experienced the days of 1914 and can only say that the declaration of war did not make the same impact on me as the reception of Hitler on 17 March. . . . Trust in Hitler's political talent and honest intentions is getting ever greater, just as generally Hitler has again won extraordinary popularity. He is loved by many . . .[62]

A report from Westphalia added that Hitler's success in the Saar and the fact that he could obviously rearm without danger had also won him favour in the working class. Even former communist supporters, previously unemployed but now earning good wages in the armaments industry, were prepared to defend the system with the argument that at least they now had work and 'the others didn't bring that about'.[63] Both the Saar triumph and the reintroduction of military service, the first spectacular successes in the foreign policy arena, seemed to confirm that Hitler was not only capable of revitalizing Germany internally, but of leading it to new recognition and success in foreign affairs—wiping out the 'shameful peace' of Versailles, and restoring German honour.

The restoration of military strength, equal right to rearm, and

---

[61] *DBS*, ii. 9, 12–14, 6 Feb. 1935.
[62] Ibid., ii. 278–9, 14 Mar. 1935.
[63] Ibid., ii. 283, 14 Mar. 1935.

independence also formed the main theme for Otto Dietrich's eulogy on Hitler's birthday in April 1935. Success on the plane of international politics now brought a further attribute to the Hitler image—the 'symbol of the nation'. Dietrich recapitulated the earlier main components of the 'Führer myth': in 1933 it had been Hitler as the 'fighter for and creator of German unity', in 1934 he was the 'statesman and architect of the new Reich', and now in 1935 he was 'the supreme Leader of the nation' who with 'incomparable strength of resolution' had restored Germany's freedom of arms. As a 'simple worker' Hitler had initially restored Germany's 'social freedom', and now the former 'simple front-line soldier' had, with a great 'soldierly achievement', restored Germany's 'national freedom'. The Führer cult attained heroic and mystical form in Dietrich's 'prose':

Just as Adolf Hitler has raised the German people to new life in heroic struggle, so we find incorporated in his own path of life the eternal rebirth of the German nation. . . . We see in him the symbol of the indestructible life-force of the German nation, which in Adolf Hitler has acquired living shape . . .[64]

Goebbels added to this as he had done in 1933 a wholly fabricated picture of Hitler's 'human qualities', aiming, as one who was close to the Führer, to present to every German 'Hitler, the man, with all the magic of his personality'.[65] Hitler, in reality a master of the art of the theatrical, was profiled as a man 'whom it was impossible to imagine posing'. Repeatedly, Goebbels stressed his personal simplicity and modesty—his 'simple' meals, and his 'simple' uniform decorated solely with the Iron Cross First Class which he had won 'as a simple soldier for the highest personal bravery'.[66] Hitler, whose 'eccentric' work-style added significantly to the administrative chaos of the Third Reich, was portrayed as a man toiling for his people while others slept, inexhaustible in his industry and endeavour. And with particular pathos, Goebbels outlined the intense loneliness and sadness of a man who had sacrificed all personal happiness and private life for his people. Incapable of human warmth, friendship, and love, Hitler was turned by Goebbels into the personal victim of his lofty position. Goebbels ended his incantation in prayer-like fashion:

[64] *Völkischer Beobachter*, north German edn., 20 Apr. 1935.
[65] The following from ibid., 21–2 Apr. 1935 (abridged version) and in full in *Münchner Neueste Nachrichten*, 21–2 Apr. 1935.
[66] According to Fest (p. 713), Hitler liked splendrous uniforms in his presence in order to emphasize to the full his own 'simple' dress.

The entire people is devoted to him not only with reverence but with deep, heartfelt love, because it has the feeling that it belongs to him, flesh from his flesh, and spirit from his spirit. . . . He came from the people and has remained among the people. . . . The smallest approach him in friendly and confiding manner because they sense that he is their friend and protector. But the entire people loves him, because it feels safe in his hands like a child in the arms of its mother. . . . Just as we do, who are gathered close by him, so the last man in the farthest village says in this hour: 'What he was, he is, and what he is, he should remain: Our Hitler!

Apart from being an exercise in pure flattery from one so dependent on Hitler for his power-base, this remarkable discourse—a eulogy which did not merely distort reality, but stood it directly on its head—can be seen as a reflection of Goebbels's own worship of Hitler. The Propaganda Minister who contributed more than anyone else to the fabrication of the 'Hitler myth' had clearly, as his diary accounts also testify, succumbed to its force. But whatever personal motives Goebbels had in constructing the legend of the warmth and protectiveness, which Hitler supposedly offered to every member of the 'people's community', it evidently tapped a vein of pseudo-religious, 'secular salvation' emotions forming a not insignificant strand of popular psychology which, alongside the naïve propensity to personalize politics and to admire political 'greatness', contributed in considerable measure to the receptivity to the Führer cult. Testimony to the chord in popular psychology struck by Goebbels is provided by the thousands of letters—together with many gifts and 'poetic' laudations—which showered daily into the Führer's Adjutancy in Berlin. The flavour of such 'correspondence', only a tiny fragment of which now survives, is indicated in the birthday greetings sent to Hitler in April 1935 by a Berlin woman: 'My fervently adored Führer! *You* have a birthday and *we* know only two ardent wishes: may everything in our Fatherland be now and in future just as *you* want it to be, and may God provide that you be preserved for us for ever. Your loyal E. E.'[67]

The year 1935 represented, however, by no means the apogee of Hitler adulation in Germany. As a remarkably bold Gestapo report from Stettin in September 1935 demonstrates, the 'human' Hitler picture which Goebbels had constructed carried for many far less than

---

[67] BAK, NS10/158, Fo. 172. Additional examples can be seen in BAK, NS10/157, Fo. 126, 138, and NS10/160, Fos. 150–150ᵛ.

total conviction. Many 'people's comrades', following the Nuremberg
Party Rally of 1935 (during which the notorious anti-Jewish laws had
been promulgated), 'could often detect only little of the particular
solidarity with the people and comradely attitude of the Führer'.
'Here and there', the report went on, 'a tone of command dominated
which was little related to being close to the people, and which is more
off-putting than attractive', adding with extraordinary frankness that
'when particularly the ordinary people's comrade in the country
misses the warmth and senses strongly the domineering, a mood of
opposition stirs in him, but not against the thing itself, rather against
the person who says it'.[68]

Above all, the mounting economic problems of the year 1935—
pegged low wages, sharply rising living costs, food shortages, and still
high levels of unemployment—pushed the rumbling discontent into
visible signs of unrest, plainest in the big industrial centres, causing
clear concern to the Nazi rulers, and threatening to undermine even
the popularity of Hitler himself. Reich Minister of the Interior Frick
sent to the Reich Chancellery extracts of the reports which were
pouring into him from all sides about the growing unrest over rising
prices, which he regarded as a 'serious danger'.[69] Among the reports
which Frick recommended to be drawn to the Führer's attention were
ones from Münster, on the edge of the Ruhr industrial belt, indicating
that 'the mood prompts fears for the worst' and drawing attention to
rumours that miners were about to go on hunger-strike in Gelsen-
kirchen, and from Minden, declaring that 'further food price rises
would be politically intolerable'. A month later the Trustee of Labour
for the North Mark—the Hamburg area—spoke of a 'devastating
picture of the mood of the working class' and 'extraordinary great
dangers' for the political situation.[70]

Low wages were the other side of the coin. 'The wage problem',
pointed out a Gestapo report from Erfurt in June 1935, was 'one of the
most important questions in determining political reliability', and had
to be solved in the imminent future since 'only a contented working
class . . . guarantees the continuance and the further development of
the National Socialist State'.[71] *Sopade* reporters pointed to reper-

---

[68] IML/ZPA, St.3/39/III, Fo. 625, LB of Stapo Stettin for Sept. 1935.

[69] BAK, R43II/318, Fo. 2, Frick to Lammers, 24 July 1935.

[70] Ibid., Fos. 28–9, 62: summary for Lammers from 8 Aug. 1935 of reports from
Arnsberg, Münster,and Minden; minutes of meeting of Trustees of Labour, 27 Aug.
1935.   [71] IML/ZPA, St.3/38/II, Fos. 312–13, LB of Stapo Erfurt, 6 June 1935.

cussions for Hitler's popularity, and began optimistically to envisage the beginning of the end of the Nazi system. 'The Hitler cult is visibly in decline', stated one report from Silesia, 'doubts are gnawing at the Hitler myth', ran another from Saxony, and there was frequent talk in the Rhineland and elsewhere that Schacht or Blomberg would be 'the coming man' and that a military dictatorship would soon replace the Nazi regime.[72]

Conditions deteriorated rather than improved during the winter of 1935–6. Symptomatic of the mood of workers, in the eyes of the Gestapo office in Magdeburg, was the reluctance to join in the 'Sieg Heil' for the Führer during visits of the mobile propaganda units of the Labour Front.[73] The frankest assessment of the mood from within the regime came, however, from a series of astonishingly forthright reports from the Gestapo in Berlin. The report for October 1935 had pointed to the fats and meat shortage (despite the fact that Berlin had been specially provisioned), the increasing cost of foodstuffs, and the again rising unemployment as the main causes of the deteriorating mood.[74] In January 1936, extensive investigations produced the conclusion that there had been a further deterioration in the mood—negatively influenced as before in the first instance by material want and an 'extraordinarily miserable' standard of living made worse by the rapidly rising prices.[75] By early March the mood of the population had worsened still further and was 'giving rise to great worry with regard to internal political conditions'. Indicative was the fact that one could go for days in Berlin without hearing the 'Heil Hitler' greeting—except among uniformed civil servants or people up from the provinces. There was widespread talk of a military dictatorship or of a second '30 June' (the day of the 'Röhm purge'), 'by which the last is meant to imply a fundamental purge of all abuses and the first the construction of a fundamentally new and clean State leadership and administration under the dominant influence of the armed forces'. The reasons for the unrest went beyond passing food shortages, it was said; these would be taken on board 'if a general trust in the State

[72] *DBS*, ii. 757–60, 895, 899, 903–5, reports for July and August 1935.

[73] IML/ZPA, St.3/44/III, Fo. 700, LB of Stapo Magdeburg, 5 Mar. 1936.

[74] BAK, R58/535, Fos. 91–6, Stapo Berlin, report for Oct. 1935. The report was signed by Graf Helldorf, the Police President of Berlin who later became involved in resistance activities and in 1944 was executed following his implication in the plot against Hitler.

[75] BAK, R58/567, Fos. 84–92, Stapo Berlin, report for Jan. 1936.

leadership and Movement existed'. The report pointed in the main to
the anti-social behaviour and life-style and blatant corruption of Party
leaders and functionaries, and of State and industry in general. It
added the striking passage:

A Morale Report written in accordance with the truth of the matter cannot
ignore the fact that the confidence of the population in the person of the
Führer is also undergoing a crisis. It is said that the Führer cannot fail to see
the effects of the human failings of a whole array of his subordinates, how now
this one and now that one is having a huge villa built, how several of his
colleagues are living a luxury existence which has a directly provocative
impact on the mass of the people. Such conversations usually end with the
question: 'Why does the Führer put up with that?' In addition, the Führer at
just the last Party Rally especially protected his subordinates which—as
generally assumed in the population—will be abused by many subordinate
leaders to retain the existing deplorable state of affairs. In broad sections of
the people the opinion has spread that the Führer is surrounded by an
invisible wall no longer penetrable by reports reflecting the truth.[76]

The unenviable task of giving Hitler a verbal summary of such
critical reports fell to his Adjutant, Fritz Wiedemann. Before he had
got past the first few sentences, Hitler cut him short in rage, snarling:
'The mood in the people is not bad, but good. I know that better. It's
made bad through such reports. I forbid such things in future.'[77]
Hitler's impatient and irrational reaction suggests an underlying
realization that the reported collapse in mood was accurate. At any
rate, his own actions between summer 1935 and spring 1936, calling for
reports on the price situation and even agreeing to a temporary
priority for consumer products above raw materials for rearmament[78]
indicate that he was well aware of the unrest.

The state of popular morale on the eve of the march into the

[76] IML/ZPA, St.3/44/I, Fos. 103–7, LB of Stapo Berlin, 6 March 1936.
[77] Fritz Wiedemann, *Der Mann, der Feldherr werden wollte*, Velbert/Kettwig, 1964,
p. 90. The fear that the negative tone of the Prussian 'situation reports', which had been
regularly submitted since mid-1934, would itself contribute to a worsening of mood
among the circle of their recipients, was expressed by Göring as the reason for indeed
terminating the reports, which ceased following the orders of Gestapo chief Heydrich
on 8 April 1936—Kulka, 'Die Nürnberger Rassengesetze', p. 595.
[78] BAK, R43II/318, Fo. 31, 204–13, 219–20; R43II/318a, Fo. 45–53; BAK, Zsg.101/28,
Fo. 331 (*Vertrauliche Informationen* for the press on a ministerial meeting on 7 Nov. 1935
about the crisis in fatstuffs provisioning; the introduction of rationing was vetoed by
Hitler, who accepted the willingness of the army to forgo a proportion of its allocation
of foreign currency until the spring in order to make currency available for the import of
foodstuffs).

Rhineland was, then, far from healthy, from the regime's point of view. It would clearly be a mistake to see the dramatic Rhineland coup of 7 March 1936 largely in terms of a diversion from domestic unrest. Obviously, diplomatic and strategic conditions played the key role. But it seems likely that domestic considerations were of some significance in determining at least the timing of the reoccupation. At any rate, that was the view of Foreign Minister von Neurath who, in private conversation with the German Ambassador to Rome, von Hassell, expressed in fact the opinion that the reasons for the Rhineland operation were solely domestic, that Hitler sensed the general drop in enthusiasm for the regime and felt compelled to look for a new national slogan to inflame the masses once more. Von Hassell agreed that domestic considerations were uppermost in Hitler's mind, and that the 'action' offered a favourable opportunity to forget the provisions difficulties and the clashes between the Party and the Catholic Church in the Rhineland.[79]

The march into the Rhineland on 7 March, despite the risk successfully calling the bluff of the allies, put earlier foreign policy triumphs in the shade. Another piece of 'Versailles', the national trauma, had been removed. Few were bothered that it marked the burial of the spirit of collective security which Stresemann had ushered in at Locarno in 1925. The spectacular coup met with almost uniform acclaim and jubilation, and was again advanced—and largely received—as the outstanding achievement of *one* man.

A new wave of elemental adulation of the Führer swept through Germany, stimulated by the surprise dissolution of the Reichstag and the propaganda campaign for the 'election' on 29 March. Though the 'election' was that of a new Reichstag, the entire Party and the propaganda machine directed their fevered campaign at the Führer himself, and at producing a massive new demonstration of loyalty to emphasize the futility of opposition at home and the strength and unity of Germany to the outside world. The long arm of propaganda did not stop at the big city, but extended even into small villages. The alpine villages of Upper Bavaria had huge banners stretching across their streets carrying slogans such as: 'Only one man can pull it off: the Führer! Stay loyal to him!' Houses were decked with garlands of flowers, pictures of Hitler, and other forms of festive decoration. On

---

[79] M. Funke, '7. März 1936. Fallstudie zum außenpolitischen Führungsstil Hitlers', in W. Michalka (ed.), *Nationalsozialistische Außenpolitik*, Darmstadt, 1978, pp. 278–9.

election day itself, the inhabitants of the villages often marched
together, accompanied by brass bands, to the polling station.[80] On 28
and 29 March the papers carried huge pictures of Hitler and his
request for the support of every German in his 'struggle for a true
peace'. Quotations from 'words of the Führer' littered the pages.
Articles and illustrations let no one forget the Führer's achievement.
'Germany is working again', trumpeted one newspaper as the caption
to a full-page illustration of a German worker and below him a motor-
way stretching into the distance: 'Everywhere hands are active in the
common work! One people, one will, one deed! The German people
has the Führer to thank for all that!'[81]

The 'election' brought the greatest plebiscitary success so far
according to the official returns, with 98.9 per cent 'for the List and
therefore for the Führer'.[82] The figures themselves were patently
absurd. Apart from the lack of alternative to the Nazi Party, and the
general fear of recrimination following secret controls at the polling
booths, there was also some outright manipulation and fabrication.[83]
The *Gauleiter* of Cologne apparently even managed to obtain a result
of 103 per cent in his area, having given his men too many duplicate
ballot papers.[84] Nevertheless, there can be little doubt that the result
did represent an overwhelming show of acclamation for Hitler and for
his foreign policy. It appeared to lend credence to a theme incessantly
rehearsed during the campaign: that Germany was a '*völkisch* Führer
State', and the Führer no dictator but an 'executor of the people's
will'. 'The approval which the people gives to the order created by the
Führer', as the constitutional lawyers explained it, did not rest upon a
contrast between ruler and ruled, a compromise between authority
and people, but was the 'expression of a trustful following'.[85] The
'Hitler myth' had become the basis of the German governmental
'system', with all the problems which that produced for the administration, for members of the government itself, and for legal theorists
seeking in vain to deduce logic and system from the essentially

[80] *Münchner Neueste Nachrichten*, 29 Mar. 1936.

[81] Ibid., 28 Mar. 1936.

[82] BAK, R18/5038, Fo. 373. This file also contains guidelines for propaganda for the
'election'. The results were published in *Statistisches Jahrbuch für das Deutsche Reich*, ed.
Statistisches Reichsamt, Berlin, 1936, p. 565.

[83] See T. Eschenburg, 'Streiflichter zur Geschichte der Wahlen im Dritten Reich',
VfZ, iii (1955), 311–16.

[84] Wiedemann, p. 74.

[85] *Münchner Neueste Nachrichten*, 14 Mar. 1936.

arbitrary 'will of the Führer' and to provide him with pseudo-democratic legitimation.

The actual dialectical relationship between plebiscitary acclamation and Hitler's policy decisions was accurately expressed in a letter of 7 March 1936 to Otto Wels, the former SPD Party Chairman, by Hans Dill, before 1933 a member of the Reichstag and now *Sopade* 'Border Secretary' for North Bavaria, residing just over the border in what was coming to be known as the 'Sudetenland': 'Hitler can no longer escape from his policy. He has himself taken away the possibility through the dissolution of the Reichstag and the new elections. On 29 March he will get approval for this, his policy, with more than 90 per cent of the votes. Then the ring will be closed and he will not be able to step out of it any longer. The Dictator lets himself be bound by the people to the policy which he wanted!'[86]

Not surprisingly, the birthday tributes to Hitler three weeks after the 'election' plumbed new depths of sycophantic unction. In his regular birthday eulogy, Otto Dietrich spoke of 'the political achievement of a titan' by which Hitler had led his people during the past three years to 'the dignity of life, the light of freedom, and the fortune of national honour'. The German people saw itself embodied in its Leader, and 'probably to no mortal being has ever so much love and trust been borne as to Adolf Hitler, the man from the people'.[87] Goebbels, as in the previous year, concentrated on 'the human Hitler', this time extolling in particular his great love of children, who in turn, with the natural sensitivity which children possess, realized 'that he belongs to them with heart and soul', perhaps subconsciously knowing 'that he alone deserves thanks for making life worth living again for German children'. Again the theme of the complete identity of the people with their Führer was the dominant one. 'Never in the history of all time', claimed Goebbels,'has one man united in his own person as he has the trust and feeling of belonging of an entire people.' Following the mass rally in Cologne which brought the 'election' campaign to a close, Goebbels intoned: 'One had the feeling that Germany had been transformed into a single great church embracing all classes, professions, and denominations, into which now its intercessor stepped before the high seat of the Almighty to provide testimony for will and deed.' And the man who was the subject of such

---

[86] ASD, ES/M33, Hans Dill to Otto Wels, 7 Mar. 1936.
[87] *Münchner Neueste Nachrichten*, 20 Apr. 1936.

adulation sat silently at the window of his compartment during the train journey back to Berlin 'and travelled through his land, travelled through his people, and probably enjoyed in this hour the happy feeling of resting deep and secure in the hearts of his nation'. The inventive Propaganda Minister and chief creator of the 'Führer myth' now added to the suggestion of intimate unison of people and Leader the image of the regal father-figure of the nation standing serenely and authoritatively above all the daily worries and cares of ordinary mortals 'like a rock in the sea'. Significantly Goebbels—who more than any other propagandist had hitherto used the name 'Hitler' in his laudations—ended his address on this occasion with the incantation not to 'our Hitler', but to 'our Führer'.[88]

By 1936, the threshold to the fully-fledged formation of the Hitler cult was crossed. Its final development to its apogee in 1938–40, as reflected in popular opinion, will concern us in later chapters. How many people actually swallowed the complete dose of the extreme Goebbels projection of the Hitler image cannot of course at any date be assessed. However, it seems certain, as the thoughtful analysts of the anti-Nazi *Sopade* reports were repeatedly prepared to accept, that many who were innately sceptical or even outrightly hostile did not remain unimpressed by the series of apparent achievements and sensational successes which the Nazi regime under Hitler could lay claim to. And hardly anyone was able completely to escape from the perpetual projection of the 'Führer myth' in the media—a practical impossibility for any German who read a newspaper, listened to the radio, or went to the cinema. Apart from the absolutely hardened opponents, it became ever more difficult to avoid the initial grudging admission that Hitler had indeed brought about a remarkable, even phenomenal, transformation in Germany: the combination of seemingly impressive deeds, appearing to speak for themselves, and ubiquitous propaganda made the drug of the 'Führer myth' hard to resist. The extent and the characteristics of the personality cult make it repeatedly clear, however, that propaganda was only effective where a gullible readiness to trust and believe in untrammelled political leadership had already been cultivated and was widespread.

Inside the Party, naturally, the Führer cult now knew no bounds. The following extract from a letter—representative of many—from an elderly 'Party Comrade' from Oppenheim on the Rhine following

[88] Ibid., 20 Apr. 1936.

Hitler's anti-Bolshevik tirade at the Party Congress in Nuremberg in September 1936, is expressive in its naïve, pseudo-religious belief in Hitler's powers of salvation, and, in the ideological sentiment it reveals, the complete accord with central tenets of Hitler's own *Weltanschauung* as conveyed through the 'Führer myth':

My Führer! . . . I feel compelled by unceasing love to thank our creator daily for, through his grace, giving us and the entire German people such a wonderful Führer, and in a time . . . where our beautiful dear Fatherland was threatened with the most horrible destruction through Jewish bolshevism. It does not bear thinking about what floods of tears, what blood after the scarcely healed wounds of the World War, would have flowed, if you, my beloved Führer, in all your anguish for such a great people had not found the courage, with at that time a small band of 7 men, to win through as the saviour of 66 million Germans, in that through your great love of every individual, from the smallest child to the most aged, you captured all, all, women, men, and the whole of German youth. . . . It is a pleasure for me, not a compliment, not hypocrisy, to pray for you, my Führer, that the Lord God who has created you as a tool for Germanity should keep you healthy, that the love of the people towards you should grow, firm and hard like the many oak trees which have been planted in love and honour to you, my Führer, even in the smallest community in Germany. . . . A Heil to the Führer for victory with all the former front-line fighters who still remain today devoted to the Führer to death. For Germany must live even if we must die. Your unto death loyally devoted front-line comrade, Adolf Dörn.[89]

What was the effect on the man who was the object of such a daily torrent of adulation? In the 1920s, as we saw, Hitler's self-image was still quite detached from the already present excesses of the Führer cult. Even in the early years of the Third Reich itself, some of this reserve is still just perceptible. Despite the forceful egocentric intolerance towards any form of criticism or opposing opinion, which was a consistent feature of Hitler's character, he appears at least in the first years of power to have retained some distance from the personality cult built up around him. It could be argued that in the years 1933–5, Hitler still saw the cult constructed around his person largely as an essential device for fostering the integration not only of Party members, but of the entire people, and approved of it, while retaining some aloofness from the cult, as a vehicle for the 'stupefication of the masses'.[90]

[89] IfZ, MA 731, NSDAP-Hauptarchiv 1/1.
[90] Weißbecker, p. 122.

It is scarcely conceivable, however, that Hitler could have remained impervious to the extraordinary cult which had been created around him, and which was now coming increasingly to envelop him. When did Hitler fall victim himself to the 'Führer myth'? Much points to the heady weeks following the Rhineland triumph as the time when Hitler became a full believer in his own 'myth'. The argument gains support from the recollections of some contemporaries who could observe Hitler from close quarters at this time. Press Chief Otto Dietrich, for example, referred to the years 1935–6 as decisive in Hitler's development, marked by a noticeable change in Hitler's personal conduct, and the memoirs of former Gestapo chief Rudolf Diels point in the same direction.[91] Apart from such testimony, the changing language of his public speeches also suggests the shift in self-perception. Before March 1936 he seldom if ever spoke of himself in the pseudo-mystical, 'messianic', quasi-religious terms which Goebbels and others used. But from the time when, in his speech in Munich on 14 March 1936, he claimed that he walked 'with the certainty of a sleep-walker' along the path which 'Providence' had laid out for him, the mystical relationship between himself and 'Providence' was seldom absent from his major speeches, and the pseudo-religious symbolism and belief in his own infallibility became ingrained in his rhetoric.[92] The style and content of his speeches—the immense claims he now regularly made on himself, and increasingly on the German people—point clearly towards a change in Hitler's self-image. At the Reich Party Rally in 1936 he now spoke himself of a mystical unity between himself and the German people: 'That you have found me . . . among so many millions is the miracle of our time! And that I have found you, that is Germany's fortune!'[93] All the signs are that this was no longer pure rhetoric. Hitler himself was a convert to the 'Führer myth', himself a 'victim' of Nazi propaganda. If one wants to put a date on the conversion, then perhaps 7 March, the date of the successful march into the Rhineland, comes as close as any. What seems certain is that the day on which Hitler started to believe in his own 'myth' marked in a sense the beginning of the end of the Third Reich.[94]

[91] O. Dietrich, *Zwölf Jahre mit Hitler*, Cologne/Munich, n.d. (1955), pp. 44–5; R. Diels, *Lucifer ante Portas. Zwischen Severing und Heydrich*, Zürich, n.d. (1949), pp. 48–50, 58–9, 61–2.

[92] Domarus, p. 606, and see also pp. 16–19.

[93] *Der Parteitag der Ehre vom 8. bis 14. September 1936*, Munich, 1936, pp. 246–7.

[94] See Fest, pp. 713–14; A. Bullock, *Hitler. A Study in Tyranny*, Pelican edn., Harmondsworth, 1962, p. 375.

3

'Führer without Sin'
Hitler and the 'Little Hitlers'

No, gentlemen. The Führer is the Party and the Party is the Führer.

Hitler, 1935

Hitler would be all right, but his underlings are nothing but swindlers.

Party Member from the Upper Palatinate, Dec. 1934

WE have so far concentrated on tracing the general development of the 'Führer myth' from its beginnings to the stage, around 1936, at which it was visibly enhancing Hitler's own over-estimation of his powers and his delusions of infallibility. In this chapter, by contrast, we focus on a single feature of the 'Hitler myth'—though one which was of considerable significance after 1933, which plainly illustrates the contribution 'from below' of 'Hitler believers' to the manufacture of the 'myth', as well as the manipulative capabilities of propaganda, and which provides also a clear indication of the functional role of the personality cult as a key element of political integration in the Nazi system. At the centre of our enquiry here is the remarkable phenomenon that Hitler's rising popularity was not only unaccompanied by a growth in the popularity of the Nazi Party, but in fact developed in some ways at the direct expense of his own Movement. To demonstrate this, we have to leave the process of manufacture of the 'Hitler myth' in the leading organs of the Nazi press and in other major newspapers, and turn to the articulation of opinion on the local level, as registered by the agencies of Party and State in their regular 'morale' and 'situation reports' and by the socialist enemies of the regime through their own information network. The available sources in Bavaria provide a rich vein to tap, but I shall also incorporate material from other parts of the Reich, indicating clearly that the reactions encountered in Bavaria were common throughout Germany.

The discrepancy between the contrasting images of the Nazi regime as reflected in the popular perceptions of the Führer and of the Party functionaries, a basic feature of political opinion throughout the Third Reich, became established in the very first years of the Dictatorship. Before turning to the image of the 'little Hitlers' themselves, however, we can observe in sharp relief the way in which Hitler's popularity expanded at the expense of his own Movement—with the strong suggestion that the 'Führer myth' served an important compensatory function in the Third Reich—by exploring popular reactions to the most dramatic events within Germany in 1934: the massacre, on Hitler's orders, of the SA leadership on 30 June 1934 following the so-called 'Röhm Putsch'.

(i) *'The Führer restores Order': 'The Night of the Long Knives', 30 June 1934*
The 'Röhm Affair' occurred at a time when the Nazi regime, following the initial euphoria—boosted by the glowing propaganda picture of early 'achievements', was visibly losing ground. Alongside the grievances arising from continuing mass unemployment and economic recession, and from disappointment at the gulf betwen the grandiose promises of the NSDAP and the dismal reality of daily life, the actual experience of the Nazi 'seizure of power' in the localities— of its impact on local government, on local church and school, farming, trade and industry, and on community relations—frequently promoted serious disillusionment. The Nazi 'revolution' was by now leaving its mark on social groups which had hitherto been generally accommodating towards Nazism—the lower middle class and the conservative social 'establishment'. And the relative calm in Church– State relations, sustained only with mounting difficulty during 1933, was being increasingly disturbed by the wave of anti-clericalism and anti-Church behaviour of local Party activists. In opposition, the NSDAP had cultivated the image of a 'Movement' embracing the whole people in national unity and 'renewal', as a direct contrast to the divisive 'politicking' of the Weimar parties. But now, in power, it revealed itself at the 'grassroots' level to be anything but a force for unity, harmony, and integration. Instead, it seemed to be a recognizable 'party' of vested sectional interests, much as the others had been, its representatives dividing and alienating opinion through their blatantly thrusting ambitions, their open, distasteful jockeying for power and influence. Local power-struggles, rows, and rivalries among the new rulers were rarely an edifying spectacle. With the

transition from a 'Movement of Struggle' to the ruling Party of the Third Reich, petty empire-building accompanied by transparent corruption became ubiquitous and was found especially intolerable where the new local bigwigs were disparaged as jumped-up social nobodies, openly on the make. Most of all, the 'unacceptable face' of the infant Third Reich was mirrored in the bullying arrogance and rowdy disturbances of the power-crazed SA, whose unsavoury behaviour—once the 'troublemakers' of the Left and other 'anti-social elements' had been 'cleared away'—was deeply offensive to the sense of public order and morality of middle-class Germans.

Popular reactions to the 'Röhm Affair' have to be seen within this context. The vast majority of the population knew little or nothing of the high-level machinations, especially within the Reichswehr leadership, aimed at removing the threat posed by the massive, pseudo-revolutionary force led by Ernst Röhm. Nor was the public aware of the smouldering crisis of confidence brewing between the SA leadership and Hitler, which was to unleash the massacre of 30 June 1934. Hardly anyone outside the inner circles of the power élite knew of the insidious fabrication of a putsch attempt in order to justify the liquidation of Röhm and other high-ranking SA leaders (as well as settling the score with some long-standing enemies such as Gregor Strasser and General von Schleicher). Even so, it might be thought that the mass shooting of former comrades without a semblance of orderly trial or sentence in a court of law could have prompted a wave of revulsion and outrage directed at Hitler and his accomplices. It is striking, therefore, that the reports on reactions of 'ordinary' people throughout Germany following the 'Röhm Putsch' tell an entirely different story.

The almost total absence of any criticism of Hitler was, in fact, already apparent even in the immediate aftermath of the events. 'Sympathy lay generally from the beginning on the side of the Führer', ran one report from Swabia as the dramatic news seeped through in the early afternoon of 30 June.[1] In Upper Bavaria 'unreserved recognition for the energy, cleverness, and courage of the Führer' could reportedly be heard everywhere.[2] The detestation for the SA, which, through the medium of Special Commissioners and Auxiliary Police, had operated in Bavaria even more overtly than elsewhere as the

---

[1] GStA, MA 106682, RPvS, 3 July 1934.
[2] GStA, MA 106670, RPvOB, 4 July 1934.

avant-garde of the Nazi 'revolution from below', was such that the shooting of Röhm and his accomplices was criticized as too mild— 'people's justice' being seen as more appropriate.[3] Extant 'situation reports' from forty-one labour exchanges all over Bavaria dating from the beginning of July 1934 and covering the mood in all sectors of the population, but especially among workers and the unemployed, concurred in their record of expressed opinion as that of overwhelming admiration for Hitler and approval of his action, together with general condemnation of Röhm, and an improvement in morale since the purge.[4] Not a few reports added that Hitler had won support and sympathy among those who had previously shown reserve towards the regime, and even among former opponents of Nazism.[5] The report from one small industrial town where the KPD had done relatively well before 1933 went so far as to claim that 'the Führer . . . is not only admired; he is deified' and that through his 'forceful action' he had won 'enormous support', especially among those who had formerly been hesitant in their attitudes to Nazism.[6]

The sentiments recorded in the Bavarian reports are echoed in the soundings of opinion taken in all parts of the Reich. According to a 'situation report' from Hanover, for example, Hitler's standing and popularity had 'never been greater'.[7] A Gestapo report from Cologne spoke of 'a massive increase in the confidence in the Führer and the government' as a consequence of the destruction of the 'enemies of the people'.[8] And from the Ruhr came the message that 'the overwhelming majority of the population fully approves of the energetic, radical, and courageous action of the Führer'.[9] Göring summed up the regime's own impressions of the positive impact on popular opinion of the liquidation of the SA leadership when, in a letter which he wrote as Minister President of Prussia to Deputy Führer Rudolf Heß, responsible for Party administration, he recorded the unanimous verdict of 'situation reports' from all the Prussian provinces that the calling of

[3] StAM, LRA 76887, GS Landsham, 12 July 1934. See also *DBS*, i. 202, 21 July 1934, report from Dresden.

[4] The reports are to be found in GStA, MA 106765.

[5] GStA, MA 106765, AA Cham, 10 July 1934; AA Marktredwitz, 9 July 1934; StAM, LRA 76887, GS Markt Schwaben, 12 July 1934; LRA 134055, BA Bad Tölz, 14 July 1934.

[6] GStA, MA 106675, AA Marktredwitz, 9 July 1934.

[7] BAK, R43II/1263, Fo. 262, LB of OP Hannover for July 1934.

[8] Ibid., Fo. 320, LB of Stapo Köln for July 1934.

[9] ZStA, Potsdam, 25732/2, Fos. 2, 7, LB or RP in Arnsberg, 10 Aug. 1934; and see ibid., Fos. 35–6, LB of OP der Provinz Westfalen, 11 Aug. 1934.

the SA to account, which Hitler had done in issuing a list of twelve demands for future conduct, had 'already attained optimal effect in all sections of the population'.[10]

Strikingly, as the reports from all over the Reich sent to *Sopade* headquarters in Prague testify, the opponents of the regime were reaching precisely the same conclusions about the impact of the 'Röhm Putsch' on Hitler's image and popularity. The general conclusions were summarized by *Sopade* in three points which recurred in most reports: '1. The broad mass has not grasped the political meaning of the events [i.e. of 30 June 1934]. 2. Large, evidently very large, sections of the population are even extolling Hitler for his ruthless determination, and only a very small portion has been set thinking or been shocked. 3. Large sections of the working class have also become enslaved to the uncritical deification of Hitler.' According to a report from Baden, Hitler was 'regarded as a hero' for his courage in acting. Reports from East and West Saxony, Silesia, Bavaria, Pomerania, Berlin, Dresden, the Rhineland, and other places told more or less the same tale, allowing the *Sopade*'s general conclusion that, far from suffering as a result of the massacre of the SA leadership, Hitler's standing had actually risen.[11]

As the *Sopade* analysts recognized, there was a notable discrepancy between the actual political significance of the events of 30 June 1934 and the ignorance of the population about what was really afoot, leading to a total misinterpretation of the purge. It was plain that there was wide acceptance of the deliberately misleading propaganda put out by the regime. Just how little 'hard' knowledge of events existed in the days immediately after the purge is revealed by the often contradictory rumours in circulation, some of which had been put about by foreign broadcasts. It was rumoured that there had been an attempt on Hitler's life in which the Führer had suffered an arm injury, that 'the last shot had not yet been fired', and that it could come to further internal unrest and to an attack on the Führer.[12] Other variants had it

---

[10] BAK, R43II/1263, Fos. 235–7, Der Preußische Ministerpräsident an den Stellvertreter des Führers, 31 Aug. 1934. The file contains the extracted reports, on which Göring's comment was based. The 'Twelve Points' were contained in a published order to the new Chief of Staff of the SA, Viktor Lutze, dated 30 June 1934. For the text, see Domarus, pp. 401–2.

[11] *DBS*, i. 197–203, 249–53, 21 July 1934. See also the detailed reports by the Bavarian Border Secretaries on the impact of the Röhm Putsch on Hitler's popular image in ASD, ES/M31, 19 July 1934, and M63, report for July 1934.

[12] StAB, K8/III, 18470, BA Ebermannstadt, 14 July 1934; GStA, MA 106765, AA

that von Papen had been shot as one of the conspirators. On the other hand, the correct news quickly spread in Bavaria that the former Bavarian State Commissar von Kahr had been among the victims. The number of those shot was subject to wild guesses—ranging from 46 to 200 according to one report.[13] Workers, said to have little sympathy for notions of a 'second revolution' which had been touted within the SA and some sections of the Party, speculated on whether the Nazi Movement would now become radicalized, or lose its edge, or move to the Left; there was talk of adherents of the former conservative and Catholic parties and of officers being involved in the 'plot'. That there had been a plot does not seem to have been doubted, and 'that the oldest fighters of the NSDAP should themselves have taken part in it, those in whom the Führer had the greatest trust, was sharply condemned'.[14]

Concern about new unrest and disturbances seems to have been one of the main reasons why Hitler's 'intervention' was so well received. But, as the scale of the rumours in circulation also suggests, there was a growing desire in early July for the Führer to speak to the people and clarify what precisely had happened.[15] After an anxious few days, Hitler himself came to the conclusion that any attempt to hush up the affair (which initially seems to have been considered,[16] but was clearly soon out of the question) would do more harm than good. Eventually, therefore, but as long as a fortnight after the events, he spoke in the Reichstag in a speech lasting several hours—not one of his best rhetorical performances but nevertheless finely tuned to the prevailing popular mood.[17] It was a remarkable speech in that the head of the German government openly accepted full responsibility for action amounting to mass murder. He described himself as the 'supreme judge' of the German people, compelled to act without hesitation in emergency conditions arising from the 'mutiny' of the SA leaders, and thus giving the command to shoot the main culprits. Those parts of the speech in which Hitler referred to the 'poisoning of

Donauwörth, 12 July 1934; and for continued rumours of an attack on Hitler, GStA, MA 106685, Pd München, 8 Dec. 1934.

[13] GStA, MA 106765, AA Marktredwitz, 9 July 1934. Almost every report mentions rumours about the number of victims and the widespread distrust of the official figures.

[14] GStA, MA 106765, AA Marktredwitz, 9 July 1934.

[15] GStA, MA 106765, AA Pfarrkirchen, 10 July 1934; AA Marktredwitz, 9 July 1934.

[16] See Fest, pp. 642–3.

[17] For the text, see Domarus, pp. 410–24.

the well within' and of the 'ulcer' of the SA's subversion which it had
been necessary 'to burn out down to the raw flesh' matched exactly the
'healthy sentiments of the people'. Two points in particular struck a
chord: the emphasis upon the immoral life-style, especially the homo-
sexuality, of the SA leadership, which Hitler claimed to be combating;
and the justification of his intervention as vital for the maintenance of
internal order and security. Both points were central to Hitler's
defence of his actions, and the latter was emphasized as the most
crucial consideration of all. And when Hitler condemned the 'destructive elements', who had regarded revolution as a permanent state of
affairs, he was certain of the acclaim not only of the mass of 'ordinary'
Germans, but also of the leaders of the army, economy, and civil
service, who had viewed the attempts to continue the Nazi revolution
with ever increasing concern.

Instead of intensifying unease at the ruthlessness of a head of
government who did not hesitate to resort to mass murder in the
interests of the state, the speech unquestionably strengthened confidence in Hitler. One typical report from provincial Bavaria claimed
that the speech—heard by many in pubs or on installed transmitters in
streets and market squares—had had a 'liberating effect' in exposing
the 'whole background' to the 'plot'.[18] Another report agreed that the
initial confusion and 'feeling of legal insecurity' had given way after
Hitler's speech to general 'admiration and gratitude'. The Führer's
intervention had been regarded as the 'liberation from a strongly felt
oppression'. The majority of the population, the report added, 'clearly
look to the Führer full of trust; he has without doubt gained significantly in respect and popularity.'[19]

Pre-conditions for the tidal wave of support for Hitler's total dis-
regard for judicial procedures were not only the widespread condemnation of the despotism and loose living within the SA, but also, as
the *Sopade* perceptively recognized, the systematic undermining of
any sense of legal rectitude which had been taking place since the start
of the Third Reich and even earlier, together with the pandering to
already existent 'strong sympathies for summary justice and as hard a

[18] StAB, K8/III, 18470, BA Ebermannstadt, 14 July 1934. For the impact of the
speech, see also GStA, MA 106670, RPvOB, 18 July 1934; MA 106677, RPvOF/MF,
21 July 1934; MA 106680, RPvUF, 20 July 1934; MA 106685, Pd München, 8 Aug. 1934.
[19] GStA, MA 106691, LB of RPvNB/OP, 8 Aug. 1934. See also MA 106693, LB of
RPvS, 8 Aug. 1934: 'The Führer enjoys a very great veneration. The people have
unshakeable belief in him.'

punishment as possible'. Accordingly, 'through his Reichstag speech Hitler has very cleverly given this mood of the masses new nourishment: without doubt, wide sections of the population have gained the impression from this speech that through his brutal energy Hitler has prevented a much greater bloodbath.'[20]

The new Hitler euphoria crossed social divides, even if it may be taken for granted that it left ideological enemies untouched. Workers and the unemployed, if they were not adherents of the proscribed left-wing parties were susceptible to the mood of acclaim, as were other social groups. A report from Ingolstadt spoke of an 'especially strong increase in and consolidation of trust in the Führer' among the unemployed, and of workers clamouring to buy pictures of Hitler.[21] As we have seen, the *Sopade* itself accepted that the admiration of Hitler penetrated deep into the working class.[22] In the countryside, the approval was even greater. Reports from rural districts of Bavaria which were certainly not Nazi strongholds commented on the 'great satisfaction' at what had taken place, and the ensuing 'high esteem' and 'sympathy' for the Führer.[23] Nor was there noticeably less praise for Hitler in Catholic than in Protestant districts, despite the fact that Erich Klausener, a prominent leader of 'Catholic Action' and in no way connected with the SA, was numbered among the victims of the 'Night of the Long Knives'.[24] Just as the Reichswehr leaders raised no protest at the murder of the two generals von Schleicher and von Bredow, so the hierarchies of both the major Christian denominations refrained from any public criticism of the events of 30 June 1934. One revivalist 'mission', held only a few days after the massacre, reportedly even went so far as to have prayers said for the Führer.[25] Although some anxiety at the arbitrary shootings (together with the likelihood of recurring purges which might endanger the lives even of non-Party members) was reported, such 'excesses' were generally not blamed on

[20] *DBS*, i. 249–53, 21 July 1934.

[21] GStA, MA 106765, AA Ingolstadt, 10 July 1934.

[22] See *DBS*, i. 197, 21 July 1934.

[23] e.g. GStA, MA 106765, AA Ingolstadt, 10 July 1934; StAM, LRA 76887, GS Markt Schwaben, GS Steinhöring, GS Zorneding, all from 12 July 1934.

[24] For signs of approval among former adherents of the Bavarian People's Party, see StAB, K8/III, 18470, GS Unterweilersbach, 1 Aug. 1934 and GStA, MA 106670, RPvOB, 18 July 1934; and for reactions in Protestant districts of Bavaria, StAN, 212/13/II, 654, BA Neustadt an der Aisch, 2 July 1934 and GStA, MA 106765, AA Marktredwitz, 9 July 1934.

[25] GStA, MA 106765, AA Ingolstadt, 10 July 1934.

Hitler himself, but were said to have taken place 'without the knowledge and against the will of the Führer and leading figures'.[26]

The 'Röhm Affair' and reactions to it took underground, left-wing resistance groups by surprise, and their own response was weak and ineffectual. Their illegal pamphlets and flysheets could make little capital out of the affair, tending to portray the purge simply as a 'butchery of associates', or to express naïve expectations that Hitler too would soon fall victim to inner-Party power struggles.[27] Some reports to the *Sopade* were equally unrealistic—one from the Rhineland claiming to perceive a widespread feeling 'that the system and the NSDAP were standing on feet of clay and that its undermining could no longer be mistaken'. 'Hitler is soon finished!', ended the note of ludicrous optimism.[28] Such comments were nevertheless exceptional among the usually realistic and balanced *Sopade* reports, and were duly ignored in the compilation of the overall analysis. On a different level, the files of the Munich Special Court, dealing with relatively minor offences which betrayed political nonconformity, provide no indication of a rise in critical remarks levelled at Hitler in the period following the purge.[29]

The two most potent features of Hitler's perceived image following the 'Röhm Putsch' were, first, that he was the executant of 'natural justice' (even if flouting all legal conventions), defending the 'little man' against the abuse of power of the 'big shots'; and, second, that he was the upholder of public morality, cleansing public life of the dissolute immorality and corruption of the SA leaders.[30] Hitler, the man of the people, so it appeared to many, was taking a courageous stance against the jumped-up petty and debauched despots in the Nazi Movement. Wishful thinking and a naïve readiness to place all trust in the presumed good intentions behind Hitler's authority are indicated in reported comments 'that the Reich Chancellor has acted against the so-called high-and-mighty' and 'that our Führer only

[26] GStA, MA 106767. AA Kempten, 9 Aug. 1934; AA Straubing, 10 Sept. 1934.

[27] H. Bretschneider, *Der Widerstand gegen den Nationalsozialismus in München 1933 bis 1945*, Munich, 1968, pp. 44, 102; StAB, K8/III, 18470, BA Ebermannstadt, 14 July 1934. For the weak and belated reactions of the underground KPD in the Ruhr, see D. Peukert, *Die KPD im Widerstand*, Wuppertal, 1980, p. 220.

[28] *DBS*, i. 202, 21 July 1934.

[29] Occasional comments leading to an indictment, such as condemnation of Hitler as a murderer (StAM, SGM 8930), seem to have been notable exceptions.

[30] See e.g. GStA, MA 106670, RPvOB, 18 July 1934; StAA, BA Amberg 2398, GS Freudenberg, 23 July 1934.

desires peace and order and acts justly'.[31] Especially the poorer and
weaker sections of the population, it was said, were grateful for their
release from torment, and it was now plainly accepted 'that the Führer
is ready at all times, without consideration for rank and status of the
guilty, to do whatever is necessary for the good of the people'.[32] The
defence of conventional morality comes across equally strongly in the
reported reactions. A *Sopade* report from Baden pointed out that
Hitler's defamation of the murdered SA leaders as homosexuals
squandering 30,000 Reich Marks on loose living was interpreted as a
heroic act. He had proved, according to a Bavarian report, that he
insisted upon a 'clean entourage'. Reported opinion in Berlin was that
Hitler 'had paved the way for a moral renewal'.[33] It is striking how
often, in the internal reports of the regime, Hitler's 'twelve points' for
'cleaning up' the SA, largely directed at the moral behaviour of the
leadership, were singled out as meeting with a particularly positive
reception.[34]

Clearly, the propaganda portrayal of Hitler as the upholder of moral
standards corresponded closely with commonly-held social values
and prejudices in its condemnation of venal corruption and homo-
sexuality. In a total inversion of reality, Hitler was widely perceived as
signalling a triumph for values associated with 'normality', acting as
the true representative of 'the common man' in cutting down to size
the high and mighty even from within his own Movement for the good
of his people. People said approvingly that no previous Reich
Chancellor would have dared act as he had done.[35] His 'morality' was
perceived as not that of the law courts, but, as the Nazis had always
claimed, that of the 'healthy sentiments of the people'. Perceptive as
usual, the *Sopade* analysts clearly recognized the effectiveness and
function of the appeal to bourgeois morality in the justification of
Hitler's 'action'. While at first sight, it was suggested, 'the revelations

[31] StAB, K8/III, 18470, GHS Ebermannstadt, 12 July 1934. A *Sopade* report from
Bavaria also pointed out how striking it was that workers in particular took satisfaction
at the thought that Hitler had shown the iron fist to the high and mighty—*DBS*, i. 200,
21 July 1934 (from ASD, ES/M63, report for June 1934, pp. 7–8).

[32] GStA, MA 106765, AA Traunstein, 11 July 1934; MA 106767, AA Ingolstadt, 9 Aug.
1934.

[33] *DBS*, i. 198–9, 201, 21 July 1934.

[34] See the reports from the Prussian provinces in BAK, R43II/1263; and in addition
M. Jamin, 'Zur Rolle der SA im nationalsozialistischen Herrschaftssystem', in
Hirschfeld and Kettenacker, pp. 349–53, and R. Bessel, *Political Violence and the Rise of
Nazism*, New Haven/London, 1984, pp. 143–6.

[35] *DBS*, i. 200, 21 July 1934.

about the moral depravity of the SA leadership clique seem to be a suicide attempt of the regime', its effect had been 'in reality a supremely clever propaganda trick' which was successful 'in diverting the attention of the great mass of the population from the political background to the action, and at the same time elevating Hitler's standing as the cleanser of the Movement all the more as the muck was raked out into full view'.[36]

Above all, it was the meeting of the traditional bourgeois demand for 'peace and quiet' and 'law and order', threatened by the unruliness, arbitrary violence, and public outrages of the SA, which gave legitimation to the State murders sanctioned by Hitler. *Sopade* reports resignedly pointed out that people were ignoring the political dimension and thinking only 'now that Hitler has restored order, things will improve again; the saboteurs, who have destroyed his work of rebuilding, are annihilated'. No doubt a small-businessman from Saxony spoke for many in seeing Hitler as 'an absolutely honest person who wants the best for the German people' but had hitherto been prevented by his subordinates from doing so. He shrugged off the argument that Hitler had sole responsibility for the murders by retorting that 'the main thing is, he has freed us from the Marxists' and has got rid of the harmful influence of 'the dreadful SA', so that now wages could indeed be reduced and industry could start to become profitable. He continued to swear by Hitler as a leader of supradimensional qualities 'even if he is a mass murderer'.[37] Ruthlessness in the interest of bourgeois 'order' was clearly a central component of Hitler's popularity.

The Nazi authorities were, however, well aware that the 'Röhm Affair' had opened the door to a torrent of criticism which did not stop at the SA, but implicated the Party itself. The illusions built into the idolization of the Führer were fully exposed in the vain hope that the purge of the SA would mark the beginning of further purges aimed at eliminating those Party functionaries 'who from their character and their past life are seen as unfit', and who were alienating people rather than winning them over to the Movement.[38] Material and personalized

[36] Ibid., i. 249.
[37] Ibid., i. 199, 201.
[38] GStA, MA 106691, LB of RPvNB/OP, 8 Aug. 1934; GStA, MA 106767, AA Marktredwitz, 7 Aug. 1934. See also ibid., AA Hof-Saale, 10 Aug. 1934; MA 106765, AA Marktredwitz, 9 July 1934; StAM, LRA 76887, GS Markt Grafing, 31 Dec. 1934; LRA 134055, GHS Bad Tölz, 27 July 1934; NSDAP 655, NS-Hago Penzberg, 6 July 1934.

motives naturally also played their part, since disappointed 'Old Fighters' of the Party were again for a while able to dream of the advancement which they had thought would be theirs by right after 1933, and which might still come their way in the event of a purge.[39] Already before the 'Röhm Putsch', reports were recording a loss of confidence even among Party members in the Party, whose leadership was felt to have 'lost touch with the people', and hopes were expressed of a coming 'great purge'.[40] It was said that people wanted to be 'freed from the oppression of small minds' and were castigating the inflated Party and Labour Front administration and their huge and unnecessary expenditure.[41] Amid the continuing economic deprivation shared by the many, the luxury of the few, paraded openly by the Nazi 'bigwigs', seemed a complete contradiction of the Führer's exhortations to 'simplicity and thrift', which his own life was depicted as epitomizing.[42]

Similar remarks were being heard and noted all over Germany in the summer of 1934. Göring's letter to Heß, cited earlier and drawing upon reports from all parts of Prussia immediately after the 'Röhm Putsch', stressed the universal expectation that 'the purge will be emphatically followed through not only in the SA, but beyond that in all affiliations of the Party', pointing out the widespread concern 'that after carrying out the action of 30 June, everything will essentially remain the same'. Göring pressed Heß to undertake a comprehensive purge, which he himself regarded as of 'paramount political significance', given the coming winter of austerity and economic difficulties, in order to 'exploit all psychological means to maintain and lift morale' and to guarantee the success of the coming Winter Aid programme. A copy of Göring's letter was sent to Hitler himself.[43]

As we have been witnessing, Hitler's own unsullied image stood only to gain from the contrast with the public profile of his Party henchmen. In the growing disillusionment of the spring and summer

[39] 'Old Fighters' in Regensburg, for example, expressed disappointment that further purges had not been undertaken, since their hopes of occupying Party positions which would thereby have become vacant had to remain unfulfilled—GStA, MA 106767, AA Regensburg, 9 Aug. 1934.

[40] GStA, MA 106765, AA Weißenburg i.B., 9 June 1934 (wrongly dated as 9 May 1934). And see the *Sopade*'s assessment of the mood just prior to the 'Röhm Putsch' in *DBS*, i. 9–14, 17 May 1934 and i. 99–122, 26 June 1934.

[41] GStA, MA 106767, AA Cham, 10 Sept. 1934.

[42] GStA, MA 106672, RPvNB/OP, 7 Aug. 1934.

[43] BAK, R43II/1263, Fos. 235–7, Göring to Heß, 31 Aug. 1934.

of 1934, the polarized images of Führer and Party were fixing themselves in popular consciousness. And the myth of 'if only the Führer knew' was already at work. Many genuinely believed that matters, especially if unpalatable, were deliberately kept from Hitler, and that if he learned of them he would act swiftly to set things right.[44] The purge of 30 June 1934 appeared to provide confirmation for this view. The Führer had, it seemed, finally learnt of the intolerable state of affairs and had acted immediately and ruthlessly to eradicate it. One report from Bavaria suggested—logically, but unrealistically—that Hitler's intervention did away with 'the ever-recurring claim that "the Führer is surrounded by a clique who keep him in the dark about the goings-on in the Party and the SA." '[45] Indeed, quite irrationally, the very fact that on this occasion Hitler was presumed to have recognized the evil and acted to remove it actually seems to have bolstered the legend, that when he did not act it was because he was being sheltered from the real evils by his underlings, who had most to lose by any discovery of the realities of misrule. 'Hitler would be all right, but his underlings are nothing but swindlers'—the comment of a Bavarian Party member in December 1934—became a cliché in the months following the 'Röhm Putsch'.[46] Many who in January 1933 had put their trust in the 'National Revolution' were prepared to distinguish between outward appearances, as reflected in the deplorable behaviour of the Party functionaries, and the 'idea' itself, embodied in the symbol of political righteousness, a man without fault, a 'Führer without sin' as one report expressively put it.[47]

The Party was evidently incapable of bringing about effective political integration in the Third Reich. But following the 'Röhm Putsch', at a point of real crisis for the regime, Hitler had been able to strengthen his own popular standing, and with it that of the regime itself, and, through playing on the 'healthy sentiments of the people' and appealing to a conventionally crude sense of morality and order, to integrate and bind the population in greater identification with the Führer, even at the expense of members of his own Movement. The affair was a propaganda coup par excellence.

[44] GStA, MA 106765, AA Weißenburg i.B., 9 June 1934.

[45] GStA, MA 106767, AA Kempten, 9 Aug. 1934.

[46] StAA, Amtsgericht Cham 72/35. See also e.g. GAtA, MA 106767, AA Cham, 9 Aug. 1934; AA Marktredwitz, 7 Aug. 1934; AA Schwandorf i.B., 10 Sept. 1934, 10 Jan. 1935; AA Straubing, 10 Sept. 1934; MA 106691, LB of RPvOB, 8 Aug. 1934; and see Kershaw, Popular Opinion, pp. 122–3.

[47] GStA, MA 106767, AA Marktredwitz, 11 Sept. 1934.

(ii) *The 'Little Hitlers': the Image of the Local Party Bosses*

How did the public image of the Nazi Party's representative figures in the localities deteriorate so markedly within the course of little more than a year following the 'seizure of power' to the stage following the 'Röhm Putsch' where, as we have seen, even Göring was demanding an extensive purge of the Party? And what were the characteristic features of the negative image of the Party functionary which enhanced in such sharp relief the unsullied image of the Führer? Answers are best found by glancing at some not untypical examples of relations between the Party and the local population at the 'grass-roots' level.

We need to be aware, of course, that vilification of Party functionaries—the 'little Hitlers' as they were frequently dubbed—did not necessarily equate with rejection of the Party itself, let alone with the ideology and aims of National Socialism. And, doubtless, many of the attacks were stirred up by those hostile to the regime (though the criticism was often shared, as we have noted, by Party members themselves). Furthermore, the local Party membership was not unpopular everywhere. Recent studies of the social profile of the Nazi Party after 1933[48] have demonstrated that the potential for political integration on the local level was considerable in areas where the Party had earlier won over representatives of the social and political élites, who already enjoyed a degree of public recognition and social acceptability and were content with a more or less 'nominal' co-ordination of local institutions following the 'seizure of power'. Similarly, things ran relatively smoothly where 'respectable' and 'moderate' local worthies, who had jumped on the Nazi bandwagon in 1933, came to occupy the leading positions in local government and in the local Party organization. Conflict was less likely to occur, finally, in communities where ideological conflict had been minimal before 1933. On the other hand, significant levels of dissension were prevalent where the break with continuity in 1933 had been sharper, where 'Old Fighters' with little social standing were catapulted into leading positions in the local

---

[48] See Z. Zofka, 'Dorfeliten und NSDAP', in *Bayern IV*, pp. 383–433; Zofka, *Die Ausbreitung des Nationalsozialismus auf dem Lande*, pp. 238 ff, 294 ff; E. Fröhlich and M. Broszat, 'Politische und soziale Macht auf dem Lande. Die Durchsetzung der NSDAP im Kreis Memmingen', *VfZ*, xxv (1977), 546–72; and E. Fröhlich, 'Die Partei auf lokaler Ebene. Zwischen gesellschaftlicher Assimilation und Veränderungs-dynamik', in Hirschfeld and Kettenacker, pp. 255–69.

government and Party, and where 'upstart' Party functionaries introduced radical attempts to attack and displace the traditional structures of social power and influence.

The 'little Hitler' type was, therefore, by no means omnipresent, but was nevertheless sufficiently widely encountered to provoke extensive criticism and to tarnish irreparably the image of the Party. In a sense, the Party functionaries were reaping the harvest of the prejudice which they themselves had helped to sow against local politicians and 'bigwigs', and had to face the daily dissatisfaction and discord as the rebound from the utopian hopes in the Third Reich which they had stirred up. The 'little Hitlers', in the forefront of the local scene, had to bear the brunt of the discontent. In stark contrast, the 'Hitler myth'—clearly in part a subconscious mechanism to compensate for the perceived shortcomings of 'everyday life' in the Third Reich—stood aloof from the dissension on a lofty and untouchable plane.

The district of Ebersberg, in Upper Bavaria, provides illustration of the development of a highly negative Party image arising from the poor standing of the local Party functionaries. As in many other Catholic areas, the NSDAP had been able to make a substantial (if still incomplete) electoral breakthrough only as late as March 1933, and the success proved, as elsewhere, transient.[49] Soon after the restructuring of village and town councils in April 1933, discord began to surface in a number of communities in the Ebersberg area. In the small market town of Markt Grafing, where friction rapidly became apparent, the scant public recognition for the new political 'élite' is plain from the local police reports. According to one report in September 1933, there was talk in the town of a massive 'popular movement against such persons who have leading positions in the national movement in the community as local base leader and so on, and who try to influence the mayor. It is in the main a case of persons who enjoy no special esteem and in whom people have no confidence'.[50] Six months later, the poor recruitment of the 'national movement' in the area was attributed to the fact that the local leadership had never enjoyed the trust of the people.[51] The town does, indeed, appear to have been run by disreputable characters after 1933.

---

[49] The NSDAP gained only 24.3% of the vote in November 1932, but almost doubled its level of support to 47.5% in March 1933—Hagmann, p. 22.

[50] StAM, LRA 76887, GS Markt Grafing, 12 Sept. 1933.

[51] Ibid., 26 Mar. 1934.

Even many Party members were highly antagonistic towards the Local Group Leader, evidently an extremely unpleasant, domineering type who engaged in a dirty fight to become mayor in June 1933, stirring up along the way a smear campaign to have his main rival for the post, the Local Peasant Leader and director of the co-operative brewery, accused of embezzlement.[52] The Peasant Leader himself, in fact, was equally disliked and enjoyed little respect among farmers because of the bad management of his own farm, while his commercial practices as director of a local brewery had formerly alienated the publicans of the town and, through his plans to develop a butchery on the premises, were now causing anger among the existing group of butchers.[53] All in all, he had little favour with leading figures among the town's commercial fraternity.

Continued hostility toward the person of the Local Group Leader and Mayor was voiced in complaints in autumn 1934 that the promised 'clearing-out' of the Party had never taken place. The report for November 1934 echoed the complaints of the farmers and local burghers of Markt Grafing that as long as those 'who understand nothing of local politics are not dismissed from their posts and replaced by genuinely competent, nationally thinking people, there will be no confidence placed in the government'. Hitler, significantly, was expressly excluded from any criticism. The report went on: 'With the orders of the Führer Hitler, whom they love above all else and who in their opinion really means well for the people, they are in complete agreement. But with the busybodies who couldn't do or understand anything then and still can't understand anything now, they are not, definitely not, in agreement.'[54]

The dichotomy between the esteem for Hitler and the disparagement of the local Party and its leadership was also a marked feature in other communities of the district. Acording to one not untypical report, 'there is great sympathy among the population for the Führer and Reich Chancellor Adolf Hitler. I have never heard any negative comment directed at his own person. Rather, one hears now and then: "Yes, if Hitler could do everything himself, some things would be different. But he can't keep a watch on everything." '[55] There could

[52] Ibid., 31 July 1934.
[53] Ibid., 12 Jan. 1934.   [54] Ibid., 30 Nov. 1934.
[55] Ibid., GS Steinhöring, 31 Jan. 1935, 1 Aug. 1935. For almost identical expressions of opinion, see also GStA, MA 106691, LB of RPvOB, 8 Aug. 1934; and StAM, OLG 127, PLG Eichstätt, 28 Dec. 1935.

hardly have been a sharper contrast with the image of the Party in the area. In Landsham, the collapse of enthusiasm for the NSDAP was put down to the recruitment of communists and criminals and the 'unbelievable conditions' within the local Party.[56] In Ebersberg itself, the meddling of the Party leadership in local government affairs had prompted a 'very tense' mood.[57] While in nearby Zorneding the loss of confidence in the local Party leadership was seen as the reason for the difficulties in winning recruits for the SA and the Nazi youth and women's organizations.[58] Alongside economic disappointments and the strong affiliation to the Catholic Church, factional squabbling and the lack of personal respect and social standing evidently played their part in undermining the authority of the Party functionaries in the Ebersberg district, where a purge was still eagerly awaited six months after the 'Röhm Affair'.[59]

Ebersberg was, however, no isolated case. Similar tendencies can be witnessed even in areas where the NSDAP had won a relatively high level of support before 1933. In Wolfratshausen, near Munich, for example, where the Nazis had attained an absolute majority in March 1933 and where the proportion of the local population who had been recruited as members was far higher than average, the Party was apparently in a miserable state by autumn 1934. In only four communities was Party morale described as favourable. Elsewhere, there was 'undiminished poor mood', 'weariness in the Party', 'mood slumping', resignations from the SA and the welfare organization, objections to the incessant collections, serious complaints about the youth organizations, and castigation of the life-style and moral standards of local Party leaders.[60]

Lack of moral standards was again the central issue in Amberg, in the Upper Palatinate, when, shortly after the 'Röhm Putsch',

[56] StAM, LRA 76887, GS Landsham, 10 Aug. 1933.

[57] Ibid., GS Ebersberg, 26 June 1933.

[58] Ibid., GS Zorneding, 13 May 1934, 1 Nov. 1934. How little the peasants of Zorneding were prepared to give to Winter Aid collections in contrast to the contributions to collections for church missions was noted in GStA, MA 106670, RPvOB, 3 Mar. 1934.

[59] StAM, LRA 76887, GS Markt Grafing, 31 Dec. 1934.

[60] StAM, NSDAP 249, report of a meeting of fifteen *Ortsgruppen-* and *Stützpunktleiter*, 18 Oct. 1934. Party membership statistics can be found in the same file, and in NSDAP 256, and compared with the figures for Upper Bavaria in *Parteistatistik*, ed. Reichsorganisationsleiter der NSDAP, Munich, 1935, i. 34–5. For voter support, see Hagmann, pp. 12–13, 22.

allegations made against six local Party leaders who were in particularly bad odour with the people of the district included drunkenness, heavy indebtedness, sexual excesses, theft, fraud, forgery, embezzlement, and acts of brutality.[61] The head of the District Administration, himself clearly disgusted with the Party leaders he had to deal with, advocated as vital an urgent and 'merciless, drastic purge', and attributed the district's poor showing in the plebiscite of 19 August 1934 to the repellent behaviour of 'countless petty "leaders" '.[62]

In the tourist area of Garmisch-Partenkirchen, where the Nazis had done rather well before 1933 and which in material terms was profiting significantly in the Third Reich, the striking loss of prestige by the Party in the first years of Nazi rule can again in part be related to the poor image of the local functionaries. Complaints about the behaviour of individual Party leaders mounted sharply in 1934 and again the following year. In August 1934 it was reported that 'the people place their hope in a strong leader and expect from him salvation and protection. People also listen gladly to this leader. On the other hand, there are still political frictions engendered by pettiness or infelicitous measures on the part of organs of the subordinate leadership, which are fitted to dampen down again the joyful approval of the new State among the population at large.'[63] In one community of the district, where tempers had risen over the Party's interference in the appointment of the Mayor, the 'leadership principle' itself came under attack, and was said to be beneficial only if capable persons with unblemished backgrounds were made leaders.[64] The repeated shows of dissension within the Party and the real or alleged scandals associated with leading personalities in the district were contributing substantially to a state of affairs where lack of interest in or outright rejection of the Party was blatantly obvious.[65] The view expressed in a report in early

[61] StAA, BA Amberg 2399, BA Amberg, 29 Aug. 1934, and see also the report of 31 July 1934.   [62] Ibid., BA Amberg, 30 Aug. 1934.
[63] StAM, LRA 61612, BA Garmisch, 2 Aug. 1934. For electoral support for the NSDAP before 1933, see Hagmann, pp. 23*, 2–3, 12–13, 22, and G. Pridham, *Hitler's Rise to Power. The Nazi Movement in Bavaria 1923–1933*, London, 1973, pp. 284–5.
[64] StAM, LRA 61613, GS Mittenwald, 30 Dec. 1934; 28 Feb. 1935.
[65] StAM, LRA 61612, BA Garmisch, 3 Nov. 1934; LRA 61613, GBF Garmisch, 3 Aprl. 1935; GS Wallgau, 28 Feb., 30 Nov. 1935. And for poor attendance at Party meetings, scant interest in news of the Nuremberg Party Rally, the ignoring of the Nazi press, apathy about the return of the Saarland to Germany, and complaints that 'the Party programme is still little known here by most people', see StAM, LRA 61612, BS Garmisch, 2 Oct., 3 Nov., 3 Dec. 1934; LRA 61613, GS Partenkirchen, 30 Dec. 1934; BA Garmisch, 6 Mar. 1935; GBF Garmisch, 3 Apr. 1935.

1935, that 'the Führer wants the best for the people, but the Party needs a real purge', was certainly not an isolated one.[66]

In the big city, it was much the same story, as reports from Augsburg in autumn 1934 bluntly make clear. The use of big cars to ferry the self-important Party bosses around the city was specified as a particular source of irritation to the poorer sections of the population. Before 1933, the allegedly corrupt and self-seeking bosses of the trade unions and Weimar parties had been a target for merciless Nazi vilification. But Augsburg workers were quick to point out that the new 'bigwigs' were far outdoing the old in their exploitation of material advantage. A strong moralistic tone was, as elsewhere, present in the condemnation of the local representatives of the Party who, it was alleged, spent their time sitting in pubs, did not pay their debts, and neglected their families. Scurrilous rumours—doubtless stirred up in many cases by foreign broadcasts or pamphlets of the underground opposition, but evidently given wide credence—provide an indication, too, of the low reputation of some national Party figures. Stories of Labour Front Leader Robert Ley's drinking habits were, of course, legion, and they also did the rounds in Augsburg. Another rumour in circulation was that Baldur von Schirach, the head of the Hitler Youth, had shot himself after having embezzled and squandered two million Reich Marks. A leading light in the Reich Propaganda Office in Berlin was accused of disgracing himself in front of numerous guests in one of Augsburg's top hotels. And another rumour, significantly exonerating Hitler from any moral taint, had the Führer, on an unexpected visit to Augsburg, discovering 'the others' in a drinking session in a hotel bar and arresting in rage twenty persons including the local *Gauleiter* Karl Wahl.[67]

The above illustrations have all been drawn from Bavaria. They can be augmented by similar evidence from many other parts of Germany which demonstrates the size of the gulf between the images of Party and Führer already in the early years of the Third Reich. According to a report from the Rhine Province in February 1935, 'the Führer constantly finds ... words fitted to create and bring about the true people's community', whereas the local leaders of the Party 'violate

[66] StAM, LRA 61613, GBF Garmisch, 4 Feb. 1935.
[67] GStA, MA 106697, LB of Pd Augsburg, 1 Sept., 1 Oct., 1 Nov. 1934. For similar criticism in other parts of Bavaria, see ibid., LB of Pd München, 3 Sept. 1934; MA 106691, LB of RPvNB/OP, 6 Sept. 1934; MA 106694, LB of RPvOF/MF, 9 Nov. 1934.

daily and hourly' his plain intention to overcome former political divisions by deepening earlier antagonisms and transferring them to current 'egotistical struggles for their personal status'. As elsewhere, people thought that Hitler was being kept in the dark about the real state of affairs, though the report alluded, vaguely but ominously, to the peril lurking in such notions. ' "Father Tsar knows nothing of it, he would not wish or tolerate it," was said before the war in Russia. But Russia's fate proves that this principle is dangerous,' it concluded in somewhat ambiguous fashion.[68]

An anonymous letter sent to Reich Minister of the Interior Frick from a Nazi sympathizer in Saxony in mid-1935 provides a hint of the material disappointments which lay behind the juxtaposition of the idealistic Hitler image and the attacks on the Party bosses. The writer pleaded with Frick to pay close attention to popular unrest about the massive outgrowth of Party positions and the rampant corruption which accompanied it, reminding him of what had been preached before the 'seizure of power' about the need for simplicity and reductions in government spending. Hitler himself was seen as embodying this 'simplicity', whereas his underlings treated people like slaves, exploited them for all they were worth, and provided jobs only for the few favoured Party members. In the event of another election, he went on, thousands would say ' "Adolf Hitler and all his men, yes, they have our full confidence. But the others, who make a nice life for themselves at the expense of the people's comrades, while so many go hungry and the middle class goes to the wall, no! No vote for them!" '[69]

First impressions are not easily shaken. In these early years of the Third Reich, attitudes of the population to the Party were formed and opinions shaped which, despite all efforts, lasted for the duration of the regime, amounting in effect to a lingering crisis of confidence in the Party and its representatives, particularly at the local and regional level.

[68] Heyen, pp. 287-8.
[69] ZStA, Potsdam, 27079/36, anon. letter to Frick, 21 June 1935. For devastating criticism of the Party's corruption and of the overbearing 'rule of the bosses' as a prominent feature of a growing crisis of confidence in the system itself, see the reports from Berlin referred to above in Chapter 2, nn. 74-6. See also the *Sopade* reports, at times clearly exaggerated in their evaluation of the crisis, from various parts of Germany in *DBS*, ii. 895, 899, 903-5, 21 Sept. 1935.

The repeated claim before the 'seizure of power', that the NSDAP, as a national, social-revolutionary 'Movement' and not simply 'another' political party, would create new bonds of unity through its elimination and transcending of the 'Party system', was highly attractive and conveyed much of Nazism's dynamic appeal. Reality after 1933 looked different. Fancy rhetoric about a national rebirth and social renewal contrasted vividly with the behaviour of Party and SA bosses and activists. Whatever the Reich Government in Berlin was doing, at the 'grass-roots' level, the Party was unable to create a convincing image of itself as a positive force in the establishment of a 'people's community'. Quite the contrary: the jobbing, pushing, and self-seeking egoism revealed the NSDAP as a 'party' much like the rest in its corrupt catering for particularist self-interest. Though many joining the flood of new entrants into the NSDAP in the first months of 1933 were socially more 'respectable' than most of the 'Old Fighters',[70] dominant positions in the local Party branches often remained in the hands of 'social upstarts' who now elbowed their way into public office. On the local level, therefore, the NSDAP was often viewed as an alien structure in the hands of a new and undeserving 'élite', the blemishes in whose personal lives and political behaviour were as a consequence all the more eagerly seized upon and castigated.

Additionally, in particular in rural areas, the often frenetic, but usually destructive, drive of the Party activists, when targeted at existing institutions—in particular the Churches—and value-systems, stirred up new or dormant conflicts and provoked much hostility. The Party was on a number of levels, therefore, perceived as intervening regularly—and negatively—in the day-to-day lives of ordinary citizens. The highly positive Führer image has to be seen in this context. Like the proverbial medieval king whose wicked counsellors took the blame, Hitler remained protected from unpopularity by the very unpopularity of the 'little Hitlers', his 'charisma' untouched by the grumbles and grievances of everyday life in the Third Reich.[71] The

---

[70] See Fröhlich and Broszat, 'Politische und soziale Macht auf dem Lande', and Zofka, 'Dorfeliten'. M. Kater, 'Sozialer Wandel in der NSDAP im Zuge der NS-Machtergreifung', in W. Schieder (ed.), *Faschismus also soziale Bewegung*, Hamburg, 1976, pp. 25–67, demonstrates the increasingly middle-class character of the Party membership after 1933. See also Kater, *The Nazi Party*, pp. 85ff, 97ff.

[71] See also M. Mayer, *They Thought They Were Free. The Germans 1933–1945*, Chicago, 1955, pp. 64–5, and Stokes, *SD*, pp. 514–16.

conviction that the Führer would intervene decisively if he once got
wind of the daily abuses of his underlings, was itself a direct product of
those abuses, the outgrowth of a psychological need for untarnished
and 'righteous' authority which functioned as an escape mechanism
for simmering discontent and therefore as a safety valve for the regime.

Hitler himself was evidently made aware of the contrast between his
own popularity and the unpopularity of the Party, though he could not
publicly admit to the disparity—least of all in the company of the Party
faithful upon whom, ultimately, the 'Führer myth' itself depended.
Hence, at the Nuremberg Party Rally in 1935 he referred directly to
the distinction drawn between himself and the Party only to disdain
such a notion: 'I must counter here ... the cliché so often heard,
especially among the bourgeoisie: "Yes, the Führer,—but the Party,
that's a different matter!" To that, I give the answer: "No, gentlemen,
the Führer is the Party and the Party is the Führer." '[72] Despite such
disclaimers, which indeed earned Hitler himself some criticism,[73] the
dichotomy between the images of Party and Führer, which we have
explored here, continued to exist. It was recognized by Goebbels,
no less, who much later, in 1941, declared that the 'Führer myth'
(whose creation he claimed for himself) was the reason 'why even now
millions of Germans drew distinction between the Führer and the
Party, refusing their support to the latter while believing in Hitler'.[74]

[72] *Der Parteitag der Freiheit vom 10.–16. September 1935. Offizieller Bericht über den Verlauf des Reichsparteitages mit sämtlichen Kongreßreden*, Munich, 1935, p. 287.

[73] See the complaints voiced at Hitler's defence of his subordinates at the Party Rally in the Berlin police report cited above in Chapter 2 (ref. in n. 76).

[74] Semmler, pp. 56–7.

4

The Führer versus the Radicals
Hitler's Image and the 'Church Struggle'

The Reich Chancellor undoubtedly lives in belief in God. He recognizes Christianity as the builder of western culture.

Cardinal Faulhaber, 1936

We thank you, Lord, for every success which, through your grace, you have so far granted him for the the good of our people.

Bishop Meiser, 1937

THE polarization of Führer and Party images was accentuated, so we suggested in the previous chapter, where ideological conflict within society was at its sharpest. The most obvious example of bitter ideological dispute in the Third Reich is provided by the confrontation of the Nazi regime with the major Christian denominations. This offers therefore the possibility of exploring the shaping of the 'Hitler myth' in a sphere of serious and lasting conflict where the leading representatives of the Churches enjoyed a very considerable influence upon the formation of opinion of that substantial proportion of the population which retained a close allegiance to the Protestant or Catholic Church.

Most of the evidence in our examination is again drawn from Bavaria which, of course, was classic terrain for the 'Church struggle'.[1] The dominant Catholicism in most of the province was a notable provocation to Nazi radicals, while the unusually devout Protestantism in the 'diaspora' conditions of Franconia also promoted acute friction with Party anti-clericals even in a hotbed of Nazi support. There is, however, little difficulty in finding parallels elsewhere in the

---

[1] I explored the nature of the popular dissent arising from the 'Church struggle' in Bavaria in *Popular Opinion*, chs. 4–5. For the general course of the conflict between Church and State in the Third Reich, see J. Conway, *The Nazi Persecution of the Churches 1933–1945*.

Reich, in both Protestant and Catholic regions, to those attitudes prevalent in the 'Church struggle' in Bavaria. To anticipate the general conclusion: all the evidence goes to suggest that the 'Church struggle', though stirring up a high level of animosity towards the Party and in a wider sense towards the Nazi regime, had a far less negative impact on Hitler's popularity than might be imagined. In escaping much of the odium the bitter conflict produced, in fact, Hitler was frequently viewed—remarkably, it seems, also by some Church leaders—as the defender of the religious values of Christianity against the ideological fanatics of the Nazi Movement.

As we saw earlier, expectations of 'heroic' leadership contained from the beginning a strong trait of 'messianism'. The mix of secular and 'godly' leadership was already being suggested by national-conservative and *völkisch* writers and theologians before the 'seizure of power', as in the following extract from a work published in 1932 by the nationalist theologian and polemicist Wilhelm Stapel:

The true statesman unites in himself fatherliness, martial spirit, and charisma. In fatherly fashion he governs the people entrusted to his care. If his people multiplies and grows, he provides it with space to live in through assembling the warlike forces of the people. But God blesses him with good fortune and glory, so that the people look up to him full of reverence and trust. In this way, the statesman holds war and peace in his hand and communes with God. His human considerations become prayer, become decisions. His decision is not only a matter of rational calculation but of the whole wealth of historical forces. His victories and defeats are not human accidents, but godly fate. Thus, the true statesman is at one and the same time ruler, warrior, and priest.[2]

At the hands of the Nazi propagandists, a streak of secular re-demptionism soaked in pseudo-religious imagery firmly attached itself well before 1933 to the growing Führer cult expanding around the leader of the NSDAP. Though, among fervent Catholics, Hitler had never managed before the 'seizure of power' to shake off the allegations that he was basically opposed to Christianity, elsewhere— and not least among significant sections of the Protestant clergy—he

[2] Cited in Sontheimer, p. 271. Like many on the national-conservative Right who were searching for an ideal 'Leader' and were instrumental during the Weimar Republic in publicizing the idea of 'heroic' leadership, Stapel eventually came to see Hitler and the Third Reich as a betrayal of his expectations. See Weinstein, pp. 11–13, 39–40 (nn. 35–7).

undoubtedly had some success in cultivating the image of one who, while not devout in a conventional church-going sense, entertained a belief in God or 'providence' and would transcend denominational divides in working for moral and ethical renewal in Germany.[3]

Once he had become Chancellor, Hitler's language became pronouncedly 'messianic' in tone, and his public addresses were frequently replete with religious symbolism. The 'awakening of the nation' was blended suggestively with religious renewal, and the source of both was located in the 'mission' of the Führer. His very first public speech as Chancellor, in the Berlin Sportpalast on 10 February 1933, ended with a remarkable rhetorical climax in which he paraphrased the last lines of the Protestant version of the 'Our Father', speaking of the 'new German Reich of greatness, honour, power, glory, and justice', even concluding with 'Amen'.[4] A few weeks later, he closed his speech on 1 May, the first 'Day of National Labour', with a direct entreaty to the Almighty: 'Lord, you see, we have changed. The German people is no longer the people without honour, of disgrace, tearing itself apart, faint-hearted, and weak in faith. No, Lord, the German people is strong again in its will, strong in its steadfastness, strong in its endurance of all sacrifice. Lord, we do not desert you. Now bless our fight for our freedom, and thereby our German people and Fatherland.'[5] A third example of Hitler's 'messianic' rhetoric, his speech to the Political Leaders of the Party assembled at the Nuremberg Rally of 1936, has been described as 'an astonishing montage of biblical texts', as allusions to the Gospels of John and Matthew as well as to other passages of the Bible abounded.[6]

How can we not once again feel in this hour the miracle which has brought us together. You have once heard the voice of a man, and it has struck your hearts, it has awakened you, and you have followed this voice. You have

---

[3] See Schweitzer pp. 68ff; Diephouse, pp. 54ff; W. Carr, *Hitler. A Study in Personality and Politics*, London, 1978, pp. 5, 132–6; and also F. Heer, *Der Glaube des Adolf Hitler. Anatomie einer politischen Religiosität*, Munich, 1966. The recent work of R. P. Ericksen, *Theologians under Hitler*, provides insights into the way in which notions of 'spiritual renewal' prompted some of the foremost theologians in the Protestant Church to accept Nazism enthusiastically and to place the greatest hope in Hitler's leadership.

[4] Domarus, p. 208; see also von Kotze, p. 41. Goebbels was thrilled with the impact of the passage—J. Goebbels, *Vom Kaiserhof zur Reichskanzlei*, 21st edn., Munich, 1937, p. 260.

[5] Domarus, p. 264.

[6] Ibid., p. 641. Stern, p. 90, analyses the Christian imagery of the speech, and for other usages in 1936, see Domarus, p. 570 and Carr, p. 135.

followed it for years, even without seeing the bearer of the voice. You only
heard a voice, and you followed it. When we meet here, the miracle of this
gathering fills us all. Not each of you sees me, and I do not see each of you. But
I feel you, and you feel me! . . . Now we are together, we are with him and he is
with us, and we are now Germany.

Eyewitnesses of such mass meetings in the presence of the Führer
have testified that for those taking part the atmosphere and effect was
closer to that of a religious revivalist meeting than that of a 'normal'
political rally.[7] There seems little doubt that for the millions who were
already 'Hitler believers' or were in the process of 'conversion', the
'religious' dimension was a powerful component of the 'Führer myth'.
At a time when Christian conventions and even forms of rather naïve
popular 'piety' remained largely intact while institutionalized
religious practices, especially among the Protestant majority of the
population, were under pressure, the secularized redemptionism and
national salvation preached by Hitler was neither unattractive nor
ineffective as a substitute faith. Goebbels appears to have grasped this
and lost little opportunity to exploit it—though here, too, it may not
have been pure cynicism on the part of the Propaganda Minister, who
himself seems to have fallen victim to Hitler's 'messianism'.
Goebbels's own descriptions of major Hitler rallies and speeches
frequently had a pronounced sacral tone, as in 1936 when he depicted
Hitler's 'election' speech in Cologne following the reoccupation of the
Rhineland as 'religion in the deepest and most mysterious sense of the
word', in which 'a nation professed its belief in God through its
spokesman and put its fate and life trustingly in his hands'.[8] Retaining
his own belief in the 'saviour' Hitler even in the make-believe world of
the Berlin bunker in 1945, Goebbels could still enter in his diary:
'When the Führer speaks, it is like a religious service.'[9]
Far more remarkable than Goebbels swallowing the religious
nimbus of the Führer which his own propaganda had helped to manufacture is the fact that even prominent churchmen—some of them
hardly won over to National Socialism—appear to have convinced

[7] See W. Shirer, *Berlin Diary 1934–1941*, Sphere Book edn., London, 1970, pp. 22–3;
Carr, pp. 5, 136.

[8] Cited in Bramsted, p. 209. In his birthday tribute two years later, Goebbels called it
'also perhaps a piece of religion' for Hitler 'to place his entire life in the service of a
people and to work and act for human happiness'—*Völkischer Beobachter*, north German
edn., 21 Apr. 1938.

[9] J. Goebbels, *Tagebücher 1945. Die letzten Aufzeichnungen*, Hamburg, 1977, p. 49.

themselves that Hitler was deeply religious in character. No less a figure than Cardinal Faulhaber himself, Archbishop of Freising and Munich, one of the dominant influences in the Catholic Church, and on numerous occasions an outspoken critic of the anti-Church policies of the Nazi regime, wrote in a confidential report following a three-hour private audience with Hitler on 4 November 1936 that he had been very impressed by him and convinced that he was a deeply religious person. 'The Reich Chancellor undoubtedly lives in belief in God', wrote Faulhaber. 'He recognizes Christianity as the builder of western culture.'[10]

Hitler's evident ability to simulate, even to potentially critical Church leaders, an image of a leader keen to uphold and protect Christianity was crucial to the mediation of such an image to the church-going public by influential members of both major denominations. It was the reason why church-going Christians, so often encouraged by their 'opinion leaders' in the Church hierarchies, were frequently able to exclude Hitler from their condemnation of the atheistic Nazi ideology and the anti-Christian Party radicals, continuing to see in him the last hope of protecting Christianity from godless Bolshevism.[11]

Before exploring the reflections of popular attitudes towards Hitler among church-goers, we need first, therefore, to consider the public pronouncements of the clergy themselves, whose continued influence in moulding opinion in the Third Reich cannot be doubted.

The ambivalence of the Churches' stance towards Nazism during the Third Reich is, of course, well established. Where Church institutions, traditions, practices, and belief were directly under attack by the Nazis, defiance was bold, resilient, and at times successful. Elsewhere, a level of accommodation and a *modus vivendi* were sought.

At the very outset of the Third Reich, the hierarchies of both Churches—even the Catholic bishops who, before 1933, had been so

[10] Cited in L. Volk, 'Kardinal Faulhabers Stellung zur Weimarer Republik und zum NS-Staat', *Stimmen der Zeit*, clxxvii (1966), p. 187; see also Lewy, pp. 207–8.

[11] Outside the major denominations, many of the small Christian sects—with the notable exception of the 'Jehovah's Witnesses'—were also frequently effusive in their acclaim for Hitler, even, on occasion, to the extent of advocating Jesus as the 'Führer ideal' and then seeing in Hitler the Führer Germany was seeking—see C. King, *The Nazi State and the New Religions*, New York/Toronto, 1983, pp. 91–3, 99, 122–4, 127, 130–1, 141, 188–9, 194.

reserved in their attitude towards the Nazi Movement—were instrumental in calming anxiety and uncertainty among the church-going
population, and in establishing respect for Hitler's authority as Reich
Chancellor. Even leaving aside the nazified wing, there was generally
far more enthusiasm for Nazism in the Protestant Church than among
the Catholic clergy. On the other hand, in the more unitary Catholic
Church there was no organized movement in which doctrinal opposition developed into political alienation in the way that it did among
the Protestant minority attached to the 'Confessing Church'. Where
Nazism did not openly threaten, it could be at least tolerated by both
major denominations, attacks on racial, social, and political minorities
accepted without demur, the expansionist foreign policy generally
applauded.[12]

Even early experience of Nazi intervention in Church affairs did not
seriously dent an approving stance towards Hitler himself, as the
example of the head of the Protestant Church in Bavaria, Bishop
Meiser, demonstrates. In autumn 1934, Meiser was deposed by commissars sent to Munich by the Reich Church Minister in Berlin,
temporarily placed under house arrest, and restored in office only
after a turbulent six weeks of widespread protest among the fervently
Protestant population of Franconia.[13] None of this, however, caused
Meiser to distance himself from Hitler. Shortly after his re-
establishment in office, he publicly declared in Munich: 'Protestants
would be ashamed if, through service to the Gospel, they were to make
themselves incapable of service to the people and incapable of offering, in all difficulties, the most loyal following to the Führer of our
people.'[14] Some while later, in a circular to clergy and teachers of
religious instruction sent out just before the 'Reichstag election' of
29 March 1936 which followed the reoccupation of the Rhineland,
Meiser hinted at his awareness of the dilemma which resulted from
such pro-Hitler comments. He acknowledged that a 'yes to the call of
the Führer' could be interpreted as approval of the anti-Christian
thrust of the Party. He nevertheless declared his 'expectation that

---

[12] For a variety of positions adopted in recent research on the levels of co-operation
and opposition by the Churches during the Third Reich, see J. Schmädeke and
P. Steinbach (eds.), *Der Widerstand gegen den Nationalsozialismus*, Munich, 1985, Pt. 3 and
pp. 1125–7.

[13] I examined the popular unrest caused by the deposition of Meiser in *Popular
Opinion*, pp. 164ff.

[14] *KL*, i. 36.

pastors and communities should, with clear resolve, support the will to liberation and peace of the man entrusted with the leadership of the people'. And in agreeing to bring the concern about the 'Church struggle' to the Führer's attention, he hoped 'to open the way for all, so that, trusting in the fact that the Führer knows of their distress, they can decide on 29 March in the way that the love of their people and the obedient and loyal bonds to the Führer command'.[15] After four years of unprecedented conflict between the Protestant Church and the State, Meiser could still, on the occasion of the fourth anniversary of the 'take-over of power' in January 1937, publicly offer prayers for Hitler, intoning: 'On this day we commend to you especially the Führer and Chancellor of our Reich. We thank you, Lord, for every success which, through your grace, you have so far granted him for the good of our people.'[16]

Loyalty to the Führer was pointedly emphasized by the Churches in the light of the 'Bolshevik danger', blown up by Nazi propaganda in extensive campaigns following the outbreak of the Spanish Civil War in 1936. Even those sharply critical of the regime's anti-Church policies were ready to offer their public support for the Führer's 'fight against Bolshevism'. This is well illustrated in the comments in June 1937 of a Bavarian Protestant pastor at a gathering of the 'Confessing Front'—the wing of the Church which had openly opposed attempts to assail the traditional basis of Protestantism. His reported words were: 'We all stand solidly behind our Führer. We all know that if the Third Reich were to collapse today, Bolshevism would come in its place. Therefore: loyalty to our Führer, who has saved us from Bolshevism and given us a better future.'[17]

The misconception that the assault on the Churches could be extracted as one negative component of Nazi policy, which might otherwise be generally accepted and often be openly welcomed, marked a basic ambivalence in the stance of the Protestant Church during the Third Reich. While more muted in the case of the Catholic Church, where the ideological clash with the regime was more

[15] Ibid., ii. 82. For other instances of public encouragement by the clergy of both major denominations to support the Führer in the plebiscite of 1936, and also in the plebiscite following the *Anschluß* in 1938, see ibid. i. 136; ii. 83, 276; iii. 100, 161; GStA, MA 106687, report of BPP, 1 Apr. 1936, pp. 16, 18; StAM, LRA 134057, BA Bad Tölz, 3 Apr. 1936; and (on the Catholic Church), Lewy, pp. 201–5, 211–18.

[16] *KL*, i. 193.

[17] Ibid., ii. 195–6.

fundamental and the 'Church struggle' a relentless war of attrition, recognition for the 'national achievements' of the regime and in particular for the person of the Führer running alongside vehement condemnation of all interference in the domain of the Church amounted, here too, to an uneasy dualism. This was plainly present in the 'Pastoral Letter of the German Bishops about the Defence against Bolshevism', issued in December 1936, which, as in earlier pastoral letters the same year, professed the bishops' unreserved co-operation in the 'religious task' of repelling the threat of Bolshevism, and of supporting the Führer whose 'thoughts and aspirations aim at averting the horrible danger', having sighted its advance from afar. 'Even where we repulse inroads upon the rights of the Church', the pastoral went on, 'we want to respect the rights of the State in its proper jurisdiction and to see also the good and great elements in the work of the Führer.'[18]

Also characteristic of the ambivalence was the advocacy by the Passau diocesan newsletter, in an area where the 'Church struggle' had raged unabatedly, of prayers 'for Führer and Fatherland' on the fourth anniversary of Hitler's accession to the Chancellorship: 'With sincere thanks to the Almighty, we look back on this day to all the greatness which has been created in these four years through the Führer's energy in building and strengthening the Reich and the people's community.'[19] In similar vein was Cardinal Faulhaber's combination—in a sermon delivered in 1936—of 'strong criticism of the present time', especially of the Nazi attacks on denominational schools and the staging of 'morality trials' involving Catholic clergy, with a concluding request to the assembled congregation to join with him in an 'Our Father' for the Führer.[20] Another leading cleric, renowned throughout Bavaria for his hostility to Nazism, was the bold Jesuit priest Father Rupert Mayer who, in a sermon shortly before his arrest and effective silencing by the authorities in 1937, diluted one of his frontal attacks on the regime with the comment that the Führer was 'a person inspired by God's grace', and Germany therefore the envy of all foreign countries.[21]

A small minority of Catholic clerics went beyond the comments so far cited in their public pro-Hitler stance. For example, the speaker at

---

[18] Cited in Lewy, pp. 209–10. See also *KL*, i. 190–1; iii. 118. The text was drafted by Faulhaber soon after his private audience with Hitler, which had made such an impact upon him—Lewy, p. 209.   [19] *KL*, iv. 115–16.

[20] Ibid., i. 148–9.   [21] Ibid., i. 195–6.

the diocesan conference of Catholic workers' associations at Bamberg in November 1936 was reported as declaring: 'We Catholics are all Germans . . . and therefore also stand solidly behind our Führer, come what may. Our Führer is recognized by the Holy Father. Also, our Führer has recognized the Concordat, and therefore every Catholic has to stand behind the Führer. The Führer has also assured both major denominations that their Faith will be upheld, and this word of the Führer is sacred to us.'[22]

It is, of course, impossible to reconstruct the atmosphere in which such sermons were given. Police observers were quite capable of mishearing or misconstruing remarks made in the pulpit, or of missing a note of intended irony in apparently loyalist sentiments. Naturally, too, the public stance of Church leaders did not necessarily match their actual sentiments. The professions of loyalty to the Führer were in part a ploy to offset criticism of the Party, the SS, or the Church's number one Nazi hate-figure, Alfred Rosenberg. It would nevertheless be stretching it too far to presume insincerity behind every laudatory reference to Hitler. And whatever the motives, the actual effect was the enhancement of the myth of the 'good' Führer detached from and set against the evil of the Party radicals. It also meant that Church opposition to Nazism could be regarded simply as criticism of the 'unfortunate' accoutrements of the system, or at best as a reflection of a conflict of two irreconcilable 'world views' in which Rosenberg's 'neo-heathenism' rather than Hitler's racial imperialism was viewed as the real enemy. Impatience with the Church's ambivalence was a hallmark of *Sopade* reporting on the 'Church struggle'. Scorning the readiness of the hierarchy, despite the hammer blows of the 'Church struggle', to offer prayers for the Führer and to seek *rapprochement* with the regime, one *Sopade* reported noted dismissively that it was 'no wonder that many socialists no longer attach any significance to the whole fuss of the clergy'.[23]

Compared with leading figures in the Church hierarchies, however, the lower clergy were often distinctly less diplomatic and conciliatory in their language. Sometimes Hitler, too, was unmistakably—if often indirectly—included in their scathing remarks about Nazism, and on occasion even subjected to open verbal attacks—though in such cases the priest normally paid the price of retribution by the authorities.

---

[22] Ibid., ii. 128.
[23] *DBS*, ii. 673–4, 15 July 1935, report from Rhineland–Westphalia.

According to one report, a Protestant pastor, alluding to the fact that in 1933 'even the Führer engaged in propaganda for the German Christians', reportedly declared that 'it dare not happen a second time that the German Christians are supported by the State' and 'that the freedom, which the Führer has guaranteed, should be granted'.[24] Other pastors were said to have 'criticized in scarcely concealed form words of the Führer' and, in praying at the altar for interned members of the clergy, to have sought intercession for the German people 'but not for the Führer'.[25]

Outspoken criticism from the Protestant clergy seldom occurred. It was more common to contrast, doubtless often for tactical reasons, the alleged righteousness of the Führer with the radicalism of Party activists. Pastor Helmut Kern, for instance, a leading representative of the 'Confessing Church' and certainly no Nazi sympathizer, invoked the Führer's word as guaranteeing a free Church election in 1937 and promised 'woe to him who makes the Führer a liar before God and the world'.[26] Another pastor, well known to the authorities for his hostility to the regime, announced in a sermon that 'we have Bolshevism in our own land', then added ambiguously that the Führer deserved thanks for recognizing Bolshevism as the arch-enemy and overcoming it.[27] It seems unlikely that such veiled comments did much to weaken Hitler's popularity. More probably, they helped to bolster the 'Hitler myth', as witnessed by the illusory statement attributed to one non-Nazi pastor that Hitler was opposed to the introduction of the bitterly contested nazified 'community schools' in place of denominational schools.[28]

The Catholic lower clergy were rather more forthright in the expression of their antipathy. One Catholic priest, for example, was quoted as stating bluntly, 'we need leaders, and those are the pope and the bishops'.[29] Another priest, criticizing the actions of the Party

[24] *KL*, ii. 165.

[25] Ibid., ii. 165, 197. According to a *Sopade* report from Saxony in 1937, at a time when the Protestant 'Church struggle' had again become heated in the wake of the announcement of forthcoming new elections (which were never actually held) to a general synod and the arrest of some clergymen (including Martin Niemöller), pastors had ceased to voice their approval of Hitler, and ' "arguments" used all too often such as: "the Führer does not want it", "if only the Führer knew, he would . . .", are no longer heard'—*DBS*, iv. 502–3, 8 May 1937.

[26] *KL*, ii. 161.

[27] Ibid., ii. 118.

[28] Ibid., ii. 73. See also pp. 144, 211, and i. 213.

[29] StAM, LRA 76887, GS Landsham, 30 June 1935.

during a religious lesson, pointed to the picture of the Führer hanging in the classroom, reportedly exclaiming, 'He's to blame as well for it.'[30] In another instance, a priest was denounced for allegedly remarking in private conversation that 'the Führer is too cowardly to act himself against the Church. That's why he needs Rosenberg and that lot.'[31] The Nazi attempt to dissociate Rosenberg's views from the official position of the Party was evidently unsuccessful. One report from Aachen also hinted that dissociation of Hitler from the attacks on Rosenberg was less than total, even going so far as to imply disbelief in the Führer's statements that the *Myth of the Twentieth Century* did not represent the Party line.[32]

According to a recent thorough investigation, as many as a third or more of the Catholic lower secular clergy were subjected to some form of political retribution during the Third Reich. Most of their 'offences' naturally occurred in connection with denominational issues, but around a third of them comprised 'criticism of the regime' (12.7 per cent), 'political unreliability' (16 per cent), and 'behaviour hostile to the State' (5.8 per cent).[33] Few of these cases, however, involved outright or even camouflaged criticism of Hitler, and, whatever their real feelings, most priests were ready to behave in public in politically conformist fashion, even if the refusal to use the 'Heil Hitler' greeting was a recurrent minor, but symbolic, expression of political dissent.[34] In public, at any rate, not much was done even by the lower clergy to undermine the myth that Hitler knew little of the excesses of Nazi Church policy and that 'the subordinates do not respect the will of the Führer'.[35]

The publicly sustained discrepancy between the most forthright criticism of Party fanatics seeking to put into practice Nazi ideology

---

[30] KL, ii. 126.

[31] Ibid., iv. 224; see also i. 127.

[32] *Volksopposition im Polizeistaat*, p. 141.

[33] U. von Hehl, *Priester unter Hitlers Terror. Eine biographische und statistische Erhebung*, Mainz, 1984, pp. xlii–iii, liii.

[34] From many examples: *KL*, i. 126–7; ii. 181; iii. 129; iv. 163; GStA, MA 106687, report of BPP, 1 July 1936, p. 42; StAB, K8/III, 18472, GS Königsfeld, 24 Feb. 1937. Instances of the Catholic lower clergy expressing outright praise for Hitler—such as the reported comment of one Catholic priest 'that the Lord God could not be thanked enough . . . for having sent us such a man as Reich Chancellor Hitler' (LRA Obernburg am Main, file 'Kirche und Nationalsozialismus', GS Sulzbach am Main, 6 Aug. 1934)—occur very seldom in the reports of the authorities and were evidently highly exceptional.

[35] LBA Obernburg am Main, file 'Kirche und Nationalsozialismus', BA Obernburg to BPP, 23 Oct. 1935, re. 'Kath. Mission in Mömlingen'.

(of which in reality Hitler was the central driving-force), and the pronounced respect for the Führer shown by Church leaders, and to a lesser extent by the lower clergy, found symbolic expression in the unsolicited order in Catholic dioceses, after six years of relentless 'Church struggle', to have church bells rung as a joyful salute on Hitler's birthday on 20 April 1939 with prayers for the Führer to be said at mass the following Sunday.[36]

What indications are there of the impact of the 'Church struggle' upon popular conceptions of Hitler among 'ordinary' church-going people? And how far did such conceptions rest upon the fiction of a Führer excluded from the opprobrium cast on his own Party, a 'moderate' prepared to defend the Churches against the 'radicals' within his own ranks? Some pointers are provided by reactions to the 'Meiser affair', to which we briefly return.

People laid the blame for the summary deposition of Bishop Meiser and the attack on the Lutheran Church in Bavaria in autumn 1934—which unleashed a remarkable, if short-lived, storm of protest—squarely at the door of the Party.[37] The traditionally pious Protestant population of the Franconian countryside, who had voted over-whelmingly for the NSDAP in 1932 and 1933, gave vent to their anger at the Party in no uncertain terms. The danger to the Party's standing and to its continued effectiveness in the region was emphasized in a communication to the Reich Minister of the Interior from the Bavarian Minister President, who had been given a firsthand impression of the explosive mood by several delegations of embittered Franconian peasants.[38] However, such delegations also showed unmistakably that Hitler's own image was completely detached from the negative image of the Party, The Führer was, in fact, scarcely drawn into the criticism at all and was directly associated with the protection of traditional religion against the attacks of the Party radicals. Demands were made for him to be informed of the real state of affairs, and he was seen as the embodiment of the true symbiosis between Christianity and National Socialism which the radicals were undermining. The only hint of criticism of the Führer was that he should permit such things to go on. But this apparent aloofness from

[36] *KL*, i. 307.

[37] See Kershaw, *Popular Opinion*, pp. 170–3.

[38] GStA, MA 107291, Siebert to Frick, 20 Oct. 1934.

the affair, followed by his decisive intervention to end the dispute by restoring Meiser in office, seemed once more to confirm the view that the Party radicals had acted behind his back, but that on discovery of their misdeeds he had acted swiftly to quell the disorder. Hitler's positive attitude towards the Church, his religious posture, and his position on the side of 'moderation' were seemingly reaffirmed. His popular standing was, as a result, strengthened rather than weakened by an affair which came close to demolishing confidence in the Party.

The effects of the tense and protracted Catholic 'Church struggle'— with its high-point before the war reached in 1936–7—upon attitudes towards the Party and the Führer can best be illustrated by way of a specific local example.

Amberg was a fairly typical district in provincial Upper Palatinate, overwhelmingly Catholic and with the great majority of its population gaining a living from agriculture or small-scale industry and commerce. The Nazis had not done too well in the region before 1933, and in Amberg had fared even somewhat worse than in most places. Despite the improvement in performance in March 1933, which occurred here as elsewhere, the NSDAP had evidently found no broad and stable basis of support in the district by the time of the 'seizure of power'.[39] And the next few years were to show a significant weakening of the Party's standing in the locality and undoubted sapping of whatever confidence had existed in the wake of the 'Church struggle'.

As early as the summer of 1934, it was plain that a propaganda campaign against 'moaners' and 'miseries'—an infelicitous attempt to combat the growing wave of disenchantment which had set in earlier in the year—had removed much of what good will there had been among the Catholic population. Not surprisingly, their patience at incessantly being labelled 'scum' or 'traitors' because of their earlier support for the Catholic Bavarian People's Party, was not unbounded. With little recourse to any self-defence in the press or in public meetings, there was not much they could do except put up with the insults and retreat into themselves. The ensuing bitterness was, however, felt to be a matter of concern by the local administration, which took the view that if the propaganda methods did not see a

[39] In the November election of 1932, the Nazis had won only 10.9% of the votes in Amberg-Land. In March 1933, the NSDAP vote in the town itself of Amberg (28.2%) was marginally lower than average (30.2%) for towns in the Upper Palatinate, while Amberg-Land (26.2%) still lagged some way behind the average (35.1%) for rural districts in the region—Hagmann, pp. 14–15, 23.

significant alteration the former party-political divides would be
replaced by a new 'division of the nation into Spartans and helots'.[40]
Reports from the localities were emphasizing that people had been far
more enthusiastic about the regime directly following the 'seizure of
power' than was the case after two years of Nazi rule, and expressed
the clear conviction that the attitude of the clergy, whose influence
was strong, had been a decisive factor.[41]

As the 'Church struggle' intensified, the local population found
itself increasingly pressed into a defence of religious practices and,
therefore, into confrontation with Party radicals. Even physical
violence against local Party functionaries was not unheard of. In one
incident, the leader of a Party 'Group' in the district, who had greatly
antagonized the population of two villages through tactless slandering
of the clergy, was beaten up in a beerhouse brawl. The report
expressly mentioned that he was wearing the uniform of a 'Local
Group Leader' of the Party, adding that he could expect the same
treatment in other nearby villages once word got round, and that as a
result he was probably finished as a Party leader.[42] Two other Party
functionaries only avoided assault, after making derogatory remarks
about the Catholic population of the neighbourhood, through a timely
escape from the hall in which they had been addressing a meeting.[43]
The head of the district administration pointed out, in a comment
passed on *verbatim* to the Bavarian Ministry of the Interior, that 'such
incidents demolish in days more goodwill and confidence than can be
built up in years', adding: 'As a result of such occurrences the suggestion, repeatedly to be heard, that the Führer wants the best but that his
underlings do what they see fit, gains a fateful appearance of reality.'[44]
The same exclusion of the Führer from blame and presumption of his
ignorance of events was voiced in the bitter complaints at the Party's
interference in the running of the traditional Corpus Christi Day
procession.[45] And as resignations from the Nazi welfare organization
and women's association took place, and the new recruitment drive for

[40] StAA, BA Amberg 2399, BA Amberg, 30 Aug. 1934, and see *KL*, iv. 30–1.
[41] StAA, BA Amberg 2398, GS Freudenberg, 21 Dec. 1934.
[42] StAA, BA Amberg, 2399, GS Freihung, 26 Jan. 1937; see also the reports for
25 Mar. 1937 and, for the prelude to the incident, 26 May 1936. The incident was singled
out for mention in the report of the Government President of Lower Bavaria and the
Upper Palatinate—*KL*, iv. 113.
[43] Ibid., GS Freihung, 26 Jan. 1937 and 'Sonderbericht' of 14 Feb. 1937.
[44] *KL*, iv. 113.
[45] StAA, BA Amberg 2398, GHS Amberg, 13 June 1936.

the Party met with refusals to join a Party which wanted to do away with religion, repeated expressions 'in favour of the Führer but as a rule against his subordinates' were reported.[46] Church-goers were heard saying that 'the Führer and the institutions of the Third Reich are gratefully acknowledged and orders gladly obeyed; it's just that the Church should not be dragged into conflict.'[47]

As the Amberg example—which could be paralleled by similar cases in other Catholic regions—makes plain, the detestation for the Party's anti-clerical and anti-Christian radicals was compatible with an essentially positive attitude towards Hitler, the authority of the State, and all major domestic and foreign policy which did not directly impinge upon the sphere of the Church. It would be going too far to imagine that Hitler escaped unscathed from the animosity stirred up by the 'Church struggle'. Criticism was implied, for example, in a report from 1937 suggesting a rather unflattering comparison with Mussolini: 'In Catholic circles there are those who say that Mussolini's policy is very clever because he has done the right thing regarding the Catholic Church, whereas this issue has not yet been solved in Germany.'[48] The removal of statues of the Virgin, Christ, and two saints from a mortuary in the same area was sufficient to prompt remarks from the pious population that they had so far believed in Hitler, 'but if he allows this, we won't believe in him any longer'.[49] A priest in Lower Bavaria even reckoned—though in the light of all the other evidence it sounds a rather exaggerated claim—that by 1935 there had been a drop of 60 per cent in confidence in Hitler within his parish because the promises of the Concordat had not been kept.[50] And according to a *Sopade* report from the Rhineland, Catholics were criticizing Hitler's 'double-dealing' in claiming to want to protect the religious denominations and yet seeking to clear away the 'inheritance of the last two thousand years'. They asked how it could be explained that he could profess his allegiance to 'positive Christianity' and yet

[46] Ibid., BA Amberg 2398, GS Schnaittenbach, 24 Aug. 1936; similar comments can be found in GHS Amberg, 13 June 1936 and StAA, BA Amberg 2399, GS Freudenberg, 28 May 1936. For resignations from Party affiliations and recruitment difficulties in the district, see StAA, BA Amberg 2399, GS Freudenberg, 22 July 1936, 22 Jan. 1937.

[47] *KL*, iv. 112 (extract from a report of the Bürgermeister der Stadt Regensburg, dating from Jan. 1937). For similar sentiments in the Amberg district, see ibid., iv. 117–18 and StAA, BA Aberg 2398, GHS Amberg, 24 Feb. 1937; BA Amberg 1 Mar. 1937.

[48] StAM, LRA 61615, GBF Garmisch, 3 Oct. 1937.

[49] StAM, LRA 61614, GS Mittenwald, 30 June 1936; BA Garmisch, 4 July 1936.

[50] *KL*, iv. 356.

'put a neo-heathen like Rosenberg in charge of the culture of the entire German people'.[51]

However, although the level of Hitler's popularity, especially in strongly Catholic areas, was evidently affected by the 'Church struggle', the discrepancy between the Führer's continued high standing and the contempt and detestation which were commonly felt for his Party remains a striking one. Given the public stance of their Church leaders, the dichotomy of attitude among ordinary parishioners is understandable. Once more, the naïvety present in the widely entertained view that 'the Führer is not informed about much that goes on, and Church policy in particular is conducted behind his back and against his wishes'[52] seems explicable only in terms of a prevailing psychological necessity to have a national leader of stature existing in an elevated sphere outside of and removed from the 'conflict sphere' of the everyday political arena. Daily reality for church-goers was the experience of local Party 'radicals' seeking to interfere with and destroy the fabric of Christian life, and behind them—singled out for attack by Church leaders themselves—the bogyman Rosenberg. Hitler's involvement in the attack on the Churches and his ultimate responsibility for it could, on the other hand, only partially and dimly be glimpsed through the miasma of Führer adulation emanating from the Nazi propaganda machine. The unwillingness to believe that the Führer himself could be lying in his professions of support for the Churches, that he could in reality be backing the anti-Christian forces in the Party, was bolstered by his intervention—as in the 'Meiser affair'—to restore order and to put the brake on the Party radicals. It meant that Hitler himself was relatively well cushioned against any serious loss of popularity as a consequence of the 'Church struggle'. As Max Weber pointed out, the basis of charismatic power lies principally outside the sphere of everyday life.[53]

[51] *DBS*, ii. 236–7, 14 Mar. 1935, report from Rhineland-Westphalia.
[52] StAM, LRA 47140, BA Bad Aibling, 5 Jan. 1937 (wrongly dated as 5 Jan. 1936).
[53] Weber, p. 246.

5

Hitler the Statesman
War and Peace in the Balance

What could I wish for other than tranquillity and peace?

Hitler, 1935

The answer to the question of how the problem 'Danzig and the Corridor' is to be solved is still the same among the general public: incorporation in the Reich? Yes. Through war? No.

The Landrat of Ebermannstadt, Upper Franconia, July 1939

THE sharp contrast between the Führer image and that of the Party, which we have documented in previous chapters in the context of the internal development of the Third Reich down to the middle of the 1930s, could, as we saw, be attributed in good measure to the fact that the Party was inextricably involved in 'everyday' political conflict and bore the responsiblity (or at least was held responsible) for measures which were at times highly unpopular. The Führer, on the other hand, appeared to be on an elevated plane far removed from the humdrum problems of everyday life and was presumed to be preoccupied with the 'mighty' issues of the nation, pondering matters of foreign and defence policy, of war and peace, holding the fate of the nation in his hand. It was a domain which, in peacetime at any rate, scarcely affected material interests in any direct or obvious way, but one which could be called upon to engender—even if only temporarily—high emotional involvement and maximum national unity.

The popular notion of a Führer standing over and above the wrangles of everyday politics was not wholly mythical. From 1935–6 onwards, Hitler did in reality withdraw increasingly from involvement in the domestic affairs of State, and did leave the ordinary business of government more and more to the overlapping and competing chancelleries, ministries, and special plenipotentiary organizations like that of the 'Four Year Plan', which turned internal government in

Germany into administrative chaos, while concentrating himself in growing measure on matters of diplomacy and foreign policy.

In the sphere of foreign policy, too, the compensatory function of the Hitler cult can clearly be seen. In contrast to the Party, the Führer, associated as he was with the spectacular foreign policy successes and the celebration of national triumphs, represented, one might say, the 'sunny side' of the regime. And for the maintenance of the 'Führer myth' it was vital that success continued, that the external 'national' policy of the regime remained 'sunny', as it effectively did for a number of years following the first major triumphs in 1935–6, and that it should not slide into the 'shady side' through failures which might have a dangerous impact on 'everyday' life and its sphere of material interests.

Hitler had always enjoyed a particular talent, approaching demagogic genius, for appealing to the populist national emotions, hopes, and aggression of increasing numbers of ordinary Germans, in particular by exploiting the deep-rooted resentments which the name 'Versailles' conjured up. But he consciously, and probably very wisely, refrained from speaking much in public and in detail about his own annexationist and imperialist '*Lebensraum*' aims which went way beyond any revision of the Versailles settlement.[1] This would have been risky not only in diplomatic but also in domestic terms, and would from the beginning have heavily burdened the politically unifying emotional desire for restoration of national 'honour' and 'greatness' with the fear of a new war and the miseries that would bring for the German people. For although the overwhelming majority of the population clearly wanted 'national success'—the restoration of Germany's power and glory in Europe—it was just as clearly unwilling to entertain the idea of major sacrifices to attain them, least of all— certainly for the older generation who remembered the suffering of 1914–18—another war. This amounted to a sort of 'working basis' of the 'Führer myth', which Hitler recognized and complied with by providing a series of rapid foreign political and diplomatic coups, and

---

[1] In the public speeches in the early 1920s, Hitler seems, in fact, seldom if ever to have used the term. The Jäckel/Kuhn edition of his speeches between 1919 and 1924 comprises upwards of 600,000 Hitler words, but, as far as I can see, the term '*Lebensraum*' does not appear once. Hitler's conception of *Lebensraum* had nevertheless been established at the latest by the end of 1922—see Jäckel and Kuhn, p. 773 No. 452, and G. Stoakes, 'The Evolution of Hitler's Ideas on Foreign Policy 1919–1925' in P. D. Stachura (ed.), *The Shaping of the Nazi State*, London, 1978, pp. 39–42.

then in the first two years of the war relatively painless victories through the lightning military attacks of the *Blitzkrieg*.

The confidential opinion reports of the regime which relate to Hitler's foreign policy, and also the reflections of opinion in the *Sopade* reports, provide clear evidence to support these conclusions. Nazi propaganda was certainly able to produce an atmosphere of wild and blind national exaltation following the foreign policy successes of the regime, but was incapable of turning this, for the majority of those rejoicing, into enthusiasm for a new war. The fear of another war was a constant, open or subliminal, accompaniment to the national euphoria which greeted Hitler's triumphs, and it placed certain limits on the rejoicing. For all the bellicose chauvinism which the Third Reich was able to stir up, especially among young Germans, the dread of war provided an element of popular feeling which remained in the 1930s even more dominant than revisionist and expansionist desires. It was a critical point in shaping popular opinion about Hitler's foreign policy.

The positive image of Hitler as statesman, national politician, and Leader of Germany indeed, of course, depicted him as a fanatical nationalist and patriot, boldly and unwaveringly striving to eradicate the perceived injustice and discrimination suffered by the German people since the First World War. At the same time, however, he was portrayed as a man of peace, seeking to attain his goals through political skill not force of arms, and building up military might as a defensive not an aggressive weapon. The strong Wehrmacht, so it was claimed and so it seemed to most Germans, was justifiable and necessary in order to put the nation once again on the same footing as its former wartime enemies and to provide a powerful base for diplomatic negotiation with the western democracies which, it was widely felt, continued to form a threat to national security. However unlikely it sounds, and however much it stands in contradiction to Hitler's actual mentality and intentions, the propaganda image of a statesman and Führer fanatically determined not only to restore Germany's greatness but also to maintain peace was not ineffective.

In his secret address to editors of the German press in November 1938, Hitler referred directly to this consciously devised 'peace image' and its consequences, which presented the propaganda apparatus with a number of problems in preparing the people for war:

Circumstances have compelled me to speak for decades almost solely of peace. Only through continued emphasis on the German desire for peace and

intentions of peace was it possible for me . . . to provide the German people
with the armaments which were always necessary as the basis of the next step.
It goes without saying that such a peace propaganda which has been cultivated
for years also has its doubtful side; for it can only too easily lead to the view
being formed in the minds of many people that the present regime identifies
with the determination and the will to maintain peace under all circumstances.[2]

With the last point, Hitler touched upon a weakness in the basis of his
mass popularity. To stir up periodic frenzies of national euphoria was
one thing. To 'school' the great majority of the German people into a
war mentality of the sort the Nazis ideally wanted was quite another. It
would have meant the conversion of the psychological basis of the
Hitler cult, which had so far been tested and proved effective only in
the 'fine weather conditions' of painless diplomatic coups, into a
fanatical ideological obsession hitherto bred and inculcated into only
a relatively small minority of the population and not even into all Party
members. Such an attempt to fanaticize the entire population would,
however, have required a Party with a wholly different propensity for
integration, and would accordingly have had to alter fundamentally
the previously existing compensatory relationship of Party and Führer
image. It is difficult to see how this could have been attainable, given
the basic premisses of the Nazi political structures, even if more time
had existed than under the prevailing conditions had been available.

These reflections already indicate underlying conditions and limits
of the 'Führer myth' which will be fully illustrated in later chapters.
They were decisive both for the further rise and for the later decline of
the 'Hitler myth'.

(i) 'Triumph without Bloodshed'

Longwinded protestations of his peaceful intentions accompanied—
or immediately followed—Hitler's early surprise moves and successes
on the diplomatic front, from the withdrawal from the League of
Nations in 1933 to the reintroduction of military service and the naval
treaty with Great Britain in 1935. He set the tone for his peace
propaganda aimed both abroad and at home in a major speech on

---

[2] W. Treue, 'Rede Hitlers vor der deutschen Presse (10 Nov. 1938)', *VfZ*, vi (1958),
182; Domarus, p. 974.

17 May 1933, in which he effusively declared that there could be 'only one great task' for himself and the German leadership: 'to secure peace in the world'. As he was on later occasions so frequently to proclaim with apparent sincerity, the goal of restoring German honour was, he stated, based on the deep respect for the rights of other nations with whom National Socialist Germany wished 'from its innermost heart to live in peace and friendship'.[3] Two years later, Hitler repeated almost word for word: 'National Socialist Germany desires peace from its innermost ideological convictions . . . Germany needs peace and desires peace.'[4] This major foreign policy speech, closely following upon the perceived threat of renewed encirclement of Germany arising from French–Soviet and Czech–Soviet agreements, reportedly made a deep impression upon the millions of Germans who clustered around radio sets and loudspeakers to listen to it. According to a report from Lower Bavaria and the Upper Palatinate, hopes of destroying the French 'network of treaties' was revived, 'belief in the calling of the Führer was strengthened anew', and fears of a war which had existed in particular in border areas were dissipated.[5] In the Ruhr District, a 'complete change of mood' was reported since the speech, which was said to have put an end to feelings that the National Socialist government would show its incapacity on the foreign policy front, and to worries about the dangers of the French–Soviet alliance.[6] Hitler's 'great foreign policy speech', which was said to have met with the 'unanimous approval and undivided acclaim of all people's comrades', and thereby to have brought Führer and people even closer together, was claimed as 'further proof that the German people, transcending all petty everyday issues, forms a single united body when matters of the life of the nation are at stake'. It was added, however, that even this speech was unable to bring about a lasting alteration to the poor mood prevailing among large sections of the population.[7] Among the people of the Aachen area, in the still demilitarized zone, Hitler's 'peace manifesto', which

[3] Domarus, pp. 273, 277.

[4] Ibid., p. 506.

[5] GStA, MA 106672, RPvNB/OP, 7 June 1935. See also Shirer, pp. 37–9. The text of the speech is in Domarus, pp. 505 ff.

[6] IML/ZPA, St.3/38/II, Fo. 198, Stapo für den Regierungsbezirk Arnsberg in Dortmund, LB for May 1935.

[7] IML/ZPA, St.3/38/IV, Fo. 695, Stapo für den Regierungsbezirk Münster in Recklinghausen, LB of 6 June 1935.

had been awaited in 'feverish tension', and the unexpectedly favourable echo it had found abroad, was said to have removed 'a nightmare' from the hearts of the population by putting an end to worries about the 'unbearable situation of the constant threat to Germany and on the other hand the continuous talk of the threat Germany posed to other states'. Hitler's speech, it was reported, left 'no further room for doubts about Germany's desire for peace', and, it was added, in a district where disagreements about Church policy had brought about considerable alienation from the Party and the State it represented, it could be seen once more that the same alienated sections of the population 'agreed with the Führer almost without exception in questions of foreign policy'.[8]

We saw in an earlier chapter what a positive impact the first major foreign policy triumphs—the result of the Saar plebiscite and the reintroduction of conscription in 1935—had made on Hitler's popularity and on political integration, and how, a year later, the next coup, the military reoccupation of the Rhineland in March 1936, had been exploited by Nazi propaganda to send admiration for the statesman Hitler soaring to a new pinnacle.[9] As with earlier foreign policy successes, the march into the Rhineland led initially to anxious and worried reactions about the likelihood of a new war breaking out. The anxiety lasted around a week; 'it needed several days until . . . people calmed down'.[10] The relief, as it became clear that the western powers would not go beyond verbal protests, undoubtedly contributed to the subsequent untrammelled jubilation over the 'liberating deed'[11] of the Führer in breaking 'the last shackles of the dictat of Versailles', amounting to a wave of enthusiasm comparable, in the eyes of some observers, with that of August 1914.[12]

The domestic impact of the triumph was immediately clear to observers. From the border zone of Aachen, in which both the staunchly Catholic and working-class population had hitherto shown themselves less enamoured with Nazism than almost any other part of

---

[8] *Volksopposition im Polizeistaat*, pp. 211–12.

[9] See above, ch. 2.

[10] StAM, LRA 99532, GHS Aichach, 29 Mar. 1936. See also GStA, MA 106670, RPvOB, 8 Apr. 1936 and *Volksopposition im Polizeistaat*, pp. 370–1. The anxious fears of war were stressed in most *Sopade* reports: *DBS*, iii. 300ff, 2 Apr. 1936.

[11] GStA, MA 106697, LB of Pd Augsburg, 3 Apr. 1936.

[12] GStA, MA 106677, RPvOF/MF, 7 Apr. 1936. See also GStA, MA 106670, RPvOB, 8 Apr. 1936; MA 106682, RPvS, 6 Apr. 1936; MA 106672, RPvNB/OP, 7 Apr. 1936; MA 106680, RPvUF, 7 Apr. 1936; MA 106687, BPP, 1 Apr. 19376; and Shirer, pp. 47–51.

the country, the Gestapo reported unprecedented shows of enthusiasm, including the spontaneous displaying of the swastika banner in house after house without awaiting the order of the Party or the authorities, and far higher participation than ever before in the innumerable parades and torchlight processions. The events had increased the standing of the Führer still further, it was added, 'and those who still have objections to the person of the Führer or his foreign policy have shrunk in number to an insignificant group'.[13] The *Sopade* concurred. The absence of any counteraction by the western powers had called forth deep depression in the ranks of the opposition: 'Hitler succeeds in simply everything, it is said, and hopes which had not quite been buried for a fall of the regime brought about from outside are again deeply disappointed.'[14]

In the frenzied acclaim which met Hitler wherever he appeared in Germany during the 'election' campaign of March 1936, jubilation at the national triumph mingled with the relief that it had been attained without bloodshed. Hundreds of thousands of Germans swarmed on to the streets of the big cities, cheering and singing as they listened to broadcasts of Hitler's speeches, or attended his campaign rallies, accompanied by torchlight demonstrations and firework displays.[15] Huge rallies were held, as in Munich, where Hitler addressed a crowd said to be 300,000 strong on the Theresienwiese, accompanied by fireworks and a 'sea of flame' arising from hundreds of thousands of torches—though *Sopade* observers in the crowd claimed the spectacle had gone wrong since the impatient and very cold masses had lit their torches early to try to keep warm![16] A depressed *Sopade* observer in the Ruhr spoke of 'ordinary citizens', 'hysterical working-class women', and 'people with limited intelligence, for whom the Third Reich raises no problems' being gripped by such rallies. 'Their number is large enough,' he added, 'The "Führer" comes to them!'[17] Internal reports spoke of a transformation in the depressed mood—the result of low wages and foodstuff shortages—of workers and consumers from the

[13] *Volksopposition im Polizeistaat*, pp. 370–2.

[14] *DBS*, iii. 460, 4 May 1936. See also the reports from the previous month in ibid., pp. 300–20.

[15] For reports on such rallies in Bavaria, see GStA, MA 106697, LB of Pd Augsburg, 3 Apr. 1936; MA 106687, BPP, 1 Apr. 1936; MA 106685, Pd München, 5 Apr. 1936.

[16] *Münchner Neueste Nachrichten*, 16 Mar. 1936; ASD, ES/M64, report for Mar. 1936, p. 9.

[17] *DBS*, iii. 304, 2 Apr. 1936.

poorer sections of society.[18] They were optimistic in expecting any
long-term change. After the short wave of national euphoria, the
worries and cares of daily life rapidly returned to dominate popular
attitudes, and demands for social improvements were soon again
heard.[19] Nevertheless, it was once again clear that Hitler's foreign
policy successes were an extraordinarily effective instrument of
political integration, at least temporarily and artificially, through
whipping up an atmosphere of national ecstasy, transcending social
divides, clashes of interest, and other areas of tension in German
society. And whatever negative feelings persisted about many unpalatable sides of Nazi rule, admiration for Hitler as the author of
Germany's new world standing and the 'simply wonderful' confidence
and trust in him, that 'he will succeed in bringing everything to a good
conclusion for Germany',[20] now knew no bounds.

Sopade observers accepted resignedly the consequences of the
coup. The 'voices of the doubters' had dwindled; the Führer had once
again shown that 'he is the supreme master of the politics of the *fait
accompli*'.[21] A thoughtful survey from Munich pointed out the climate
of opinion in which the Rhineland triumph had taken place. The
many enthusiastic 'Hitler worshippers' were fully convinced that
Hitler wanted peace, and saw no alternative to his unyielding policy of
upholding Germany's rights against a ring of hostile nations which
wanted to deny those rights. The 'indifferent mass'—the majority of
the population—were horrified at the thought of another war, but felt
helpless, and there was no condemnation of Hitler. That he had led
German into 'fateful isolation' scarcely occurred to the mass of the
population: 'Almost all, who are otherwise ready with their criticism,
accept that the government is right in its foreign policy measures.'
Most of the workers, it was claimed, could be accredited with such
attitudes, and for all that they complained about economic matters
and other things accepted that Hitler had done much that was right.
Catholics saw Hitler as the lesser evil compared with Bolshevism.
Those rejecting the regime—'opposition would be too much to

[18] GStA, MA 106687, BPP, 1 Apr. 1936; MA 106670, RPvOB, 8 May 1936. *Sopade*
reporters acknowledged the diversionary effect of the Rhineland coup—AdSD, ES/
M33, 18 Mar. 1936; ES/M64, report for April 1936.
[19] See GStA, MA 106686, Pd Augsburg, 30 Apr. 1936.
[20] StAM, LRA 47140, BA Bad Aibling, 6 Apr. 1936, and see GStA, MA 106687, BPP,
1 May 1936.
[21] *DBS*, iii. 304, 2 Apr. 1936, report from the Ruhr District.

claim'—were unclear in their ideas, except that they reckoned increasingly with the inevitability of war. And youth had its own place in the scenario, becoming ever less critical, seeing the world only through the eyes of National Socialism, and coming in increasing measure to accept the 'great power ideology' which was being pumped into them daily. In this climate of opinion, Hitler's surprise Rhineland coup and his bold defence of his action 'impressed all, who are otherwise less than enthusiastic about him. . . . Everyone felt that there was an element of justification in Hitler's demands. The spirit of Versailles is hated by all Germans. Hitler has now torn up this cursed treaty and thrown it at the feet of the French.' ' "What a guy, Hitler. He had the courage to risk something," ' was a frequently encountered expression but 'that this new deed of Hitler is another milestone on the way to the hell's jaws of destruction seems hardly to have entered the consciousness of anyone'.[22]

During the two following years, foreign policy retreated somewhat as a dominant factor in shaping popular opinion. No new breathtaking national triumphs took place in this period, though the beginning of the Spanish Civil War, the deployment of the German 'Condor Legion', the stepped-up anti-Bolshevik campaign, and the state visit of Mussolini in September 1937 as the celebration of the German–Italian 'axis' provided new occasions for bolstering national-chauvinist identity feelings and the closely related Hitler cult. Among the anti-Nazi minority, of course, these same events provided ominous foreboding of the growing certainty of a new massive conflagration. The population in general, however, knew nothing of the actual reflections of Hitler and the German leadership on future German aggression and imperialist intentions, as revealed in the Hoßbach memorandum of November 1937 and in Goebbels's diaries for this period.[23] Rumours did seep out, however, about clashes between Hitler and the leaders of the armed forces related to war aims, following the Blomberg–Fritsch crisis and reorganization of the Wehrmacht leadership in February 1938. It was said, for instance, that Hitler had wanted to send in 20,000 soldiers to Spain or to Austria, or that a war had been planned, which the dismissed generals had

---

[22] Ibid., pp. 306–8, from AdSD, ES/M64, report for March 1936.
[23] The Hoßbach memorandum is in Noakes and Pridham, pp. 521 ff; some relevant extracts from Goebbels's diary notes can be found in I. Kershaw, *The Nazi Dictatorship*, London, 1985, p. 123.

strongly advised against.²⁴ With an effective speech on 20 February 1938, however, Hitler was quickly able to calm the unease,²⁵ and the march into Austria and *Anschluß* of the *'Ostmark'* which took place three weeks later took admiration for the Führer onto a new plane. Probably, this new triumph marked the overall high-point of Hitler's prestige and popularity, and of the massive extent of consensus and approval for his actions which he had been able to construct in the previous years.

As with the reoccupation of the Rhineland, however, the first, dominant wave of feeling was intense fear about the outbreak of a new war. Internal reports and *Sopade* observations in all parts of Germany emphasize the widespread anxieties, particularly prominent in border regions, which followed the partial troop mobilization on 10–11 March 1938. The press was commanded on no account to mention, either in positive or negative sense, the word 'war', to report any 'mood of panic', or to suggest that German–British relations were endangered by the action.²⁶ Only once it was plain that the western powers were again prepared to stand by and do nothing, that Hitler had once more pulled off without bloodshed a major coup—the unification of Germany and Austria and realization of a 'Greater Germany' which since the nineteenth century had always retained some appeal, especially in Catholic southern Germany—did the initial war psychosis give way to a tumult of jubilation. The relief is apparent in the assessment of opinion provided by reports from Bavarian localities bordering on Austria, where the fears of war had been especially acute. From the Berchtesgaden area, 'heartfelt jubilation everywhere' was reported, 'above all because our Führer has pulled it off without bloodshed'.²⁷ Similarly, from the Garmisch-Partenkirchen

---

²⁴ GStA, MA 106673, RPvNB/OP, 8 Mar. 1938; see also, StAA Amberg, BA Amberg 2398, GS Schnaittenbach, 24 Feb. 1938; StAM, NSDAP 983, NSLB Kreis Erding, 8 Feb. 1938; LRA 61616, GBF Garmisch 2 Mar. 1938; GS Mittenwald, 26 Feb. 1938.

²⁵ Text in Domarus, pp. 792–804. For reactions, see GStA, MA 106671, RPvOB, 10 Mar. 1938; MA 106673, RPvNB/OP, 8 Mar. 1938; MA 106678, RPvOP/MF, 9 Mar. 1938. Not everyone was preoccupied by Hitler's clarification of the changes in the government and army command. In the Berchtesgaden area, three hundred 'Strength through Joy' visitors from Düsseldorf and Berlin explained that they were too busy with their winter sport to break off and listen to the Führer's speech—StAM, LRA, 29654, GS Markt Schellenberg, 28 Feb. 1938.

²⁶ H. Auerbach, 'Volksstimmung und veröffentlichte Meinung in Deutschland zwischen März und November 1938', in F. Knipping and K.-J. Müller (eds.), *Machtbewußtsein in Deutschland am Vorabend des Zweiten Weltkrieges*, Paderborn, 1984, p. 278.   ²⁷ StAM, LRA 30678, GS Anger, 31 Mar. 1938.

district it was noted that many who had previously not supported Nazism were now completely in favour of the National Socialist State 'because the Führer has succeeded in uniting Austria with Germany without bloodshed', and that the people have 'unlimited trust in our Führer' because the *Anschluß* had taken place 'so smoothly and without loss of blood', so that 'the affair' did not have to be taken 'so seriously'.[28]

Once the danger of war was past, Hitler's accomplishment of 'the German miracle' unleashed, not least in such border areas, what government agencies, straining for new superlatives, described as 'an elemental frenzy of enthusiasm'.[29] In the Berchtesgaden district, directly on the Austrian border, crowds stood for hours on the road waving in jubilation to the passing troops.[30] Elsewhere, for instance in the Protestant parts of northern Bavaria where there had been no close historic or religious attachment to Austria, feelings about the *Anschluß* seem to have been more muted. One report from the area stated laconically that 'special enthusiasm could not be registered' and that 'here and there silly comments were heard that Austria was a poor country and its people not reliable'.[31]

Lack of interest and enthusiasm was also noted in some of the *Sopade* regional reports, though some of these have a tone of wishful thinking rather than stark reality and in many cases clearly represent disproportionately the feelings of opponents of the regime.[32] Alongside the deep depression in such circles about the weakness and inactivity of the western democracies, the *Sopade* reports nevertheless recognized that Hitler's popularity—and with it the central political base of the Nazi regime—had been strengthened still further. Nazi supporters in Bavaria claimed Hitler was greater than Napoleon: unlike the French emperor, he conquered the world without war. Even among the less exultant, there was great admiration for Hitler: 'what a guy' was a commonly heard sentiment.[33] In Westphalia, where the Austrian triumph was interpreted as a necessary diversion from

[28] StAM. LRA 61616, GS Mittenwald, 29 Mar. 1938; GS Wallgau, 30 Mar. 1938.
[29] GStA, MA 106683, RPvS, 8 Apr. 1938.
[30] StAM, LRA 30678, GS Anger, 31 Mar. 1938.
[31] StAB, K8/III, 18473, GS Unterweilersbach, 26 Mar. 1938; see also GBF Ebermannstadt, 29 Mar. 1938; BA Ebermannstadt, 1 Apr. 1938; GS Heiligenstadt, 25 Mar. 1938; GS Waischenfeld, 25 Mar. 1938; and GStA, MA 106678, RPvOF/MF, 8 Apr. 1938.
[32] *DBS*, v. 256ff., 9 Apr. 1938.
[33] Ibid., p. 260.

growing internal tensions and amounted to Hitler's 'greatest success' so far, it was reckoned to signify that there would now be 'no further worthwhile opposition to new adventures', since 'the country is now fully prepared for the fact that the "Führer" can do everything he wants to'.[34] In the Ruhr, where the report offered a somewhat over-simplistic class division in reactions to the *Anschluß*, workers were said to have been enraged at the lack of intervention of the western democracies, while chauvinism, 'childish pride in the army', and the feeling that Hitler was 'a devil of a fellow who controlled Europe and now would not stop at Czechoslovakia' dominated among the bourgeoisie.[35]

A thoughtful report from Saxony also distinguished between a first phase of war psychosis, followed by boundless jubilation when it was recognized that there would be no war. The joy of the second phase, it was said, arose partly from relief at the peaceful outcome of the affair, but intermingled with this was undoubtedly also 'a great deal of admiration and recognition of Hitler's success'. Even sections of the population which had previously been cool towards Hitler or rejected him entirely were now sufficiently carried away to admit 'that Hitler is a great and clever statesman who will raise up Germany from the defeat of 1918 to greatness and standing again'. The Saxony report then pointed to a third phase in opinion formation when, after a further two weeks or so, interest in Austria declined despite the imminent plebiscite.[36] Though rightly regarded as a foregone conclusion, this plebiscite unquestionably represented, for all the farcical nature of the official result of over 99 per cent, which broke all previous records, a massive consensus in Hitler's 'achievements' in the sphere of foreign policy.[37]

(ii) *Tension*

The *Anschluß* was the last of the great foreign policy successes which Hitler was able to attain almost effortlessly, without the intervention of the western powers. The lightning, dramatic coup, which had proved so successful in the cases of the Rhineland and Austria and had faced the German people as well as foreign powers with a *fait accompli*, had scarcely provided time for the real build-up of a 'war psychosis'.

---

[34] Ibid., pp. 267–8.
[35] Ibid., pp. 268–9.
[36] Ibid., pp. 263–4.
[37] On the plebiscite, see Auerbach, 'Voklksstimmung', p. 279.

Though, as we have seen, anxiety about a new war was the dominant sentiment as the news of those events broke in Germany, the crisis in each case rapidly passed and gave way to boundless jubilation, not only at the triumph itself, but at the fact that it had been attained peacefully. In the Sudeten crisis of 1938 there was for the first time a difference. The population was subjected during the course of the summer of 1938 to a war of nerves which lasted for weeks and was conducted in an ever shriller press campaign attacking the alleged Czech atrocities against the Sudeten Germans. The indications are that the anti-Czech propaganda was not without effect, and that it was widely felt that Germany was justified in assisting the 'repressed' Sudeten population. Initially, at least, there appears also to have been some optimism that the Sudetenland would soon come 'home to the Reich' and that this would be accomplished without recourse to arms. However, the longer the crisis lasted, the more dominant the anxiety became that war would be the outcome. Unquestionably, this dread of war, reaching at times almost panic levels, was the central feature of opinion among the majority of the population, far outweighing annexationist aspirations, and threatening for the first time to cast a major shadow over Hitler's own popularity.

In its annual report for the year 1938, the SD spoke of a 'war psychosis' which began with the Czech mobilization in May and lasted until the Munich Agreement at the end of September and described the mood of the population as 'serious and depressed' and strongly pessimistic.[38] *Sopade* reports for the whole of Germany, and internal reports of the Nazi administration (which are more plentifully available at this date for Bavaria than for any other part of the Reich), provide more than adequate amplification of the SD generalizations.

Reports from Bavarian authorities spoke of 'a real war psychosis', especially in the towns of areas bordering on Czechoslovakia in Lower Bavaria and the Upper Palatinate in the eastern parts of the province.[39] One *Landrat* even reported 'panic' in the population of his locality.[40] Among the older generation in particular, for whom the memory of the First World War was still a vivid one, it seems clear that dread of a new conflict outweighed nationalist fervour and readiness to follow the Führer blindly. Numerous reports in summer 1938, and

[38] *MadR*, ii. 72–3.
[39] GStA, MA 106673, RPvNB/OP, 8 Sept. 1938.
[40] StAA, BA Amberg 2399, GS Hahnbach, 21 Sept. 1938.

especially in the acute phase in September, indicated significant differences in attitude mainly according to generation and Party affiliation. One observer felt able, for example, to distinguish three main currents of opinion. Reckless 'go-getters' asked what was the use of having a strong army if it was not going to be used, and thought there should not be just talk, but immediate release of the Sudetens from their 'distress and subjugation'. The 'anxious' set, on the other hand, were certain that there would be a war which Germany, with its economic weakness, was incapable of winning against the might of the entire world. The result would be that Russia would reduce Europe, as it had Spain, to ashes. Their view was that the Sudetens should have given in to the Czechs, and they asked how the Führer could contemplate plunging them into another war. The third group, however, members of the Party and its affiliates, took the confident line that 'the Führer is always right', had always proved right so far, and would do so again, and that one could rely upon him blindly in this case too to bring the matter to a conclusion favourable for Germany.[41]

Though crude, the views cited in this and in other reports suggest that the confidence in Hitler in considerable sections of the population rested above all upon the hope that he would now be able to solve the Sudeten problem too without a war. It is of course clear from such reports that the chauvinist aggression stirred up by Nazi propaganda had also left its mark on opinion and had produced a strain of impatient expectation of an early strike against the Czechs, as reflected, too, in the reported voicing in some sections of the population of admiration for the Führer's patience.[42] Such feelings were particularly prominent among younger Germans, who had not experienced the war and had undergone the formative years of their 'socialization' during the Third Reich itself. One report on the 'morale of youth in the critical days', compiled by a local Hitler Youth leader in Upper Bavaria, claimed that among the young, in contrast to the older generation, there were no doubts about the outcome of a war. All believed unshakeably in victory, and regretted only that they could not take part, hoping nevertheless that they might serve the Führer in some capacity. About his own generational group of the 16–20-year-olds, he had also 'only the best' to report. Though aware of the consequences of war, they stood 'united behind the Führer—even if

[41] StAM, NSDAP 983, NSLB Kreis Weilheim, Abschnitt Peißenberg, 3 Oct. 1938.
[42] Ibid., report to NSLB Kreis Traunstein, 23 Sept. 1938.

some were not so enthusiastic—and were prepared to do their utmost for the Führer'. His conclusion was that 'the Führer can rely upon his youth' of Germany, and that if he could depend upon all 'people's comrades' to the same extent, 'victory would have been ours right at the beginning of a war'.[43]

Even these nazified comments of a fanatical youth leader illustrate, however, that the majority of the population thought differently. For the first time in the Third Reich, serious doubts about Hitler's policy were revealed. Signs of a potential crisis of confidence in Hitler are recognizable, even if they have to be read between the lines of official reports. The anxious reactions to the Sudetenland crisis demonstrate the superficiality of the belief in Hitler in extensive sections of the population, and how much the popularity of the Führer depended upon continued success. Even Party functionaries were prepared to admit as much, as in the case of a District Leader of the NSDAP who confessed that when the danger of war appeared acute during the critical days in September, 'the necessary unconditional trust in the Führer was lacking among many Party members, who could not be counted on if things became serious'.[44] In similar vein, the leader of the Nazi women's organization, the *NS-Frauenschaft*, in one Bavarian locality claimed that some women 'had no trust in our Führer when the chips were down', while a Block Leader from the same district reported that some were resting their hopes for peace on Mussolini and the western statesmen, and two reservists on their way home had declared to him that England and France could be thanked for the fact that war had been avoided.[45] The fragility of trust in the Führer in the case of a war over the Sudetenland was hinted at in a number of reports from other Bavarian districts.[46] Further reports suggested that the population, especially former wartime soldiers, were 'inwardly not

[43] StAM, NSDAP 440, 'Bericht über die Stimmung der Jugend in den kritischen Tagen', n.d., presumably Oct. 1938.

[44] StAM, NSDAP 126, KL Erding, report for Oct.–Dec. 1938. A line was put through the comment cited, which was replaced in the finished report by a more neutral formulation.

[45] StAM, NSDAP 440, NS-Frauenschaft Ebersberg, 31 Oct. 1938 and the undated *Blockwart*'s 'Stimmungsbericht über die ereignisreichen Tage im September 1938 vor dem Einmarsch ins Sudetenland'. Defeatist and critical comments from the middle class, and complaints from farmers about the commandeering of their horses, were mentioned in another report in the file, from the 'Reichsbund der Deutschen Beamten' to the 'Ortsgruppe Ebersberg', 29 Oct. 1938.

[46] StAM, LRA 59595, BA Schrobenhausen, 4 Nov. 1938; LRA 47140, GS Feilnbach, 18 July 1938; LRA 134059, BA Bad Tölz, 2 Sept. 1938.

ready' to fight, that the 'psychological readiness' for a war was lacking, that 'not a man should be sacrificed on behalf of the Sudeten Germans', and that, while the people stood solidly behind the Führer, 'they preferred peace to be maintained'.[47]

Sopade observers depicted a similar mood of the population in the summer of 1938. A report from north-west Germany claimed that even most of Hitler's fanatical supporters were against a war, believed Hitler's peace protestations and thought he was bluffing in the Sudeten question. The Saxony report distinguished between the victory mood of the Nazi section of the population, the war fears especially of those who had fought in the 1914–18 war, and the feeling of opponents of the regime that only a war could liberate Germany from fascism. There was, it was added, a general conviction that Germany could not win a long war. The Bavarian reporter speculated—quite mistakenly as things turned out—that a potential loss of prestige for the regime would occur if it became clear that Hitler had been forced to withdraw from the brink of a conflict which would amount to the opening of a world war.[48] Summarizing the gist of reports from all parts of the Reich, *Sopade* headquarters in Prague reckoned that in terms of morale, the 'war potential' of the German people was far smaller than 1914. As regards the general attitude of the population towards war, it could be stated that the great majority feared war and no one thought Germany could win; but that most of youth had been won over by propaganda to the idea of war; and that many opponents welcomed a war as a means to end the dictatorship.[49]

Reports of the regime's authorities and also the files of the political 'Special Courts' show that in these critical weeks there was also a sharp rise in instances of outright criticism of Hitler and attribution to him of sole guilt for the outbreak of any war which might occur as a result of the Sudeten question. Some negative comment came from former sympathizers of the KPD or SPD, but records of the Munich 'Special Court' provide no indication that most of those arraigned came from such a background.[50]

---

[47] StAA, BA Amberg 2398, GS Hirschau, 22 Aug. 1938; StAM, LRA 99497, BA Aichach, 1 Sept. 1938; GStA, MA 106681, RPvUF, 7 Sept. 1938.

[48] *DBS*, v. 685–9, 24 Aug. 1938.

[49] Ibid., pp. 684–5; see also pp. 913–39, 10 Oct. 1938.

[50] On a rough count, Hitler was the direct target of criticism in 81 out of 448 'malicious practices' (*Heimtücke*) cases (18.1%) of the Munich 'Special Court' in 1937, but 297 out of 1,302 cases (22.8%) in 1938, 290 out of 1,269 cases (22.9%) in 1939, and 234 out of 812 cases (28.8%) in 1940. Whereas the comments about Hitler in the early years of

How widespread the unease about Hitler's policy was among those who nevertheless held their tongues was revealed by the enthusiastic greeting given to the British Prime Minister Neville Chamberlain on his visits to Bad Godesberg and Munich at the height of the crisis in September 1938.[51] It was graphically illustrated, too, by the sullen response of the Berlin population to a military parade in Berlin on 27 September. According to eyewitness accounts, instead of enthusiastic applause for the massive motorized procession rolling down the Wilhelmstraße, which had been deliberately timed to catch the thousands of Berliners pouring out of their offices, most 'ducked into subways, refused to look on, and the handful that did stood at the curb in utter silence unable to find a word of cheer for the flower of their youth going away to the glorious war'. Hitler, watching from a balcony, was reported as being 'disgusted with the crowd for their apathy'.[52]

Certainly, it would be going much too far to speak of a dramatic collapse of the 'Führer myth', which had been built up for years by Nazi propaganda and had evidently established strong psychological foundations in wide sections of the population. Even presuming that most Germans would have been prepared to abandon claims to the Sudetenland in order to preserve peace, this would not in itself have signified a turn of opinion against Hitler, since he himself was regarded by so many as engaging in bluff and brinkmanship but not prepared to take Germany into war over the issue. And it seems that most, influenced by the propaganda campaign, were convinced that Germany had right on its side in its defence of Sudeten Germans.

Even so, in the wake of the Sudetenland crisis Hitler's popularity was threatened for the first time. In the event of war, the possible army coup which was being contemplated in the summer of 1938 might have

the Dictatorship tended to be unspecific insults, including a significant minority of remarks about his sexuality—especially around the time of the 'Röhm Putsch'—those between 1938 and 1940 were far more concerned with Hitler's responsibility for specific international issues—the *Anschluß*, Sudetenland, and the beginning of the war. Jokes and comments about his sexuality disappear almost completely, and the unspecific insults decline in percentage terms. Directly on account of their anti-regime comments on the Sudetenland issue, 79 persons—mostly unskilled labourers, skilled workers and craftsmen, and farmers—were arrested for trial before the 'Special Court' in Munich—SGM material in StAM.

[51] N. Henderson, *Failure of a Mission*, London, 1940, pp. 154, 161, 166.
[52] Shirer, p. 117; Stokes, *SD*, p. 272; R. Andreas-Friedrich, *Schauplatz Berlin. Ein deutsches Tagebuch*, Munich, 1962, pp. 5–6; see also Steinert, pp. 77–9.

possessed a distinct chance of finding popular support. In this respect, too, the Munich Agreement by which the western powers handed over the Sudetenland to Germany was a fateful step. Not only was a possible coup against Hitler robbed of any hope of success, the Führer's prestige was also more than recovered: the settlement provided him with 'almost legendary standing'[53] among the German people; and every opponent of the regime was disarmed, every basis of criticism removed. All reports from the days following the Munich Settlement reflect the new wave of relief, admiration, and gratitude which now poured out for Hitler. With a single blow, the Führer had eliminated all doubts and had established a new basis of trust and confidence in his genius as the statesman who had triumphed once more through keeping his nerve while all around him faltered.

The euphoria arose primarily out of the relief following weeks of great tension. Such was the joy at the preservation of peace that the 'home-coming' of the Sudeten Germans was at times almost forgotten, and 'the world historical significance of the German success not fully taken in'.[54] The German press was instructed explicitly not only to lay especial stress on the solidarity of the German people with the Führer during the days of utmost crisis, but also to avoid in expressions of gratitude, praise, and blind obedience to the Führer the sense that this was out of pure relief.[55]

Hardly anyone imagined then that Hitler, in his moment of triumph over the Sudetenland, was actually furious at being manœuvred into a diplomatic settlement of the question.[56] Again, the popular image of Hitler was far removed from reality. While he berated the longing for peace among the population, his own prestige was reaching new heights through attaining yet another triumph without bloodshed. As one report put it, 'people's comrades, who up to now have not been fully convinced by National Socialism, now see that no other leadership of state could possibly have attained this success.' Amid the general political jubilation, people were thrilled at the 'statesmanship of our Führer'.[57] His brilliant diplomatic success in Munich had the

[53] Steinert, p. 79.
[54] GStA, MA 106671, RPvOB, 10 Oct. 1938. See also Stokes, *SD*, pp. 270, 273; Steinert, pp. 78–9; Shirer, p. 122.
[55] Auerbach, *Volksstimmung*, p. 285.
[56] See Henderson, pp. 175, 179.
[57] GStA, MA 106671, RPvOB, 10 Nov. 1938. See also MA 106681, RPvUF, 10 Nov. 1938.

accompanying effect of taking all the wind out of the sails of internal opponents. The deep disappointment, anger, and depression at the behaviour of the western democracies is a prominent feature of all *Sopade* reports from the period following the Munich settlement.[58] Even in the most critical conditions—it must have seemed to many— the supreme genius of the Führer could be relied upon to do the best for Germany. This enhanced belief in Hitler's powers of statesman- ship was certainly a major factor in the relative composure of the popular mood during the Polish crisis of the following year, when the fears that it would lead to war were nowhere near so extensive as they had been in 1938. The Führer image had evidently attained through the preceding successes, and especially through the triumph following the Sudeten crisis, a new dimension of legendary infallibility in the sphere of diplomatic activity. The *Sopade* perceptively commented in early October 1938: 'Hitler has again reached his goal without war. This too will not remain without impact on the mentality of the German people. Until recently, the fear of war was growing in the broadest sections of the population. Must not this anxiety finally yield following Hitler's new bloodless victory to the conviction that Hitler can demand what he wants, the others will always give way? Must not the megalomania of the Führer extend to ever wider sections of the population?'[59]

(iii) *War*

Hitler's last foreign policy successes before the war, the march into Prague on 15 March 1939 and, a week later, the incorporation of the Memel district into the Reich, took place so rapidly that there was little time for the build-up of any anxiety in the German population about a possible outbreak of hostilities. The first reaction was one of surprise,[60] followed by renewed admiration for the statesmanly genius of the Führer, not least for accomplishing yet another triumph without bloodshed.[61] However, these new German successes scarcely released a wave of euphoria comparable to that following the *Anschluß* and the

---

[58] *DBS*, v. 939–47, 10 Oct. 1938.

[59] Ibid., p. 940.

[60] See *DBS*, vi. 281, 14 Apr. 1939, report from south-west Germany; StAM, NSDAP 126, KL Wasserburg, report for Jan.–Mar. 1939. See also LRA 29654, GS Bad Reichenhall, 28 Mar. 1939, and StAB, K8/III, 18473, GS Königsfeld, 27 Mar. 1939.

[61] Expressly pointed out in StAB, K8/III, 18473, GS Waischenfeld, 26 Mar. 1939. And see the *Sopade* reports in *DBS*, vi. 278ff, 14 Apr. 1939.

Munich Agreement the previous year. As one Bavarian District Leader of the NSDAP expressed it, 'people are glad about the great deeds of the Führer and look to him full of confidence, but the needs and cares of daily life are so great that the mood is very quickly gloomy again.'[62] While allegedly even many former SPD supporters accepted the justification of incorporating the largely German-speaking Memel district into the Reich, the occupation of Czechoslovakia, where for the first time there was no question of the 'home-coming' of German lands, prompted some criticism, puzzlement, and scepticism, and naturally little of the sense of identity which had accompanied earlier extensions of the Reich to territories which shared German language and culture.[63] Even so, as a *Sopade* report from Rhineland-Westphalia pointed out, the German march into Prague was above all another prestige success for Hitler, and in the face of the successes which he could muster, the argument that there was no moral justification for the occupation of Czechoslovakia carried little weight.[64] The summary of the *Sopade* analysts, who had rapidly had to move their headquarters from Prague to Paris, accepted that a new gain in prestige for Hitler was the dominant impact of the destruction of Czechoslovakia, accompanied by the feeling that the Führer succeeded in everything he attempted while the 'others' were ready, in the face of Germany's strength, to give way to any demands without a fight.[65]

When, a few weeks later, Hitler's fiftieth birthday on 20 April 1939, was celebrated with proud display of the might of the Wehrmacht at a spectacular military parade in Berlin, it provided a special occasion for demonstrations of unbounded devotion to the Führer. Outside those groups of the population who still held firmly to their former socialist and communist beliefs, and those fundamentally alienated from the Nazi regime through the 'Church struggle', it would be not going too far to suggest that at this date the great majority of Germans

---

[62] StAM, NSDAP 126, KL Aichach, 31 Mar. 1939. See also GStA, MA 106683, RPvS, 7 Apr. 1939; MA 106678, RPvOF/MF, 10 Apr. 1939; MA 106673, RPvNB/OP, 11 Apr. 1939; MA 106681, RPvUF, 11 Apr. 1939; MA 106671, RPvOB, 12 Apr. 1939, for reactions reported by the Bavarian Government Presidents.

[63] See *DBS*, vi. 282, report from south-west Germany.

[64] Ibid., p. 278, report from Rhineland-Westphalia.

[65] Ibid., p. 275. 'Dull indifference', criticism of German imperialism—now for the first time going beyond any pretence at liberating 'repressed German minorities', and worry that war was now one step nearer, were noted (p. 276) as the other general reactions.

could find some point of identification with Hitler and his 'achievements'. A *Sopade* assessment of the Führer cult, following the birthday celebrations, noted that although notions of 'heroic' leadership had a long pedigree in Germany, Hitler was unique not only in coming from the lower ranks of society and in his populist demagogic talents, but also in the strength of the faith in him which he had stirred up. And though anyone who knew Germany was aware that a large section of the population had, during Hitler's rise to a 'mythical figure', remained cool and sceptical, the internal terror which suppressed any critical action, and the foreign policy of the western democracies, 'which handed the Führer one success after another', had undermined this reserve. Despite the pervading fear of a war, belief in the Führer was still vitally present in wide sections of the population. To demonstrate this, the report included a substantial selection of letters, poems, and adulatory outpourings from 'ordinary' citizens published in German newspapers at the time of Hitler's birthday, and expressing—often in the most extraordinary language—devotion to the Führer. The *Sopade* analysts added that such shows of devotion could not simply be put down to propaganda, but 'certainly in part arise from a naïve faith which is not so easily destroyed'.[66]

Despite the increasing tension associated with the 'Danzig Question' in summer 1939, the basic mood of the German population was far less nervous and anxious about the threat of war than it had been during the Sudeten crisis of the previous summer. Since the Munich Agreement, there was, it seemed, little room for doubts about Hitler's diplomacy, and his speeches in the spring and summer of 1939—especially his highly effective rebuff of President Roosevelt on 28 April[67]—made a considerable impact, seeming to confirm to many Germans that his underlying aims were to preserve peace, not to wage war. Moreover, few thought that having sacrificed the Sudetenland and then the rest of Czechoslovakia without a fight the western powers would be prepared to risk a war over Danzig. The mood, in contrast to the previous year, was therefore on the whole one of confidence. Many thought that this time, too, Hitler would get what he wanted without

---

[66] Ibid., pp. 435–54, 10 May 1939.
[67] Text in Domarus, pp. 1148ff. Some observers thought the rejoinder to Roosevelt was Hitler's 'most brilliant' rhetorical performance—see Fest, pp. 795–8.

bloodshed.[68] One seventeen-year-old German girl, who believed that 'Hitler was a great man, a genius, a person sent to us from heaven', undoubtedly reflected the views of many that summer: 'Rumours of an impending war were spreading steadily but we did not worry unduly. We were convinced that Hitler was a man of peace and would do everything he could to settle things peacefully.'[69]

Even so, fears of a new, impending conflict were far from absent and continued to form a central component of popular opinion, as practically all reports—internal or those of the *Sopade*—in summer 1939 clearly indicate. The reports of the particularly outspoken *Landrat* of Ebermannstadt, in Upper Franconia, provide a good illustration of the prevailing mood. At the end of June 1939, he wrote: 'The desire for peace is stronger than that for war. Among by far the overwhelming proportion of the population, therefore, there is agreement with the solution of the Danzig question only if this proceeds in the same swift and bloodless fashion as the previous annexations in the east. . . . Enthusiasm such as there was in 1914 cannot be reckoned with today.'[70] A month later he encapsulated in a few words the feelings of millions of Germans towards the growing Polish crisis: 'The answer to the question of how the problem "Danzig and the Corridor" is to be solved is still the same among the general public: incorporation in the Reich? Yes. Through war? No.'[71] As war became imminent, then began on 1 September with the invasion of Poland, these sentiments were confirmed in all contemporary assessments of opinion and morale. Compared with the heady days of August 1914, all observers concurred in registering only anxiety and lack of enthusiasm.[72] Despite weeks of relentless propaganda, many people, according to some reports, were still not sure what the war was all about; a 'deeper understanding of the necessity of the war' was missing, and many were unclear about the 'full significance of the action against Poland'.[73] Another report from Ebermannstadt, on the very last day of peace, had emphasized once more that trust in the Führer depended to a con-

---

[68] GStA, MA 106673, RPvNB/OP, 7 Aug. 1939, and see MA 106671, RPvOB, 10 Aug. 1939, and Steinert, pp. 84–5.

[69] I. McKee, *Tomorrow the World*, London, 1960, p. 27.

[70] StAB, K8/III, 18473, LR Ebermannstadt, 30 June 1939; and see GI Ebermannstadt, 29 July 1939.

[71] StAB, K8/III, 18473, LR Ebermannstadt, n.d. (end of July) 1939.

[72] See e.g. Shirer, pp. 152, 158–9; Steinert, pp. 91–2; Stokes, *SD*, p. 471; Fest, p. 849.

[73] GStA, MA 106671, 11 Sept. 1939. See also MA 106678, RPvOF/MF, 7 Sept. 1939, and MA 106683, RPvS, 8 Sept. 1939.

siderable extent upon whether or not he could prevent a war: 'Trust in the Führer will now probably be subjected to its hardest acid test. The overwhelming proportion of people's comrades expects from him the prevention of the war, if otherwise impossible even at the cost of Danzig and the Corridor.'[74]

According to this, Hitler's popularity still rested upon his preservation of peace. Yet war was what the Germans got in autumn 1939. Despite their unmistakable dread of another conflagration, shown so clearly over the previous years and above all during 1938 and 1939, they followed their Führer into a new war without enthusiasm, but also without protest or opposition. And far from going into decline, Hitler's popularity was by the end of the year, four months into the war, as solidly based as ever. It had survived unscathed both the shock volte-face of the pact with the ideological enemy, Soviet Bolshevism, and the beginning of hostilities with the West.[75] Though the years of terror and repression account in good measure for the lack of any open opposition to Hitler's war, they can only in small part help to explain why the 'Führer myth' remained intact. The main factors have to be sought elsewhere. First of all, it seems clear that although Nazi propaganda had not succeeded—outside fanaticized youth and sections of the faithful in the Party and its affiliations—in evoking outright enthusiasm for a war, it had proved far more successful in denigrating anti-war sentiments as unpatriotic and defeatist and effectively banning them from public discourse. And though there was a fear of war, there was a general readiness to fight, as had been the case in 1938, if it came to the worst. This readiness was bolstered by the success of propaganda in spreading the conviction that the war against Poland was justified and necessary in a conflict which had been forced upon Germany. General credence, not only in Party circles, was attached to the propaganda reports about the persecution of the German minority in Poland.[76] It was an easy matter for German propaganda to play upon deep-seated anti-Polish prejudice and convince people that German armed intervention had been the only

[74] StAB, K8/III, 18473, LR Ebermannstadt, 31 Aug. 1939.

[75] See *DBS*, vi. 985–9, for reactions to the Non-Agression Pact with the Soviet Union; and ibid., pp. 975–83 for early reactions to the war. The report was completed on 24 Oct. 1939.

[76] See e.g. Shirer, p. 138.

remaining option to put an end to the provocation of the Poles.[77] In addition, Nazi propaganda had repeatedly appealed to long-standing anxieties about the danger of 'encirclement' and the need to break the threat—an element of basic consensus between people and regime undoubtedly more extensive than that derived from the specific ideological dogmas of Nazism. And once war had broken out, there was, as in all countries, some closing of ranks and rallying round the government, and basic feelings of loyalty strengthened the bonds with the Führer. Opposition during the war was now tantamount to treason. Hitler's war was Germany's war, and even ideological opponents of National Socialism were prepared, for patriotic reasons and 'duty to the Fatherland'—which it was now difficult to distinguish from duty to the Führer—to follow Hitler to war, however unwanted the war itself had been.[78]

Nor should the continued belief that Hitler was anxious for a rapid peace be underestimated. Evidently, many still believed that Hitler had done all he could to avoid a war.[79] The propaganda construct of Hitler's desire for peace, which had been built up over the past years, clearly still had an effect on a population deprived of contrasting interpretations available in the foreign press.[80] Hitler was quite frank in private about the fact that he had used his 'peace image' as an alibi towards the German people, 'in order to show them that I had done everything to preserve peace'.[81] After hostilities had begun, he sought to sustain this 'peace image' in stressing his most heartfelt desire for a rapid end to the conflict, culminating in his 'peace offer' to the western powers in his Reichstag speech of 6 October 1939, following the victorious end of the Polish campaign.[82] Though undoubtedly many Germans were sceptical about the seriousness of the call for peace,

[77] For such convictions, see e.g. GStA, MA 106673, RPvNB/OP, 9 Oct. 1939; MA 106681, RPvUF, 10 Feb. 1940; MA 106678, RPOF/MF, 7 Apr. 1940; StAM, LRA 29655, GS Bad Reichenhall, 29 Dec. 1939.

[78] See e.g. GStA, MA 106673, RPvNB/OP, 8 Sept. 1939: 'It has already emerged . . . from all reports that the people do not want to know about a war, but that, despite lack of enthusiasm for war such as in 1914, in the event of war they will bear whatever is unavoidable calmly and confidently, trusting in the Führer.' See also GStA, MA 106678, RPvOF/MF, 7 Sept. 1939; Shirer, pp. 165, 173; and Steinert, pp. 95–7.

[79] GStA, MA 106671, RPvOB, 11 Sept. 1939. See also Stokes, *SD*, p. 472: 'There is no reason to suppose that the bulk of the population did not accept Hitler's portrayal of himself as a frustrated peace-seeker.'

[80] See Shirer, p. 138.

[81] P. Schmidt, *Statist auf diplomatischer Bühne*, Bonn, 1953, p. 469.

[82] Text in Domarus, pp. 1377ff. See the comments on the speech in Shirer, pp. 182–4.

which effectively demanded that the western powers accept yet
another *fait accompli* on German terms, the prompt rejection of the
'offer' by Chamberlain and Daladier could be exploited by
propaganda to confirm, apparently yet again, what many Germans had
already been prepared to believe: that the western powers were to
blame for the prolongation of the war. One report among many
emphasizing this feeling stated that, after Germany's enemies had
rejected 'the outstretched hand' of peace, the people had recognized
'that England only desired the destruction of Germany' and were
consequently 'more united than ever in their unlimited trust in their
Führer to carry through the struggle imposed on Germany to its
victorious conclusion'.[83]

Finally, the continuing naïve belief that Hitler only wanted the best
for his people was not undermined by the events of the war itself in its
early stages. The scenes which the newsreels relayed of the modern
German Wehrmacht in action and the brilliant *Blitzkrieg* strategy
which the Führer supervised in person enhanced Germany's prestige
still further, and, given the minimal losses and speedy victories in
Poland, the widespread depression which had been felt at the
beginning of September soon lifted.[84] It was widely felt that the
western powers would be forced to negotiate peace and that the war
would soon be over.[85] And there were few moral scruples about the
brutal devastation of Poland. William Shirer noted: 'I have still to find
a German, even among those who don't like the regime, who sees
anything wrong in the German destruction of Poland. . . . As long as
the Germans are successful and do not have to pull in their belts too
much, this will not be an unpopular war.'[86]

All in all, there was little in the autumn of 1939, despite the fact that
Germany was now involved in another war, to shake confidence in
Hitler's leadership. One young soldier, just home from Poland,
doubtlessly reflected the views of many Germans at the time. In a
conversation reported by a sympathizer of the socialist *Neu Beginnen*
group travelling in Germany at the time, he was reported to have had
unconditional trust in the military leadership, an uncritical admiration

[83] GStA, MA 106678, RPvOF/MF, 7 Nov. 1939. And see Stokes, *SD*, pp. 473–6;
Steinert, pp. 108–9.
[84] StAB, K8/III, 18473, GKF Ebermannstadt, 29 Sept. 1939.
[85] See e.g. BA/MA, RW20–13/8, 'Geschichte der Rüstungs-Inspektion XIII', p. 35;
Meldungen, p. 8.
[86] Shirer, p. 173 (entry for 20 Sept. 1939).

for Hitler's boldness, the strong hope that England and France would not pursue the war in the light of German military superiority, and the conviction that Hitler would get his way.[87]

An indication that Hitler's popularity had suffered few setbacks in the first months of the war is provided by the reactions to the assassination attempt in the Bürgerbräukeller in Munich on 8 November 1939. Shock, anger, and relief at the outcome were recorded on all sides in internal opinion reports, even from areas where there had been earlier conflict between the Party and the local population arising from the 'Church struggle'.[88] The SD claimed that 'the assassination attempt in Munich has greatly strengthened the identity feelings of the German people', that 'devotion to the Führer has deepened still further', and that 'the attitude towards the war, too, has become even more positive in many circles in the light of the attack'. A mood of great hatred towards Britain, alleged by Nazi propaganda to have instigated the attempt, was said to be prevalent.[89] And according to a *Sopade* report from Berlin, a prominent line of thought after the attempt was that its success would only have resulted in internal confusion in Germany, to the benefit of the nation's enemies, bringing in its train the loss of the war, misery greater than after Versailles, and the negation of all the efforts since 1933. The incident was, therefore, turned into a propaganda success by the Nazis: 'The political result of the bomb attack, according to our general observations, is a strengthening of determination.'[90]

At the end of 1939, the German people experienced the first winter of the war, and with it the first hardships and deprivation. Enthusiasm for the victory of Poland had long since died away. And discontent caused by shortages of some commodities, especially the failures in

[87] WL, 'Deutsche Inlandsberichte', No. 56, 1 Nov. 1939.

[88] For responses within Bavaria, see e.g. GStA, MA 106678, RPvOF/MF, 7 Dec. 1939; MA 106683, RPvS, 9 Dec. 1939; MA 106681, RPvUF, 11 Dec. 1939; StAB, K8/III, 18473, GP Waischenfeld, 26 Nov. 1939; StAM, LRA 61616, GKF Garmisch, 28 Nov. 1939; GP Mittenwald, 24 Nov. 1939. Even though the reports naturally elaborated upon the sympathy for Hitler, the view of one contemporary observer—whose own Christian conservatism made him highly antagonistic towards the regime—that there was hardly anyone in Munich who was not tearing his hair out over the failure of the attempt on Hitler's life, has to be put down to pure wishful thinking—F. P. Reck-Malleczewen, *Tagebuch eines Verzweifelten*, Frankfurt a.M./Hamburg, 1971, p. 68.

[89] *MadR*, iii. 449. The report, from 13 Nov. 1939, added that the attendance in Munich for the funeral ceremony for the victims of the explosion was thin and its expressions of sympathy muted.

[90] *DBS*, vi. 1024–5, 2 Dec. 1939.

provisioning of coal during the hardest winter for years, was readily apparent in the poorer sections of the population, particularly among workers whose attitude towards the war was recognized as being pessimistic.[91] Nevertheless, Hitler's own assessment, which he had made in a speech to the Wehrmacht leadership just before the start of the war, justifying his determination to move, seems to have been equally well-founded four months later: that he had united the people, possessed their confidence, and that his authority was accepted by them to a degree which no successor would be capable of achieving. Alongside other reasons, Hitler gave this as an important factor in favour of waiting no longer to begin the war.[92] Only a short time later, he repeated in a speech to his generals that an internal revolution was impossible, and that the German people stood behind him, arguing that the time was ripe for war since the morale of the population 'can only grow worse'.[93] More than any other exponent of propaganda, Hitler had an extremely sensitive awareness of the tolerance level of the mass of the population—of whom he was at one and the same time both contemptuous and distrustful.[94] He sensed in autumn 1939, as his comments show, that, despite the new potential for patriotic loyalty which the war had created, and the extended apparatus for repression of nonconformist attitudes, the time of easy popularity was limited. However, for the time being at least, Hitler's own authority and immense popularity—the obverse of the apparatus of repression and terror—formed the central vehicle for consolidating and integrating society in a massive consensus for the regime, if a consensus based at least in part on misconceived notions of Hitler's war aims. Additional elements of the Führer cult—in particular the image of the war strategist of unparalleled genius—arose following the triumphant western campaign of 1940. But the longer the war lasted, and the greater the German sacrifices, the more inexorable was the inevitable, if at first surprisingly slow, decline and ultimate demise of the 'Führer myth'.

---

[91] *Meldungen*, pp. 34–6; and see Stokes, *SD*, pp. 379–95; Steinert, pp. 110–22.

[92] Domarus, p. 1234; Noakes and Pridham, p. 562.

[93] Domarus, p. 1426; Noakes and Pridham, p. 575.

[94] See A. Speer, *Erinnerungen*, Frankfurt a.M./Berlin, p. 229, for Hitler's concern to uphold popular morale, and in particular to avoid a fall in his own popularity from which internal crises for the regime could develop.

PART TWO

The Breaking of the 'Hitler Myth', 1940–1945

6

Blitzkrieg Triumph
High Peak of Popularity, 1940–1941

Germany is Hitler, and Hitler is Germany.

Nazi propaganda slogan, 1939

It is safe to say that the entire nation is filled with a believing trust in the Führer such as has never before existed to this extent.

The District Leader of Augsburg City, 1940

BY the time of Hitler's last national triumphs before the outbreak of war, the making of the 'Führer myth' was almost complete. Only one major attribute was still missing: that of the military genius. However, even before war broke out, the regime's propaganda experts were also at work on that strand of Hitler's image. The 10,000 metres of film recording Hitler at the grandiose military parade and celebrations for his fiftieth birthday in April 1939 consciously sought to portray him not only as a 'statesman', but also as 'the future military leader, taking muster of his armed forces'.[1] Once in the war, the image of Hitler as supreme war leader and military strategist came to dominate all other component parts of the 'Führer myth'. And although, as we saw, initial anxieties about another war were largely overcome by easy and painless victories, the start of the war can nevertheless be seen to mark a caesura in the development of the 'Hitler myth'.

From the earliest weeks, euphoria about military success was quickly dissipated by the economic restrictions and the material impact on daily life, even though, compared with the later years of the war, these appear in retrospect to have been minor forms of interference.[2] The psychological basis of Hitler's popularity as a national leader standing above and outside of the troubles of everyday life, was,

---

[1] F. Terveen, 'Der Filmbericht über Hitlers 50. Geburtstag. Ein Beispiel national-sozialistischer Selbstdarstellung und Propaganda', *VfZ*, vii (1959), 82.

[2] See Stokes, *SD*, pp. 375–95; and Kershaw, *Popular Opinion*, ch. 7.

however, not substantially affected by these material concerns. On the contrary: emotional attachment to Hitler was rooted in the notion that he represented the ideal of national community and national greatness, that he was leading Germany to greater prosperity, and that, whatever the immediate sacrifices, a bonanza for all was only just over the horizon. Exactly how this wonderland would be brought about was, of course, seldom systematically thought out.

However, the aura of the military genius paving the way for lasting prosperity through final victory could almost by definition last only so long as one glorious triumph after another—and all without significant material sacrifice and loss—was attained. As victory turned to defeat, domestic conditions deteriorated, belts had to be tightened and hardships increased, and the vision of utopia turned into the reality of total war and impending disaster, the function of the Hitler image as a compensation for the mounting miseries and sacrifices of daily existence gradually lost its effectiveness then collapsed almost completely. This second part of the book deals mainly with the progressive phases of this decline and fall, charted through the surviving traces of the changing popular receptivity to the propaganda image of Hitler during the war. Before turning to the decline of the 'Hitler myth', however, we need to sketch it at its absolute zenith, in the years when *Blitzkrieg* victories brought almost the whole of Europe under Hitler's command.

Most Germans were in expectant but uneasy mood during the first months of 1940. Despite the surprising ease of the victory over the Poles, the real test, it seemed clear, was yet to come. Daily life continued much as normal. Some new measures had, of course, been necessary, but on the whole changes brought about by the war were less incisive than they had been in 1914. Not least, the absence of any serious rationing of consumer goods, and the large number of exemptions from military service for skilled workers and farmers made it appear that the regime was well in control of developments, did not fear a war on the 1914–18 scale, and was even rather generous in its provisioning arrangements. Nevertheless, all this could not completely conceal the tension. There was a feeling that something was in the air, that it was the lull before the storm.[3] Few imagined at this stage the scale and speed of the German victories which over-

---

[3] On the general mood, see Stokes, *SD*, pp. 284 ff., 395 ff.; and Steinert, pp. 121 ff.

whelmed western Europe in the spring and early summer, culminating in such a comprehensive defeat of the old enemy, the French, in June, and prompting the toadying Field Marshal Keitel to declare that Hitler's strategic brilliance in preparing the campaign made him 'the greatest military commander of all time'.[4]

Hitler himself contributed in no small measure to the further enhancement of his image during these months of triumph. Between January 1940 and June 1941 he broadcast no fewer than nine major speeches, demonstrating his unshakeable confidence, strengthening morale, and giving further hope for an early end to the war. In later years, by contrast, he came to speak in public less and less frequently, despite being repeatedly urged to do so by Goebbels and others, evidently realizing only too well how closely the effectiveness of his rhetoric was dependent on being able to report success and to hold out hope for an end to the war.

Already during the uncanny calm of the 'phoney war' in the winter of 1939–40, Hitler had hinted at a successful end to the conflict during 1940, and at the same time had further blamed England and France for deliberately prolonging the war through their influence on previously neutral countries.[5] Such allegations paved the way for justification of the German occupation of Denmark and Norway in April 1940— justification made all the more credible by the appearance, at almost exactly the same time as the German navy, of British warships in Norwegian waters and of British troop landings at Narvik and Trondheim. The German explanation that the risky Scandinavian operation had been made necessary by the planned British landing and breach of neutrality had, therefore, the ring of plausibility and seems to have been largely accepted by the German population.[6] The occupation of Denmark and Norway, carried through with unexpectedly low losses and seen as a major blow for Britain, was celebrated as a 'great success for the bold, determined policy of the Führer',[7] whose birthday in April 1940 saw propagandists struggling to find new superlatives to express the 'unshakeable loyalty' of his 'following'.[8] In the last reports they were able to compile, in April 1940, *Sopade* observers were still

---

[4] Fest, p. 862.
[5] See Stokes, *SD*, pp. 282–8.
[6] The German claim was not unfounded. See D. Irving, *Hitler's War*, London, 1977, pp. 82–6. See also Steinert, pp. 123–4; and Stokes, *SD*, pp. 481–2.
[7] GStA, MA 106683, RPvS, 7 May 1940.
[8] e.g. GStA, MA 106678, RPvOf/MF, 8 May 1940.

noting that 'many prefer to keep Hitler than to envisage what could come after a defeat', that fear of chaos and revolution still pre-dominated among the bourgeoisie, but that 'there is no doubt that up to now the majority of the people is still convinced of Germany's victory'.[9] A report from around the same time which reached the London bureau of the *Neu Beginnen* organization, based on conversa-tions with an elderly, formerly active member of the SPD, living in a central German city, painted a similar picture of opinion. Most workers, it was claimed, thought that it would be much worse for Germany if it lost the war, that a more draconian Versailles, the dismembering of Germany, and massive unemployment would be the consequence. German youth stood united behind the Nazis, and 'believe unconditionally in Hitler'. They thought him a genuine socialist who had tackled the capitalists—something the SPD had failed to do, and had hopes for a brighter future when the war was won.[10] And ordinary soldiers, writing to relatives from the Front in April 1940, spoke naïvely of their belief that 'as long as we have the front soldier Adolf Hitler, there will be only loyalty, bravery, and justice for his people', and that 'the most beautiful day in the life of our Führer has still to come', the day on which 'all peoples have recovered their freedom, peace, and equality'.[11]

The German explanation for the invasion of Belgium and Holland on 10 May 1940—that it had been necessary in order to forestall a breach of neutrality by the enemy—carried less conviction than it had done in the Scandinavian operation.[12] This was in itself, however, of little significance in an atmosphere impregnated with tension, and anxiety that the western offensive could not conceivably go as smoothly as the Polish and Scandinavian campaigns.[13] The 'special announcements' on the German radio of the rapid, almost un-impeded, advance of the Wehrmacht in the west could therefore scarcely be believed. A month after the offensive had begun, a fairly typical internal report—from the Government President of Swabia—eulogized: 'All followed the burgeoning world-historical success with

[9] *DBS*, vii. 221–2, 8 Apr. 1940, reports from Berlin and Rhineland-Westphalia.

[10] WL, 'Deutsche Inlandsberichte', No. 61, 29 Apr. 1940.

[11] *Das andere Gesicht des Krieges. Deutsche Feldpostbriefe 1939–1945*, ed. O. Buchbender and R. Sterz, Munich, 1982, p. 51.

[12] The SD nevertheless adjudged German propaganda on the breach of neutrality to have been effective. See Steinert, pp. 125–6.

[13] *Meldungen*, p. 66.

breathless tension, proud admiration, and praise for the brave troops and the Führer's genius. This was even more the case, since our losses were again relatively small. The Führer's call to fly flags on 5. 6. 1940 met with a joyful response everywhere. In the peal of bells resound the prayers for Führer and army and for a happy end to the struggle for Germany's freedom and future.'[14]

In his report a month later, when the entry of German troops in Paris on 14 June and the official French capitulation in Compiègne on 22 June—symbolically wiping out the humiliation of the German capitulation in the same spot in 1918—had raised Hitler's standing to unsurpassed heights, the same Government President of Swabia provided his own description of the mood. The 'most glorious and mighty victory of all time' had brought forth a tide of 'jubilation, admiration, awe, pride, competitiveness in achievement and devotion, certainty of victory and hope for peace', as 'the entire people, together with the Führer, humbly thanked the Lord God for his blessing'. All 'well-meaning' citizens were said to have recognized 'wholly, joyfully, and thankfully the superhuman greatness of the Führer and his work', and, confronted with this 'greatness', 'all pettiness and grumbling is silenced'.[15] The, by contrast, normally sober reports of the District Leader of Augsburg City added that belief and trust in the Führer had reached an unprecedented level, and that 'if an increase in feeling for Adolf Hitler was still possible, it had become reality with the day of the return to Berlin' from the western Front.[16]

The function of the victories in providing the regime with even more extensive popular backing seems undeniable. The SD reported 'a previously unprecedented inner solidarity' and close bonds between *Front* and *Heimat* following the triumph, which had 'everywhere removed a receptive ground for the activity of opposing groups' and produced a hostile climate for any criticism.[17] Opponents of the regime themselves wrote later of the difficulties they faced in this climate of opinion, and some even admitted that it was hard to remain aloof from the jubilant victory mood.[18] Reports from the Wehrmacht

[14] GStA, MA 106683, RPvS, 10 June 1940.

[15] Ibid., 9 July 1940.

[16] StANeu, vorl. LO A5, KL Augsburg-Stadt, 10 July 1940.

[17] *Meldungen*, pp. 77–8. See also GStA, MA 106671, RPvOB, 8 June 1940; MA 106678, RPvOF/MF, 8 July 1940.

[18] See e.g. the remarks of Carl Severing, cited in Stokes, *SD*, p. 399; and the recollections of a foreman in the Messerschmitt works in Augsburg, cited in W. Domarus, *Nationalsozialismus, Krieg und Bevölkerung*, Munich, 1977, p. 90.

'Armaments Inspectorates' claimed that workers on reserved occupations in armaments factories did not want to be left out of the army and were pressing to join up.[19] A drop in cases coming before the political 'Special Courts' can also be seen as a reflection of the fall in expression of critical opinion in the summer of 1940.[20]

It seemed clear to many that with the defeat of France a glorious peace was imminent. A letter to a Front soldier from a citizen of Görlitz in late June or early July 1940 undoubtedly spoke for many in stating that, following the 'unimaginably great' events which had been seen each week in the newsreels, 'we will never be able to thank the Führer and brave army enough for sparing us at home the horrors of war', and that an 'immensely great' future awaited Germany 'in the construction of Europe after the final victory'.[21] Only the defeat of Britain—now widely presumed to be a matter of course—stood in the way, it seemed, of that final victory, and the intoxication of the triumph over the French mingled with a widespread desire, whipped up by almost hysterical anti-British hate propaganda, for the total destruction of Britain. For the first and almost the only time in the Second World War, there was what can fairly be described as a generally pervading popular 'war mood', disdaining any premature and presumed over-generous peace with Britain, and even somewhat disappointed with Hitler's new and 'final' peace offer of 19 July, aimed at assuaging world opinion. According to one report, people could hardly wait for the attack to start, and everybody wanted to be present at Britain's impending defeat. And if there had been a degree of sympathy with the other defeated peoples—a doubtful claim, it has to be said, particularly with regard to the Poles—in this case 'the entire population took the view that England should at all costs be destroyed'.[22]

In the event, of course, the great invasion never took place, and as the second war winter approached, the mood in autumn 1940 began to sag. Reports still spoke of the impatience with which people awaited the final attack on Britain. But whatever the extent of anti-British

[19] BA/MA, RW 20–7/16, 'Geschichte der Rüstungsinspektion VII', p. 105.

[20] Steinert, p. 137; BAK, R22/3379, OLGP München 3 Sept. 1940.

[21] *Das andere Gesicht des Krieges*, p. 62.

[22] StANeu, vorl. LO A5, KL Augsburg-Stadt, 10 Aug. 1940. A violently anti-British mood was also highlighted in the reports of the Bavarian Government Presidents: GStA, MA 106678, RPvOF/MF, 7 Aug. 1940; MA 106681, RPvUF, 10 Aug. 1940; MA 106683, RPvS, 8 Aug. 1940; MA 106673, RPvNB/OP, 8 Aug. 1940.

feeling, the impatience was first and foremost a sign that the final peace showed no immediate signs of becoming reality. The euphoria of the summer gradually gave way to the pessimistic feeling that it might after all be a long war. Hitler's standing was as yet unaffected. Most were confident that his military and political genius would once again pick out the correct moment for the decisive blow against Britain, and had no inkling in autumn 1940 that 'Operation Sealion' had been postponed indefinitely.

The continued unbroken trust in the Führer down to spring 1941 rested in no small measure on the lack of serious interference of the war in the conditions of 'everyday life'. And it was given new nourishment by a series of Hitler speeches in late 1940 and early 1941 which aimed to strengthen confidence in final victory and create the impression that the decisive strike to end the war—people still presumed that it would be against Britain—would take place in the course of the next twelve months.[23]

The function of the 'Führer myth' in deflecting from 'everyday' concerns and in bolstering the basis of support for the regime comes across clearly in reports on the impact of Hitler's speeches, which the SD was keen to monitor. In November 1940, for example, 'personal economic worries' in the light of the coming second war winter were said to be widespread and to have given rise to 'discontented and sceptical thoughts'. Reports from all over Germany indicated, however, that Hitler's speech to the 'Old Fighters' of the Movement on 8 November had dispelled such feelings and reinvigorated 'extensive sections of the population'. One comment from Schwerin, cited as typical, stated that 'When the Führer speaks, all doubts fall away and one is ashamed of ever doubting whether the right moment for our actions would be exploited.'[24] Similar reactions were registered by SD agencies in Lower Franconia in early 1941. Pessimists had been saying that the war could last between four and seven years, and that Britain, which had never lost a war, would not lose this one either. After Hitler's speech of 24 February 1941, such views were said to have disappeared, and the dominant opinion was that 'the war would be victoriously concluded in summer 1941'. Hitler's confidence in early victory made a deep impression, and it was widely believed that the

[23] The text of speeches by Hitler on 10 Dec. 1940, and 30 Jan., 24 Feb., and 16 Mar. 1941 is in Domarus, pp. 1626–34, 1667–70, 1674–5.

[24] *MadR*, v. 1763, 14 Nov. 1940.

final push would begin in March or April.[25] One woman, remarking on 'how wonderful it was, with what faith the Führer spoke', was reported as saying it took just such a speech to show 'how faint-hearted one had become through the routine of everyday life', and that she could now look to the future with confidence again.[26] After Hitler had again suggested in a speech in mid-March 1941 that Britain would be conquered and the war ended finally in Germany's favour within the next year, people were heard to remark that 'the Führer had never held out a prospect of something which had not happened', and that one could therefore unquestionably rely upon the imminent defeat of Britain and end of the war.[27] The naïve, almost religious basis of belief in Hitler is clearly visible in such reports, which show too, however, that people were above all listening in Hitler's speeches for hints of an early end to the war, and that his popular standing depended heavily upon the fulfilment of such hopes. The war fever of summer 1940 was a passing phase, which by the end of that year had again been replaced by the dominant tone of impatient longing for the end of the war.

When the coup in Yugoslavia in spring 1941 interfered with Hitler's plans for an attack on the Soviet Union (Britain's last potential Continental ally) and a deterioration in mood set in owing to the threatening extension of the war to the Balkans, SD soundings of opinion again registered 'with what childlike trust the most ordinary people in particular look up to the Führer and our leadership of state', convinced that ' "the Führer has taken it into account and will deal properly with it" '.[28] 'The Führer' had become like a drug for the people, needed for reassurance whenever doubts, worries, and uncertainties began to mount. The SD in the industrial town of Schweinfurt in Lower Franconia reported complaints in March 1941 from the poorer sections of the population that badges bearing a picture of the Führer could only be obtained through a sizeable contribution to Winter Aid collectors, and that there were too few to satisfy the demand.[29] And there were reports from many parts of the Reich that 'a newsreel without pictures of the Führer was not regarded

[25] StAW, SE/13, AS Bad Kissingen, 25 Feb. 1941.
[26] StAW, SD/22, AS Schweinfurt, 4 Mar. 1941.
[27] StAW, SD/35, HAS Würzburg, 25 Mar. 1941; SD/23, AS Würzburg, 18 Mar. 1941; and see SD/22, AS Schweinfurt, 18 Mar. 1941; SD/17, AS Kitzingen, 18 Mar. 1941.
[28] StAW, SD/17, AS Kitzingen, 1 Apr.1941. See also *Meldungen*, p. 129; Steinert, pp. 125–6.
[29] StAW, SD/22, AS Schweinfurt, 7 Mar. 1941.

as up to standard'. 'People always want to see how the Führer looks, whether he is serious or laughing,' and had expressed disappointment that they had not even heard his voice for a long time in the newsreels, for, as one report put it, 'the words of the Führer are gospel for the people'.[30]

Orders went out for only simple celebrations of Hitler's birthday on 20 April 1941 on account of the war. Even so, such crowds gathered that in parts of Lower Bavaria and the upper Palatinate halls reserved for the ceremonies were overfilled and had to be closed off by the police.[31] The tone of the festivities was set by Göring's public eulogy, stating: 'We . . . look back to an unbroken chain of glorious victories such as only one man could attain in a single year of his life, one who is not only a statesman and military commander, but at the same time also Leader and man of the people: our Führer . . .'[32] Ten-year-olds being sworn into the *Deutsches Jungvolk* and *Deutsche Jungmädelschaft* on that day had to pledge an almost religious vow: 'You, Führer, are for us our command! In your name, we stand. The Reich is the goal of our struggle. It is beginning and end.'[33]

Confidence in Hitler was unbounded. The central digest of SD reports, soon after the beginning of the Balkan campaign on 6 April 1941, registered 'unconditional confidence' that the campaign in Yugoslavia and Greece would rapidly end in victory. Some thought it might last as little as three weeks, as in Norway; hardly anyone reckoned on longer than six to eight weeks.[34] And its successful conclusion indeed took less than three weeks. Though the campaign scarcely gripped the imagination as the victories in the west had done—some reports hinted that the significance of the campaign had not been properly grasped, and that the victories had been unable to affect the popular mood for more than a very short time—it seemed to provide yet another example of Hitler's strategic genius. But, as it turned out, it was the last instance of a complete *Blitzkrieg* triumph accompanied by the minimal losses which were once more a central element in the popular response to the Balkan success.[35] Also more significant than the somewhat diminished jubilation for the victories

[30] *Meldungen*, pp. 116–17; StAW, SD/17, AS Kitzingen, 21 Mar. 1941.

[31] GStA, MA 106674, RPvNB/OP, 8 May 1941.

[32] *Rheinisch-Westfälische Zeitung*, 20 Apr. 1941.

[33] Heyen, p. 228.

[34] *Meldungen*, p. 133; Steinert, p. 187; Stokes, *SD*, p. 334.

[35] GStA, MA 106674, RPvNB/OP, 8 May 1941; MA 106681, RPvUF, 12 May 1941.

was the 'hope and urgent desire that the war can still be ended in this year' [36] The extension of the theatre of war to south-eastern Europe had, despite the German triumph, led to increased concern that the war could now drag on for a long time.[37] The shadow darkened through rumours about worsening relations with the Soviet Union and news of troop movements on the eastern borders of the Reich. And the fears were not lessened by comments in recent Hitler speeches hinting at a 'hard year of struggle' ahead, and promising better weapons for the Wehrmacht 'next year'.[38] On the eve of the invasion of the Soviet Union, however, Hitler's popular standing was undiminished, and confidence in his leadership among the great majority of the population unbroken.

The gulf between Hitler's immense popularity and the generally low standing of the Party had nevertheless if anything widened still further in the first wartime years. While the war certainly strengthened affective notions of patriotic unity, this never remotely matched up to the ideal of the 'people's community' proclaimed and preached by the Party. The field-grey of the Wehrmacht and a new generation of military heroes made the brown-shirted Party functionaries stand out in even more unattractive light than before the war. The contrast between the enthusiasm for the Wehrmacht and the disdain for the Party was striking. The Führer, too, had demonstratively donned field-grey at the start of the war, to emphasize his unity with his troops and his image as the first soldier of the Reich, whereas the unpopular Party hacks were often seen as shirkers, avoiding their duty at the Front. The complaint of farmers in one district of Upper Franconia already in September 1939, about the 'Old Fighters' of the Party who were 'hanging about' at home in Party uniform and occupying 'unimportant Party offices' when they now had a good 'opportunity to fight' for something, was not the expression of an isolated sentiment.[39]

[36] GStA, MA 106681, RPvUF, 12 May 1941.

[37] GStA, MA 106674, RPvNB/OP, 8 May 1941.

[38] Domarus, pp. 1692, 1708 ('Aufruf zum 2. Kriegshilfswerk für das Deutsche Rote Kreuz', 18 Apr. 1941; report on the Balkan campaign to the Reichstag, 4 May 1941). For reactions, see GStA, MA 106674, RPvNB/OP, 8 May 1941; MA 106684, RPvS, 10 June 1941; MA 106671, RPvOB, 10 June 1941; *Meldungen*, p. 143; Steinert, pp. 188 ff.; Stokes, *SD*, pp. 337, 490.

[39] StAB, K8/III, 18473, LR Ebermannstadt, 30 Sept. 1939; see also BAK, R22/3355, OLGP Bamberg, 1 July 1940.

Despite frequent references in the press to the number of Party functionaries in leading posts at the Front, such criticisms persisted.

Though they were the inexhaustible propagandists of the 'Führer myth', the Party functionaries were unable to bask in the reflected glow of Hitler's own popularity. While he was perceived to be concerned with the great strategic issues of war leadership, the representatives of the Party had to tackle the tedious, and often unpopular, workaday matters affecting daily life in the *Heimat*. And while the Führer and his army could claim the glory for military successes, the increased—and often voluntary—efforts of members of Party affiliates to cope with the social problems of individuals or groups particularly affected by the war tended to bring contact with disgruntled 'people's comrades' but few plaudits and little prestige.[40] The inability of the Party substantially to improve its image despite the personal sacrifices frequently shown by individuals in, for instance, the NSV (the Party's welfare organization), had its roots in the unpopularity of so many manifestations of the Party's social and political role during the 1930s: the alienation produced by the attacks on the Christian Churches, the overbearing arrogance of the 'little Hitlers', the hooliganism and loutish vulgarity of the organized mobs, and the irremovable taint of corruption and venality. All this stood in marked contrast to the, in many senses, basically conservative and pseudo-religious feelings so frequently underlying and characterizing belief in Hitler. As strange as it sounds, the great popularity of Hitler already before the war had for the most part little to do with fanatical belief in the central tenets of the Hitlerian racial-imperialist 'world-view', and even less to do with belief in the Party, whose leader he was. And during the war, while the Party failed to increase its own popularity, Hitler could benefit as the focus of a widespread consensus between 1939 and 1941 among the vast majority of the population about the successful course of the war and the favourable prospects for an early and glorious peace.

Although in the first war years the Party substantially cut down the number of meetings devoted to 'training' in ideological matters—which had never enjoyed much popularity—and concentrated in its regular work in the localities on trying to fulfil 'the popular demand for a more lively participation in the events of the day', as one report

[40] See Stokes, *SD*, pp. 499ff.

put it, it was unable to build up much interest in Party work or to enhance the popularity of the local Party organizations. Party members and SA men, who in 1933 had seen themselves as posing a radical, populist alternative to the conservative Reichswehr, now took a back seat and simply provided the setting for the triumphant reception of young officers of the Wehrmacht, heroes home on leave from the Front recounting tales of stirring deeds which had earned them the *Ritterkreuz*.[41] At one function staged by the Party in Schweinfurt in October 1940, for example, the local population turned out in force to welcome U-Boat veterans at a recruiting session for the navy, but the same people 'were almost entirely missing at the other functions of the NSDAP'.[42] SD reporters in Lower Franconia referred a few months later to a 'tiredness' with ideological 'education' among Party members as well as the general public, and remarked that the winning over of those people who still stood aloof from the Party was 'still an unsolved problem'.[43] People were largely interested only in the Wehrmacht and 'how things were out there' at the Front.[44]

In the war, the Party had, in fact, to take on a number of new tasks, some of them important in the context of social welfare and organization, though not necessarily guaranteed to increase the popularity of the local functionaries. For instance, Local Peasant Leaders or Mayors (who were often also Party functionaries) had to adjudicate on the 'reserved occupation' applications of farmers in the neighbourhood. This was, of course, an open invitation to trivial forms of corruption and bribery, and the decisions, however reached, invariably caused bad blood among the families of those whose applications had been turned down. Policing of black-out restrictions was another task which fell to local Party representatives and, in the early war years when air raids seemed scarcely a menace, frequently formed another source of irritation. The undertaking of the welfare of illegitimate children of soldiers who had been killed, the organization of accommodation and support for those evacuated from the western borders of the Reich already in autumn 1939, or the administration of packages to be sent to relatives at the Front, were all tasks which fell to the Nazi welfare organization, the NSV. However, such activities at

[41] GStA, MA 106674, RPvNB/OP, 8 Mar. 1941.

[42] StAW, SD/31, SD-Abschnitt Würzburg, 4 Nov. 1940, 'Volksleben und National-sozialismus'.

[43] StAW, SD/10/12, AS Würzburg, 13 Feb. 1941.

[44] StAW, SD/19, AS Lohr, 25 Mar. 1941.

best brought some credit to the NSV itself, with little rubbing off onto the main organization, the NSDAP.[45]

Some Party reports interpreted the increased claims on the Party as a sign of growing confidence in its activities.[46] These seem highly optimistic, however, in the light of numerous reports, especially from country districts, in which the extended interference of the Party in everyday affairs, especially in welfare and economic matters, was subjected to fierce criticism.[47] And in the big cities—to go from the relatively sensitive and 'socially conscious' reports of the District Leader of Augsburg-Stadt—the old attacks on the parasitic existence of Party functionaries gained new strength in wartime conditions; the extravagance of Party buildings was set alongside the slums in which it was said the great mass of the population still had to live; and 'especially unfavourable note is taken of the feudal life and dwelling of leaders of Party and State'. The same population which hero-worshipped Hitler would not tolerate 'little tin-pot gods (*Nebengötter*) alongside the Führer', and wanted an end to 'this glorification of persons who would otherwise practically be nobodies' and to the uncalled for luxury-living in a Party which had come to power stating that it would wipe out such corruption.[48] Such strong feelings about the Party 'bigwigs', whose life-style was seen to clash so vividly with the austere living conditions of the bulk of the population, were commonplace in the Germany of early 1941.[49]

An indicator of popular views of Party leaders can be seen in the wild rumours which circulated from time to time about prominent figures in the NSDAP. These rumours were no doubt often started by foreign broadcasts or opponents of the regime within Germany. But

[45] On the NSV and Nazi wartime 'welfare' and 'social work', see C. A. A. Smith, 'The National Socialist organisation NSV: "NS-People's Welfare"', propaganda and influence, 1933–1945', Univ. of Edinburgh Ph.D. thesis 1986, ch. 7.

[46] e.g. StANeu, Vorl. LO A5, KL Augsburg-Stadt, 9 Mar., 10 Aug., 10 Oct. 1940.

[47] Selective economic support granted by the Party or NSV to specific individuals or families and the level of family allowances were the subject of envy and criticism in rural areas. And perceptions of over-generous financial support for evacuees, such as those from the Saarland, who apparently showed little aptitude for hard labour on the farm, prompted farmers to threaten to end contributions to the NSV. See e.g. StAB, K8/III, 18473, GKF Ebermannstadt, 31 July, 30 Aug. 1940; LR Ebermannstadt, 31 July 1940; GStA, MA 106671, RPvOB, 10 May 1941.

[48] StANeu, vorl. LO A5, KL Augsburg-Stadt, 10 Aug. 10 Nov. 1940.

[49] See Steinert, p. 174. A particular target of abuse was the high life of Party officials, amid the general austerity enjoying themselves in top hotels, and prompting comparisons with the state of affairs during the First World War—StAW, SD/23, AS Würzburg, 8 Apr. 1941; StAM, LRA 61618, GP Mittenwald, 25 Feb. 1941.

they were evidently believed by a great many people. In 1940, for example, there were widespread rumours that Julius Streicher, the detestable Jew-baiter of Nuremberg who at that time had to come before Göring—of all people—to face charges of corruption, had fled across the border with 30 million Reichmarks.[50] Above all, the flight of Rudolf Heß to Scotland gave rise to every conceivable kind of speculation—so much so that one report in Bavaria dubbed May 1941 'the month of rumours',[51] as tales surfaced everywhere about the disloyalty, corruption, theft on a grand scale, and flight abroad of Reich notables such as Himmler and Ley and various Bavarian Party bosses, among them Gauleiter Adolf Wagner, said to have been caught trying to get across the Swiss border with 22 million Reichmarks he had stolen from the confiscated property of dissolved monasteries.[52] A similar 'flood of rumours and speculation, such as had hardly been the case after any other event',[53] also spread like a bushfire in other parts of Germany. According to different versions, Count Helldorf, Police President of Berlin and later implicated in the July plot of 1944 against Hitler, Julius Streicher, Alfred Rosenberg, Adolf Wagner, and the 'blood and soil' guru of Nazi agricultural policy Walther Darré, had been arrested for complicity in Heß's 'treason', and some of them already shot. Lists of 'intolerable' local leaders of Party, Labour Front, and NSV were also rumoured to have been drawn up.[54] Clearly, the Party's public standing was extraordinarily low, even in this victorious phase of the war. It was evidently widely felt that its representatives were capable of more or less any form of major misdemeanour.

In contrast, a basic component of the Hitler image was his presumed innocence of any of the corruption and self-centredness with which his underlings were tainted. It is remarkable, for instance, how seldom allegations of Hitler's material corruption occur in the 1,400 or so cases among the Munich 'Special Court' files in which people stood specifically accused of a wide variety of insulting comments about the Führer.[55] The continued belief in the 'untainted

[50] GStA, MA 106678, RPvOF/MF, 7 Apr. 1940; BAK, R22/3381, OLGP Nürnberg, 8 Mar., 8 May, 4 Nov. 1940; GenStA Nürnberg, 11 Apr. 1940; StAB, K8/III, 18473, GKF Ebermannstadt, 29 Mar. 1940; LR Ebermannstadt, 30 Mar. 1940.

[51] GStA, MA 106671, RPvOB, 10 June 1941.

[52] StANeu, vorl. LO 15, Fo. 168, KL Memmingen, n.d. (end of May 1941). Such rumours were mentioned in almost all reports around this time.

[53] *Meldungen*, p. 146.   [54] Stokes, *SD*, pp. 511–12.

[55] SGM files in StAM.

Führer' alongside the castigations of Party corruption blinded people now as earlier to the fateful path of destruction along which the institutionalized undermining of constitutional and legal norms in the 'Hitler State' and the fanatical pursuit of the Führer's 'selfless' goals was taking Germany. Compared with such an inexorable path to disaster, still camouflaged by the 'Hitler myth', the self-seeking aggrandisement of Party bosses, however much it offended social and political sensitivities, was only of fringe importance.

In the euphoria which had followed the victory over France, there was even some talk that when the war was over the Party would be dissolved by the Wehrmacht and Germany would become a 'pure military state'.[56] A few months later, in November 1940, a report from the Würzburg SD agency devoted its attention squarely to the impact of the war on the Party's standing. It concluded that in the light of the great events of the war, Party affairs had necessarily been forced into the background, and divided reactions into three groups. The first group, that of ordinary soldiers, had found a new cameraderie at the Front, which had led 'to a loosening of ties to the Party and its affiliations at home'. Some soldiers had said that when the war was over they did not want to take up Party work any longer: 'Many of them think that they have done enough through their service at the Front or also behind the front-lines, and point to those of similar age or younger who were not soldiers.' The second group, of those—even including some Party members—who had previously been apathetic or negatively disposed towards the Party, thought that the time had now come when they could air their feelings. Among the things they criticized were the arrogant behaviour of Party leaders, their lenient treatment when misdemeanours came to light, the fact that 'the awaited purge in the Party had not taken place', the wringing of money out of the people in constant collections, and the 'large, elegant cars' in which Party functionaries travelled to and from work. The third group comprised the Party activists and functionaries themselves, who were finding it increasingly difficult to recruit new willing Party workers at the same time that their own work-load was being considerably enlarged. 'Political Leaders' in the localities, and especially the Block and Cell Leaders (that is, those who most directly came into contact with ordinary citizens and most plainly encountered popular

---

[56] StAW, SD/31, SD-Abschnitt Würzburg, 13 June, 12 Sept. 1940, 'Volksleben und Nationalsozialismus'.

feeling), were, the report stated, suffering from the fact that 'their work was not properly appreciated and acknowledged either by people's comrades or by superior Party offices'.[57]

An even more devastating depiction of the unpopularity of the Party and of many aspects of the Nazi regime was provided by the Würzburg SD office three months later. A 'new illegal Party', it was somewhat picturesquely alleged, seemed in the process of creation out of all those—evidently disparate individuals and groups—united in their opposition to National Socialism and forming on that basis their assessment of domestic politics and the war situation. Even some members of the Party and its affiliates were said to be included. Critics of the regime were reported to be openly venting their displeasure 'at new laws, announcements of the government about future Party buildings, the planned social legislation, school reform, etc.', and pointed to 'the higher taxes, the restrictions on personal freedom, the "threat to the Christian philosophy", the promotions in the civil service almost solely on the basis of attitude and Party membership without any consideration of ability, the activity of the Gestapo, the "reign of terror" (*Schreckensregiment*), the "corruption"', and the mismanagement of Party hacks and bosses, and were said to be conveying their discontent and doubts 'to ever wider circles'.[58]

Poor mood and deep distaste for the Party and its representatives were evidently, then, current before the 'Heß affair' had its dramatic impact in May 1941. But as the astonishing news broke of Heß's flight to Scotland, the popular response ran true to type: the 'Heß case' was catastrophic for the Party's image, but there were hardly any negative repercussions on Hitler's prestige. In fact, there was much sympathy expressed for the Führer who had this to suffer on top of all his other worries.[59]

The central SD digest of all the regional reports received at headquarters indicated 'great dismay' and, among Party members in particular, 'deep depression'.[60] Bavarian reports spoke of 'paralysing horror' at the news,[61] and—with typical exaggeration—of a mood

[57] Ibid., 25 Nov. 1940.

[58] StAW, SD/23, AS Würzburg, 25 Feb. 1941.

[59] *Meldungen*, pp. 145–6; Steinert, p. 195; Stokes, *SD*, p. 511; GStA, MA 106684, RPvS, 10 June 1941; MA 106679, RPvOF/MF, 8 June 1941; StAM, LRA 29655, GP Anger, 29 May 1941; LRA 135114, LR Mühldorf, 4 June 1941.

[60] *Meldungen*, pp. 145–6.

[61] GStA, MA 106684, RPvS, 10 June 1941.

comparable to that of 1917,[62] while others commented that workers were thinking it was the beginning of the end of the Party and the Third Reich, and that rumours were abroad about disturbances in Munich.[63] According to a lengthy and differentiated report from the SD in Leipzig, Party members were 'completely shocked' and regarded the affair as 'a lost battle', taking the view that the blow to the Party was at least twice as bad as that of the SA crisis of 1934. Business circles condemned Heß's action as treachery against Führer and people, and regarded press and radio reports—which were universally scorned—as a 'Party swindle'. There was sympathy for Hitler himself, who was continually being let down by his old compatriots. Some saw it as the beginning of the end of Nazism, which had again almost 'run itself to death with victories'. The commencement of the major attack on Britain and 'the complete destruction of the island' was now seen as urgent; Germany, it was felt, could last a third war winter, but sabotage would increase, and it would not be surprising if another 'November 1918' was the result. The reported comments among Leipzig workers also hinted at a possible prolongation of the war through the entry of America into the conflict, and it was seen as vital that the Führer bring about 'a lightning quick destruction of England—with gas if necessary'. Finally, the 'intelligentsia' and scholarly circles—presumably attached to Leipzig University—in condemning Heß reportedly included some reproaches for Hitler for selecting such a 'mentally disturbed person as his possible successor', though it was immediately added that most members of such circles were 'nevertheless convinced that the Führer no longer hears at all about the actual mood and situation within the Reich itself and that most things are kept from him'.[64]

The essential basis of the 'Führer myth'—his ignorance of the 'dark side' of Nazism—was evidently still functioning. 'The Führer, yes! The Party, no!'[65] amounted to a widely prevailing view on the eve of

[62] StAM, LRA 61618, GP Mittenwald, 24 May 1941.

[63] StAM, LRA 135114, GP Kraiburg, 29 May 1941. See also GStA, MA 106674, RPvNB/OP, 8 June 1941; MA 106679, RPvOF/MF, 8 June 1941; MA 106671, RPvOB, 10 June 1941; MA 106681, RPvUF, 11 June 1941; BAK, R22/3355, OLGP Bamberg, 1 July 1941.

[64] IWM, 'Aus deutschen Urkunden', unpublished documentation, n.d., pp. 243–6. For Nazi propaganda on the 'Heß affair', and its impact, see M. Balfour, *Propaganda in War, 1939–1945*, London, 1979, pp. 217–21.

[65] H. Picker, *Hitlers Tischgespräche im Führerhauptquartier 1941 bis 1942*, Stuttgart, 1963, p. 132.

the invasion of the Soviet Union. Trust in Hitler was scarcely affected by the lapses in morale, the poor mood, and the daily antagonisms generally predominant in shaping popular opinion during the spring and early summer of 1941. Hitler's extraordinary popular standing, built up in the peacetime years on the foundations of his perceived personal achievement in overcoming economic and political crisis, ridding Germany of unemployment, and making the nation great again through an astonishing series of diplomatic coups, was maintained in the first phase of the war; it was then even further elevated through the scarcely conceivable run of military victories attained with minimal loss and sacrifice and, not least, through the prospect he continued to hold up of an imminent glorious end to the war. But, despite initial successes in the eastern campaign, the military setbacks of the first winter in Russia marked the end of the 'sunny Hitler weather'—the run of the easy triumphs which had formed the corner-stone of the 'Führer myth'. It was the beginning of the downward spiral in Hitler's popularity.

7

The War turns Sour
The 'Hitler Myth' starts to crumble

Now it is especially the occupation of Stalingrad itself which will
be completed. . . . And you can be sure that nobody will get us
away again from this place!

Hitler, 30 Sept. 1942

The Führer has also spoken himself about how important
Stalingrad is, and now he has gone and lost it.

Augsburg salesman, 3 Feb. 1943

FOLLOWING the eighteen months of German victory and triumph in
Poland, Scandinavia, the west and south-east of Europe between
September 1939 and April 1941, the next eighteen months from the
beginning of the Russian campaign on 22 June 1941 to the German
defeat in Stalingrad at the end of January 1943 brought the decisive
change in the course of the war and the downturn of Germany's
military fortune. In autumn 1941 the German advance into Russia,
which had begun so spectacularly, ground to a halt on the approach to
Moscow, and a disastrous retreat in the icy wastes of the Russian
winter could only be staved off with difficulty and at high human cost,
leaving an ill-equipped army to endure the arctic conditions. On
11 December 1941, Germany declared war on the United States of
America. An early end to the conflict was now hard to imagine. And in
1942 the first major bombings of German cities were carried out by
allied air flotillas, and as the Luftwaffe lost control of the skies many
Germans began to experience with dread the sort of terror-bombing
which their own airforce had inflicted on numerous European cities
since 1939 and which the allies were now returning with immeasurably
greater force and concentration.

In this phase, too, the ideological obsessions, the immorality and
criminality of the regime, and—as Germany came under pressure for
the first time—the draconian repression of the police state, were

becoming more and more evident, and could increasingly be recognized by the ordinary civilian population. Information filtering back home from soldiers on leave told of the unparalleled barbarity of the ideological warfare on the eastern Front, where Soviet commissars were being shot on capture and Jews massacred in their thousands. Inside the Reich, worrying stories leaked out about the mentally ill and incurably sick being gassed in asylums; the regime's anti-Christian thrust was unmistakable again in the reopened struggle with, especially, the Catholic Church; and attacks on the conservative forces in army and State, and the defamation of civil servants and judges, reflected the strengthening of the forces of naked power and repression as ordered administration and the remnants of the constitutional State were undermined by the expanding network of the Security Police.

Only the very perceptive and those with clear information and a wide perspective over events could fully grasp the interrelationship of these developments. And given the brutalizing effect of the war itself and the undeniable impact of at least parts of the ideological message which had been hammered into Germans for years, by no means all of what was taking place and would lead Germany into the abyss was unwelcome or unpopular. Nevertheless, though the currents of genuine popular opinion are now even more difficult to evaluate than they had been earlier, given the intensified persecution from 1942 onwards of even relatively trivial 'offences' of criticizing the regime or 'subverting' the wartime ordinances, every sign points towards the growth in this period of a 'silent majority' increasingly critical of the Nazi regime—even if the criticism was often only obliquely expressed—and ready to blame it for the mounting miseries of the war.

The tightening net of repression and the increased care taken to avoid 'risky' remarks naturally had a direct effect on expressions of opinion about Hitler himself. Negative comment about the Führer had, of course, always been dangerous, but now it was tantamount to high treason and was punished accordingly. This has to be taken into account in assessing the significance of the recorded attitudes towards Hitler in the 'opinion reports' of the regime's agents. The usually veiled criticism contained in the report material, and the open comment coming to light in denunciations and court prosecutions, have necessarily to be regarded as the tip of the iceberg. Nevertheless, the dominant impression to be gleaned from all the available evidence in this period is that, despite the decisive transformation in the balance of military power and the massive worsening of the mood of the bulk of the German population, the 'Hitler myth'—though unquestionably starting to crumble and lose its aura of untouchability—still retained much strength and potency. Since trust in Hitler had owed a great deal to the belief that he would lead Germany to a rapid and glorious peace, since despair of an early end to the war was the essential reason for the waning morale, and since the failure of the *Blitzkrieg* in the USSR and the declaration of war on the USA made it difficult in logic to hold anyone other than Hitler responsible for the prolonging of the war, it is worth enquiring why the 'Hitler myth' did not collapse more quickly than was evidently the case.

The first part of an explanation would be the extent of belief in Hitler which had built up in the years before 1940. Although the extremes of the personality cult had probably gripped only a minority of the population, it was a minority with power and influence. Moreover, *elements* of the personality cult had attained far wider resonance and, as we have seen in earlier chapters, can be said to have affected the vast majority of the population, leaving completely untouched only sections still wholly anchored ideologically in left-wing philosophies of life, those totally alienated by the attacks on the Churches, and a few exceptional individuals among intellectuals and members of the upper bourgeoisie who despised the irrationality of the Führer cult, were entirely nauseated by the populist vulgarity of Nazism, and could see national disaster looming. For most of the remainder, Hitler stood for at least *some* things they admired, and for many had become the symbol and embodiment of the national revival which the Third Reich had in many respects been perceived to accomplish. He had evoked in extreme measure and focused upon himself many irrational, but none the less real and strong, feelings of selfless devotion, sacrifice, and passionate commitment to a national ideal—emotions which had developed enormous, elemental force during and after the First World War. As such, Hitler had become in a way the projection of national aspirations to greatness which reached back into the imperial ambitions of the Wilhelmine era, and which in added strength under Nazism had found an echo among much of the German population, not least as a compensation for a far greyer reality. Given the size of Hitler's following and the level of confidence in his leadership which his 'achievements' and the outpourings of propaganda had built up, it would have been remarkable had the 'Hitler myth' collapsed completely overnight.

Furthermore, while 'logically' it might appear that at least from summer 1941 only Hitler could be blamed for the extension and prolongation of the war, a sufficient platform had been constructed by years of propaganda and ideological indoctrination to buttress the transfer of the blame to Germany's external enemies—the Bolsheviks, the Jews, the British, the Americans—or to internal incompetence, naturally stopping short of the Führer, as when Field Marshal von Brauchitsch was made the scapegoat for mistakes in strategy and provisioning on the eastern Front in the winter of 1941–2.

Moreover, trust in Hitler was not simply based upon an early end to the war, but on an early *victorious* conclusion, and all the indications are that before late 1942 and early 1943—centring around Stalingrad, the North African reverses, and the mounting allied air supremacy— only a minority of Germans (around a third of the population accord- ing to American surveys carried out in 1945) were prepared to concede that the war was lost.[1] Around the same proportion of the population, according to the same surveys, never thought of giving up the struggle to the end—or recovered from such defeatist notions—and it is fair to presume that for them Hitler remained the symbol of continued hope and determination.[2] Here, too, Nazi propaganda had succeeded in good measure in inculcating into large sections of the population the fear of what a new defeat would bring. Certainly, many imagined life after a defeat would be substantially worse than under Nazism, and this notion continued to form a negative base of Hitler's support.

Finally, the material as well as the affective side of the 'Hitler myth' has to be taken into account. Hitler's rule had provided golden open- ings for armies of opportunists to 'better themselves' by pulling on the Party uniform and obtaining the profits and trappings of minor office. Such petty apparatchiks had burnt their boats with Hitler, and were as dependent upon his continued popularity—upon the continued reten- tion of the 'Hitler myth'—as were the leading figures in the Party. And for the mass of the petty bourgeoisie, which had from the beginning provided a backbone of the 'Hitler myth', the period when, materially, the Third Reich turned to unmitigated disaster only seems to have set in from 1942 onwards.[3]

[1] *USSBS*, iv. 16.
[2] Around a half of the German population was unwilling to entertain unconditional surrender until the very end. And a remarkably high proportion even after the war admitted their confidence at the time that the German leaders had the best interests of their people at heart—ibid., pp. 14–18.
[3] See Kershaw, *Popular Opinion*, p. 329.

For all these reasons, the 'Führer myth' could not be dismantled instantaneously, but underwent a lengthy process of decline accompanying the gradual but chequered disillusionment and alienation of the mass of the population. In the context of the rapidly deteriorating popular mood, already visible in the winter of 1941–2, the slow deflation rather than the swift puncture of the 'Hitler myth' becomes all the more evident.

Unlike the case in earlier phases of the war, the German people were not systematically prepared by propaganda for the opening of the war against the Soviet Union. The Russian campaign started, in fact, while most people were still expecting the final show-down with Britain to begin in the near future. The Armaments Inspectorate at Nuremberg, commenting on the successful concealment of preparation for the invasion, noted that 'the concentration of numerous troops in the eastern areas had allowed speculation to arise that significant events were afoot there, but nevertheless probably the overwhelming proportion of the German people did not think of any warlike confrontation with the Soviet Union'.[4] One woman, writing to a relative at the Front on the day of the invasion itself, said she had been 'speechless' as, wholly unawares, she had turned on the radio and caught Hitler's proclamation about the campaign in the east. But on reflection, she had realized that no one had taken the friendship with the USSR wholly seriously, and now the realization of how much worry it must have caused the Führer and 'the greatness of his diplomacy' made her feel 'quite small'.[5] Immediately following the invasion and on the basis of reports from all over the Reich, the SD registered 'the greatest surprise' and 'a certain dismay' (though no major shock) at the news. People were aware of the hard struggle ahead and of its significance, but were generally calm and confident, apart from a few nervous expressions of the difficulties involved in conquering 'these vast spaces'.[6]

Just how little the opening of a new Front in the east matched the widespread desire for a rapid end to the war, and how risky the extension of the conflict was felt to be, can be seen in the admission, a few months later, by Adolf Wagner, *Gauleiter* of Munich and Upper

[4] BA/MA, RW 20–13/9, 'Geschichte der Rüstungsinspektion XIII', p. 156.
[5] *Das andere Gesicht des Krieges*, p. 70. For Hitler's proclamation on 22 June 1941, announcing the invasion of the Soviet Union, see Domarus, pp. 1726–32.
[6] *Meldungen*, pp. 155–6.

Bavaria, at a meeting of Party functionaries, that if Hitler had consulted the German people before the start of the war in the east about its readiness for the Russian campaign, the vast majority of the population would have said: 'My God, keep your hands off, my dear Adolf Hitler. You are our dear Führer, but for God's sake keep your hands off, don't undertake the campaign.'[7]

Early anxieties about the Russian campaign were soon dispelled by the growing confidence arising from the rapid and impressive successes of the Wehrmacht in the initial advances. The first 'special announcements' about the encirclement and capture of huge numbers of Soviet prisoners and the seizure of Russian war material seemed to support the propaganda line that the superlative German troops would swiftly destroy the inferior Red Army, and that a new *Blitzkrieg* victory was already in sight. It seemed as if the Führer was right yet again, and that the end of the Russian campaign was only a few weeks away. Hitler himself provided encouragement for such opinion when, in his major speech in the Berlin Sportpalast on 3 October 1941,[8] he not only defended the invasion of the Soviet Union as a preventive war, pre-empting in the nick of time a planned Bolshevik assault on the Reich,[9] but also gave the impression that the back of the Soviet fighting capability had already been broken. Anyone with ears to hear must have noted Hitler's words, that 'we had no idea, how gigantic the preparations of this enemy were against Germany and Europe, and how immensely great the danger was, how narrowly we have avoided this time the destruction not only of Germany, but of the whole of Europe'. But the most significant phrases appeared to denote that Russia was 'already broken' and would 'never rise again'.[10] The conclusion was drawn that the 'war in Russia can be regarded as over already', and the coming major offensive, which Hitler had announced, could be viewed as the decisive 'strike of the German Wehrmacht against the last Bolshevik armies still capable of fighting'.[11] The Reich Press Chief, Otto Dietrich, also conveyed the

[7] BDC, Personalakt Adolf Wagner, address of Wagner given at the 'Kreisappell der Ortsgruppenleiter und Bürgermeister' in Rosenheim, 22 Oct. 1941.

[8] Text in Domarus, pp. 1758–67.

[9] A few days after the speech, the Government President of Swabia referred to 'growing recognition that the war with Russia was necessary, and that Bolshevism was prepared for an invasion of the whole of Europe'—GStA, MA 106684, RPvS, 8 Oct. 1941.   [10] Domarus, pp. 1762–3; *Meldungen*, p. 180.

[11] Domarus, p. 1758, StANeu, vorl. LO A5, KL Augsburg-Stadt, 10 Nov. 1941; GStA, MA 106674, RPvNB/OP, 8 Nov. 1941.

impression, in comments made on 9 October, that the end of the Russian campaign was imminent, and newspapers carried banner headlines such as 'Eastern Campaign Decided—Bolshevism militarily finished'.[12] Many were amazed that the war against Bolshevism was already more or less over,[13] but no less a person than the Führer himself had again lent support to such notions with his proclamation to the soldiers on the eastern Front on 2 October, in which he spoke of 'the last mighty blow to smash the enemy even before the onset of winter'.[14] One non-commissioned officer, writing home, said he presumed that by the time his letter arrived 'the bells throughout the whole of Germany would be announcing the victory over the mightiest enemy of civilization. For it cannot last much longer, and for us the words of the Führer are gospel.'[15]

The premature declarations of imminent victory and raising of empty hopes contained the germ of the inevitable decline in confidence which set in during the following weeks, as the news from the eastern Front told a different story. Already in November 1941, the SD was reporting 'disappointment that the final smashing of Bolshevism is not taking place as rapidly as hoped and that no end of the eastern campaign is in sight', a dampening of optimism at the news of the first falls of snow and the feeling that further advancement might be extremely difficult, puzzlement at the failure to advance further when the Russian troops were allegedly so poor and so badly equipped, concern at the reports of continued tough resistance of the Soviet army, and pessimism that 'the way to the Urals was still a long one, and the partisan war could still last a good while'. In discussions about the military situation in the east, the SD noted, the question was constantly being raised about how an end to the war against Russia would be possible at all.[16] There were complaints when Hitler's speech to the Party 'old guard' in Munich on 8 November was not broadcast, for it was said that in the disappointment about the unfulfilled expectations from the Russian campaign many people 'had

---

[12] *Meldungen*, pp. 182, 184; GStA, MA 106684, RPvS, 8 Nov. 1941.

[13] *Meldungen*, pp. 182–3. The SD report noted the scepticism and 'wait and see' attitude of a population distrustful of German propaganda.

[14] Domarus, p. 1757.

[15] *Das andere Gesicht des Krieges*, p. 84.

[16] *Meldungen*, pp. 184–6; Steinert, pp. 234–5; see also GStA, MA 106671, RPvOB, 10 Nov. 1941; MA 106674, RPvNB/OP, 8 Dec. 1941; MA 106684, RPvS, 8 Nov. 1941; MA 106679, RPvOF/MF, 7 Oct., 6 Nov. 1941; StANeu, vorl. LO A5, KL Augsburg-Stadt, 10 Nov. 1941.

felt the need to hear the voice of the Führer again and to derive new strength from his words'.[17]

The reaction to the sudden call, just before Christmas 1941, for a collection for winter clothing for the German troops in the east was one of profound shock and bitterness. It seemed scarcely conceivable that the leadership had not made sufficient provision for the troops wintering in Russia.[18] The simultaneous news that the Commander in Chief of the Army, von Brauchitsch, had been relieved of his duties and that Hitler himself had taken over the direct military leadership of the army, together with the undeniable fact that the German advance had come to a halt and the Soviet counter-attack close to Moscow could only be staved off with partial retreats, and, not least, the entry of the United States into the war, combined to produce the first major shock to the German population during the Second World War.[19] One report spoke of 'a low in public opinion'.[20] Another, already in November 1941 explaining the drop in morale, remarked that 'the hope of an early peace had been too general', and, within a few weeks, that 'the hope of an early end to the war has been abandoned'.[21]

The Party, of course, touted the line that 'the Führer had been badly informed by his generals in the east'.[22] But, even though direct criticism of Hitler seldom surfaced, the excuse must have sounded somewhat hollow. The conclusion could hardly be avoided that the Führer, who only a short while before had been speaking so confidently of imminent victory, had been mistaken. His extra-ordinary run of successes had been halted, the links of his apparent infallibility for the first time broken. But recognition of this dawned only slowly on the still immense proportion of 'Hitler believers' among the population. The set-back was hardly sufficient to dent their faith, though the number of doubters was beginning to grow.

The sagging morale and worsening of mood in the second half of 1941 was not solely determined by the changing fortunes on the

¹⁷ *Meldungen*, pp. 191–2.

¹⁸ Ibid., p. 202; GStA, MA 106671, RPvOB, 9 Jan. 1942; MA 106679, RPvOF/MF, 5 Jan. 1942; MA 106681, RPvUF, 12 Jan. 1942; MA 106674, RPvNB/OP, 8 Jan. 1942; BAK, R22/3355, OLGP Bamberg, 1 Jan. 1942; R22/3381, GenStA Nürnberg, 10 Feb. 1942.

¹⁹ GStA, MA 106684, RPvS, 12 Jan. 1942; *Meldungen*, p. 203.

²⁰ StAB, K8/III, 18474, GKF Ebermannstadt, 30 Jan. 1942.

²¹ GStA, MA 106684, RPvS, 8 Nov. 1941, 9 Feb. 1942. See also *Meldungen*, pp. 200–1.

²² StAW, GL Mainfranken II/5, Kreispropagandaleiter Brückenau-Hammelburg, 26 Jan. 1942. See also GStA, MA 106679, RPvOF/MF, 5 Jan. 1942; MA 106684, RPvS, 12 Jan. 1942; and Steinert, pp. 264–8.

eastern Front. Events at home were also playing their part. The gathering force of worrying rumour about the killing in asylums of mentally sick and incurably ill patients was one factor which, especially but not solely among practising Christians, was giving rise to grave concern and threatening to alienate support for the regime.[23] In August 1941, news of the courageous open denunciation of the 'euthanasia action' by Bishop Galen of Münster spread rapidly and seems to have persuaded Hitler to halt the killing, at least inside the Reich itself.[24] Some reports by the Nazi authorities on the unrest which had arisen claimed that it was having an impact on confidence in Hitler himself.[25] It may even have been the case—a suggestion emanating, admittedly, from a piece of post-war testimony—that the Reich Propaganda Ministry deliberately started off a rumour that the Führer, on discovering what was taking place (in an 'action' which, in reality, he himself had authorized in writing), had given the order to halt it immediately.[26] According to this interpretation, the protection of the 'Führer myth'—of the legend that Hitler was kept in the dark about the misdeeds of the regime, and acted promptly on learning of them—was a crucial component in bringing the 'euthanasia action' to an end.

Opinion in Catholic parts of the Reich in particular was greatly influenced by the new wave of attacks on the position of the Church which had begun in spring 1941 and gathered momentum during the summer and autumn. They appear to have been initiated by the head of the Party Chancellery, Martin Bormann, probably under pressure from anti-Christian activists at *Gau* level, for whom the apparent strengthening of the Church's hold over the population during the war was a notable provocation. New measures against the Church— including the confiscation of monastic property, further restrictions on provision of religious instruction and on publications, the removal of the last nuns from any form of social or educational work, and inter- ference with holy days and with the form of school prayers—were guaranteed to stir up antagonism and unrest in Catholic regions.[27]

In Bavaria, most of which was overwhelmingly Catholic, by far the

[23] See Kershaw, *Popular Opinion*, pp. 334 ff.

[24] E. Klee, *'Euthanasie' im NS-Staat. Die 'Vernichtung lebensunwerten Lebens'*, Frankfurt a.M. 1983, pp. 333 ff.

[25] See e.g. Kershaw, *Popular Opinion*, p. 336.

[26] Klee, p. 341.

[27] See Conway, pp. 232, 259–60, 383–6; and Kershaw, *Popular Opinion*, pp. 332 ff.

greatest unrest was provoked by the crude attempt to remove crucifixes from school classrooms. On this highly emotional issue, an extraordinary wave of protest forced the Nazi authorities into retreat.[28] The episode casts interesting light on the 'Hitler myth' at this juncture, where the Party had made itself unpopular as never before.

Hitler was by no means altogether excluded from the angry storm of criticism which arose from the 'crucifix action'. An anonymous letter sent to one Local Group Leader of the NSDAP, castigating him and his District Leader, threatened that 'if our Führer lets such scoundrels rule, it will soon all be over with Heil Hitler'.[29] Farmers in Lower Bavaria and the Upper Palatinate were reported to have removed pictures of Hitler from their houses in reaction to the 'crucifix action'.[30] From an Upper Bavarian town, it was noted that anti-Church measures had prompted 'the wish for the reconstruction of the monarchy and the formation of a State comprising Bavaria and Austria'.[31] Similar sentiments could be heard elsewhere, too, and people in Munich were arrested for saying they preferred 'Wilhelm by the grace of God' to the 'idiot from Berchtesgaden'.[32]

The 'crucifix action' was one of the first indicators that massive criticism of the Party no longer necessarily excluded Hitler. Nevertheless, there are clear signs of the continued exemption of Hitler from blame and the belief—as it happens not altogether misplaced in this particular case[33]—that he had had nothing to do with the 'action' and would disapprove of it. For example, one woman who was prominent in a demonstration against the removal of crucifixes was heard to shout out: 'I am a hundred per cent Hitler supporter and have been a National Socialist since 1923. But this is going too far. The Führer doesn't want this, and certainly knows nothing of this removal of the crosses.'[34] Like so many others, this woman was acting purely on the basis of her naïve belief in Hitler's good intentions and ignorance of

[28] See Kershaw, *Popular Opinion*, pp. 340 ff.

[29] LRA Neumarkt in der Oberpfalz (Registratur), LRA Parsberg 939, anon. Letter to the Ortsgruppenleiter of Hemau, received on 20 Sept. 1941.

[30] *KL*, iv. 290.

[31] *KL*, i. 328.

[32] StANeu, vorl. Slg. Schum. Anh. 3, KL Augsburg-Land, 20 Oct. 1941; StAM, SGM 5659, 8634. The offence was the repetition of the neat rhyming couplet: 'Lieber Wilhelm von Gottes Gnaden, als den Depp von Berchtesgaden.'

[33] Hitler was allegedly furious with *Gauleiter* Wagner for his stupidity in provoking the unrest—E. N. Peterson, *The Limits of Hitler's Power*, Princeton, 1969, p. 219.

[34] LRA Neumarkt in der Oberpfalz, LRA Parsberg 939, 'Durchführung des Kreuzerlasses in Parsberg', 19 Sept. 1941.

what was going on. Others even took the view that the Party was deliberately exploiting the situation, with the Führer away at the Front leading the struggle against Bolshevism, to destroy the basis of Christianity at home 'behind his back'. A Catholic woman—and evidently a Hitler fanatic—in the Berchtesgaden vicinity wrote, in a crude anonymous letter to the local mayor and Party leader: '. . . You wear brown shirts on top, but inside you're Bolsheviks and Jews. Otherwise you wouldn't be able to carry on behind the Führer's back. . . . For what you cowardly heroes are doing isn't helping Adolf Hitler. Our Führer doesn't order such things. He's bothering daily about his soldiers in the field and not about the crosses in the school . . . Heil Hitler. . . .'[35] Another woman, repeating with incredulity that such things could happen while the Führer was standing by his soldiers at the Front in the fight against Bolshevism, said blessings would go out from the crucifixes in the schools 'not only for the children themselves, but also for our Führer and his soldiers, who are our sons, fathers, and brothers'.[36] And in one village, a protest demonstration of thirty to forty inhabitants, ended in the local school, where in front of the crucifix and a picture of Hitler they prayed for 'the warriors, the fallen warriors, and for Führer, people, and Fatherland'.[37] The fact that Hitler was out of Germany, at the Führer Headquarters in the east, and engaged in the conduct of the war against the Bolshevik arch-enemy—a war which he had long prophesied as inevitable in order to defend Christian Europe—evidently made it unthinkable for many that he could have anything to do with the 'godless Bolshevism' of the brownshirts at home. The Government President of Swabia formulated what was undoubtedly widely felt in September 1941, when he wrote that 'from here, the proceedings in the homeland must appear "Bolshevistic", the blatant contradiction incomprehensible; people cannot believe that the Führer approves of this.'[38] The 'crucifix action' illustrates how strong the 'Führer myth' still remained. That was again demonstrated in 1942, as Germany's fortunes in the war deteriorated still further, despite some success in specific military operations, and the prospects of an early end to the war receded rather than improved.

[35] StAM, LRA 31933 GP Ramsau, 9 Oct. 1941.
[36] StAM, LRA 48235, Letter to Bezirksschulrat Pfaffenhofen, 17 Sept. 1941.
[37] StAL, 164/14, 5731, Pfarramt Ulbering to the LR Pfarrkirchen, 3 Sept. 1941; GP Triftern, 3 Sept. 1941; LR Pfarrkirchen, 26 Sept. 1941.
[38] *KL*, iii. 223.

After the first winter of the war in the east, Hitler's popularity was unbroken, if not completely unscathed. The 'Bolsheviks' had proved a far tougher enemy than German propaganda had led people to expect; German losses had mounted alarmingly; material restrictions on the home front were beginning to bite; and the end of the war was nowhere in sight. The basis for the easy triumphs which had over and again given new nourishment to the 'Hitler myth' was gone, even if trust in the Führer was still generally strong. Also, the direct experience of 'contact' with the Führer through his major speeches, which for years had served as the ritualistic form of plebiscitary 'meeting' between the Leader and his people, to be repeated at regular intervals, took place only infrequently after 1942. Withdrawn into the isolation of his headquarters in the east, Hitler became an increasingly distant figure. Without new triumphs to proclaim, he appeared less and less in public, and seldom made speeches. The Führer was no longer present among his people; he played the part increasingly of a *deus ex machina*, turning up every now and then in Berlin or Munich, but mostly a distant war-lord conducting military affairs in faraway parts but scarcely having any real further contact with the German people themselves. Such contact was still wanted. An SD report at the end of January 1942 noted that 'the pictures from the Führer Headquarters were felt to be the high-point of the newsreel', and that 'not enough pictures of the Führer could be shown'. Comments such as 'A smile of the Führer. His look itself gives us strength and courage again,' were said to have occurred in almost all reports received.[39] But the earlier propaganda image of a 'human' and even 'family' Hitler, coming from the people, sharing its worries and cares, and understanding 'the little man' seemed to have less and less to do with reality. The propaganda had to be adjusted accordingly to the new, and more distant, relationship with the Führer which the Russian campaign had brought about. Early in 1942, and in conjunction with the première of the new film *The Great King*, Goebbels depicted Hitler as a modern Frederick the Great, isolated in distant majesty, conducting a heroic—and against all odds ultimately victorious—struggle far from home on behalf of nation and people.[40] This monumental image was designed

[39] *MadR*, ix. 3225, 29 Jan. 1942.
[40] See Bramsted, pp. 222–3. The press had in fact been instructed in March to avoid, in commenting on the film, all comparisons of Frederick the Great with the Führer, and all analogies with the present, especially in connection with the pessimistic note which dominated the early scenes of the film and was in no way to be identified with the

to stir up emotions of awe and respect, but could scarcely evoke feelings of warmth and affection. Hitler was increasingly the war-lord, at first seen in a positive and 'heroic' sense, but later more and more in terms of an unyielding, scarcely human harshness which was out of touch with the interests and problems of ordinary people.

Despite the reported 'need to hear the voice of the Führer again', Hitler's traditional speech on 30 January 1942, the anniversary of the 'seizure of power', left some feelings of disappointment, since people were looking for comforting or encouraging words about the state of the war in the east and not for just another stereotype repetition of the Nazi Party's glorious history.[41] The SD in one Catholic locality in northern Bavaria reported that 'the population did not listen to the Führer, but went to church' and held a rosary.[42] Nor could Hitler's speech on 'Heroes' Memorial Day'—the nazified remembrance of the dead of the First World War—on 15 March do much to improve morale. People were more preoccupied with rumours about an imminent sharp reduction in food rations than by the speech of the Führer, noted the SD.[43] And from previous experience it was for some no longer a matter of automatic belief when Hitler declared that 'the Bolshevik hordes ... will be smashed into oblivion by us in the coming summer'.[44] More optimistic and uncritical comments, that the Führer would not say something he was not sure about, could also be heard.[45] But they sounded more hollow than they had done a year earlier, and were certainly less widespread. Jokes circulating in Bavaria at the time told a different tale. One joke had a candidate for

bearing of the German people in the current war—*'Wollt ihr den totalen Krieg?' Die geheimen Goebbels-Konferenzen 1939–1943*, ed. W. A. Boelcke, dtv edn., Munich, 1969, pp. 287, 298. Nevertheless, Goebbels himself explicitly made the comparison of Hitler with Frederick in the context of the film. See *MadR*, x. 3660–2, 23 Apr. 1942. As Frederick had had to do in the darkest days of the Seven Years War, Goebbels spoke of the Führer now 'bearing the heavy burden of responsibility on his shoulders alone', and provincial newspapers, referring to Hitler as the 'first soldier of the Reich', attuned to the new image by stating that 'the politician, the statesman, now steps seemingly into the background' as 'the iron laws demand the soldier, the military commander'—*Völkischer Beobachter*, north German edn., 20 Apr. 1942; *Rheinisch-Westfälische Zeitung*, 20 Apr. 1942. For the film, *Der große König*, see Welch, pp. 174 ff.

[41] *Meldungen*, pp. 216–17.
[42] StAN, LRA Hilpoltstein 792, SD Schwabach, 2 Mar. 1942.
[43] *Meldungen*, pp. 239–40.
[44] Domarus, p. 1850; *Meldungen*, p. 239.
[45] StAM, LRA 29656, SD Berchtesgaden, 31 Mar. 1942. See also GStA, MA 106679, RPvOF/MF, 7 Apr. 1942; MA 106674, RPvNB/OP, 10 Apr. 1942; MA 106684, RPvS, 10 Apr. 1942.

the Waffen-SS being asked at the muster whether he was willing to sign on for the duration of the war; to which, he replied: 'No, at first only for twelve years.' Another joke posed the question about how long the war would go on, to which the answer ran: 'Until Goebbels's trousers fit Göring.'[46]

Hitler's most dramatic speech in 1942, following the surprising recall of the Reichstag, took place on 26 April that year.[47] After a long-winded description of the historical background to the war, and survey of the situation in the east—hinting that the war would continue to drag on over the coming winter—Hitler, in the part of the speech which attracted most attention, demanded full powers to act immediately and ruthlessly 'independent of person and status' where anyone was found not to be fulfilling his duties to the 'people's community' and failing in the war effort and promised an 'inexorable challenge to every form of corruption and omission of duty'. In an astonishing verbal assault on the justice administration and on the civil service, Hitler—allegedly voicing the exact sentiments of a great proportion of the population—made it clear whom he thought the main culprits were, and threatened to remove their privileged position and 'well-established rights' and to dismiss offenders instantaneously. The speech provoked varied and in part contradictory, reactions, which cast light on Hitler's popular standing and image in early 1942.

First reactions, the SD had to admit, contained disappointment at what Hitler had to say.[48] Rumours had been rife about the recalling of the Reichstag, and what dramatic events were to be disclosed. As it was, people felt left in the dark about what the weighty causes of such an unusual step might have been, and remained worried about the seriousness of the situation in the east and that in the Reich itself 'something is not right', suggesting conflict in the leading positions within the Wehrmacht and dissatisfaction of the Führer with prominent figures at home, whose life-style did not match the gravity of the times. There was also disappointment that no immediate action had followed such strong words, and lack of comprehension that Hitler needed any further powers to be granted. Further disappointment arose from Hitler's promise of retaliation for the bombing of German cities, when, in the days that followed, only English towns

---

[46] StAN, LRA Hilpoltsein 792, SD Schwabach, 2 Mar. 1942.
[47] Text in Domarus, pp. 1865–77.
[48] For the following, see *MadR*, x. 3671–4, 3685–8, 27 Apr., 30 Apr. 1942.

such as Bath, Norwich, and York were reported as bombed. Few results were expected 'from the bombing of these British spa and provincial towns' which were not seen as fitting retaliation for the destruction in Germany.[49] Above all, there was disappointment at Hitler's remarks that he had made full provision for the coming winter—the logical conclusion being drawn 'that the struggle in the east, in contrast to the hopes entertained up to now by the over-whelming majority of the population, cannot be ended before the next winter'.[50] Even Party reports had to accept that the speech, at least in this point, had 'not found everywhere the response it deserved'. 'Despondent souls,' it was said, 'and there are not a few of these, seem to have been struck only by one part of the Führer's speech: where he spoke of the preparations for the winter campaign in 1942–43. The more the homeland has become aware of the cruelty and hardship of the winter struggle in the east, the more the longing for an end to it has increased. But now the end is still not in sight. Many wives and mothers are suffering as a result.'[51]

By far the most popular parts of the speech, to go from the reactions reported by the SD, were those in which Hitler, claiming new plenipotentiary powers, attacked judges and civil servants and threatened draconian measures to root out corruption and parasitic privilege whatever the rank and status of those involved. The enthusiastic response of the 'great mass' of 'ordinary' people to such populist rhetoric recalls in some ways the popular reactions to Hitler's actions following the 'Röhm Putsch' of 1934. This time, however, conservative, bourgeois, and intellectual circles were said to be voicing 'still carefully expressed fears about a certain legal insecurity in future'.[52] And among those in the front-line of attack—the civil servants, lawyers, and judges—there was deep shock and dismay. While the shame of the public defamation felt by the typical Nazi lawyer was allegedly almost enough to drive him to suicide, reactions of astonishment, disbelief, anxiety, and criticism can be read between the lines of the responses from judges and the justice administration, and the most outspoken reaction was that the Führer had been badly

[49] Ibid., p. 3687.

[50] Ibid., p. 3672.

[51] StANeu, vorl. LO 30/35, KL Nördlingen, 11 May 1942. See also vorl. Slg. Schum. Anh. 3, KL Augsburg-Land, 23 May 1942.

[52] *MadR*, x. 3687. And see BAK, R22/3355, Fols. 63a–b, OLGP Bamberg, 29 June 1942.

misinformed and his 'wholly unexpected attack on justice' much 'discussed and cricitized'.[53]

It was the first time during the Third Reich that a Führer speech had provoked such direct criticism in the reportage of upper civil servants. In attempting to deflect opinion from the disappointments of the previous winter and the lack of prospect of an early end of the war and to revamp morale through blaming others for Germany's misfortunes—much as he had done in the years before 1933—Hitler had lifted a corner of the veil of the 'Führer myth' and revealed a glimpse of the arbitrary, dictatorial, and irrational way he responded to the first reverses he and the nation had had to suffer. The speech of 26 April 1942, held against the theatrical back-cloth of the summoning of the Reichstag, had not lived up to expectations. It illustrated the diminished effectiveness of Führer speeches where no successes could be announced. And it demonstrated that Hitler's instinctive grasp of the 'gut feelings' of the population, on which his effectiveness as a speaker greatly rested, was also beginning to leave him as a result of his isolation in his distant field headquarters.

However, Hitler's popular base of support was still massive. An anonymous letter from an opponent of the regime in Franconia, condemning the 'puppet show' of the Reichstag and claiming ninety per cent of Germans shared his own desire, that Hitler 'disappear from the face of the earth as fast as possible', was an absurd exaggeration.[54] The offensive which began in summer 1942 on the southern wing of the eastern front and carried German troops over the Crimea and into the Caucasus, and the successes of the Afrikakorps and U-Boats in the Atlantic offered new opportunities to admire the exploits of the Wehrmacht. Many hoped and believed that Hitler would prove right in his prophecies, and that the decisive blow to the Russian colossus was imminent. And the Japanese advances in eastern Asia nourished the hopes that the United States would be completely tied down in that theatre of war.

The 'easy' times of war were over, however, and even the still notable military successes could no longer evoke untrammelled enthusiasm. The human losses mounted rapidly, and the extension of

[53] *MadR*, x. 3686. See also BAK, R22/3355, Fos. 62c–d, 63a–d, OLGP Bamberg, 30 Apr., 29 June 1942; and Steinert, pp. 289–92, Kershaw, *Popular Opinion*, p. 327.

[54] StAB, LRA Münchberg, vorl. ohne Signatur. I am grateful to Dr Karl-Heinz Mistele (Staatsarchiv Bamberg) for referring me to this document.

recruitment to those just eighteen years old and those already forty-five extended the worries about loved ones at the Front into almost every family, while at home their losses to farming and industry had to be made good, as far as possible, with more prisoners-of-war and 'foreign workers'. Shortages of foodstuffs and consumer goods were also making themselves felt, and the bombing—now affecting south-German cities, too—was causing widespread and constant anxiety. In this initial phase of allied bombing, it was less the material damage than the psychological shock of the helplessness of the Luftwaffe either to prevent the attacks or to retaliate in due measure which was harmful to morale. This touched upon a sensitive nerve with regard to confidence in the leadership. Göring's popularity in particular suffered as it became evident that, whatever successes German troops were having in distant parts, as head of the Luftwaffe, he was unable to guarantee the protection of the homeland. Gradually, too, Hitler's own massive prestige began to suffer under the ceaseless bombing-raids.

For the time being, however, Hitler was able to exploit the successes of the summer offensive to raise spirits at home again in his next major speech in the Berlin Sportpalast on 30 September 1942. The speech came generally as a surprise, and many presumed, when it was announced that Hitler would speak, that he would report the capture of Stalingrad. In the absence of anything so spectacular, the most impressive parts of the speech were those which declared how Germany had successfully surmounted the most severe test in the previous winter, and those indicating the exploitation of the material resources of the occupied territories and giving rise to hopes of improved foodstuff provisioning at home.[55] A further boost was given to these hopes by Göring's speech, four days later, at the Harvest Thanksgiving Festival, promising an improvement in the availability of foodstuffs.[56] Since, for much of the civilian population at home, material conditions were more directly relevant than distant military events, Göring's remarks were regarded, according to some reports, as even more significant than those of the Führer himself.[57] Hitler's speech, in fact, though according to one local report in Bavaria said to have brought about a 'direct miracle' and from SD soundings to

[55] *MadR*, xi. 4259, 1 Oct. 1942. Text of Hitler's speech in Domarus, pp. 1913–24.

[56] *MadR*, xi. 4291–3, 8 Oct. 1942.

[57] e.g. StAM, LRA 61619, SD Garmisch, 27 Oct. 1942; StAW, SD/36, HAS Würzburg, 8 Oct. 1942.

have prompted the standard wish that the Führer would speak to the people more often since his words provided greater stimulation than anything else, was reported as provoking less discussion than usual.[58] Nor did it have any lasting effect on morale. A month later, its impact had gone; 'the war weariness is just too strong.'[59] The SD agency in Würzburg even reported criticism of the fanaticism shown by Hitler and Göring which dispelled any hope of coming to terms with the enemy and meant the continuation on all sides of the 'war of annihilation'.[60]

In almost all reports in 1942, this 'war weariness' and longing for peace, now by no means always linked to expectations of glorious victory and often highly pessimistic, dominates much more strongly than it had done a year earlier. Frank reports from Bavarian localities where the government and police agencies were in closer touch with reality than many of their superiors give a clear impression of the mood. People were 'especially despondent' ran one report in early 1942. Another, compiled in June, stated that no one believed any longer in an early end to the war in Russia, and that soldiers on leave had said they would not go through a second winter there. The population, it was added, was for the most part interested only in their daily problems of work and getting sufficient provisions, and there was little talk about military events.[61] From the same area—around Garmisch-Partenkirchen in the Bavarian alps—it was said that the mood was getting 'noticeably worse by the day' on account of the provisioning difficulties.[62] Two reports from Oberammergau heavily criticized the German leadership, implicitly including Hitler even though his name was not directly mentioned. The war could not be won because so many irredeemable mistakes had been made by a leadership unwilling to accept expert advice; recent decrees and 'many speeches' were said to have contradicted the 'true will of the people'; and the leaders had underestimated Russia and other countries.[63] The war had not been necessary at all, and could have been prevented. It was pure idiocy for countries to destroy each other

---

[58] StAM, LRA 29656, LR Berchtesgaden, 3 Oct. 1942; *MadR*, xi. 4279–80, 5 Oct. 1942.

[59] StAB, K8/III, 18474, LR Ebermannstadt, 2 Nov. 1942.

[60] StAW, SD/36, HAS Würzburg, 8 Oct. 1942.

[61] StAM, LRA 61619, GP Mittenwald, 25 Feb., 24 Mar. 1942; GP Kohlgrub, 24 June 1942; GKF Garmisch, 29 June 1942.

[62] Ibid., GP Etal, 25 Aug. 1942.

[63] Ibid., GP Oberammergau, 25 June 1942.

on account of the few responsible for causing the war; 'there was always talk of a long peace, and things were only really being made ready for this war.' How little pacifist or humanitarian feeling was behind such notions is revealed by the concluding remark that 'it is only worth while waging war if the enemy can be destroyed with the first blow, which we did not manage.'[64] But these and similar reports indicated that, at any rate in such traditionally Catholic conservative areas where Nazism had only partially penetrated the existing sub-culture though where approval of Hitler had for the most part been completely unreserved between about 1938 and 1940, the gulf between propaganda image and actual reality was now rapidly becoming blatantly obvious.

In spring and summer 1942, the number of cases brought before the Munich 'Special Court' as a result of alleged critical remarks made about the regime also increased sharply. People were accused of spreading rumours about soldiers with weapons at the ready standing watch at stations in Munich and other big cities because of popular unrest. Others had been saying that nobody wore the Party badge any longer in Munich and that 'for a long while not a single person had believed anything the Führer had said'. Here, as elsewhere, Hitler was dubbed 'the carpet-biter' because of rumours of his blind fits of rage.[65] Stories that he was physically or mentally ill had, in fact, spread rapidly in summer 1942. Even the previous November there had been isolated rumours that he had suffered a nervous breakdown.[66] Now the rumours were widespread about Hitler's fits and frenzies of rage, that he had to be accompanied everywhere by a doctor specializing in mental illness and Himmler had given orders to allow no one to see him, and that he was wounded and in hospital.[67] It took his appearance and speech on 30 September 1942 to dispel such rumours,[68] only for them to recur in the winter of 1942–3 and especially after the Stalingrad disaster. Such rumours suggest at the very least a readiness to believe that the highest leadership of State and military was—to put it mildly—no longer in control of the situation. The 'Führer myth' was now plainly on the defensive.

[64] Ibid., 24 July 1942.
[65] StAM, SGM 11316, 12573.
[66] e.g. ibid., 11298.
[67] *MadR*, xi. 4190, 10 Sept. 1942; StANeu, vorl. Slg. Schum. Anh. 3, SD Friedberg, 28 Sept. 1942; StAM, LRA 29656, SD Berchtesgaden, 28 Sept. 1942.
[68] *MadR*, 4259, 1 Oct. 1942.

Another indicator of this—long before Stalingrad—is provided by an interesting source: the death-announcements for 'fallen heroes' which from autumn 1941 filled longer and longer columns in the German newspapers. Within limits, the family of the dead soldier could form the wording of the announcement without censorship, making the death-columns (alongside advertisements) the only non-'co-ordinated' parts of German newspapers (though the SD kept an eye on them, apparently aware of their potential as an index of opinion).[69] In practice, a number of conventional formulations were regularly used. People commonly chose between the two most frequently cited phrases—'For People and Fatherland', and 'For Führer, People, and Fatherland'—to praise and justify the sacrifice of their loved ones. Sampling of three prominent Bavarian newspapers shows that mention of the Führer sharply declined in private death-announcements between 1940 and the end of 1942. In the *Fränkischer Kurier*, for example, a newspaper with extensive circulation in and around Nuremberg and Fürth in Franconia, the Führer was mentioned in 41 per cent of the death-announcements for 'the fallen' between May and August 1940, in 25 per cent between July and December 1941, and in only 12 per cent between July and December 1942. In the *Augsburger Nationalzeitung*, the main Party organ for the region of Swabia, 62 per cent of announcements mentioned the Führer in June 1940, only 29 per cent in November and December 1941, and only 11.5 per cent in the last two months of 1942. And in the *Münchner Neueste Nachrichten*, by far the largest 'bourgeois' newspaper in the Munich area but also with much wider circulation, the 44 per cent of May and June 1940 had dropped by June and July 1941 to 29 per cent, reached 15 per cent for the period October to December 1941, and sank to only 7 per cent by October and November 1942. While such figures cannot, of course, be seen as precise indicators of opinion, the downward trend apparent in all of them does suggest that devotion to the Führer—or at least the readiness to declare such devotion in public—had fallen rapidly by the time of the Stalingrad débâcle. Presumably in order to counter even such indirect expressions of opinion, the free choice of wording for death-announcements

---

[69] A central directive of 19 June 1940 from the *Reichssicherheitshauptamt* to all *SD-Leitabschnitte* ordered a watch to be kept on the composition of death-announcements of fallen soldiers in the newspapers—StAW, SD/41/6, RSHA-SD Nr. 17766, 19 June 1940. William Shirer claimed even as early as the Polish campaign that the non-mention of the Führer in the death-announcements had political overtones—Shirer, p. 176.

for fallen soldiers was abruptly ended in September 1944. Instead, from now on all 'heroes' deaths' were placed in the newspapers under a uniform heading at the top of the columns, reading: 'For Führer, People, and Reich gave their lives. . .' In the preceding weeks, the figure of those mentioning the Führer in death-announcements in the *Münchner Neueste Nachrichten* had been around 4 per cent.

Though clearly, whatever the logic of the situation, Hitler could still rely upon substantial bonds of undying allegiance among his most loyal supporters, especially of course those who for years had been exposed to the full brunt of Party organization and indoctrination, there seems little doubt that the mass base of unquestioned trust in Hitler was already in 1942 beginning to give way. The most fundamental reason was evidently that Hitler was proving incapable of bringing about the fervently desired end to the war, either victoriously or even through a creditable compromise peace.[70] It was not the catastrophic defeat at Stalingrad, as often presumed, which saw the turning-point in Hitler's popularity. Rather, it was his inability to end the war which, already in the first months of the Russian campaign and ever more strongly during 1942, began inexorably to undermine the image of the far-sighted, infallible, and well-intentioned Führer. The contribution of the massive shock unleashed by 'Stalingrad', and the enormous loss of prestige accruing to Hitler as a result, was to open the flood gates to the criticism which was already present just below the surface and which—despite the obvious risks involved— now openly allotted blame to the Führer himself.

The loss of confidence which set in after Stalingrad was not least a consequence of the totally misleading and outrightly mendacious German propaganda which had preceded the catastrophe. For propaganda as well as for the military effort, Stalingrad was a débâcle.

The facts of the Stalingrad drama are well known.[71] At the begining of September 1942, the German 6th Army under General Paulus had reached Stalingrad—a city whose capture would have had symbolic significance; on 19 November a major Soviet counter-offensive had begun and led, within only a few weeks, to the encirclement of the 250,000 men of the 6th Army; by Christmas 1942 the situation was as

[70] Already in the late summer of 1942, Bavarian reports were noting that many people were now longing for peace even without victory—StANeu, vorl. Slg. Schum. Anh. 3, SD Friedberg, 14 Sept. 1942.
[71] See e.g. L. Gruchmann, *Der Zweite Weltkrieg*, Munich, 4th edn., 1975, pp. 190–4.

good as hopeless; on 10 January, the last Russian assault commenced; on 31 January Paulus—disobeying orders of the Führer that the troops had to fight to the last man—surrendered, and almost 90,000 survivors entered Soviet captivity, from whom only a small minority were to return.

The story told by German propaganda, however, betrayed nothing of the mounting hopelessness of the 6th Army's position.[72] Early press reportage, in fact, raised hopes of imminent German victory. The people of Augsburg, for example, could read in their local press on 18 September 1942 that the fate of the Russians in and around Stalingrad was sealed; the hour was near 'in which the city of Stalin with its surrounded great Soviet armies and with enormous quantities of war material will be doomed to destruction. . . . The finale of one of the greatest epics in German history has begun.'[73] Not surprisingly, the mood in the area—as elsewhere—was full of optimism. The SD station at nearby Friedberg noted that people were 'convinced that the fall of Stalingrad could take place any day', even if with a presumed heavy toll of German lives.[74] Hitler himself had lent support to such optimism, as we saw earlier, in his speech on 30 September 1942, by stating emphatically that German troops would 'overrun Stalingrad and take it'. 'You can depend on that!', he added, 'Nobody is going to get us away from this place again.'[75]

Goebbels instructed German press representatives on 19 October that 'it would still be a few days before the fall of Stalingrad' and recommended caution in reporting. He was critical of the 'illusions' and false optimism which the Wehrmacht reports were prompting. Only two days previously, the Supreme Command of the Wehrmacht had suggested lines of propaganda to be carried out after the expected triumph in Stalingrad 'in the next days', and took pride in the excellent planning of the Reich's military leadership after the mistakes of the previous winter.[76] But when no announcements of conclusive victory emerged in the following few weeks, people began—as was reported towards the end of October—to express their impatience that

[72] For a good account of the propaganda mythologizing of Stalingrad, see J. W. Baird, *The Mythical World of Nazi War Propaganda 1939–1945*, Minneapolis, 1974, ch. 11.

[73] *Augsburger National-Zeitung*, 18 Sept. 1942.

[74] StANeu, vorl. Slg. Schum. Anh. 3, SD Friedberg, 28 Sept. 1942.

[75] Domarus, p. 1914.

[76] *'Wollt ihr den totalen Krieg?'*, pp. 383–5.

the struggle for Stalingrad was taking too long and costing too many lives.[77]

The theme of Stalingrad was becoming rapidly a major embarrassment to the propagandists, especially those on the Wehrmacht staff, who had prematurely whipped up the victory atmosphere in September. From the time of the Russian counter-offensive in mid-November 1942, the Wehrmacht reports—seen and amended by Hitler himself—were largely silent about Stalingrad, and Goebbels, probably not fully informed of the true situation, confined himself largely to warnings about the severity of the struggle and the need to avoid the impression that a decisive stroke was imminent.[78] The Russian counter-offensive was not mentioned. However, the more 'realistic' mentioning of the hard fighting taking place gave rise to deepening depression in November and December, and despite the silence of the official media rumours could be heard by the end of the year about the encirclement of the 6th Army.[79] After a lengthy silence, the report of the Supreme Command of the Wehrmacht spoke ominously on 16 January 1943 about the 'heroically courageous defensive struggle' of German troops against an 'enemy attacking from all sides'.[80] Goebbels learnt the grim truth about the situation in a visit to the Führer Headquarters on 22 and 23 January. And on 23 January, the Reich Press Chief, Dietrich, gave instructions to the press which spoke suddenly, and without any prior warning to the public, of 'the great and stirring heroic sacrifice which the troops encircled at Stalingrad are offering the German nation'.[81] A day later, he spoke of the imminent 'heroic epic' of Stalingrad.[82] Finally, on 3 February, to the accompaniment of the opening bars of Beethoven's Fifth Symphony, came the now dreaded 'Special Announcement': 'The struggle in Stalingrad is over. Loyal to their oath down to the last

---

[77] StAM, LRA 61619, SD Garmisch, 27 Oct. 1942.

[78] *'Wollt ihr den totalen Krieg?'*, pp. 399–400; Balfour, pp. 290, 305–6; Bramsted, p. 260.

[79] *MadR*, xii. 4619, 4 Jan. 1943; GStA, MA 106679, RPvOF/MF, 8 Jan. 1943; MA 106681, RPvUF, 9 Jan. 1943; *Das andere Gesicht des Krieges*, p. 19; and see Balfour, p. 307.

[80] *'Wollt ihr den totalen Krieg?'*, p. 422. A planned edition of last letters from the heroes of Stalingrad had to be quashed since the tone of most of the letters scarcely matched the tone of heroic sacrifice demanded by Nazi propaganda—Steinert, p. 328. For soldiers' letters from Stalingrad, see *Das andere Gesicht des Krieges*, pp. 95–107, and *True to Type. A Selection of Letters and Diaries of German Soldiers and Civilians collected on the Soviet–German Front* London, n.d. (?1944), pp. 71–8, 109–10.

[81] *'Wollt ihr den totalen Krieg?'*, p. 426.

[82] Steinert, p. 327.

breath, the 6th Army, under the exemplary leadership of General Field Marshal Paulus, succumbed to the superior force of the enemy and the unfavourable conditions. ... Generals, officers, non-commissioned officers, and men fought shoulder to shoulder down to the last shot. They died so that Germany might live. . .'[83] Even here, the propaganda had to lie. News of the surrender of Paulus and 90,000 soldiers of the 6th Army—which would have provided some relief for their distraught relatives—had to be kept quiet to maintain the legend of total and selfless sacrifice for the nation in the 'greatest epic in German history'. This, too, proved to be a mistake. Rumours were soon in circulation about the surrender, and a few days later it was announced that 47,000 wounded had been saved.[84]

Stalingrad was the greatest single blow of the war. Deep shock, dismay, and depression were recorded everywhere. It was correctly viewed as the low point of wartime morale on the home front. There was lack of comprehension at how it could have happened and why the 6th Army could not have been relieved, and little consolation for bereaved relatives in the official interpretation of 'heroic sacrifice'.[85] Psychologically as well as militarily, Stalingrad was a turning-point in the war. It also gave a decisive boost to the decline of the 'Führer myth'. Reports at the turn of the year 1942–3 referring in the usual glowing terms of undiminished confidence of the people in 'its beloved Führer' and claiming that 'the person of the Führer was as always put beyond criticism' had been speaking in the conventional exaggerations of the regime's apparatchiks.[86] Even so, it seems evidently to have been the case that before Stalingrad the voicing of direct criticism of the person of the Führer and his leadership was a rarity. With the defeat at Stalingrad this altered abruptly.

---

[83] Domarus, p. 1985. For an interesting eye-witness account of reactions of people in the city centre of Nuremberg to the stunning news, see F. Nadler, *Eine Stadt im Schatten Streichers*, Nuremberg, 1969, pp. 71–6.

[84] *'Wollt ihr den totalen Krieg?'*, p. 437.

[85] *MadR*, xii. 4750–1, 4760–1, 4 Feb., 8 Feb. 1943; GStA, MA 106684, RPvS, 11 Feb. 1943; MA 106681, RPvUF, 10 Mar. 1943; MA 106679, RPvOF/MF, 8 Mar. 1943; MA 106671, RPvOB, 8 Feb. 1943; MA 106674, RPvNB/OP, 10 Feb. 1943; StAW, SD/36, HAS Würzburg, 1 Feb., 8 Feb. 1943; BAK, R22/3355, OLGP Bamberg, 29 Mar. 1943; StAM, LRA 29656, LR Berchtesgaden, 1 Feb. 1943.

[86] GStA, MA 106679, RPvOF/MF, 8 Jan. 1943; MA 106684, RPvS, 10 Dec. 1942; StANeu, vorl. Slg. Schum. Anh. 3, SD Friedberg, 4 Jan. 1943; *MadR*, xii. 4618, 4 Jan. 1943.

Already towards the end of January, when it was made known that German troops were encircled in Stalingrad, the unease registered in numerous reports merged into critical comment expressing fundamental doubts about the necessity of the war with Russia and now also about the truth of Hitler's explanations for the war.[87] Many spoke with respect and admiration for the soldiers of the 6th Army, but took the view that the losses suffered had been in vain. Whereas on earlier occasions where bad news or unfavourable developments had occurred, the view had prevailed—at least in public utterances—that the Führer had been badly counselled or had been kept uninformed, in the case of Stalingrad Hitler was directly implicated in the catastrophe. The former ambassador to Rome, Ulrich von Hassell, executed in July 1944 for his involvement in the plot to kill Hitler, wrote on 14 February 1943 of the crisis 'symbolized in the name "Stalingrad" ':

For the first time Hitler was not able to get out from under the responsibility; for the first time the critical rumours are aimed straight at him. There has been exposed for all eyes to see the lack of military ability of 'the most brilliant strategist of all time', that is, our megalomaniac corporal. This was concealed up to now by a few intuitive master strokes, the lucky results of risks that were in themselves unjustified, and the short-comings of our enemies. It is clear to all that precious blood has been shed foolishly or even criminally for purposes of prestige alone. Since strictly military affairs are involved this time, the eyes of the generals were opened, too. . . . It is significant that Hitler did not dare to speak on January 30! Who would have believed this a short time ago? . . .[88]

According to Albert Speer, Goebbels referred around this time not just to a 'leadership crisis', but to a 'Leader crisis'.[89] Party reports—usually more coloured and 'loyal' than any other type of report in their avoidance of criticism of the leadership—from all parts of Germany confirmed the 'especially dangerous' signs that people were now 'daring to express open criticism of the person of the Führer and to attack him in hateful and mean fashion'.[90] The head of the regional justice administration in Bamberg had also observed 'a sharp increase and intensification in criticism of the political and military leadership' and, 'what had never been the case before, to a growing extent of the

[87] StAW, SD/36, HAS Würzburg, 25 Jan. 1943.
[88] U. von Hassell, *The von Hassell Diaries 1938–1944*, London, 1948, pp. 255–6.
[89] Speer, p. 271.
[90] Cited in Steinert, p. 348.

person of the Führer, who is made responsible especially for the events in Stalingrad and in the Caucasus'. Rumours spoke of Hitler ignoring all warnings, and of major differences between him and his military advisers.[91] An Augsburg salesman was brought before the 'Special Court' in Munich for spreading one such rumour. He was accused of asserting that Hitler had rejected the army's suggestions of an airlift to remove the encircled troops, and of saying: 'The Führer has always spoken himself about how important Stalingrad is, and now he's gone and lost it.'[92] Reports from local officials in numerous districts leave no doubt that the blame for risking, then losing, the 6th Army was attributed to Hitler. His earlier much-fabled 'ruthless determination' and fanatical single-mindedness were now becoming to be regarded as a major liability, and the command to the 6th Army to fight to the last man was seen as its fateful demonstration.[93] Stalingrad was being interpreted as the consequence of what was now becoming to be widely viewed as Hitler's catastrophic policy and leadership. The *Landrat* of Ebermannstadt in Upper Franconia, frank as usual in his comment, reported that people in his area were too careful to say such things as 'Hitler will give us no peace till everything has had it', but said instead 'there won't be any peace before . . .', and meant the same thing. It was squarely concluded that Hitler, through the over-estimation of his own strength and rejection of all overtures for peace from neutral states, 'bears himself in the last resort the blame for the retrograde development which has now set in'.[94]

Opponents of the regime took new heart from the Stalingrad disaster, and their limited revival resulted in a spread of illegal broadsheets and surreptitiously daubed graffiti, attacking Hitler 'the Stalingrad Murderer'.[95] In Munich, the Stalingrad disaster prompted the group of students who, largely inspired by moral and religious idealism, had the previous year formed the 'White Rose' movement and circulated anti-Nazi leaflets in Munich University, to stage a suicidally brave public demonstration of their detestation for Hitler and Nazism in a defiant manifesto displayed all over the university buildings:

[91] BAK, R22/3355, OLGP Bamberg, 29 Mar. 1943.
[92] StAM, SGM 12443.
[93] StAN, LRA Hilpoltstein 792, SD Schwabach, 6 Mar. 1943.
[94] StAB, K8/III, 18475, LR Ebermannstadt, 2 Feb. 1943.
[95] GStA, MA 106671, RPvOB, 10 Mar. 1943; see also MA 106684, RPvS, 11 Feb. 1943; StAM, LRA 29656, LR Berchtesgaden, 1 Feb. 1943; and Steinert, p. 347.

Fellow Students! The nation is profoundly shaken by the defeat of our troops at Stalingrad. Three hundred and thirty thousand Germans have been senselessly and irresponsibly led to death and destruction through the cunning strategy of a corporal from World War I. Our Führer, we thank you! . . .

Fellow Students! The German people look to us! As in 1813 the people looked to us to destroy the Napoleonic terror, so today in 1943 they look to us to destroy the terror of National Socialism. Beresina and Stalingrad are burning in the east; the dead of Stalingrad adjure us . . .[96]

Though open opposition, as the 'White Rose' showed, was futile against the might of the Gestapo and resistance groups were necessarily compelled to continue their work in secrecy and isolation, their hostility to the Nazi regime was now far less out of touch with the climate of opinion than had been the case even a few months earlier, before Stalingrad. Reports were now reaching the SD that people—especially those attached to the Churches—were expressing the hope that the Wehrmacht would take over running the State, and that there would be a final victory for Germany but not for National Socialism.[97] The 'White Rose' itself evidently gave rise to rumours, widely circulating in Bavaria and in many other parts of Germany 'about large demonstrations of Munich students', unrest, and even revolutionary feeling in Munich, 'and people were talking about graffiti and fly-leaf propaganda with a Marxist content on public buildings in Berlin and in other cities'.[98] In a play on the official Nazi designation of Munich as 'Capital of the Movement', it was now dubbed unofficially the 'Capital of the Counter-Movement'; it was said that propaganda advocating the restoration of the monarchy was increasing, that it was no longer advisable to use the 'Heil Hitler' greeting or wear the Party arm-badge, and that 'sooner or later' a revolution could break out in Munich.[99] Various reports confirmed that the 'German Greeting' was indeed seldom used now in southern Bavaria, and was sometimes demonstratively refused by relatives of 'fallen' soldiers.[1] Jokes and witticisms about the Führer proliferated. One man was brought before the 'Special Court' for saying Germans

[96] Noakes and Pridham, pp. 319–20.
[97] StAW, SD/23, AS Würzburg, 23 Apr. 1943; SD/37, HAS Würzburg, 29 May 1943.
[98] *MadR*, xiii. 4944, 15 Mar. 1943.
[99] StAW, SD/36, HAS Würzburg, 15 Mar. 1943; StAM, LRA 29656, SD Berchtesgaden, 25 Feb. 1943.
[1] StAW, SD/37, HAS Würzburg, 8 May 1943; StANeu, vorl. LO 30/35, KL Nördlingen, 10 Apr. 1943.

had no need to fear starvation in this war, because Hitler had the biggest farm in the world 'followed around by 90 million cattle and running an enormous pigsty'.[2] To the popular hit melody with the first line, 'It all passes by, it all fades away,' people added a second line: 'Hitler falls in April, the Party in May.'[3] And there was a new out-pouring of rumours about Hitler's health: that he was ill, mad, blind, had suffered a nervous breakdown, or that as a result of mental illness he had been forced to hand over the leadership of the State to the military, and had been shot.[4]

Rumours about Hitler's health and mental condition had been further prompted by the rescheduling of his speech on 'Heroes' Memorial Day', 14 March, to the following week, 21 March. According to the central SD digest, the speech dispelled the rumours about his health.[5] This was an exaggeration. The SD station at Kitzingen in Lower Franconia, for example, which in its special report directly on the speech had declared that 'the rumours about the Führer are presumably disposed of' mentioned in its regular report a few days later that some workers had been heard saying that, from the speed and tone of voice, it had not been the Führer himself, but a substitute who had spoken, and Hitler himself had suffered such a shock from Stalingrad that he had to be kept under closely guarded house arrest on the Obersalzberg.[6] The speech, an undeniable disappointment, had indeed been given in an unusually dull monotone and at great speed. It was criticized as rhetorically poor, depressing in its tone, and not matching the occasion—especially in the absence of any special reference to the dead of Stalingrad.[7] Above all there was rank disbelief at the figure of 542,000 dead which Hitler gave as the total German

[2] StAM, SGM 12443. Other jokes about Hitler at this time are referred to in: StAW, SD/37, HAS Würzburg, 29 May, 15 June 1943; SD/23, AS Würzburg, 22 May 1943; and Steinert, p. 348.

[3] StAW, SD/22, AS Schweinfurt, 16 Apr. 1943; StAM, SGM 12506, 12513; LRA 135116, GP Neumarkt-St. Veit, 25 June 1943.

[4] *MadR*, xiii. 4944, 15 Mar. 1943; StAW, SD/14, AS Bad Neustadt, about 21 Mar. 1943; SD/36, HAS Würzburg, 15 Mar., 31 Mar. 1943.

[5] *MadR*, xiii. 4981, 22 Mar. 1943.

[6] StAW, SD/17, AS Kitzingen, about 21 Mar., 2 Apr. 1943. People claimed to recognize in the tone of the speech 'clear symptoms' of a nervous disorder—StAW, SD/37, HAS Würzburg, n.d., (early April) 1943. For the persistence of rumours about Hitler's health, see also: StAW, SD/37, HAS Würzburg, 29 May, 15 June 1943; StAM, LRA 29656, GKF Berchtesgaden, 27 Mar. 1943; LR Berchtesgaden, 3 May 1943; SD Berchtesgaden, 27 Apr. 1943; LRA 61619, GKF Garmisch, 30 Mar., 28 July 1943.

[7] *MadR*, xiii. 4981-2, 22 Mar. 1943; StAW, SD/36, HAS Würzburg, 22 Mar. 1943; SD/13, AS Bad Kissingen, about 21 Mar. 1943. Text in Domarus, pp. 1999-2002.

losses for the whole war. Some thought the Führer must have meant only the losses on the eastern Front, not including Stalingrad and those missing, and put the real figure at something like one and a half million.[8] A letter to the Reich Propaganda Ministry from a former employee currently in a military hospital, dealing with the mood among soldiers, stated that he had yet to meet a single one who accepted the Führer's figures. Their own experiences at the Front, and the fact that in many of their villages and townships heavier losses had already been recorded than in the First World War, contradicted what Hitler had had to say. The letter concluded: 'Convinced Nazis who are really inwardly certain of our final victory don't seem to be too plentiful even among people who have otherwise courageously held their own at the Front. Their doubts can be seen over and over again from their words.'[9]

That hardly anyone was prepared to accept the Führer's word on the losses suffered by Germany is a clear indication of how far the decline in confidence had reached. The mood was despairing, despondent, and war-weary—apathetic rather than rebellious.[10] But the great national hopes built around the figure of Hitler were now falling in ruins; fewer and fewer looked to a future under his leadership.

Outwardly much appeared to remain the same. Hitler's birthday was celebrated with most of the usual trappings and in 'dignified and serious fashion' as befitted the war situation. It was said to have brought new expressions of trust and gratitude for the Führer, 'the greatest gift for the German people'. But the SD added that in the areas tormented by allied bombing the trust of the people was expressed 'with more reserve', and non-attendance at the celebrations was carefully excused by saying 'that it shouldn't be taken amiss if,

[8] *MadR*, xiii. 4982. While the central digest recorded 'surprise' and 'relief' at the low losses, hinting at rather than explicitly registering the outright scepticism, local reports made no bones about the incredulity. As one such report put it, 'the figure, mentioned only in passing by the Führer, of 542,000 men lost was hardly believed by a single comrade of the people'—StAW, SD/13, AS Bad Kissingen, about 21 Mar. 1943.

[9] BAK, R55/583, Fo. 8–8ᵛ.

[10] Reports around this time described the prevailing mood in terms of 'war-weariness', 'petty-mindedness', 'doubts', 'listlessness', 'inner rejection of the war', 'psychological depression', and 'indifference'—e.g., StAW, SD/37, HAS Würzburg, 5 June 1943; SD/17, AS Kitzingen, 9 Apr. 1943; SD/22, AS Schweinfurt, 7 May 1943; SD/12, AS Bad Brückenau, 14 May 1943; *MadR*, xiii. 5202–3, 5215–16, 5285–6, 3 May, 6 May, 30 May 1943.

despite all our love for the Führer, we can't celebrate his birthday this year with the usual joy'.[11]

Where it was still highly risky and dangerous to speak negatively of the Führer, people frequently vented their wrath on the Party and its representatives. Here, too, of course, a misplaced word could result in a denunciation and draconian 'punishment', but plainly the massive growth in the number of critics of the Party made possible a wide range of devastating comment. Relatively 'self-contained' and cohesive social groups such as peasants and church-going Catholics, generally knowing whom to trust and with a low level of organization in the NSDAP, were now often unrestrained in their attacks. The hope that at least the disappearance of the Party might be one thing to emerge from a lost war was said in one report to be more widespread in rural areas than appeared to be so on the surface.[12] Aware of their worsening position, many local functionaries no longer felt as sure of themselves and were less anxious to emphasize their Party loyalties.[13] Goebbels's rousing 'total war' speech on 18 February 1943 stirred the Party faithful again for a short time.[14] But outside their ranks its reception was a mixed one; some, in circles of the 'intelligentsia', reportedly labelled the speech a piece of 'theatre' and a 'comedy' designed for those who had always screamed 'Ja' to everything.[15] And what impact it had made was soon dissipated when it was realized that the 'total' war was still only partial after all, and that the well-to-do and high-and-mighty were still able to avoid the burdens which fell on ordinary people.[16] Some wits even suggested that the answer to the

---

[11] *MadR*, xiii. 5157–8, 22 Apr. 1943. Local reports noted the low attendance at official ceremonies, indifference reflected in the poor displays of bunting, and the lack of resonance of Goebbels's customary birthday address—StAW, SD/12, AS Bad Brückenau, 22 Apr. 1943; SD/17, AS Kitzingen, 23 Apr. 1943; SD/19, AS Lohr, 23 Apr. 1943.

[12] StAB, K8/III, 18475, GKF Ebermannstadt, 22 Mar. 1943; see also GP Waischenfeld, 19 Mar. 1943; GKF Ebermannstadt, 27 Feb. 1943; LR Ebermannstadt, 2 Feb. 1943.

[13] StAM, LRA 29656, GKF Berchtesgaden, 27 Mar. 1943; StAW, SD/36, HAS, Würzburg, 22 Feb. 1943.

[14] Text in *Goebbels-Reden*, ed. H. Heiber, Düsseldorf, 1972, ii. 172–208. For an analysis of the speech, see G. Moltmann, 'Goebbels' Speech on Total War, February 18, 1943', in H. Holborn (ed.), *Republic to Reich*, Vintage Books edn., New York, 1972, pp. 298–342. In addition, and for the reception of the speech, see *'Wollt ihr den totalen Krieg?'*, pp. 23–4, 444–6; *MadR*, xii. 4831, 22 Feb. 1943; Steinert, pp. 331–7; Balfour, pp. 322–4.

[15] StAW, SD/36, HAS Würzburg, 21 Feb., 22 Feb. 1943; SD/17, AS Kitzingen, about 18 Feb. 1943; SD/23, AS Würzburg, about 18 Feb., 19 Feb. 1943.

[16] See Steinert, pp. 354–6; Kershaw, *Popular Opinion*, p. 308.

labour shortage which the 'total war' measures were seeking to combat was to be found by closing down the Propaganda Ministry and combing out Party offices.[17] By March and April morale in the Party had fallen again, and a wave of propaganda meetings aimed at reviving the post-Stalingrad gloom were practically a total failure. The propaganda was described as 'ridiculous' and attendance was frequently 'catastrophic'.[18]

A report from the Lower Franconian town of Kitzingen in May 1943, dealing particularly with opinion among academics, salespeople, and the bourgeoisie—groups which had earlier tended to be pro-Nazi in their sympathies—stated that 'a disgust about the Party was building up among the people, and a rage which would one day boil over'. The same report, reversing the earlier legend excusing the Führer because he was being kept in the dark by his underlings in the Party, added: 'Even the Führer has lost much sympathy among the people because he has apparently let himself be taken in by his Party people and does not seem to notice what things are like in the State today.'[19]

The images of Führer and Party, which for almost a decade after the 'seizure of power' had been largely separate and even diametrically opposed, were now starting to blur in public consciousness. But a diminishing, though still powerful, minority ensured that the 'Hitler myth' was kept alive and could even be temporarily revitalized from time to time when there was a transient upturn in Germany's fortunes or the promise of suitable retaliation for people's miseries. The total collapse of the 'Hitler myth' was reserved for the last phase of the war.

[17] StAW, SD/23, AS Würzburg, 19 Feb. 1943; SD/36, HAS Würzburg, 25 Jan., 8 Feb. 1943.

[18] StANeu, vorl. Slg. Schum. Anh. 3, SD Friedberg, 29 Mar., 23 Apr. 1943; vorl. LO 30/35, KL Neu-Ulm, 2 Apr. 1943; KL Nördlingen, 10 Apr. 1943; StAW, SD/22, AS Schweinfurt, 7 May 1943.

[19] StAW, SD/17, AS Kitzingen, 14 May, 1943.

8

Defeat and Disaster
The 'Hitler Myth' collapses

The Führer has it easy. He doesn't have to look after a family. If the worst comes to the worst in the war, he'll leave us all in the mess and put a bullet through his head.

A woman in an air-raid shelter in Schweinfurt, April 1944

If people had imagined in 1933 that things would have come to such a pitch, they'd never have voted for Hitler.

An anonymous German, March 1945

ACCORDING to Max Weber's 'model' 'charismatic leadership' could not survive lack of success.[1] And indeed, as we have seen, as 'his' astonishing run of victories turned gradually but inexorably into calamitous defeat, the tide of Hitler's popularity first waned rather slowly, then ebbed sharply—a decline accelerating decisively after Stalingrad, when Hitler's personal responsibility for the catastrophe was widely recognized. The German propaganda machine—and Hitler himself in his speeches—continued, of course, to hammer home the theme that, in contrast to the First World War, *Front* and *Heimat* were indivisibly united, and the bonds between leadership and people unbreakable. However, the reports on morale and popular opinion which were reaching the regime's leaders painted a different picture. Only a minority of the population, it seems, as yet contemplated capitulation.[2] Fear of the consequences of defeat and the absence of any clear alternative but to continue fighting, especially following the allied stipulation of 'unconditional surrender', were sufficient to ensure that.[3] But, as Stalingrad showed, even fewer were

[1] See Weber, pp. 1114–15.
[2] According to post-war surveys, around a third of the population did not want to go on with the war by the time of the Normandy landings, and between 50% and 60% eventually became ready to accept unconditional surrender—*USSBS*, iv. 14–16.
[3] For the propaganda exploitation of the allied demand for 'unconditional surrender', and its impact, see Balfour, pp. 316–17.

moved by the notion of heroic self-sacrifice in a glorious *Götter-dämmerung* along the lines that Hitler and Goebbels had lauded as the fate of the 6th Army. The desire for peace was the increasingly dominant and constant theme of popular opinion. In the face of mounting defeats, personal losses, misery, and sacrifice, Hitler's earlier successes began to be seen in a new light, and he was now increasingly blamed for policies which had led to the war, and for his failure to terminate the war and produce the desired peace. And the gap which had to some extent been there from the beginning in popular consciousness between 'Hitler's war' for racial empire and territorial aggrandisement, and the patriotic defence of the 'Fatherland' was widening.[4]

Whatever the distressing news coming from afar, from the battlefields in Russia, North Africa, and elsewhere, for growing numbers of people in cities and towns on the home front the latter half of the war was increasingly dominated by the threat from the skies, as Luftwaffe defences crumbled and allied air supremacy became as good as total. A key component of Hitler's image had formerly been that the build-up of Germany's military might would bring the strengthening of defence against outside threat: a policy of 'peace through strength'. Now those enemies were pouring through non-existent defences and laying waste the cities of the Reich.

Mastery of the skies over large parts of Germany had already passed to the allies in 1942, and heavy raids, chiefly by the Royal Air Force, had been carried out on cities mainly in northern and north-western Germany (Hamburg, Lübeck, Rostock, Cologne, Essen, Bremen, and others). Smaller raids which followed on the south-German cities of Munich, Augsburg, and Nuremberg, had a disproportionate psychological effect in demonstrating the extent of allied air supremacy in the capacity to reach so far south, and in illustrating that few could now consider themselves immune from the dangers of bombing.[5] After the

---

[4] This was implicitly recognized by Goebbels. See ibid., p. 316. Despite a reasonably clear notion among British intelligence of Hitler's diminishing popularity (see ibid., p. 293), allied propaganda continued successfully to portray an image of the German people fanatically prepared to fight to the last for its Führer—ibid., p. 320.

[5] Numerous SD reports indicated the reactions to the stepped-up allied bombing campaign from March 1942. See e.g. *MadR*, ix. 3506, 23 Mar. 1942; ibid., x. 3544–5, 3567, 3597–8, 3615, 3687, 3697, 3708, reports for 31 Mar., 2, 9, 13, 20, 30 Apr., 4, 7 May 1942; and for reactions to the 1942 raids on south Germany, see ibid., x. 3640–1, 20 Apr. 1942; GStA, MA 106684, RPvS, 9 May 1942, 10 Oct. 1942; Reichsstatthalter 694, RPvOB, 5 Sept. 1942, and anon. letter to Reichsstatthalter Epp, dated 22 Sept. 1942; StANeu,

directives following the Casablanca Conference of January 1943 had linked the British 'area bombing' by night to the American daytime 'precision raids' in a 'round-the-clock bombing' strategy, which formed the allied combined-bomber offensive, the raids—described, in this case aptly, by German propaganda as 'terror-bombing'— escalated rapidly in extent and ferocity. A total of 41,440 tons of bombs were dropped on Germany in 1942, rising to 206,000 tons in 1943, and 1,202,000 tons in 1944. The first four months of 1945, which brought the total devastation of the city centres of Nuremberg, Würzburg, and Dresden, saw a further 471,000 tons dropped.[6] Roughly a third of the population are estimated to have suffered directly from the bombing: more than a quarter of homes in Germany were damaged in some way; fourteen million persons lost some property through bombing; between seventeen and twenty millions were deprived at some time of electricity, gas, or water; nearly five millions had to evacuate because of 'air terror'; 305,000 people were killed.[7]

As the above figures show, the year 1943 brought a major stepping-up of the bombing campaign. Now, as before, the industrial heartland in and around the Rhine–Ruhr area bore the heaviest brunt of the attacks, as British Bomber Command launched a series of forty-three major raids in the 'Battle of the Ruhr' between March and July 1943. An SD digest of reports on the effects of the raids of late May and early June 1943 on towns and cities in western Germany, culminating in a devastating incendiary attack on Wuppertal-Barmen on 30 May, provides an indication of the impact on political attitudes.

Many people were said to said to have lost their nerve in the 'catastrophe' and in the heat of the moment to have given voice to 'comments hostile to the State'. One man in Düsseldorf allegedly remarked, even in the presence of a member of the SS, that 'we have the Führer to thank for this'. Here, as was reported in many other bombed areas, people were making a point of refusing or avoiding the 'Heil Hitler' greeting, which had almost disappeared.[8] More damaging still were the many tales of the poor morale and 'hostile

vorl. LO A5, KL Augsburg-Stadt, 10 Sept. 1942; vorl. Slg. Schum. Anh. 3, SD Friedberg, 31 Aug. 1942; W. Domarus, pp. 140–5; F. Nadler, *Ich sah wie Nürnberg unterging*, 2nd edn., Nuremberg, 1959, p. 270.

[6] Gruchmann, pp. 198, 280–1, 414.

[7] *USSB*, iv. 7–10.

[8] *MadR*, xiv. 5356, 5427, 17 June, 2 July 1943; and see G. Kirwan, 'Allied Bombing and Nazi Domestic Propaganda', *European History Quarterly*, xv (1985), 351.

attitude' of the bombed-out population. Among other stories, it was rumoured that a gallows had been set up in Düsseldorf with a picture of the Führer hanging from it. And a joke doing the rounds in various parts of the Reich had a Berliner complaining about the severity of a raid which caused all the glass to fall out of window-frames as much as five hours later and his partner from Essen retorting that that was nothing at all: pictures of the Führer were still flying out of the window fourteen days after the last attack on Essen.[9]

When, at the end of July and the beginning of August 1943, four RAF raids practically wiped out the centre of Hamburg—Germany's second city—in fire-storms, killing some 40,000 people,[10] rumours spread that unrest had had to be put down by the police and SA or Wehrmacht, and that there was a 'November mood'—an allusion to the revolutionary mood of November 1918—in the Reich which would rise up against the unbearable air raids. In the light of such reflections of opinion, stereotype reports that people 'with insight' were saying the Führer could not be aware of the extent of the damage, otherwise more extensive rescue operations would have been deployed, or that people were looking 'full of trust' to the Führer and expressing the wish that he should stir them up and strengthen their faith, have a hollow ring to them.[11]

Although their 'defeatist' tone was highly unwelcome to the regime's leadership, the SD central digests were usually milder in their statements than many of the reports which were coming into headquarters from the provincial SD stations. The reports of the SD station in Würzburg and its subsidiary agencies in the area offer an opportunity to explore the changing mood of the population of Lower Franconia in the light of the five air raids on the local town of Schweinfurt, an important centre of ball-bearing production, so crucial for the armaments industry, between August 1943 and April 1944.

Already after the first raid in August 1943, SD agencies in Lower Franconia reported widespread shock and depression among the population, even among the previously 'reliable' sections who had been convinced of German victory. Party members themselves were now avoiding the 'Heil Hitler' greeting, and the Party badge was being

[9] *MadR*, xiv. 5354–7, 17 June 1943.
[10] See Kirwan, 'Allied Bombing', p. 350.
[11] *MadR*, xiv. 5562–3, 2 Aug. 1943.

worn less and less frequently.[12] More serious than the actual material damage in Schweinfurt itself were the psychological effects of the first raids. These were made worse by the tales and rumours which had been spread by evacuees about the devastation in north German cities, especially following the destruction of Hamburg.[13] The 'most dreadful' feeling was being completely exposed to the bombing, powerless to do anything about it, and with no sign of any retaliation.[14]

The second raid on Schweinfurt in October 1943 prompted many inhabitants of the town to take flight and seek accommodation in nearby villages. Some people in Würzburg saw the raid as revenge for the pogrom against the Jews in November 1938, and 'intellectual circles' reportedly took the view that Germany 'should stop the war, if one was not in a position really to prevent attacks on towns and industrial centres'. People in Schweinfurt itself who had suffered directly from the bombing were said to be completely demoralized and had declared that they would not hold out much longer in 'such nerve-racking days'.[15] Women from the 'lower classes' demanded an end to it all, saying '1918 had not been so bad, and things would now too surely not be so bad'. The SD regarded the 'terror raids' and the rumours about them as 'a negative morale factor of the first order' which had unquestionably produced 'a danger for the will to resist', especially among women.[16] Fear and panic gripped people in the nearby countryside and small towns, too, and many took flight into fields and woods at the air-raid warning.[17] The impression in one village was that foreign broadcasts were being listened to everywhere, and that the 'text of leaflets, accusing Hitler of having started the war with every country, was approved, and the Führer cursed and damned'. Since enemy planes had been over the village, 'they have all lost their heads'.[18]

[12] StAW, SD/37, HAS Würzburg, 17 Aug. 1943, and also 20 July 1943; SD/17, AS Kitzingen, 2 Aug. 1943; SD/20, AS Lohr/Marktheidenfeld, 2 Aug. 1943.

[13] StAW, SD/37, HAS Würzburg, 15 June, 19 June, 22 June 1943. And see, partly referring to Franconia, Kirwan, 'Allied Bombing', 350–2.

[14] StAW, SD/37, HAS Würzburg, 17 Aug. 1943.

[15] StAW, SD/37, HAS Würzburg, 24 Aug. 1943. See also ibid., 7 Sept. 1943; SD/22, AS Schweinfurt, 6 Sept. 1943; SD/23, AS Würzburg, 24 Aug. 1943; BAK, R22/3355, OLGP Bamberg, 27 Nov. 1943.

[16] StAW, SD/37, HAS Würzburg, 31 Aug. 1943.

[17] StAW, SD/13, AS Bad Kissingen, 29 Aug. 1943.

[18] StAW, SD/37, HAS Würzburg, 24 Aug. 1943; and see SD/23, AS Würzburg, 24 Aug. 1943; SD/17, AS Kitzingen, 1 Sept., 13 Sept. 1943; SD/12, AS Bad Brückenau, 20 Sept. 1943; SD/19, AS Lohr, 29 Aug. 1943.

According to rumours circulating in Würzburg, Party representatives in Nuremberg were finding it difficult to carry out their functions following the recent raids on the city. Their uniform 'acted like a red rag to a bull' on the population; people had lost all respect for them, held them to blame for their plight, and vented their anger on them.[19] At the beginning of September, the SD agency in Kitzingen felt that the loss of confidence in the Party and the regime's leadership was rapidly moving towards a dangerous level. Göring was a particular target of popular displeasure for allegedly neglecting the build-up of the Luftwaffe, but the criticism extended to 'the person of the Führer' himself.[20] This was the case, too, after the heavy raid on Frankfurt in October 1943. Inhabitants of the stricken city taking refuge in adjacent parts of Lower Franconia, where many had relatives, asked 'how it was possible for the Führer to allow a systematic destruction of our German Fatherland'. He must know, they added, that German industry would be left in complete ruins if the raids continued unhindered. If the weapons for a retaliatory strike were to hand, then it was 'damned high time' to hit back. But if—and that was the general fear—that was not the case, then it was time to stop all the futile talk of coming retaliation and to end the war as soon as possible.[21]

After the fourth and fifth raids on Schweinfurt on 24 and 25 February 1944, a new wave of criticism of the Party functionaries arose. It was greatly taken amiss that they were not to be seen in the bombed vicinities.[22] In mid-April the SD in Schweinfurt reported: 'The people curse quite openly. If the District Leader and *Landrat* or the Mayor can't be torn to pieces any more, they go on to the State leadership and the Führer himself. Thus, a woman with two small children in the air-raid shelter is said to have commented: "The Führer has it

[19] StAW, SD/23, AS Würzburg, 24 Aug. 1943. Compare this with the assessment of D. Orlow, *The History of the Nazi Party, 1933–1945*, Pittsburgh, 1973, pp. 438ff: 'There is little doubt that the bombing of German cities had counterproductive propaganda consequences for the Allies. The population as a whole did not blame the party for the bombs, but the allied pilots, and the Hoheitsträger could well reinforce their popular standing by impressive feats of Betreuung after a severe raid.'

[20] StAW, SD/17, AS Kitzingen, 6 Sept. 1943; SD/37, HAS Würzburg, 31 Aug. 1943.

[21] StAW, SD/12, AS Bad Brückenau, 11 Oct. 1943. For the propaganda on 'retaliation' and popular responses to it, see G. Kirwan, 'Waiting for Retaliation—A Study in Nazi Propaganda Behaviour and German Civilian Morale', *Journal of Contemporary History*, xvi (1981), 565–83.

[22] StAW, SD/22, AS Schweinfurt, between 28 Feb. and 8 Apr. 1944. Labour Front boss Robert Ley's high-speed dash through the damaged Schweinfurt factories was a particular target of criticism.

easy. He doesn't have to look after a family. If the worst comes to the worst in the war, he'll leave us all in the mess and put a bullet through his head! He's always said himself that he won't experience defeat!" This interpretation of the words of the Führer was frequently voiced.'[23]

One of the last extant reports of the SD agency in Schweinfurt, from May 1944, attributed the defeatist attitude of the population, especially of the workers, directly to the effects of the bombing. Workers were reported as saying: 'Our government ought to reach a peace before our entire villages and towns are destroyed, since we can't do anything about it anyway.'[24] By this time, according to the findings of the *United States Strategic Bombing Survey*, more than three-quarters of the German people regarded the war as lost, and for a large proportion of these the raids played a major part in their loss of hope.[25]

It is commonly assumed that the strategy of 'area bombing'—indiscriminate attacks on largely civilian target 'areas', usually in city centres—failed in its express aim of undermining and destroying the morale and will to resist of the German people and instead merely stimulated such an intense hatred of the enemy that the bonds between regime and people were strengthened, not weakened.[26] Of course, German propaganda was keen to emphasize that the 'gangsters of the sky' had only made the resolve and unity of the people stronger than ever, a point indeed underlined in some SD reports.[27] And no doubt some 'inner cohesion' of the 'community of fate' was stimulated by the intensification of feelings of hatred towards the allied bombers and especially the thirsting for retaliation against Britain.[28] The majority of opinion reports from the SD and other agencies of the regime reaching the Nazi leadership point nevertheless towards conclusions about the impact on morale similar to those we have witnessed for the Schweinfurt area.[29] And Goebbels's own diary jottings leave little doubt that he thought morale was severely shaken by the bombing, and the will to resist potentially weakened.[30]

---

[23] Ibid., report compiled between 11 and 22 Apr. 1944.
[24] Ibid., 27 May 1944.
[25] *USSBS*, iv. 1, 16–17.   [26] See Steinert, pp. 317, 434.
[27] Ibid., p. 434; Kirwan, 'Allied Bombing', pp. 343–4.
[28] See Kirwan, 'Waiting for Retaliation'; and Balfour, pp. 339 ff.
[29] e.g. *MadR*, xii. 4652, 4761, 5277–8, 11 Jan., 8 Feb., 24 May 1943; and especially ibid., xiv. 5426–34, 2 July 1943. See also Steinert, pp. 362 ff; Kirwan, 'Allied Bombing', pp. 350–1, 355–7; and H. Schnatz, *Der Luftkrieg im Raum Koblenz 1944/45*, Boppard a.R., 1981, pp. 324–5, 479–82, 515–18.   [30] See Balfour, pp. 340–1.

Post-war interviews carried out by the *United States Strategic Bombing Survey* confirmed such impressions: one out of three Germans indicated that his morale was affected by bombing more than any other single factor; nine in ten of those interviewed mentioned bombing as the greatest hardship they had to suffer in the war; three in five admitted to war-weariness on account of the bombing, and the percentage not wanting to go on with the war was significantly higher in heavily bombed than unbombed towns; more than two-fifths said they lost hope in German victory when the raids did not stop; and the percentage of people with confidence in the leadership was fourteen per cent lower in heavily bombed than in unbombed towns. In twelve per cent of cases people volunteered comments such as: 'In the bunker, people cursed the Führer.' The overall conclusion was that bombing did not stiffen morale, but seriously depressed it: fatalism, apathy, defeatism, and other psychological effects were all more strongly encountered among bombed than umbombed sections of the population. And much of the hate and anger aroused by the bombing was channelled against the Nazi regime which was blamed for its failure to ward off the attacks.[31]

It seems clear, therefore, that demoralization caused by the bombing raids was considerable, the damage inflicted upon the standing of the German leadership substantial. The mistake of allied strategists was in imagining that such a regime could possibly be brought to a state of collapse by a decline in popular morale. Apathy and a 'retreat into the private sphere' rather than mounting opposition characterized the mood of the vast majority. And escalating repression by the Nazi State—according to one calculation, roughly one in every 1,200 Germans was arrested by the Gestapo for a political or religious 'offence' in 1944[32]—was a heavy deterrent to any 'deviant' activity. What political integration still remained had now for the most part little to do with Nazi idealism or belief in the genius of the Führer, but in the common fear of the consequences of defeat and hatred of the enemy coupled with reserves of patriotic defiance.

In three important—and partially overlapping—groups, however, the 'Führer myth' was still disproportionately strong, even if here too there were distinct signs of its decay.

A large proportion of the younger generation, growing up during

---

[31] *USSBS*, iv. 1, 7, 13–18.
[32] Ibid., p. 2.

the Nazi era and highly impressionable, had been fully exposed to the
suggestive force of propaganda and had succumbed more uncritically
than any other section of the population to the emotional appeal of the
'Führer myth'. The 'socialization' in school and in the Nazi youth
movement—eleven-year-olds were told on their induction in the
Jungvolk that 'from today onwards your life belongs to the Führer'[33]—
kept alive the heroic image of the Führer in many young Germans
even when their parents were becoming increasingly critical of Hitler.
An SD report on youth in August 1943 suggests a continuation of the
old detachment of Hitler from the Party. The report painted a bleak
picture of attitudes towards the Nazi Party. Members of the Hitler
Youth itself allegedly saw the Party already as a piece of history, had
no feelings of loyalty towards it, and had no reservations about
criticizing it. Hitler's image, however, stood apart from this: 'For
many of these young ones, the Führer is not the representative of the
Party, but in the first instance Führer of the State and above all
Supreme Commander of the Wehrmacht.'[34]

Even so, there can be little doubt that by the middle of the war, the
hold of the 'Hitler myth' was among German youth, too, in a process
of disintegration. Though the majority of youth continued outwardly
to behave in a conformist manner, the growth in numerous big cities of
deliberately non-conformist and sometimes actively oppositionist
youth groups delighting in physical as well as verbal attacks on Hitler
Youth brigades, wearing 'western' clothes, aping English mannerisms,
and listening to jazz, showed that Nazism was losing ground among
what had been its strongest area of support. These youth cliques, with
picturesque names like *Edelweißpiraten* or, based on their taste in
music, *Swing*, were regarded as a political menace by the regime, and
for the most part their behaviour did contain a distinct political
dimension—rejection of the Party, the Hitler Youth, the regime, and
the Führer himself and the lack of freedom and dull uniformity which
his rule represented.[35]

[33] Heyen, p. 228.

[34] *MadR*, xiv. 5603–7, here esp. p. 5606, 12 Aug. 1943. See also Steinert, pp. 400 ff.

[35] See L. Gruchmann, 'Jugendopposition und Justiz im Dritten Reich', in W. Benz
(ed.), *Miscellanea. Festschrift für Helmut Krausnick*, Stuttgart, 1980, pp. 103–30; M. von
Hellfeld, *Edelweißpiraten in Köln*, Cologne, 1981; A. Klönne, *Jugend im Dritten Reich. Die
Hitler-Jugend und ihre Gegner*, Düsseldorf, 1982; H. Muth, 'Jugendopposition im Dritten
Reich', *VfZ*, xxx (1982), 369–417; D. Peukert, 'Edelweißpiraten, Meuten, Swing.
Jugendsubkulturen im Dritten Reich', in G. Huck (ed.), *Sozialgeschichte der Freizeit*,
Wuppertal, 1980, pp. 307–27; and also Steinert, pp. 402–3.

Even among the great majority of youth who bowed more readily (or with forced conformity) to the demands imposed on them in wartime conditions, the 'Führer myth' was losing its potency. The findings of a recent sociological study, based on retrospective reflections of former 'flak helpers', then fifteen- or sixteen-year-olds and called up from their schools from the beginning of 1943 to assist in the manning of anti-aircraft batteries, suggest that the 'Hitler myth' was in rapid decline from 1942–3 onwards. The 'flak helpers' had been little more than children at the time of Hitler's great 'triumphs', and in the hail of bombs, the destruction, and the retreating armies, the remaining image of the Führer as the military genius bore scant relation to their daily experience of reality.[36]

The 'Führer myth' remained relatively strong in a second important group—that of ordinary Front soldiers. Based on letters from the Front, the SD station in Halle reported in June 1943 on the strong morale among soldiers compared with that at home, and on the critical attitude of many soldiers to the poor morale in the *Heimat*.[37] Such assertions have to be viewed with some scepticism. Because of the censorship, and the obvious need to avoid dangerously critical comments about the regime and the war, the correspondence to and from the front provides no easy guide to political attitudes. However, it was not necessary to be effusively positive about Hitler or the regime in order to escape the censor's wrath, and it seems significant, there-fore, that many letters home continued to emphasize trust in the Führer, often accompanied by outrightly Nazi sentiments.[38] Interro-gations of German prisoners-of-war captured in 1944 and 1945 on the western Front also revealed surprisingly high rates of continued trust in the Führer, almost down to the very end of the war.[39] On the other hand, the soldiers' correspondence demonstrates, too, in spite of the known censorship, some highly critical comments about Hitler. One soldier, in June 1943, spoke of a growing indifference among his comrades. More than half of the men, at a recent inspection, did not know when Hitler had come to power and 'nobody cares any longer about it'. Among the ordinary soldiers, he said, everything could be

---

[36] R. Schörken, *Luftwaffenhelfer und Drittes Reich. Die Entstehung eines politischen Bewußtseins*, Stuttgart, 1984, pp. 202–4.

[37] Steinert, pp. 388–9.

[38] e.g. *Das andere Gesicht des Krieges*, pp. 112–14, 126, 154.

[39] I. M. Gurfein and M. Janowitz, 'Trends in Wehrmacht Morale', *Public Opinion Quarterly*, x (1946), 81–3.

spoken about: 'The time of fanaticism and non-toleration of the views of others is past, and gradually one begins to think more clearly and coolly.'[40] Another letter, from February 1944, asked how many would still be alive to enjoy the day the Führer had always promised them, when 'the sun would shine again'.[41] By mid-1944, a fifth to a quarter of the 'Front correspondence' was negative in tone.[42]

The third group, and the one where the 'Führer myth' still prevailed most strongly of all, was that of the Party activists themselves. For those 'Old Fighters' who had been enthusiastic Hitler supporters even before the demise of the Weimar Republic, for the direct beneficiaries of Nazism—the careerists, power-seekers, and apparatchiks who had the Third Reich to thank for their offices and careers in Party and State, and for the ideologically committed who had 'burnt their boats' with the Nazi regime, the belief in the Führer's powers to bring about a miracle and achieve final victory in the face of all the odds was the blind faith rooted in self-interest and fear of the future. Morale among the Party faithful declined more slowly than among the rest of the population.[43] The process of disillusionment with the Führer also took place only gradually, and was subject to temporary reversals when the war situation momentarily seemed brighter and to stubborn remarks of wholly irrational but unshakeable belief even when the odds were hopeless.

In the six months following Stalingrad, Germany's fortunes worsened still further as a result of the reversals in the east, the allied landing in Sicily and Calabria, and the fall of the Mussolini regime in Italy. The last of these in particular sent shock waves running through those still loyal to Nazism, produced new hope among illegal opposition groups in Germany, and stirred up more widely the feeling that the seemingly impregnable Nazi regime might after all suddenly be toppled. 'The argument that in certain circumstances a similar development could take place in Germany can be heard constantly', reported the SD in August 1943, and 'the idea that the form of government thought in the Reich to be unshakeable could in Germany, too, suddenly be altered, is very widespread.' As usual, the finger was pointed at cases of corruption among leader figures in the Party, the State, and the

---

[40] *Das andere Gesicht des Krieges*, p. 117.
[41] Ibid., p. 153.
[42] Ibid., pp. 22–3.
[43] *USSB*, iv. 33–4.

economy. And new jokes about Hitler sprang up: in one, the Führer had gone into retreat to write a new book called 'My Error'; in another, the capsizing of a U-Boat carrying the Führer and Dr Goebbels led not to their rescue, but instead to the rescue of the entire German people.[44]

Nevertheless, according to SD reports, the reception of Hitler's speeches on 10 September and 8 November 1943 was far more positive than that of his speech the previous March. As usual, the central SD digest recorded comments after the September speech indicating that Hitler had revived morale and confidence in victory. The most striking point was the announcement of imminent retaliation against Britain for the bombing raids. After hearing from the Führer himself, many were said to believe in it for the first time. His comment that the Party had to be a 'model' in everything prompted the usual naïve remarks that things would be different if all were like the Führer, and that much would be achieved if the Party leaders took his words to heart.[45]

The impact of the November speech in Munich to the Party 'Old Guard' on the anniversary of the 1923 Putsch was apparently even greater. It was 'the old' Führer again, in contrast to the rumours circulating about the state of his health, and back to his speaking form of the *Kampfzeit*, the 'time of struggle' before 1933, stated the reports.[46] A revival of the will to resist and strengthening of the general fighting morale were said to be the main effects of the speech.[47] Again, the part of the speech which really struck a chord was the unequivocal announcement of imminent retaliation. A promise from the Führer was said to be worth more than all the declarations in the press, radio, and Party meetings. His promises that destroyed cities would be rebuilt within three years were also well received in bombed-out areas, it was reported; but there was a certain ambivalence in comments that such assurances would not be believed if the Führer himself had not announced them.[48]

[44] *MadR*, xiv. 5560–2, 2 Aug. 1943.
[45] Ibid., xv. 5753–4, 13 Sept. 1943; see also StAW, SD/37, HAS Würzburg, 11 Sept., 14 Sept. 1943; SD/20, AS Lohr-Marktheidenfeld, 13 Sept. 1943. Text of the speech in Domarus, pp. 2305–9.
[46] *MadR*, xv. 5987–9, 11 Nov. 1943; StAW, SD/37, HAS Würzburg, 9 Nov. 1943; SD/23, AS Würzburg, 9 Nov. 1943; SD/22, AS Schweinfurt, 10 Nov. 1943. Text of the speech in Domarus, pp. 2050–9.
[47] *MadR*, xv. 5988–9, 6022–3, 11 Nov., 18 Nov. 1943.
[48] Ibid., p. 5988.

The reactions to the speech were an indication of reserves of 'charisma' which Hitler still possessed. A craftsman in Kitzingen (Lower Franconia) commented: 'It's remarkable what power the Führer has. The same people who said on Tuesday morning that Germany was defeated didn't want to know any more of this on Tuesday evening.'[49] However, the strong suspicion seems justified that the speech, and the one before it in September, mainly warmed the hearts of the depressed Party faithful, and that the central SD digests were mainly recording reactions from the dwindling number of Party diehards. The crudity of the 'opinion research' of some SD agents was not designed to elicit critical comment. In one recorded instance, the agent approached a farmer (and Party member) with the question: 'Well then, didn't the Führer speak well?', and received the reply: 'Things must be tough in the east.'[50] And given the extensive fear of denunciation for critical or defeatist comment, it is hardly surprising that negative remarks about the speeches rarely came to light. One local SD report stated frankly that after the November speech hostile opinon could hardly be registered because of the fear 'of being brought to reckoning'.[51] The conclusion that the speeches largely appealed to long-standing victims of the 'Führer myth' also seems justified on the basis of an examination of the more nuanced reports from local SD agencies, which, while generally positive, provide a somewhat more varied picture of reactions.

The September speech was said to have disappointed many in the Würzburg area because it provided no comforting words about the situation on the eastern Front.[52] A sizeable proportion of the population did not even listen to the speech. Schweinfurt people who had suffered from the bombing avoided the speech, saying they 'didn't want to know any more of the war' and that 'the Führer is mentally disturbed and megalomaniac'.[53] Those attached to the churches also boycotted the speech.[54] The same section of the population remarked

[49] StAW, SD/17, AS Kitzingen, 15 Nov. 1943; SD/37, HAS Würzburg, 16 Nov. 1943.

[50] StAW, SD/13, AS Bad Kissingen, 13 Nov. 1943.

[51] StAW, SD/23, AS Würzburg, 9 Nov. 1943.

[52] StAW, SD/37, HAS Würzburg, 11 Sept. 1943; SD/20, AS Lohr-Marktheidenfeld, 13 Sept. 1943; SD/17, AS Kitzingen, about 10 Sept. 1943; SD/12, AS Bad Brückenau, about 10 Sept. 1943; AS Schweinfurt, 12 Sept. 1943; SD/14, AS Bad Neustadt, about 10 Sept.. 12 Sept. 1943; SD/13, AS Bad Kissingen, about 10 Sept. 1943.

[53] StAW, SD/22, AS Schweinfurt, 20 Sept. 1943.

[54] StAW, SD/13, AS Bad Kissengen, about 10 Sept. 1943; SD/13, AS Bad Neustadt, about 10 Sept. 1943.

in November 'that the Führer had spoken more than normally about God', that 'apparently even among the old Nazis there's nothing more doing without God', which accorded badly, however, with the way the Party was treating the Church.[55] Hitler's remarks stressing the work of 'Providence' on Germany's side prompted only shaking of the head among 'academics' and the 'higher circles' of society.[56] Others interpreted the troop withdrawals in the east not as the tactical manœuvres devised by Hitler, but as moves 'dictated' by the Russians, and many were disappointed that no precise details were given about retaliation.[57] In any case, hardly anyone in the countryside was said to believe in 'the so-called retaliatory strike against England'.[58]

Though the morale of the Party faithful had been temporarily resuscitated by Hitler's rhetoric, it is clear that rhetoric alone was no longer sufficient to restore the confidence of the considerable sections of the population who had only superficially been won over in previous years by the magnitude of Hitler's seemingly undeniable 'achievements' and who had suffered irreversible disillusionment since 1941–2. For these, Hitler's words were little consolation for the increasingly depressing outlook for Germany in the war. Only a fundamental improvement in the military situation, the implementation of drastic retaliation against Britain, and the creation of an effective defence against allied bombing—a decisive transformation in war fortunes, in other words—could have refurbished Hitler's tarnished popularity.

In fact, however, new disappointments followed on Hitler's confident promises: the bombing, almost unimpeded by German defences, intensified; the situation on the eastern Front worsened almost by the day; and in the west an invasion was expected at any time. Accordingly, Hitler's credibility suffered still further. No central SD reports were compiled on the celebrations for the Führer's birthday on 20 April 1944. Local reports from Bavaria, however, especially from rural areas, mentioned very sparse flagging. It was

[55] StAW, SD/22, AS Schweinfurt, 10 Nov. 1943. The passage found its way, via the report of HAS Würzburg (SD/37, 9 Nov. 1943), into the central 'SD-Bericht zu Inlandsfragen' of 11 Nov. 1943—*MadR*, xv. 5989. For the relevant part of Hitler's speech, see Domarus, p. 2057.

[56] StAW, SD/12, AS Bad Brückenau, 9 Nov. 1943.

[57] Ibid., 9 Nov. 1943.

[58] StAW, SD/13, AS Bad Kissingen, 13 Nov. 1943. On the other hand, the passage about retaliation was said to have been particularly well received by urban dwellers, especially workers.

especially noticeable that no swastika banners were to be seen on
houses where news of fallen relatives had been received.[59] Goebbels's
rhetoric that 'the German people has never looked up to its Führer so
full of belief as in the days and hours that it became aware of the entire
burden of this struggle for our life', and that far from being discouraged 'it stood all the more firmly and unerringly behind his great
aims', sounded even emptier than usual.[60]

Goebbels's propaganda had by this time in any case lost practically
all credibility. Even some Party functionaries were heard to say that it
would be better if Goebbels stopped writing and speaking
altogether.[61] The overwhelming majority of the population now
accepted that the war was irretrievably lost, and some voiced the
feeling that its continuation, with the inevitable accompanying great
losses, served only the interest of the leadership of the Reich, since it
was obvious that the coming catastrophe would mean their own
destruction.[62]

In May 1944, the mood was shaped above all by the expectations of
the invasion in the west. Everyone was aware that the war was now
about to enter its decisive phase. When, on 6 June, the allied operation
'Overlord' finally commenced, there was a remarkable short-lived
phase of almost euphoric relief after the tension of the previous
weeks.[63] And new hope—'utopian expectations' according to one
report[64]—arose again following the announcements on 16 June that
the long-awaited retaliation had begun with the firing of the first VI
missiles on London and parts of southern England.[65]

It was the last temporary lifting of morale in the final phases of the
war. Already after a few days it became clear that the German troops
had not suceeded in repulsing the Normandy landing, and that the
deployment of the VI—rapidly dubbed '*Versager 1*' ('Failure
No. 1')[66]—could not live up to the high expectations created by

[59] StAW, SD/12, AS Bad Brückenau, 24 Apr. 1944.

[60] *Völkischer Beobachter*, 20 Apr. 1944.

[61] StAW, SD/23, AS Würzburg, 6 June 1944; see also SD/22, AS Schweinfurt,
22 Apr. 1944.

[62] StAW, SD/22, AS Schweinfurt, 22 Apr. 1944.

[63] *MadR*, xvii. 6576–80; GStA, MA 106696, RPvNB/OP, 10 July 1944; MA 106695,
RPvS, 15 July 1944; MA 106695, RPvOF/MF, 9 June, 6 July 1944; MA 106696, RPvUF,
7 July 1944.

[64] GStA, MA 106696, RPvUF, 7 July 1944.

[65] Steinert, pp. 459–60.

[66] GStA, MA 106695, RPvOB, 7 Aug. 1944.

German propaganda.[67] The mood immediately sank back into deep depression, especially in the light of the Soviet summer offensive, which had pushed as far as the Vistula, and, in August, the accelerating advance of the western allies through France. The allied advance in Italy, and a new wave of massive air raids on German cities in June and July, added to the demoralization.

In this situation, the bomb placed by Oberst Claus Graf Schenk von Stauffenberg exploded in the Führer Headquarters near Rastenburg in East Prussia at 12.45 p.m. on 20 July 1944. The reactions to the attempt on Hitler's life provide a veiled reflection of the Führer's popular standing at this low ebb in Germany's fortunes.

In view of the rapid drop in morale in the first half of 1944—with a short interruption in the first half of June—and the evidently growing unpopularity of the Nazi regime, the registered popular response to news of the plot against Hitler appears surprising. The two central summary reports compiled by the SD, based on observations of reactions in all parts of the Reich immediately following the attack, provide a more or less uniform picture of deep shock, dismay, anger, and outrage about the attempt on the Führer's life, and immense relief at the outcome. 'Very many people's comrades', continued the SD digest, 'connect directly mystical, religious notions with the person of the Führer.' No comments whatsoever could be found in the first soundings of reactions 'which even provided so much as a hint that some or other people's comrade was in agreement with the attempted assassination'. Even parts of the population known not to be well disposed towards the regime, such as workers in the northern districts of Berlin, were said to be horrified at the attack. Hatred of the 'officer clique' responsible, and shock that such treachery could occur were equally common responses. Three days later, in marginally more restrained tone, it was said that 'only in absolutely isolated cases' was there an instance of the attack not being vociferously condemned. In several cities—Berlin and Königsberg were specifically mentioned— women were seen to burst into tears on the streets in their joy at the Führer's safety. 'Thank God, the Führer is alive,' was a sigh of relief

---

[67] See Balfour, pp. 377–83; and Kirwan, 'Waiting for Retaliation', for the propaganda failure. In all, some 9,300 V1 missiles were fired on England, of which 29% reached their target. Little damage of military significance was achieved, the loss of life—6,184 persons were killed in the raids—was relatively low, the psychological impact one of initial shock but no serious effect on morale—Figures from Gruchmann, p. 284.

which could be heard everywhere.[68] The same picture is supported by a
mass of reports from many different localities, where, within a few
days, the Propaganda Ministry had organized well-attended
demonstrations of the 'spontaneous expression of will of our people
about the foul attempt on the Führer's life'.[69] The bonds with the
Führer were said to have been deepened, the trust in the leadership
strengthened.[70]

Given the state of the war, the undeniable growth of anti-Nazi
feeling, and the rising criticism of Hitler himself, which we have been
able to document for the years 1942–4, such reports can hardly have
been an accurate reflection of existing attitudes. Intimidation was, of
course, at its height with regard to comments on the attempt on
Hitler's life, an act of 'high treason' for which those involved, and their
families, suffered the most draconian reprisals. Remarks coming to
the ears of SD agents were, therefore, to a large extent self-selective in
their conformity. Long before the assassination attempt, in fact,
reports of the SD and other agencies had pointed out that people were
becoming more wary about voicing their opinions in public.[71] With
regard to the events of 20 July 1944, the silences were frequently more
evocative than the comments which the reporters were allowed to
catch. Finally, of course, the regime's agents often added their own
unctuous gloss to the popular mood they were reporting, anxious, in
the light of the conspiracy against the Führer, to put their own
unswerving loyalty beyond question. Given these reservations about
the nature and value of the reportage, it is not surprising that any
dissenting opinion has to be found 'between the lines'. Local reports
in Bavaria do, however, apart from registering 'loyal' opinion, provide
some indications that the reactions depicted in the central SD reports
were not the only ones to be observed.

---

[68] The above is based on the reports in *Spiegelbild einer Verschwörung*, ed. Archiv
Peter, Stuttgart, 1961, pp. 1–10. For a critical review of this edition of the reports sent
from Kaltenbrunner to Bormann, see H. Rothfels, 'Zerrspiegel des 20. Juli', *VfZ*, x
(1962), 62–7; and Steinert, pp. 475–9.

[69] BAK, R55/614, R55/678, ' "Treukundgebungen" nach dem 20. 7. 44'; IWM, 'Aus
deutschen Urkunden', pp. 289–92; *MadR*, xvii. 6684–6, 28 July 1944; Steinert, pp. 475 ff;
Balfour, p. 388.

[70] *MadR*, xvii. 6684, 28 July 1944; GStA, MA 106696, RPvOF/MF, 8 Aug. 1944.

[71] e.g., StAB, K8/III, 18475, GP Heiligenstadt, 26 Nov. 1943; BAK, R22/3355, OLGP
Bamberg, 27 Nov. 1943; R22/3379, OLGP München, 28 Mar. 1944; StAM, LRA 113813,
LR Bad Aibling, 1 Dec. 1943, 31 Jan. 1944; GP Feldkirchen, 24 Nov. 1943; StAW, SD/
23, AS Würzburg, 24 Apr. 1944.

Even the Government President of Upper Bavaria felt compelled to admit that the relief about Hitler's survival was not unanimous, but that 'part of the population would have welcomed the success of the assassination attempt in the first instance because they would have hoped for an earlier end to the war from it'. Such people, he added, were dominated by the notion of 'an end with horror, rather than a horror without end'.[72] The view that the assassination of Hitler would have brought the end of the war was reported as the opinion of many inhabitants of the town of Bad Aibling in his administrative region.[73] Other reports in this district spoke of the reluctance of the population to express any opinion; in one place, farmers, hearing the news of the attempt in a pub, sat 'dumb at the tables' and 'no one dared to say anything'.[74] A police report from a village in the Garmisch-Partenkirchen area stated: 'While the failure of the assassination attempt has unleashed enthusiasm among Party comrades and those sections of the population who sympathize with the Party and the National Socialist State, the other section of the population refrains from any comment or opinion. The wish for a quick end to the war is expressed generally.'[75] In the Berchtesgaden district, most recorded comment—as elsewhere—was loyal in tone, but there were difficulties in getting anything out of the rural population. The view that 'the war might have been over today' was said to be common among women in country localities. And the report included one directly negative remark. From the darkness of an air-raid shelter, a women's voice was heard, saying: 'If only they'd have got him.'[76]

The difficulties of reaching an unequivocal evaluation of the impact of the bomb-plot on attitudes towards Hitler can be seen, too, from a consideration of letters of ordinary soldiers from the Front, where evidence can be found both of a revival, if temporary, of faith in Hitler, and of extreme anti-Hitler feelings expressed despite the censorship. The report of the censor for August 1944, based on an examination of 45,000 letters, ran:

[72] GStA, MA 106695, RPvOB, 7 Aug. 1944.

[73] StAM, LRA 113813, Schupo Bad Aibling, 23 July 1944.

[74] Ibid., LR Bad Aibling, 31 July 1944; GP Feldkirchen, 24 July 1944; GP Ostermünchen, 24 July 1944; GP Bad Aibling, 25 July 1944; GP Feilnbach, 23 July 1944.

[75] StAM, LRA 61619, GP Kohlgrub, 25 July 1944; see also GP Garmisch, 26 July 1944; GKF Garmisch, 28 July 1944; and GStA, MA 106695, RPvOB, 7 Aug. 1944.

[76] StAM, LRA 29656, SD Berchtesgaden, 3 Aug. 1944.

The high number of joyful expressions about the salvation of the Führer, which is emphasized as a true stroke of fortune for the German people, is not only proof of the devotion and loyalty of the soldiers to the Führer, but of the firm determination of the soldiers to fight and conquer for him, which is also brought out in the letters. . . . The treachery of the conspiratorial clique is rejected by all as the greatest crime against the German people. . . . The letters of all good soldiers show that the military duties of the soldier and his good military bearing are indivisibly bound up with the loyalty to the Führer and thus with a genuine National Socialist attitude in general. . .[77]

Extant letters provide ample evidence of wholly loyal, nazified sentiments of officers and men.[78] While anti-Hitler remarks were obviously dangerous, it was not necessary to write in glowing praise of him, or even to mention him and the attempt on his life at all. The examples of strong pro-Hitler feeling cannot, therefore, simply be ascribed to the need to conform and the censorship control. Indeed, other evidence also points to a revival of faith in Hitler among soldiers following the bomb-plot. For example, belief in Hitler among German prisoners-of-war captured in France increased from 57 to 68 per cent between mid July and early August 1944.[79]

The trend was not, however, all in the same direction. The censor recorded an increase from 20 to 25 per cent of negative comments in soldiers' letters between July and August.[80] And despite the censorship, some letters were bold to the point of foolhardy. One private soldier wrote home on 4 August: 'You write in your letter of the attack on the Führer. Yes, we heard of it even on the same day. Unfortunately, the gents had bad luck. Otherwise there'd already be a truce, and we'd be saved from this mess.'[81] This letter passed through unnoticed. A lance-corporal who wrote the following letter was more unlucky: 'Last Sunday when I was in church, the preacher actually thanked God that He had graciously protected and safeguarded the Führer. I'd have liked best of all to have stuffed his mouth with hay. Our people doesn't see how it is run by satanic power.' The letter was marked down to be followed up; the death sentence was the likely result.[82]

[77] *Das andere Gesicht des Krieges*, pp. 21–2. The number of letters checked by the censor marked a huge increase on the 17,332 letters examined the previous month.
[78] See ibid., pp. 142–8.
[79] Gurfein and Janowitz, p. 81; Balfour, p. 389.
[80] *Das andere Gesicht des Krieges*, pp. 22–3.
[81] Ibid., p. 146.
[82] Ibid., pp. 24, 147–8.

We can infer from the available evidence, unsatisfactory though it is in many respects, that, as had been the case in 1939, the attempt on Hitler's life polarized sentiments. It seems a justifiable inference, too, that, even more than had been the case in 1939, a sizeable proportion of the population would not have been saddened by Hitler's assassination, and viewed his survival as a hindrance to the ending of the war. Even so, the evidence is consistent with a short-lived, but still powerful, backlash of support for Hitler, especially but not only among the Party faithful. Substantial reserves of support for Hitler still remained. Given the circumstances, the 'Hitler myth' still retained a remarkable potency. Members of the conspiracy were themselves well aware in advance that their attempt would have little popular backing.[83] Many clearly accepted the propaganda version of events and, even if they had begun to have their doubts about Hitler, regarded the plot as a sacrilegious and treasonable act against the head of State, and an attempted sabotage of the war effort. Certainly, a successful coup would have offered potential for a dangerous new version of a 'stab-in-the-back' legend.[84] As it was, the objective function of the massive shows of loyalty to Hitler, however contrived they were, was to reveal to waverers that the 'Führer myth' was still very much alive, that the regime still enjoyed a formidable degree of support, focused as ever around the bonds with the Führer. Combined with the drastically increased level of control and repression, the size of the Führer's mass following continued to act as a deterrent to further thoughts of active resistance.

Hitler was never again to be at the centre of public attention as he was for a while following the plot of 20 July 1944. In the months thereafter he sank almost completely from view. In most opinion reports from the last months of the war, there is little or no mention of the Führer and the attitudes of the population towards him. He had become for most a distant, shadowy figure, only seldom to be seen now in newsreels, hardly ever speaking to the nation, and no longer being seen in public. Complaints from the regional Propaganda Offices that neither press, nor radio, nor newsreels were reporting anything about the Führer any longer were to no avail.[85] The continued silence about him

[83] H. Mommsen, 'Social Views and Constitutional Plans of the Resistance', in H. Graml *et al.*, *The German Resistance to Hitler*, London, 1970, pp. 59, 63.

[84] See Conclusion, below, for the relatively high level of condemnation of the assassination attempt and positive opinion on Hitler even in the 1950s.

[85] BAK, R55/601, Fos. 212–13.

gave rise to new rumours about his health and mental condition, and that he had been relieved of his duties by Himmler and Goebbels.[86] Some still claimed the Führer was not being told the truth by those around him, and received a far too rosy depiction of the situation. But even the heavily biased reports from the Propaganda Offices were obliged to admit that criticism of Hitler and grave doubts in his alleged 'strategic genius' were mounting sharply, and that those still believing his words that 1945 would bring a 'historic turning-point' in Germany's fortunes had a hard time against the doubters.[87] And though some reports, particularly from higher officials, absurdly continued to state that the belief in the Führer, despite all setbacks, had not diminished,[88] SD regional and local reports provided a much more devastatingly realistic impression of the Hitler image in the last phase of the war.

A number of reports of the SD station at Stuttgart provide a particularly frank account of Hitler's standing in the period between August 1944 and January 1945.

The report of 8 August 1944 pointed out bluntly that apart from a tiny proportion of the population and Party activists, no one believed in victory. Only a miracle could save Germany, and belief in miracles was a thing of the past. Hitler's speech on 20 July after the attempt on his life was turned into a criticism of him and the regime. The Führer's claim that his work had been sabotaged for years, and that the German war machine could run at full stretch now that the last plot had been foiled, was seen to demonstrate that the people had long been lied to in earlier statements that time was on Germany's side and war production increasing. Either the Führer's statement, the report went on, meant that he had allowed himself to be badly deceived and was not, therefore, the genius he was always alleged to be; or he had intentionally lied to the people about rising war production, knowing all the time that saboteurs were at work. 'The most worrying aspect of the whole thing', it concluded, 'is probably that most people's comrades, even those who up to now have believed unwaveringly, have lost faith in the Führer.'[89]

[86] V. Berghahn, 'Meinungsforschung im "Dritten Reich": Die Mundpropaganda-Aktion der Wehrmacht im letzten Kriegshalbjahr', *Militärgeschichtliche Mitteilungen*, i. (1967), 99.

[87] BAK, R55/601, Fos. 123–4, 295–6. The relevant passage from Hitler's proclamation of 24 Feb. 1945 is in Domarus, p. 2205.

[88] GStA, MA 106695, RPvOB, 7 Dec. 1944, 9 Jan. 1945.

[89] IWM, 'Aus deutschen Urkunden', p. 264.

Two months later, the growing recognition of the terrible price people were paying for their belief in Hitler—that the 'hope of millions' had become Germany's ruin—was reflected in bitter allusions to the Führer's 'mission'. The SD at Stuttgart recorded a comment, said to be frequently encountered in differing variants: 'It's always claimed that the Führer has been sent to us from God. I don't doubt it. The Führer was sent to us from God, though not in order to save Germany, but to ruin it. Providence has determined the destruction of the German people, and Hitler is the executor of this will.'[90]

By early January 1945, observers in the Stuttgart area were pointing out that *Mein Kampf* was being—rather belatedly—cited to prove that Germany had itself to blame for the war, that Hitler's expansionist aims which he had laid down twenty years earlier were the cause of the war, and that it was therefore clear that 'the Führer has worked for war from the very beginning'.[91] Goebbels's eulogy of Hitler in an article in *Das Reich* on 31 December was said to have been well received by 'only a few people's comrades and naturally the old loyal fighters'. 'Hardly ever has a Goebbels article stood so much in the public eye as this one,' added the report, 'but his articles have probably never been so criticized.' The 'human' virtues of Hitler, a side of the 'Führer myth' which Goebbels had always particularly stressed, were now scorned. The lauding of Hitler's modesty was compared with the tone of self-praise with regard to his own work and effort which had been a feature of his New Year address. Great exception was now also taken to the mystical aspect of the Hitler image. It was claimed that Goebbels had raised up the Führer to be the 'German god'. The statement of the Propaganda Minister that Hitler had a 'sixth sense' for seeing what remained hidden to ordinary mortals was sarcastically said by a young secretary to explain his choice of Italy as an ally. With regard to the war itself, Hitler's 'sixth sense' ought to have enabled him to foresee that other countries would not simply bow down to German expansion. Therefore, he was not the genius depicted by Goebbels, and had 'intentionally unleashed this world conflagration in order to be proclaimed as the great "transformer of mankind" '.[92]

Special reports from the regional Propaganda Offices on the echo of Hitler's New Year address admitted to a little disappointment about

[90] Ibid., p. 276.
[91] Ibid., pp. 276–8.
[92] Ibid., pp. 66–7.

the lack of details of deployment of retaliatory weapons or the combating of the bombing, but otherwise resorted yet again to the usual empty clichés about restored morale. Many people were said to have had tears in their eyes at hearing the Führer's voice again. No sarcasm was intended.[93] Again, the picture from local SD reports is a contrasting one. In Berchtesgaden, where Hitler had his home on the Obersalzberg, and where he had enjoyed special veneration in former days, the SD reported that his speech on New Year's Eve merely elicited the response that it 'brought nothing new',[94] and there was 'hardly any credibility worth mentioning' left for his last broadcast speech on 30 January 1945.[95] The last public declaration to his people on 24 February 1945, the anniversary of the promulgation of the Party Programme, was not given by Hitler himself, but was read out as a Führer Proclamation by his old Munich comrade, Hermann Esser.[96] With its tirades against the 'unnatural alliance' between capitalism and Bolshevism, it appealed to the last remaining hope—the belief in the miracle of a split between the eastern and western allies and a new alliance between the Reich and the West against Bolshevism. However, people were heard to say that only the Führer himself now believed in a miracle.[97] 'Among the overwhelming majority of people's comrades,' reported the SD in Berchtesgaden, 'the content of the proclamation whistled by like the wind in the empty boughs.'[98] The greatest demagogue in history no longer had an audience.

Numerous reports from all over Germany make clear how little the German people in the last months of the war was attuned to the heroic strains of the message preached above all by Goebbels. 'The people has completely lost its nerve and is dreadfully wound up and frightened', ran a report from Upper Bavaria in March 1945, as once again an 'enemy air armada' in full flight formation crossed the skies completely unimpeded.[99] Other reports spoke of 'lethargy' and

---

[93] BAK, R55/612, Fos. 19–21. See also Berghahn, p. 101.

[94] StAM, LRA 29656, SD Berchtesgaden, 5 Jan. 1945; text of Hitler's speech in Domarus, pp. 2179–85.

[95] StANeu, vorl. Slg. Schum. Anh. 3, SD Friedberg, 3 Feb. 1945. Text in Domarus, pp. 2195–8.

[96] Text in Domarus, pp. 2203–7.

[97] Berghahn, p. 105.

[98] StAM, LRA 29656, SD Berchtesgaden, 7 Mar. 1945. See also GStA, MA 106695, RPvOB, 7 Mar., 7 Apr. 1945.

[99] StAM, LRA 113813, LR Bad Aibling, 1 Mar. 1945; and see Schupo Bad Aibling, 24 Jan. 1945.

'disconsolate mood, bordering on apathy'.[1] Even the highly coloured reports sent in to the Propaganda Ministry had to accept in March 1945 that the crisis of confidence in the leadership did not stop at Hitler,[2] and the point was underlined much more forcefully in final reports from the 'opinion research' office of the SD.[3]

Since the beginning of the year, Germany's enemies had penetrated the borders of the Reich in east and west. For many, the worst agonies of the war were now beginning. The horror stories about the Red Army transported by thousands of refugees from the east whipped up new anxieties. 'If only the Russians don't come here, we could bear everything else', was a commonly heard sentiment.[4] But few were ready to engage in heroic resistance to the last. A Goebbels article in *Das Reich* at the beginning of March, in which he had emphasized 'the great honour of the victims and of holding out for the new Europe', for which it was worthwhile 'fighting to the last man in order to go down in history', met with heavy criticism. An SD report from Berchtesgaden noted: 'The broad mass couldn't care less what the future Europe looks like. It can be gathered from every conversation that the people's comrades from all walks of life want a return to the living standard of the pre-war era as soon as possible, and don't lay the slightest value on going down in history.'[5] The attempt to 'educate' the people to heroic self-sacrifice for historic deeds and ideological aims had led ultimately to an even stronger yearning for material satisfaction and personal happiness. What was said by a single inhabitant of Berchtesgaden in March 1945 was a sentiment undoubtedly close to the hearts of most Germans at this time: 'If we'd have imagined in 1933 how things would turn out, we'd never have voted for Hitler.'[6]

The moral condemnation of the Third Reich emerged for the most part only after the end of the war when the most barbaric crimes of the regime were fully exposed. In the first months of 1945, the German people regarded itself as Hitler's main victim.

---

[1] StAM, LRA 61620, GP Oberammergau, 24 Feb. 1945; LRA 113813, Schupo Bad Aibling, 24 Jan. 1945; LR Bad Aibling, 31 Jan., 1 Mar., 31 Mar. 1945; LRA 29656, SD Berchtesgaden, 7 Mar. 1945; GStA, MA 106695, RPvS, 9 Apr. 1945. And see Steinert, pp. 554–5.   [2] *MadR*, xvii. 6732–4, 28 Mar. 1945.

[3] Ibid., xvii. 6734–40, end of Mar. 1945; Steinert, pp. 572–7.

[4] StAM, LRA 113813, GP Brückmühl, 24 Feb. 1945; see also GStA, MA 106695, RPvS, 9 Mar. 1945; MA 106695, RPvOB, 7 Apr. 1945; StAM, LRA 29656, SD Berchtesgaden, 7 Mar. 1945.

[5] StAM, LRA 29656, SD Berchtesgaden, 7 Mar. 1945.

[6] Ibid., 7 Mar. 1945.

The potency of the 'Hitler myth' had vanished. Silent bitterness replaced the earlier adulation of the Führer. Eloquent testimony is provided by a report on a remembrance ceremony at the war memorial in the little Bavarian alpine town of Markt Schellenberg on 11 March 1945:

When the leader of the Wehrmacht unit at the end of his speech for the remembrance called for a 'Sieg Heil' for the Führer, it was returned neither by the Wehrmacht present, nor by the Volkssturm, nor by the spectators of the civilian population who had turned up. This silence of the masses had a depressing effect, and probably reflects better than anything the attitudes of the population.[7]

Anyone going beyond silent forms of disaffection had still to be prepared for the worst from the servants and supporters of a regime now *in extremis*. Genuine 'believers' in the Führer might now be few, but it was dangerous to ignore their presence. A shopkeeper in Nuremberg who said to a customer what 'in these days was common to almost everybody in Nuremberg', that Hitler was set on continuing the war, tried to deceive the people into thinking that he still had a miracle weapon, and was 'nothing more than a criminal', was denounced by the customer, taken away by the police, and shot for 'subversion of the military power'.[8]

In the absence of any 'situation reports' for a country now almost entirely under enemy occupation, there are no indications of popular reactions to the news of Hitler's death on 30 April 1945. It is hard to imagine that it was the cause of much sadness. With the end of Hitler, the outward signs of National Socialism also disappeared, seemingly overnight, from the face of the earth. Pictures of the Führer and Party emblems, uniforms, and literature had been thrown away or burnt before the arrival of the Russian, American, or British troops. Like the 'Führer myth', they had outlived their purpose even before the end of the Third Reich and were now a liability. The new *Landrat* of Gunzenhausen, a former Franconian bastion of National Socialism, wrote in his first monthly report after the end of the Third Reich, in

---

[7] Ibid., LR Berchtesgaden, 4 Apr. 1945, citing the report from GP Markt Schellenberg. The incident was mentioned in the report of the Government President of Upper Bavaria—GStA, MA 106695, RPvOB, 7 Apr. 1945.

[8] Nadler, *Ich sah wie Nürnberg unterging*, p. 110. Similar comments at this date can be found in StAM, SGM files.

August 1945: 'Although the war has only been over for a few months, National Socialism is hardly ever spoken about, and when at all, only in a negative sense. There's no sign of any emblems of the National Socialist State in any form whatsoever among people who had displayed them in their homes.'[9]

[9] StAN, BA Gunzenhausen 4346, GKF Gunzenhausen, 25 Aug. 1945.

PART THREE

The 'Hitler Myth' and the Path to Genocide

9

Hitler's Popular Image and the 'Jewish Question'

HITLER'S twin ideological obsessions, it is universally recognized, were *Lebensraum* and anti-Semitism. Paranoid hatred of the Jews was the dominant strain, though the two themes fused in Hitler's mind in the vision of Jew-infested Bolshevik Russia, ripe for German expansion. We saw in earlier chapters that there was a substantial disparity between Hitler's actual expansionist aims and what his public image suggested he stood for. Certainly there were affinities between popular aspirations favouring a growth in Germany's national prestige and power, and Hitler's racial-imperialist aims. Expansion of German's borders, especially the incorporation of 'ethnic' German territory into the Reich, was massively popular, as long as it was attained without bloodshed. But enthusiasm for war itself and for an apocalyptic struggle for 'living space' was difficult to raise outside circles of nazified youth, the SS, and Party fanatics. And once the war had come, the overriding sentiment was the desire for an early peace, despite the readiness to benefit in every way possible from the acquisition and exploitation of the occupied territories. There were affinities, therefore, but nothing like a total identity between the Hitler version of *Lebensraum*-expansionism and the hopes and expectations of the mass of the German population.

A parallel disjuncture can be claimed with regard to anti-Semitism. Certainly, dislike or suspicion of the Jews was widespread even before Hitler took power. Jews had to experience forms of discrimination in many walks of life. And among a minority of the non-Jewish population, though a growing one which after 1933 came to occupy positions of power, dislike of Jews became vicious and violent hatred. In the climate of the Third Reich itself, it goes without saying that the barrage of Nazi propaganda could not be without effect in extending and deepening already prevalent anti-Semitic attitudes. Many, probably the great majority of the population, were convinced by 1939 if not before that the Jews had been a harmful influence in German society, and that it would be better if those still remaining left (or were forced to leave) as soon as possible. But prevailing attitudes towards the Jews at this time among all but a small proportion of the population, discriminatory though they were in different degrees, did not remotely match the anti-Jewish paranoia of Hitler and the activist Jew-baiting elements within the Nazi Movement. In fact, much points towards the conclusion that, despite its centrality to Hitler's own thinking, anti-Semitism was for the most part of no more than secondary importance as a factor shaping popular opinion in the Third Reich.[1]

This raises the difficult question about the place of anti-Semitism in Hitler's popular image. Could anti-Semitism, so pivotal in Hitler's 'world view', have been of only minor significance in forming the bonds between Führer and people which gave the Third Reich its popular legitimation and plebiscitary base of acclamation? Was the Hitler image, in this centrally important area, again largely detached from reality? And what function do we accord, then, to Hitler's public *persona* in explaining the process which led to Auschwitz? The evidence available for trying to answer such questions is, it has to be admitted, difficult to assemble, and even more difficult to interpret. The conclusions arrived at in the brief analysis which follows have necessarily, therefore, to be seen as no more than tentative and hesitant deductions.

The recent publication of all known speeches and writings of Hitler between 1919 and 1924 provides for the first time an opportunity to observe the self-image profiled in his public statements. In the present context, what is significant, if not altogether surprising, is that hardly a speech or publication went by between 1920 and 1922 without the most concentrated vitriol being poured upon the Jews. In the first speeches, the Jews were above all at the heart of Hitler's ferocious attacks on war 'profiteers', 'racketeers', and 'parasites'—an expression of his brand of

[1] This is now widely accepted in the literature—see Steinert, p. 263; I. Kershaw. 'The Persecution of the Jews and German Popular Opinion in the Third Reich', *Yearbook of the Leo Baeck Institute*, xxvi (1981), 281, 287; W. S. Allen, 'Die deutsche Öffentlichkeit und die "Reichskristallnacht"—Konflikte zwischen Werthierarchie und Propaganda im Dritten Reich', in Peukert and Reulecke, pp. 401–2; D. Bankier, 'German Society and National Socialist Antisemitism, 1933–1938', Hebrew University of Jerusalem Ph.D. thesis, 1983, Engl. abstract, p. xi; O. D. Kulka and A. Rodrigue, 'The German Population and the Jews in the Third Reich', *Yad Vashem Studies*, xvi (1984), 435.

populist anti-capitalism. From mid-1920, possibly influenced by Rosenberg, Hitler became preoccupied in his speeches with Bolshevik Russia. The picture of the brutal rule of the Jews, for which Social Democracy was said to be preparing the way in Germany, provided the catalyst in the link-up of anti-Semitism and anti-Marxism. In February 1922, Hitler told his SA that the 'Jewish Question' was the only thing that mattered, and a few months later he summed up the entire Party Programme in the one point: that no Jew could be a 'people's comrade'.[2] The ubiquity of the Jewish theme in his public addresses at this time makes it impossible to imagine that early converts to Nazism could fail to regard violent anti-Semitism as a leading feature of Hitler's image.

From late 1922, however, extreme anti-Marxism—now often without the express linkage to the Jews—began to take over as a dominant theme of his speeches. He now declared the aim of the NSDAP to be simply the 'annihilation and extirpation of the Marxist world view',[3] and during 1923, as the notion of a heroic, final struggle between two opposed *Weltanschauungen* seemed to grow in his mind, the Jews played a less overt role in Hitler's public statements, whereas the sole, mortal enemy of the Nazi Movement was now proclaimed to be Marxism.[4] When the press noted the change in tone, Hitler agreed that he had altered his stance, but only to the extent, he said, that he had earlier been too mild, and had realized while at work on *Mein Kampf* that the 'Jewish Question' was one not solely for the German people, but for all peoples, 'for Juda is the world plague'.[5] There had been no change of basic thinking, then, merely an adjustment of emphasis. But even at this date the alteration in emphasis can only have been a conscious attempt to attune to the wider audience, if still at that time mainly within Bavaria, which was beginning to show interest in Hitler in 1923, and an awareness that anti-Marxism had a wider potential appeal than the mere repetition of anti-Jewish paroxysms of hate.

We know little in any systematic fashion about the ideological motivation of the rank-and-file membership (approximately 55,000 strong in November 1923) of the pre-Putsch Nazi Movement. Since anti-Semitism was such a prominent feature of the Party's public

[2] Jäckel and Kuhn, pp. 568, 727, nos. 357, 421.
[3] Ibid., p. 704, no. 411.
[4] Ibid., e.g. pp. 1210, 1226, 1232, nos. 625, 626, 636.
[5] Ibid., p. 1242, no. 654.

image, and that of its leader, whom many must have heard speak in person in the Munich beerhalls, it seems certain that the 'Jewish Question' ranked highly as a motivational factor at this date for the Movement's recruits, often coming to the NSDAP from other anti-Semitic organizations and *völkisch* groups. Impressionistic evidence provided in a number of studies of the early Nazi Movements supports the suggestion that those entering the Party earlier rather than later were more likely to be strong anti-Semites.[6]

It is unlikely that anti-Semitism was as powerful in its motivational force for recruits in the Party's 'mass phase' after 1929–30 as it had been for the early activist core of the NSDAP. A striking feature of the Abel material—and more than half of the sample came from members who had joined the Party before its 'take-off' in 1930—is indeed that even among 'Old Fighters' of the Movement—according to Merkl's ranking of 'main ideological theme'—only about one-eighth saw anti-Semitism as their most salient concern, while what he calls 'strong ideological antisemites' comprised only 8.5 per cent of the total sample.[7] Merkl summarized his findings as follows: 'A breakdown by dominant ideological theme . . . shows about one-third to be primarily preoccupied with the solidaristic *Volksgemeinschaft* and over one-fifth to be superpatriots. Nearly that many are devotees of Hitler's personal charisma. About one-seventh appears to be motivated mostly by their antisemitism. . . . Ranked by the chief object of their hostility, Abel's early Nazis by two-thirds turned out to be anti-Marxists.'[8] Merkl pointed out, of course, that these other categories by no means excluded anti-Semitic feelings, which were encountered in around two-thirds of the 'biographies'.[9] In fact, one could go further and claim that the negative image of the Jew provided a common denominator which was able to combine and provide justification for all these ideological themes. However, the figures are certainly compelling enough to suggest that features other than anti-Semitism dominated

[6] e.g. Noakes, ch. 1; R. Hambrecht, *Der Aufstieg der NSDAP in Mittel- und Oberfranken, 1925–1933*, Nuremberg, 1976, ch. 2. The same deduction is supported by the 'Abel Material'—the 581 'autobiographies' of rank-and-file Nazis later processed by Peter Merkl—though it contains only 20 *vitae* of members who joined before 1923, and is weighted in the sample towards Berlin rather than towards the earliest Nazi homelands around Munich and in Franconia. The war, and especially the revolution, had played a formative role in the prejudice of a relatively high proportion of the extreme anti-Semites in the sample—see Merkl, pp. 498ff., 556–7; and Gordon, pp. 57–65.

[7] Merkl, pp. 33, 453, 566–7.

[8] Ibid., p. 33, and see also pp. 453, 522–3.

[9] Ibid., pp. 33, 499. See also Gordon, pp. 55ff.

the image of the Nazi Party in the eyes of its pre-1933 membership. If we accept that Hitler was regarded by most if not all as the embodiment of the Party, it would seem that, for most new recruits to the Nazi Movement during the rise to power, his own undoubted extreme anti-Semitism formed a secondary rather than primary component of his image and appeal.

In the absence of modern opinion-surveys, the motivation of Nazi voters can only be inferred. But if we extend the above argument, drawn from the motivation of 'Old Fighters' of the Party to the wider electorate, we would have to conclude that here—probably to an even greater extent—Hitler's image was not dominated by his obsession with the 'Jewish Question'. This inference gains some backing from the comparison of the content of Hitler's speeches—revealing his self-profile—in the early 1930s, when the Nazi Movement was making huge electoral gains, with the early 1920s, when it was a fringe *völkisch* sect. Examination of election propaganda before the 1930 'breakthrough' poll has indicated that attacks on Jews provided more of a background than a main theme, and it appears that Hitler's speeches tended not to tackle the 'Jewish Question', especially if dealing with an upper middle-class audience.[10] By 1932, when Hitler was running for Reich President and the Nazi Movement was gaining the support of over a third of the population, the 'Jewish Question' scarcely featured in Hitler's public addresses. Jews and the 'Jewish Question' were mentioned as such neither in Hitler's New Year exhortation to his Party at the beginning of 1932, nor in his notorious speech to the Düsseldorfer Industrieklub in January, nor in his 'Appeal to the Nation', sold as a record in July and typical of his election addresses in the first half of the year.[11] The main target was clearly 'Marxism' and the Weimar 'system', and the main message that he alone and his Movement offered the hope of salvation from these and from the disaster which they had brought upon Germany. Of course, for Hitler himself—and for some of his oldest and most fanatical supporters—all these ills were reducible solely to the 'Jewish Question', a point of dogma which was a fundamental premiss within the Nazi Movement. But the public image of Hitler at this time did not reflect the pre-eminence of the 'Jewish Question' in his own thinking. Though his popular image undoubtedly embodied the broad

[10] Gordon, p. 68.
[11] Domarus, pp. 59–117.

ideological prejudices and aspirations of the masses—including anti-Semitism—it appears hard to argue that at the time that Hitler was gaining his widest electoral support the 'Jewish Question' was the decisive element in his growing appeal.

The absence of verbal onslaughts against the Jews is also a striking feature of Hitler's public speeches in the years 1933 and 1934. The 'Jewish Question' is not touched upon in a single major public address by Hitler in this period of the 'seizure' and consolidation of power—a time, as we saw earlier, in which his popularity was greatly extended and the 'Führer myth' massively enhanced.[12]

Only the exhortation to 'all Party organizations' on 28 March 1933 to carry out a nation-wide boycott aimed at Jewish businesses, goods, doctors, and lawyers, starting on 1 April, concentrated explicitly on the 'Jewish Question'.[13] Proclamations to the Party after the 'seizure of power' generally went out under Hitler's name. In this case, however, though the style is recognizably Hitlerian (apart from the accompanying specific instructions for implementing the boycott, which seem to have been composed by Goebbels), the 'appeal' was signed collectively by 'the Party Leadership'.[14] No one, of course, could have imagined that the boycott was proceeding without Hitler's express support. But the wording of the 'appeal' couched the action solely in terms of justifiable retaliation for the 'campaign of agitation' and 'lies' in the foreign press allegedly initiated by Jewish emigrants, and the claim that 'hardly a hair had been touched' on Jewish heads in the course of the 'national revolution' was meant to suggest that the Party Leadership (including Hitler) was ignorant of the daily maltreatment of Jews which had taken place at the hands of the Party rank-and-file. It was possible, therefore, so far as Hitler was specifically linked to the boycott at all, to see him only in connection with presumed justifiable action, and detached from the 'unfortunate excesses' of Party activists.

As is well known, the boycott was less than a resounding success in terms of popular reactions, and, as an organized nation-wide affair, was called off after only a single day. The relative lack of resonance of the boycott can only have indicated to Hitler that he had been right to keep a fairly low public profile on the 'Jewish Question'. For the lack

---

[12] Nor did the 'Jewish Question' feature in either *Sieg des Glaubens* or *Triumph des Willens*, the films of the first two Party rallies after the 'seizure of power', in which the Führer cult was so prominently projected.

[13] Domarus, pp. 248–51.

[14] Ibid., p. 251.

of overt reference to the 'Jewish Question' in his major speeches, and the omission of his name as a signatory to the boycott 'appeal' can only be seen as a deliberate policy to detach the Führer himself in his public image from the violent anti-Jewish rhetoric and actions of which he privately approved. As we have seen, it appears that, despite his own obsessions, Hitler was politically aware from an early date—perhaps as early as 1923—that a wider currency than anti-Semitism was needed to distinguish the NSDAP from the purely sectarian politics of other *völkisch* groups, to extend the Party's appeal, and to make a serious bid for power. The closer he came to attaining power, the more, purely for presentational purposes, anti-Semitism had to be subordinated to or subsumed within other components of the Hitler image. And once he had become Head of Government, the need to detach himself in public from the distasteful gutter tactics of his activist anti-Semites was prompted above all by foreign political considerations as well as by the necessity to avoid gratuitous alienation of the conservative German establishment around Hindenburg, whose own ingrained anti-Semitism nevertheless stopped short of arbitrary open violence. Moreover, by 1935, if not before, it was being made abundantly clear that anti-Semitic outrages and terroristic hooliganism aimed at Jews by Party activists were generally unpopular among the public at large. Nevertheless, by this time the violence provoked by the new anti-Semitic wave and incited by propaganda had put the 'Jewish Question' back in a high place on the agenda, and pressure was mounting from within the Party for anti-Semitic legislation to fulfil the aims of the Party programme, and from the public for regulations to put an end to the 'individual actions' which had characterized the summer of violence.[15] Hitler could no longer remain aloof from the 'Jewish Question'.

In his address to the assembled Reichstag at the Nuremberg Party Rally on 15 September 1935, Hitler took up the 'Jewish Question' in a major public speech for the first time since becoming Reich Chancellor, recommending acceptance of the three laws placed before it—the 'Flag law', and the two notorious anti-Jewish 'Nuremberg Laws' (the Reich Citizenship Law, preventing Jews from becoming citizens of the Reich, and the 'Law for the Protection of German Blood and German Honour', banning marriage and sexual relations between Jews and 'aryans'). As in 1933, he accused the Jews abroad of

[15] See Kulka, 'Die Nürnberger Rassengesetze', pp. 608–24.

stirring up agitation and boycotts against Germany, and claimed that
this had made an impact on Jews inside Germany itself, whose public
provocative behaviour had stirred up countless complaints and calls
for action by the government. He justified the 'legal regulation of the
problem' as the only way of heading off the likelihood of spontaneous
'defensive actions of the enraged population', and claimed the
German government had been compelled 'by the idea of being able,
through a once and for all secular solution, of perhaps creating a basis
on which the German people might possibly be able to find a tolerable
relationship with the Jewish people'. If this hope was not fulfilled, and
international agitation continued, he threatened, the situation would
have to be re-examined.[16] In subsequent speeches the same day,
Hitler exhorted the Party and nation to maintain discipline, and not to
depart from the path of legality in the matter. He emphasized that the
laws opened up to Jews the possibility of their separate existence
within Germany in all spheres of life, and renewed the command
forbidding all 'individual actions' against Jews.[17]

The hypocrisy of Hitler's expressed sentiments needs no emphasis.
But in terms of his public image as seen at the time, he had been
careful to distance himself from the unpopular anti-Jewish terror of
the Nazi mobs and had placed himself on the side of legality.
Reactions among Party members varied. Some activists were disappointed at the emphasis on legal measures and discouragement of
'direct action' and felt that legislation did not go far enough in tackling
the 'Jewish Question'.[18] Others suspected the truth: that Hitler's
public stance did not represent his real feelings on the issue. A
situation report from Hesse in March 1936 expressly mentions the
opinion, allegedly widely held among the population in the area,
though undoubtedly reflecting above all the views of Party activists,
'that the Führer had for outward appearances to ban individual
actions against the Jews in consideration of foreign policy, but in
reality was wholly in agreement that each individual should continue
on his own initiative the fight against Jewry in the most rigorous and

---

[16] Domarus, p. 537. Hitler used the same arguments and justification, making
substantially the same points, in an interview with a representative of the American
press in late November 1935—ibid., pp. 557–8.

[17] Ibid., pp. 538–9.

[18] Kulka, 'Die Nürnberger Rassengesetze', p. 623; Kulka and Rodrigue, p. 426.
H. Mommsen, 'Die Realisierung des Utopischen: Die "Endlösung der Judenfrage" im
"Dritten Reich"', *Geschichte und Gesellschaft*, ix (1983), 388–9, n. 20, speaks of a 'serious
defeat' for the Party.

radical form'.[19] Outside the ranks of the Party activists, the most common reported positive responses to the promulgation of the Nuremberg Laws were of approval for the formal legal framework for segregating Germans and Jews and regulating the treatment of the 'Jewish Question'. Negative reactions were recorded among church circles, ideological opponents of the regime, the liberal intelligentsia, and some businessmen who feared the economic consequences of the laws.[20] The image Hitler portrayed of himself at the Nuremberg Rally was clearly consonant with the wide accepance of the broad principles of legal discrimination and racial segregation, and with the satisfaction generally felt at the ending of the open brutality and pogrom-like anti-Jewish disturbances of the vulgar anti-Semites.

For two years after the Party Rally of 1935, Hitler again scarcely touched upon the 'Jewish Question' in his major speeches. Even following the assassination in February of the leading Nazi functionary in Switzerland, Wilhelm Gustloff, by a young Jew, the proximity of the Winter Olympics and foreign policy considerations confined him to a single and, in his terms, relatively 'moderate', speech at the funeral, attacking Jewry in generalized terms as the stimulus behind practically every political 'martyr' of the Right since the Revolution of 1918.[21] In his speech on 1 May 1936, he merely spoke of 'elements' sowing the seeds of international unrest, but his hints were immediately recognized by the audience, which howled: 'the Jews'. Hitler's next words, 'I know', were followed by applause lasting minutes.[22] A few months later, on 30 January 1937, he referred briefly to the beneficial effects for German culture which had been derived from the removal of Jewish influence,[23] and at the opening of the 'House of German Art' in Munich the following July he again scorned the Jewish contribution to the arts.[24] However, it was only in September 1937, at the Party Rally, that he returned to a frontal attack on Jewry, framed in general terms, in connection with his main attack on Bolshevism, which he explicitly dubbed a Jewish creation. With characteristic phraseology, he alleged that eighty per cent of Soviet

[19] ZStA Potsdam, RMdI, 27079/71, Fo. 52, LB of RP in Kassel, 4 Mar. 1936.
[20] Kulka, 'Die Nürnberger Rassengesetze',pp. 622–3; O. D. Kulka, ' "Public Opinion" in Nazi Germany and the "Jewish Question" ', *Jerusalem Quarterly*, xxv (1982), 124–5.   [21] Domarus, pp. 573–5.
[22] When the tumult died down, Hitler repeated the words 'I know', but now as the first part of a platitudinous sentence in which the Jews were not again mentioned—ibid., p. 621 and n. 121.
[23] Ibid., p. 666.   [24] Ibid., p. 708.

leaders were Jews, that the former leaders of the Bavarian *Räterepublik*, the Spartakus League, and the Communist Party, had been Jews, and that the Jews were now plotting to plunge the whole of Europe into 'Bolshevik chaos'.[25]

Despite this glimpse of vintage anti-Semitic paranoia, setting the tone for the new wave of anti-Jewish action and propaganda which began in the last months of 1937 and continued throughout the following year, the 'Jewish Question' was scarcely touched upon in Hitler's speeches throughout the critical year of 1938. Once more among his Party faithful in Nuremberg in September 1938, his proclamation contained the usual cliché about the infant Nazi Party beginning the fight against the greatest enemy threatening the German people, international Jewry, and a few days later, still at the Party Rally, he attempted to justify Germany's attempts to rid itself of its Jews by the stereotype reference to an over-populated country.[26] Other than this, he hardly mentioned the Jews in his public statements in 1938. His speeches were, of course, dominated by the great foreign political issues of the year, but there can be no doubt that Hitler was deliberately steering clear of the 'Jewish Question', and that there was a continued conscious attempt to dissociate his public image from the seamier side of anti-Semitism visible in the renewed growing violence of Party activists.

Press directives in 1938 prohibited discussion of the 'Jewish Question' in newspapers in connection with Hitler's visits to various parts of Germany.[27] Above all, Hitler's deliberately intended low profile with regard to action against Jews is demonstrated by the total absence of any public statement with regard to the *Reichskristallnacht* pogrom of 9–10 November 1938. Although the attack by a young Jew on the German Legation Secretary in Paris, Ernst vom Rath, had taken place just the day before his usual address to the Party 'old guard' in Munich on 8 November 1938, Hitler avoided all mention of it in his speech.[28] Nor did he refer to it in his address to new SS recruits at midnight on 9 November, and not a word relating to the pogrom was contained in his confidential speech—not meant for public consumption—to leaders of the German press on the evening of 10 November, less than twenty-four hours after the burning of the

[25] Ibid., pp. 727–32.
[26] Ibid., pp. 890, 899.
[27] Gordon, p. 153.
[28] Text in Domarus, pp. 966–9.

synagogues and the destruction of Jewish property throughout the length and breadth of Germany.[29] The violence and destruction of the pogrom aroused much criticism,[30] but the unpopularity was mainly incurred by Goebbels and the Party rather than by Hitler—even if, according to one *Sopade* observer from Saxony, Hitler himself, 'whose name had formerly scarcely been mentioned in such discussions', was 'increasingly reproached with having to bear the main responsibility because of his silence, his toleration, or even his blatant backing for all the events'.[31]

During the 1930s, then, in the years when his popularity was soaring to dizzy heights, Hitler's public pronouncements on the 'Jewish Question' were less numerous than might be imagined, and, while certainly hate-filled, were usually couched in abstract generalities in association with western plutocracy or Bolshevism. Where he did intervene in public, it was generally to lend support to 'legal' discriminatory measures—for the most part popular and meeting with widespread approval—excluding Jews from German society and the economy. But as we have seen, he was extremely careful to avoid public association with the generally unpopular pogrom-type anti-Semitic outrages. If considerations of foreign diplomacy, unquestionably influenced by his personal fears of the international power of world Jewry, were paramount, the protection of his prestige and standing among the German public was clearly also a matter of concern to Hitler.

In the peacetime years of the Third Reich, the 'Jewish Question' did not rank prominently on the scale of priorities of most of the German population. At certain times, notably in the spring of 1933, the summer of 1935, and above all in the autumn of 1938, the 'Jewish Question' had a high profile. But for the most part interest in it was relatively low—except for Party activists—and subordinated to other far more pressing matters in the formation of popular opinion. There is no doubt that Hitler's anti-Semitism, perceived as it was chiefly in connection with legal discrimination against Jews, was acceptable to the millions of his admirers. But it is striking how little, either in internal reports or in those of the *Sopade*, the 'Jewish Question' figures

[29] Ibid., pp. 970–3.
[30] See Steinert, pp. 74–6; Kershaw, 'The Persecution of the Jews', pp. 275 ff.; Allen, 'Die deutsche Öffentlichkeit', pp. 398 ff.; Kulka, ' "Public Opinion" in Nazi Germany and the "Jewish Question" ', pp. 138 ff.
[31] *DBS*, vi. 10, 9 Feb. 1939.

in remarks about Hitler's popular standing, and it seems unlikely that it formed, for most 'ordinary' Germans, the main reason for their adulation of the Führer.

Between the pogrom and the start of the war, Hitler dealt with the 'Jewish Question' in only one speech. This was, however, his notorious Reichstag speech on 30 January 1939, when, in far more menacing fashion than ever before, Hitler made his threatening 'prophecy' that a new war would bring 'the destruction of the Jewish race in Europe'.[32] It was the first in a series of brutal references to the 'Jewish Question' which Hitler came to make during the following years.

Hitler's speech had its background in Germany's strengthened position since the Munich settlement, in his determination to force the pace in foreign policy in 1939, and—in its tone of heightened aggression towards the Jews—in the anger he felt at the increasingly strong anti-German feeling in the USA and in Britain which the *Reichskristallnacht* pogrom had greatly fuelled. Hitler's threats against the Jews, whose hand he of course saw behind the British and American 'war-mongerers', were an attempt to retaliate at what he regarded as Jewish-provoked anti-German public opinion and, by depicting Jews in the position of hostages as the certain victims in any new war, to exert pressure on Britain and the USA to leave Germany a free hand in Europe.[33]

Hitler's 'prophecy', a brief moment in his two-hour speech, was singled out as the central point of the newsreel coverage on 3 February. Remarkably, however, neither internal opinion reports nor the reports of the *Sopade* mentioned the passage on the Jews in their comments on the impact of Hitler's speech. The SD report for the first quarter of 1939 mentioned the speech only in the context of factors influencing the German press to fix attention firmly on foreign policy developments, and made a brief reference to Hitler's remarks on the 'Church problem'.[34] The reports of the Bavarian Government Presidents all record the resounding impact of the speech—one called

[32] Domarus, p. 1058, and see pp. 1055 ff.

[33] Mommsen, 'Die Realisierung des Utopischen', p. 396, and see also p. 392 n. 36.

[34] *MadR*, ii. 228, 287, 'SD-Vierteljahresbericht 1939'. Hitler had said that he would protect the German priest as the servant of God, but destroy the priest who acted as the political enemy of the Reich, and attacked the sympathy shown abroad for members of the clergy who had 'come into conflict with the law' in Germany—Domarus, p. 1061.

it 'mighty', another 'epoch-making'—but interpreted this solely in terms of anxiety about an imminent war being eased by Hitler's emphasis on his desire for peace.[35]

The *Sopade* reports also centred on the implications of the speech for war or peace, but, in contrast to internal reports, asserted that it had substantially increased the fears in Germany of war in the near future. According to an observer in Silesia, the speech focused the general discussion of the population, even in Nazi circles, almost exclusively upon the coming war.[36] But again, there was no mention of the passage on the Jews. The lengthy section in the same report on the persecution of the Jews in Germany began by stating that what was currently taking place was the 'irresistible extermination of a minority', comparable to the genocide against the Armenians by the Turks during the First World War but carried out in Germany against the Jews 'more slowly and in more planned fashion', adding accurately that 'in reality a lawless situation has long prevailed, through which every act of force against the Jewish minority is sanctioned'. Again, there was no direct reference to Hitler's 'prophecy' about the destruction of European Jewry, though the whole section of the report was placed under a quotation from the speech which led up to the passage on the Jews: that in the light of the suffering of the Germans at the hands of others, people should 'keep well away from us with their humanitarianism'.[37]

Recorded reactions suggest that the German public was pre-occupied not with Hitler's remarks on the 'Jewish Question', but with the implications for war or peace contained in his speech. The threats against the Jews were no doubt correctly 'read' in government and Party circles as an indication that a war would somehow bring about a final show-down with the Jews. But Hitler's prophecy, highly significant though it appears in retrospect, was at the time probably taken much for granted by most 'ordinary' Germans in the context of the ever more overtly radical anti-Jewish policy of the regime—a 'prophecy' so commonplace in its sentiments that it scarcely prompted the need for exultant expressions of praise, just as it failed to

---

[35] GStA, MA 106671, RPvOB, 8 Feb. 1939; MA 106673, RPvNB/OP, 9 Feb. 1939; MA 106683, RPvS, 7 Feb. 1939; MA 106678, RPvOF/MF, 8 Feb. 1939; MA 106681, RPvUF, 10 Feb. 1939. See also Steinert, p. 80 for glowing tributes paid to Hitler after his speech, but again without reference to the 'Jewish Question'.

[36] *DBS*, vi. 123, 10 Mar. 1939.

[37] Ibid., vi. 201 ff., 10 Mar. 1939.

stir up any animosity or repulsion.[38] What is, however, abundantly clear is that, unlike the 1930s, Hitler was prepared, indeed anxious, to be publicly associated during the war with the most radical steps in the 'Jewish Question', even though, of course, his horrific statements remained couched in vile generalities, avoiding any specific reference to the details of the 'Final Solution', which were intended to remain entirely secret.

The nauseating 'documentary' film, *Der ewige Jude* (*The Eternal Jew*), receiving its première in November 1940—a year which also saw the production of two other anti-Semitic films, *Jud Süß* and *Die Rothschilds*, in a concentrated attempt to 'educate' German opinion and harden attitudes on the 'Jewish Question'—provides an illustration of the way in which propaganda was now directly linking Hitler himself with the need for a most radical 'solution' to the 'Jewish problem'. It also reveals some of the difficulties in relating this to the popular reception of Hitler's image.

The film, which concentrated on depicting the 'real' ghetto Jew behind the 'mask of assimiliation', and, using trick photography, likened the migrations of Jews to the spread of a plague of bacillus-carrying rats, closed 'in shining contrast', as the film programme put it, with a clip from Hitler's Reichstag speech of 30 January 1939, 'prophesying' the annihilation of Jewry. The aim was to 'fill the viewer with a feeling of deep gratification for belonging to a race whose Führer is fundamentally solving the Jewish problem'.[39] The film ran in every major city of Germany in late 1940 and early 1941, and simultaneously in no fewer than sixty-six Berlin cinemas.[40] An SD report, summarizing reactions to the film from numerous cities, noted an overwhelmingly positive reception. According to the report from Munich, enthusiastic applause broke forth at the scene from Hitler's Reichstag speech. Interestingly, however, the SD went on to note that after unusually large audiences, prompted by heavy propaganda, had attended the film at the outset, the numbers rapidly dropped off, and there were comments that the film would bring nothing new, that people had had enough of the Jewish theme, and that many were

---

[38] The cases coming before the Munich 'Special Court' show a rise in criticism of Nazi anti-Jewish policy in late 1938 and early 1939, mainly in connection with the *Reichskristallnacht* pogrom, but the total number of such cases was still extremely small—SGM files in StAM.

[39] Welch, *Propaganda and the German Cinema*, pp. 293, 299.

[40] D. Sington and A. Weidenfeld, *The Goebbels Experiment*, London, 1942, p. 213.

nauseated by the depiction of ritual slaughter scenes—some fainting, and others leaving the cinema in disgust. It was added that 'the typical film public' was avoiding the film and even engaging in 'verbal propaganda' against it, while in a number of cities—including Munich—it was expressly stated 'that frequently only the politically more active section of the population attended the documentary film'.[41] It would seem from these comments that Hitler's association with the solution of the 'Jewish problem' was regarded as a highly positive attribute in the eyes of mainly the 'politically active' part of the population which formed the bulk of the film's viewers, but that among 'ordinary' Germans there was also a considerable degree of disinterest in the 'Jewish Question'.

From 1941 onwards, and particularly so in 1942 when the 'Final Solution' was in full swing, Hitler repeatedly harked back to his 'prophecy' of 1939, which he consistently misdated to the day of the outbreak of war, 1 September, not 30 January. This in itself could scarcely be accidental, and reflects Hitler's own identification of the war with the destruction of the Jews.[42] Hitler reminded his audience of his grim 'prophecy' for the first time in his Reichstag speech on 30 January 1941, and in 1942 returned to it in no fewer than four major addresses, on 30 January, 24 February, 30 September, and 8 November, as well as hinting at the destruction of the Jews in the war in his 'New Year Appeal'.[43] In his most dire reference to 'the extermination of Jewry in Europe', in his November speech to the Party 'Old Guard', he stated: 'I've always been scorned as a prophet. Of those who laughed then, there are countless numbers who are no longer laughing today, and those who are still laughing now, will perhaps also not be doing it any longer in the time to come.'[44] Twice more, on 24 February and 21 March 1943, Hitler repeated his threat

---

[41] *MadR*, vi. 1917–19, 20 Jan. 1941. I am grateful to Prof. O. D. Kulka (Jerusalem) for drawing my attention to this report.

[42] See Domarus, pp. 1058 n. 119, 1663 n. 54; H.-H. Wilhelm, 'The Holocaust in National Socialist Rhetoric and Writings', *Yad Vashem Studies*, xvi (1984), 102 n. 8; E. Jäckel, 'Hitler und der Mord an europäischen Juden', in P. Märthesheimer and I. Frenzel (eds.), *Im Kreuzfeuer: Der Fernsehfilm 'Holocaust'*, Frankfurt a.M., 1979, pp. 161–2; E. Jäckel, *Hitler in History*, Hanover/London, 1984, p. 56. Unlike Hitler, Goebbels dated the 'prophecy' correctly—Wilhelm, p. 105, referring to a Goebbels editorial of 16 Nov. 1941.

[43] Domarus, pp. 1663, 1821, 1828–9, 1844, 1920, 1937; Jäckel, 'Hitler und der Mord an europäischen Juden', pp. 160–1.

[44] Domarus, p. 1937. See also Wilhelm, p. 111 n. 23.

that the war would bring about the extermination of Jewry, and came back to it again in one final reference—which produced 'lively applause'—during an address to generals and officers at Berchtesgaden on 26 May 1944.[45]

It has been rightly said that these remarkable statements can only be seen as Hitler's wish to make manifest his work in the eyes of history.[46] At the same time, however, he had agreed with Rosenberg in late 1941 that it was inappropriate to speak of extermination in public.[47] And by late 1942 Bormann was anxious to end rumours circulating about the 'Final Solution' in the east.[48] The striking contrast between Hitler's deliberate flaunting hints—barbaric, but nevertheless generalized and abstract—of the dire events unfolding in the east and the suppression of 'hard' information about the actual mechanics of mass murder, mirrors the manner in which Hitler, as the driving force behind genocide, even privately combined massive threats against the Jews with a taboo on the details of extermination.[49]

The reactions provoked by Hitler's chilling public statements about the coming end of Jewry cannot, of course, be established with precision. A few days after Hitler's repetition of his 'prophecy' on 30 January 1942, the SD reported that his words had been 'interpreted to mean that the Führer's battle against the Jews would be followed through to the end with merciless consistency, and that very soon the last Jew would disappear from European soil'.[50] However, it seems likely that the open expression of opinion on such matters coming to the ears of the SD informants was over-representative of the overtly nazified section of the population. Moreover, Hitler's vicious but unspecific remarks about the Jews were clearly not the centre-point of the speech for most people. According to the SD report itself,[51] the main interest of the population in Hitler's speech lay in his assessment

[45] Domarus, pp. 1992, 2001; Wilhelm, p. 102. Goebbels also referred explicitly to the 'prophecy' in at least two 'leading articles' (of 16 Nov. 1941 and 9 May 1943) in *Das Reich*—regarded as a 'quality newspaper' with a circulation, by early 1944, of one and a half millions—ibid., pp. 104–5, 111.

[46] Jäckel, 'Hitler und der Mord an europäischen Juden', p. 161.

[47] Cited in Jäckel, *Hitler in History*, p. 55.

[48] Cited in Steinert, p. 252.

[49] See Mommsen, 'Die Realisierung des Utopischen', pp. 391–5.

[50] *Meldungen*, pp. 218–19; see also O. D. Kulka, ' "Public Opinion" in Nazi Germany: the Final Solution', *Jerusalem Quarterly*, xxvi (1983), 147; and Kulka and Rodrigue, pp. 433–4.

[51] *Meldungen*, pp. 216–20. The response to the passage on the 'Jewish Question' takes up only five lines in a report of almost four printed pages.

of the military situation in the east, and the generalized response to the 'prophecy' passage was summed up in the single sentence quoted above. For the majority of the population, it seems that, now as before, the 'Jewish Question' was of no more than secondary interest.

The point seems reinforced by the fact that the SD reports following the further repetition of the Hitler prophecy in the speeches of 24 February, 30 September, and 8 November 1942, and 24 February and 21 March 1943, make no mention of any reaction to the passage about the Jews. Hitler's proclamation on 24 February 1943 was, in fact, hardly noticed at all by the population,[52] while reactions to the low-key speech on 21 March 1943 were dominated by the speculation over the astonishingly low figures for German war casualties which Hitler had given.[53] The suspicion must be that for all their draconian nature, Hitler's comments on the Jews were regarded as stereotype repetition, and of little interest compared with his assessment of the war situation.

There are, nevertheless, sufficient indications to suggest that attitudes towards the Jews hardened during the war, and that among those Party members and others who shared radical Nazi views on the 'Jewish Question', Hitler's pronouncements were welcomed as endorsement of the most ruthless destruction of the 'racial enemy'.

The climate had worsened significantly for the remaining Jews in Germany following the invasion of the Soviet Union, in a period of stepped-up hatred towards the 'Jewish-Bolshevik' arch-enemy and heightened tension, as Party activists agitated with renewed pressure for action in the 'Jewish Question'. The introduction of the 'Yellow Star', publicly branding the Jews as outcasts, in September 1941—a direct outcome of such pressure—and the beginning of the deportations in the autumn that year, brought the 'Jewish Question' temporarily into the limelight. In this climate, Goebbels's essay, 'The Jews are Guilty', in *Das Reich*, with its express reference to Hitler's 'prophecy', was said by the SD to have 'found a strong echo' in the population, with critical comments coming from church-going circles.[54] A few weeks later, the deportation of Jews from Minden in Westphalia provoked reported mixed reactions from the local population, ranging from sympathy for the Jews to outrightly nazified

[52] *MadR*, xiii. 4869, 1 Mar. 1943.

[53] Ibid., xiii. 4981–3, 22 Mar. 1943; and see above ch. 7 for disbelief in the figures for German losses provided by Hitler.

[54] Ibid., viii. 3007, 20 Nov. 1941.

comments thanking the Führer for freeing the people of the plague of Jewish blood, claiming that had it been done half a century earlier the First World War would not have been necessary, and including rumours that the Führer wanted to hear by 15 January 1942 that there were no more Jews in Germany.[55]

These and other reports make it plain that attitudes were divided on the 'Jewish Question', now as before. Whether positively, or—in a minority of the population—negatively, it seems plain that Hitler was now, to a far greater extent than in the pre-war period, directly associated with the radical anti-Jewish actions of the regime. And for those, especially within the Movement, for whom it ranked as a burning issue, Hitler's words were clearly taken as a signal and sanction for further radical action and were increasingly treated as a literal description of what was actually taking place.[56]

The extreme anti-Jewish sentiments expressed in letters from soldiers at the Front, though evidently a small minority of the overall services' mail, also sometimes included direct references to Hitler's stance on the 'Jewish Question', interpreting the war in classical Nazi fashion as a struggle brought about by the Jews and destined to end in their destruction. One, stating that 'the great task imposed on us in the struggle against Bolshevism resides in the annihilation of eternal Jewry', went on: 'Only when you see what the Jew has brought about here in Russia, can you really understand why the Führer began the struggle against Jewry. What sort of suffering would not have fallen upon our Fatherland if this beast of mankind had retained the upper hand?'[57] Another, this time from a lance-corporal serving on the western Front and evidently of an extreme Nazi mentality, expressly

[55] SD-HAS Bielefeld, 16 Dec. 1941; SD-AS Minden, 6 Dec., 12 Dec. 1941. I am most grateful to Prof. O. D. Kulka (Jerusalem) for his kindness in allowing me to consult these reports prior to publication in his *The 'Final Solution' and the German People*, Wisconsin Univ. Press, forthcoming.

[56] The day after Hitler had repeated his 'prophecy' in his 'message', read out (in his absence, for the first time) to the 'faithful' assembled for the annual Party foundation celebration in Munich on 24 Feb.1942, the *Niedersächsische Tageszeitung* headed the relevant paragraph of its report: 'The Jew is being exterminated' (*Der Jude wird ausgerottet*). A cutting from the newspaper was kept with his diary jottings by Karl Dürckefälden, an ordinary citizen opposed to Nazism, living near Celle in Lower Saxony, who evidently took the heading in its literal sense—H. Obenaus, 'Haben sie wirklich nichts gewußt? Ein Tagebuch zum Alltag von 1933–1945 gibt eine deutliche Antwort', *Journal für Geschichte*, ii (1980), 29; see also H. and S. Obenaus, '*Schreiben, wie es wirklich war!' Aufzeichnungen Karl Dürkefäldens aus den Jahren 1933–1945*, Hanover, 1985, pp. 107ff.

[57] *Das andere Gesicht des Krieges*, p. 171, no. 351, 18 July 1942.

referred to Hitler's 'prophecy' in a malevolent tirade, thanking *inter alia* the *Stürmer* for remaining true to its principles on the 'Jewish Question' and applauding the introduction of the Yellow Star now also in the western occupied territories: '. . . Things have now finally reached the point which our Führer at the outbreak of this struggle prophesied to world Jewry in his great speech: ". . . should Jewry once more succeed in again plunging the nations into a new world war, it would be the end of that race, and not ours." Gradually, therefore, this race is being ever more reminded of these words. . . . All its efforts won't any longer be able to alter its fate.'[58] Other soldiers sent letters with similar sentiments direct to the *Stürmer*, which, with its circulation during the war estimated at still over 300,000, continued as before to publish a selection of the most repulsively anti-Jewish readers' letters.[59] When, under the hail of bombs in the last phase of the war, some Nazi cranks and fanatics sent letters to the Propaganda Ministry, extraordinary even for the Third Reich in the depths of inhumanity they plumbed, suggesting the shooting or burning of Jews in retaliation for allied air raids, it was occasionally specifically requested that the 'suggestions' be sent on to Hitler. Others addressed their propaganda 'suggestions' directly to the Führer himself.[60]

The evidence we have considered, patchy though it is, suggests a number of generalized conclusions.

The growing barbarization of the war, especially following the invasion of the Soviet Union,[61] led to an increasing dehumanization of the abstract image of the 'Jew' and a corresponding 'internalization' of the justification of the need to search for a radical solution to the 'Jewish Question'. As the forthright proponent of the 'destruction of European Jewry', Hitler's image was enhanced among a minority— though a growing and powerful minority—of the German population (especially, though by no means exclusively, those 'organized' in the Nazi Movement and, presumably, those who already before the war

[58] Ibid., p. 172, no. 352, 22 July 1942.

[59] F. Hahn, *Lieber Stürmer. Leserbriefe an das NS-Kampfblatt 1924 bis 1945*, Stuttgart, 1978, pp. 114, 149, 188–227.

[60] BAK, R55/1461, Fos. 38–40, 301; and see Steinert, pp. 260–1.

[61] See O. Bartov, 'The Barbarisation of Warfare. German Officers and Men on the Eastern Front, 1941–1945', *Jahrbuch des Instituts für Deutsche Geschichte*, Tel Aviv, xiii (1984), 305–39; and also H. Krausnick and H.-H. Wilhelm, *Die Truppe des Weltanschauungskrieges*, Stuttgart, 1981; and C. Streit, *Keine Kameraden. Die Wehrmacht und die sowjetischen Kriegsgefangenen*, Stuttgart, 1978.

had been active, whole-hearted Nazis and convinced ideological anti-Semites) by his open association with extreme anti-Jewish measures. For the committed exponents of Nazi rule, Hitler's public statements on the destruction of the Jews provided sanction and legitimation for their own 'private initiatives' taken against Jews, backing and support for their own involvement in the escalating criminality of the regime.

For another, smaller and by now entirely powerless, minority, the barbarous anti-Jewish measures and policies were one component in their criticism or outright rejection of Nazism. Practising Christians were the most visible group, singled out by many Nazi reports as voicing objections to the treatment of the Jews. But many anonymous individuals whose traits of basic humanity had not been eradicated even by years of Nazism revealed through small acts or gestures of kindness of sympathy that they were out of step with mainstream Nazi attitudes towards the Jews.[62] For these, it seems obvious, Hitler's public association with the radical 'solution of the Jewish Question' and the linking of the Führer to the widespread knowledge and rumours of the extermination of the Jews in the east, can only have been a further negative feature of his image. The same can probably be claimed for those who for reasons which had little to do with humanitarian concern—fearing Jewish revenge in the event of a lost war, or blaming Hitler for bringing on the war through attacking the Jews, attitudes which of course themselves betrayed the influence of Nazi 'Jewish conspiracy' propaganda—were voicing criticism of Nazi anti-Jewish policy.[63]

The identification of Hitler with the 'struggle against the Jews' was most probably seen in a more positive light by the far wider sections of the population, who, though never rabid or violent anti-Semites, had accepted the basic justification of discrimination and expulsion of Jews, and who were largely persuaded of the responsibility of world Jewry for the war. At the same time, although feelings towards the Jews undoubtedly hardened in such circles during the war years, it would be easy to exaggerate the significance of the 'Jewish Question' in the

[62] For notable instances of aid to Jews, see K. Kwiet and H. Eschwege, *Selbstbehauptung und Widerstand. Deutsche Juden im Kampf um Existenz und Menschenwürde 1933–1945*, Hamburg, 1984, pp. 159ff.; and also H. D. Leuner, *When Compassion was a Crime*, London, 1966; A. M. Keim (ed.), *Yad Washem. Die Judenretter aus Deutschland*, Mainz/Munich, 1983; I. Deutschkron, *Ich trug den gelben Stern*, 4th edn., Cologne, 1983; and L. Gross, *The Last Jews in Berlin*, London, 1983.

[63] See Kershaw, *Popular Opinion*, pp. 368–70; and SD-AS Minden, 6 Dec. 1941 (cf. above n. 55).

formation of popular opinion. The evidence suggests, in fact, that, during the war as before it, the 'Jewish Question' did not rank highly, relative to other factors shaping German popular opinion.

There was, it seems clear, much deliberate or subliminal exclusion of the treatment of the Jews from popular consciousness—a more or less studied lack of interest or cultivated disinterest, going hand in hand with an accentuated 'retreat into the private sphere' and increased self-centredness in difficult and worrying wartime conditions. As has been aptly stated, the fate of the Jews 'was an unpleasant topic, speculation was unprofitable, discussions of the fate of the Jews were discouraged. Consideration of this question was pushed aside, blotted out for the duration.'[64]

This conclusion is supported by the replies which Michael Müller-Claudius, formerly a psychologist, received to his unique, camouflaged small sample of opinion of sixty-one Party members (all of whom had joined either the NSDAP or the Hitler Youth before 1933) in 1942. In response to his prompting remark that 'the Jewish problem still hasn't been cleared up' and 'we hear nothing at all about what sort of solution is imagined', only three Party members (5 per cent) expressed open approval of the right to exterminate the Jews, with comments such as: 'The Führer has decided upon the extermination of Jewry and promised it. He will carry it out.' Thirteen persons (21 per cent) showed some signs of ethical and moral sense, though accepting much of the Nazi claim that the Jews had caused Germany harm. Their replies also revealed resigned attitudes—washing of the hands for whatever brutalities were taking place. Three persons (5 per cent) revealed what he called a 'clear detachment from anti-Semitism'. Finally, 42 of the Nazis (69 per cent of the 'sample') provided responses which could be classed as 'indifference of conscience', and pointed to disinterest or internal suppression of knowledge and responsibility for the fate of the Jews. Characteristic replies included: 'There's no point in thinking about it. The decision lies with Hitler alone.' 'I prefer not to speak of it. It's simply not possible to form an opinion on it.' 'Have a cigarette instead. I'm busy twelve hours a day, and can't be concerned with that as well. . .' And 'I'm just about up to here with the war. I want a regulated situation. What part the Jews play in that isn't my concern.'[65]

[64] W. Laqueur, *The Terrible Secret*, London, 1980, p. 201.

[65] M. Müller-Claudius, *Der Antisemitismus und das deutsche Verhängnis*, Frankfurt a.M., 1949, pp. 166–76.

Though of course Müller-Claudius's 'sample' was hardly a representative one, the responses have more than a ring of plausibility about them, and, coming from Nazis who had been in the Party since before Hitler's 'seizure of power', can be extended *a fortiori* to 'non-organized' Germans. It would seem fair to conclude that while for the bulk of the population Hitler's image was no doubt related in an abstract fashion to finding a 'solution to the Jewish Question', this was an issue which people either gave little thought to or deliberately turned their minds from, and that, correspondingly, Hitler's public attacks on the Jews were something absorbed with little deliberation, forming no central part in explaining either the high peaks of his popularity or the collapse of the 'Führer myth' in the last years of the war.

Returning to the questions we posed at the outset of this enquiry, we would, therefore, have to conclude that anti-Semitism, despite its pivotal place in Hitler's 'world view', was of only secondary importance in cementing the bonds between Führer and people which provided the Third Reich with its popular legitimation and base of plebiscitary acclamation. At the same time, the principle of excluding the Jews from German society was itself widely and increasingly popular, and Hitler's hatred of the Jews—baleful in its threats but linked to the condoning of lawful, 'rational' action, not the unpopular crude violence and brutality of the Party's 'gutter' elements—was certainly an acceptable component of his popular image, even if it was an element 'taken on board' rather than forming a centrally motivating factor for most Germans.

Clearly, the Hitler image, in this fundamentally important area, was again largely detached from reality. Though at the very beginning of his political 'career', Hitler had emphasized the need for anti-Semitism derived from 'reason', not pure 'emotion',[66] there were—as is well known—no measures in the 'Jewish Question' which were too extreme for him, except on occasions where tactical considerations prevailed. His consistent defence of Streicher and *Stürmer* anti-Semitism, together with his sanctioning of the Goebbels initiative to unleash the November pogrom of 1938—to which he never publicly admitted—demonstrate the extent of the gulf between image and reality. And the replacement of anti-Semitism by anti-Marxism as early as 1922–23 as the main 'hate-theme' of his public addresses, and

[66] Noakes and Pridham, pp. 36–7.

the relatively low profile of anti-Semitism in his speeches during the 1930s, can again only be explained in terms of a conscious decision to limit the public expression of his own phobias and paranoia for political and diplomatic purposes, to provide a wider appeal and to avoid gratuitous alienation at home and abroad. His Reichstag speech of 30 January 1939 marks the point at which public image and reality started to approximate, although during the war, too, however violent his rhetoric, he avoided any explicit connection with the actual processes of mass murder.[67]

The third question to which we sought an answer was the function of Hitler's public *persona* in an explanation of the radicalization of the 'Jewish Question' and genesis of the 'Final Solution'. Here it seems important to distinguish between Hitler's image as portrayed to and perceived by the mass of the population, in which anti-Semitism was no more than a subsidiary component of the 'Führer myth', and his image as viewed from within the Nazi Movement and sections of the State bureaucracy, where his 'mission' to destroy the Jews functioned as a symbolic motivating force for the Party and SS, and an activating and legitimating agent for government initiatives to 'force the pace' in finding a 'radical solution' to the 'Jewish Question'.[68] It is in this last capacity that Hitler's image as perceived by his loyal 'following'— functioning within the framework of 'charismatic politics'—played its crucial role, as not only the leaders of Party and State, but those in responsible intermediary positions—whether for ideological reasons or for a variety of careerist or other motives little related in essence to principled hatred of Jews—'read' Hitler's vaguely expressed 'intent' as a green light for radicalizing actions which developed their own dynamic and momentum.

For the top and intermediate Party leadership, Hitler's image stood therefore in far closer relationship to reality than it did for the broad mass of the population. In private or semi-private conversation and 'confidential' addresses to the Party faithful, Hitler left no doubt of his feelings on the 'Jewish Question'. A case in point was his speech to Party *Kreisleiter*, the indispensable link with the Party activist base at the district level, at Sonthofen in 1937, in which, in contrast to the carefully cultivated image portrayed in his public addresses, he spoke

[67] See Mommsen, 'Die Realisierung des Utopischen', pp. 391-8.

[68] See Broszat, 'Soziale Motivation', pp. 402 ff., 408; Mommsen, 'Die Realisierung des Utopischen', esp. pp. 389-90, 399-400; M. Broszat, 'Hitler and the Genesis of the "Final Solution" ', *Yad Vashem Studies*, xiii (1979), esp. 81, 83-5, 97-8.

openly and frankly about his methods and aims.[69] With direct reference to the 'Jewish Question', and in response to a 'demand' for more radical action which he had read in a newspaper, Hitler made clear that he had at the time to proceed tactically and in stages, but that his strategy was to manœuvre his enemy into a corner before destroying him completely.[70] In such ways, Hitler set the vicious tone for discrimination and persecution, providing the touchstone and legitimation for initiatives which largely came from others at various levels of the Party, the State bureaucracy, and not least the SS-SD-Gestapo complex, where the 'Jewish Question' had a key functional role.

Hitler's image functioned, therefore, on two different levels. Within the Nazi Movement and the coercive apparatus of the State, symbolizing the struggle to rid Germany of its Jews, and increasingly the struggle to destroy Jewry itself once and for all, it had a significance which can hardly be overrated. But outside the Nazi Movement, the objective function of the 'Führer myth' was rather to integrate into the Third Reich, through association with the far more popular and attractive aspects of Nazi rule symbolized by Hitler, the mass of 'ordinary' and 'non-organized' Germans for whom the 'Jewish Question' retained only a relatively low level of importance. This in itself distracted attention from Hitler's involvement in the 'seamier' side of Nazi policy. Hitler's massive personal popularity enhanced at the same time the readiness to accept uncritically his proclaimed struggle against the immense (but anonymous) power of world Jewry, and to welcome the increasing levels of 'legal' discrimination against Jews which he publicly advocated. This in turn ensured at least passive acquiescence in if not outright approval for the escalating inhumanity of Nazi anti-Jewish policy, and provided the regime with an extensive sphere of autonomy, free from any constraints of popular disapproval, in adopting ever more radical measures towards providing a 'final solution' to the 'Jewish Question'.

---

[69] Text and commentary in von Kotze, pp. 111–77.

[70] Ibid., pp. 147–8. See also the instance of the *Kreisleiter* who, following a court case in which a Jew had triumphed at the expense of an 'aryan', said he would have doubts about justice 'if one did not know that at the head of our people stands a leader who will dry out this swamp when he finds time'—Hahn, p. 193.

CONCLUSION

WE have explored the main components of the popular image of Hitler and their blending into a leadership 'myth' of remarkable potency and resilience. The gulf between the fictive figure, manufactured by propaganda on the foundations of pre-existing 'heroic' leadership ideals, and the genuine Hitler is striking. Difficult though it is to evaluate, the evidence of the receptivity to the portrayal of Hitler's image which we have examined has pointed to seven significant bases of the 'Hitler myth'. In each case the contrast between image and reality is stark, the 'mythical' content unmistakable.

Firstly, Hitler was regarded as the personification of the nation and the unity of the 'national community', aloof from the selfish sectional interests and material concerns which marked the normality of 'everyday life' and created the damaging divisions in society and politics—the selfless exponent of the national interest, whose incorruption and unselfish motives were detachable from the scandalous greed and hypocrisy of the Party functionaries. Secondly, he was accepted as the single-handed architect and creator of Germany's 'economic miracle' of the 1930s, eliminating the scourge of mass unemployment which continued to plague other European nations, revitalizing the economy, providing improved living standards, and offering a new basis of lasting prosperity. Thirdly, as shown most clearly in the popular reactions to the massacre of the SA leadership in 1934, Hitler was seen as the representative of 'popular justice', the voice of the 'healthy sentiment of the people', the upholder of public morality, the embodiment of strong, if necessarily ruthless, action against the 'enemies of the people' to enforce 'law and order'. Fourthly, as the example of the 'Church Struggle' showed, Hitler was widely viewed— even by prominent Church leaders with a reputation for hostility to Nazism—as personally sincere, and in matters affecting established traditions and institutions as a 'moderate' opposed to the radical and extreme elements in the Nazi Movement, but largely kept in the dark about what was actually going on. Fifthly, in the arena of foreign affairs, Hitler was commonly regarded as an upholder and a fanatical defender of Germany's just rights, a rebuilder of the nation's strength, a statesman of genius, and for the most part, it seems, not as a racial imperialist warmonger working towards a 'war of annihilation' and limitless German conquest. Sixthly, in the first half of the war Hitler appeared to be the incomparable military leader who, nevertheless, as a former Front soldier and one distinguished for bravery knew and understood the 'psychology' of the ordinary soldier. Even after the war turned sour he continued to be seen by many as the epitome of Germany's unwavering will to certain victory. Finally, there was Hitler's image as the bulwark against the nation's perceived powerful ideological enemies—Marxism/Bolshevism and, above all, the Jews. This image presumably registered most strongly among those sections of the population whose exposure to ideological 'schooling' was greatest—particularly, therefore, among committed members of the Party and its affiliates. Fear of Bolshevism and the prevalent anti-Marxism in the German middle classes, made even more acute through the shrill tones of Nazi propaganda, unquestionably formed a wide negative base of Hitler's popularity. But, strikingly, Hitler's personal preoccupation with 'the struggle against the Jews' does not appear to have figured as a leading component of his image for the bulk of the population.

That the crass inversion of reality caricatured in these aspects of the popular image of Hitler was in large measure a product of the deliberate distortions of Nazi propaganda has been made abundantly clear in the preceding chapters. Even though at best only partial success was attained in 'imposing' this image on the still unbroken socialist/communist and catholic subcultures, where there were strong ideological counters to acceptance of the 'Hitler myth', and on sections of the upper classes whose status-conscious élitism provided a continuing barrier to the appeal of populist leadership images, there can be no doubt that the penetration of the propagated 'Hitler myth' was deep, especially, but by no means only, among the German middle classes. After 1933, Nazi propaganda, largely uncontested now that opponents within Germany had been silenced, could almost deify Hitler. Goebbels, as we saw, ranked his creation of the public Hitler image as his greatest propaganda triumph. Yet, cynical though its 'manufacture' was, the excesses of the Führer cult after 1933, and the extent of its penetration, are inconceivable without the realization that, in the crisis conditions of the early 1930s, it had touched upon and articulated (even if in extreme and distorted fashion) long-standing and pervasive elements of the bourgeois political culture in Germany.

Of these, the most crucial arose from the disparities between the superficial attainment of national unity and the internal divisions of the German nation-state since its creation in 1871, and the gulf between the immense world-power aspirations and the modesty of Germany's actual achievements in international relations. From Bismarck's time onwards, 'national unity' in the new nation-state not only received exaggerated emphasis, but was focused on the rejection of internal 'enemies of the Reich' (Catholics, socialists, ethnic minorities) and, increasingly under Wilhelm II, was linked to varying notions of German expansionism. The internal divisions grew more rather than less apparent, however, enhanced by the populist politics from the 1890s onwards, and the imperialist ambitions, though more and more strident, were gravely disappointed. The ideological basis was there for the fundamental divides which the war, defeat, and revolution openly exposed, and which provided the Weimar Republic from its inception with an extremely weak base of legitimation, especially among the bourgeoisie and élites. The extensified fragmentation of Weimar politics and eventual decline into little more than interest politics[1] in the face of mounting internal crisis, entirely delegitimized the State system itself, wholly discredited pluralist politics, and paved the way for a full acceptance—already by 1932 of around 13 million Germans—of a new basis of unity represented in an entirely novel political form personalized in Hitler's 'charismatic' leadership.

In such conditions as prevailed in the last phase of the Weimar Republic, of the total discrediting of a State system based upon pluralist politics, the 'functional' leadership of the bureaucrat and the Party politician as the representatives of the impersonal 'rational-legal' form of political domination, imposing laws and carrying out functions for which they are not personally responsible and with which they are not identifiable, lost credibility. Salvation could only be sought with a leader who possessed *personal* power and was prepared to take *personal* responsibility, sweeping away the causes of the misery and the faceless politicians and bureaucrats who prevail over it, and seeming to impose his own personal power upon the force of history itself.[2] In reality, of course, the fascist variant of 'charismatic

---

[1] See T. Childers, 'Interest and Ideology: Anti-System Politics in the Era of Stabilization 1924–1928', in G. Feldman (ed.), *Die Nachwirkungen der Inflation auf die deutsche Geschichte*, Munich, 1985, pp. 1–20.

[2] See A. Gorz, *Farewell to the Working Class*, London, 1982, pp. 58–9, 62–3.

leadership'—there are obvious parallels in the Mussolini cult—was not only superimposed on existing bureaucratic power, but created new, extensive apparatuses of bureaucratic administration, and led not to diminished but to massively increased bureaucratic interference in all spheres of daily life. In this paradox, we see the essence of the heightened detestation of the new breed of Party 'functionaries', the agents—along with the traditionally disliked State civil servants—of this bureaucratized control, and the popularity of the Führer, whose personal power was idealized and elevated to a plane where it seemed to be executed outside the realms of 'everyday life'.

An extract from a speech to the Reichstag in April 1939 illustrates well the personalized claims Hitler made for 'his' great 'achievements' and how far these rested on 'national' rather than specifically Nazi ideals and aspirations. These 'achievements' provided the basis on which Hitler, more than any politician before him, had been able to integrate not only the German middle classes, but the vast majority of the population who, on particular aspects of policy, could often reveal heated antagonism to the specific manifestations of Nazi rule affecting their daily lives. In his speech, on 28 April 1939, Hitler provided the following catalogue of achievements which, in the view of most ordinary Germans, could only be taken as a breathtaking list of personal successes:

I have overcome the chaos in Germany, restored order, massively raised production in all areas of our national economy ... I have succeeded in completely bringing back into useful production the seven million unemployed who were so dear to all our own hearts, in keeping the German peasant on his soil despite all difficulties and in rescuing it for him, in attaining the renewed flourishing of German trade, and in tremendously promoting transportation. I have not only politically united the German people, but also militarily rearmed them, and I have further attempted to tear up page for page that Treaty, which contained in its 448 articles the most base violations ever accorded to nations and human beings. I have given back to the Reich the provinces stolen from us in 1919. I have led back into the homeland the millions of deeply unhappy Germans who had been torn away from us. I have recreated the thousand-year historic unity of the German living-space, and I have attempted to do all this without spilling blood and without inflicting on my people or on others the suffering of war. I have managed this from my own strength, as one who twenty-one years ago was an unknown worker and soldier of my people.[3]

---

[3] Domarus, p. 1178; see also Haffner, p. 44.

For the great mass of Hitler's audience, the political and economic recovery of Germany, which he was trumpeting as his own personal achievement, was a goal in itself. For Hitler and the Nazi leadership, it provided only the base for racial-imperialist conquest and a war of annihilation. It remains for us to ask how the popular Hitler image we have examined contributed towards the growing strength of the regime and towards making possible this war, which, from what we have seen, most Germans—though prepared to fight if necessary—had been only too anxious to avoid.

The 'Hitler myth' can be seen as providing the central motor for integration, mobilization, and legitimation within the Nazi system of rule. Its functional significance has to be examined in the context of its importance for the 'non-organized' masses, whose image of Hitler has been the central concern of this work, for the Party faithful, and for the Nazi and non-Nazi élites.

No one was more aware of the functional significance of his popularity in binding the masses to him, and hence to the regime, than Hitler himself. He pointed out that the strength of the regime could not depend on 'the laws [!] of the Gestapo alone', and that 'the broad mass [of the population] needs an idol'.[4] On another occasion, he commented that the ruler who was dependent only upon executive power without finding 'the way to the people' was destined to failure.[5] His well-documented fear of loss of personal popularity and the corresponding growth in instability of the regime[6] is further testimony of his awareness of the centrality of the integratory force of his role as Führer. This integration was largely affective, for the most part forging psychological or emotional rather than material bonds. But its reality can scarcely be doubted. And at moments of internal crisis— such as in June 1934—the regime was stabilized and its leadership given extended room for manœuvrability through the surge in Hitler's popularity and the strengthening of bonds of identity between people and Führer. In his portrayed public image, Hitler was able to offer a positive pole in the Third Reich, transcending sectional interests and grievances through the overriding ideal of national unity, made

---

[4] Picker, *Hitlers Tischgespräche*, p. 478; cited in von Kotze, p. 46.

[5] Cited in von Kotze, p. 46.

[6] See Speer, p. 229; and also T. W. Mason, 'The Legacy of 1918 for National Socialism', in A. Nicholls and E. Matthias (eds.), *German Democracy and the Triumph of Hitler*, London, 1971, pp. 215–39.

possible through his necessary aloofness from the 'conflict sphere' of daily politics, separating him from the more unpopular aspects of Nazism.

Hitler recognized that enthusiasm and willingness for self-sacrifice could not be conserved, and were bound to fade when confronted with 'the grey daily routine and the convenience of life'.[7] He saw, therefore, that the masses could be bound to him only through constant psychological mobilization, demanding ever recurring successes. Until the middle of the war, the successes came, and spectacularly so, especially in the arena of foreign policy and military affairs, bringing many Germans who were far from Nazis into close identification with Hitler, revamping sagging morale, forcing open acclaim, prompting active participation—if shallow and largely ritualized—in support of 'his' achievements, disarming potential opponents, making objections to Nazi policy difficult to formulate. This was, for example, un-doubtedly the effect of the plebiscites staged in 1933, 1934, 1936, and 1938, in which the massive acclamation, though the product of intense propaganda and coercion and obviously in no sense a true reflection of the state of opinion, nevertheless reflected genuine widespread approval and admiration for Hitler's accomplishments and persuaded waverers to fall in line.[8]

The plebiscitary acclamation which could always be mobilized by Hitler provided him with an unassailable base of popularity, and as such offered the regime legitimation both within Germany and in the eyes of foreign powers, allowing the scope for further mobilization and a gathering momentum of Nazi policy. The massive popularity of Hitler, recognized even by enemies of the regime, formed therefore a decisive element in the structure of Nazi rule in Germany. It goes far towards helping to account not only for the high and growing degree of relative autonomy from non-Nazi élites enjoyed by Hitler and the Nazi leadership, but also—as the counterweight to terror, repression, and intimidation—for the weakness of resistance to the regime. The 'Hitler myth' and terror were in this sense two indispensable sides of the same coin, ensuring political control and moblization behind the regime. It is no coincidence, therefore, that terroristic repression escalated wildly in the final phase of the waning regime as the binding force of Hitler's popularity weakened and collapsed.

[7] *Lagebesprechungen im Führerhauptquartier*, ed. H. Heiber, Berlin, 1962, p. 287.
[8] See Schweitzer, pp. 86–7.

For the mass of 'non-organized' Germans, the 'Hitler myth' functioned through the stimulation of popular acclaim—recurrent but always temporary—for *faits accomplis*, for coups which had been brought about, successes already attained, rather than for a clear set of policies in train. One main role of the Party was to ensure that the appropriate degree of acclamation was produced. But for the activists in the Party and its affiliates, the integratory and mobilizing functions of the 'Hitler myth' were not confined to support for current attainments, but rested on the incorporation in Hitler of the 'idea' of Nazism itself, determining future utopias to be won as well as past glories achieved. The centrifugal forces of the Nazi Movement were held together in great measure by the ideals embodied in the image of the Führer; social disappointments and disillusionment could be transcended and overcome by participation in the Führer's great 'struggle' and ultimate satisfaction in the brave new world to come. For the activist and 'committed' core of the Movement, especially for the younger element, the perceived Führer image stood symbolically for ideological precepts—preparing for a show-down with Bolshevism, acquisition of *Lebensraum*, 'removal of Jews'—which were 'directions for action'[9] long before they were realizable objectives. Without such ideological precepts bound up in the 'representative figure' of the Führer, the dynamism built into the permanent mobilization of the Party and its affiliates is largely unthinkable. Not detailed plans of a Party programme, but his role as the embodiment of a cosmic struggle against irreconcilable internal and external enemies of immense power and magnitude ultimately bound the Party faithful to Hitler.

And where the coming mortal conflict with Bolshevism sharpened among Nazi activists the preparedness and taste for uncompromising and brutal struggle, and the idea of *Lebensraum* and limitless German expansionism provided a future panacea for all national ills and current personal dissatisfactions, the 'removal of the Jews' offered a current, existing target to be attained, even if the road to the goal was unclear. Based as it was on principles of race, with the figure of the Jew as the focal point of all hatred, and with the Führer as its ideological and organizational fulcrum, the Nazi Movement needed no regular orders or directions from Hitler to step up the pace of anti-Jewish

---

[9] Broszat, 'Soziale Motivation', p. 405. The following reflections owe much to this stimulating article.

actions and discrimination, pushing the government and the State bureaucracy into action, and always therefore increasing the radicalizing momentum of racial policy.

In such ways, the Führer image functioned, in integrating the potentially disintegrative forces within the Nazi Movement on a different plane among the Party 'faithful' than among the broad mass of 'non-organized' Germans, in mobilizing the boundless energy and misplaced idealism of the fanatics and activists through orientation towards long-term 'cosmic' and 'utopian' goals, and through offering legitimation for action undertaken against ideological and racial 'enemies of the State'.

The significance of the 'Hitler myth' has to be seen, finally, on a third level which preceding chapters have not sought to explore systematically: that of its function for the élites—both the non-Nazi 'national-conservative' élites and the power-groups within the Movement itself.

For non-Nazi, 'national-conservative' power-élites in the economy and in the army, Hitler's 'charisma' had in itself never been a decisive factor, even though by the early 1930s it seems clear that substantial sectors of especially the 'intellectual élite' had succumbed in varying degrees to the Führer cult.[10] For the traditional élites, it was not charisma but pragmatic power considerations which aligned them with Hitler. The erosion of their political and social 'basis of legitimation', stretching deep into the pre-war era, had reached a critical level during the Weimar Republic.[11] Hitler was able to offer them a new mass base for the apparent consolidation of their leadership positions within the framework of an authoritarian system, together with the prospect of Germany attaining a position of hegemony within Europe and even world power status. For his part, Hitler needed their support to gain and consolidate power. This was the well-known basis of the *entente* between the dominant forces of the traditional 'power-élite' and the Nazi leadership in January 1933.[12]

[10] See Struve, p. 433; Weinstein, pp. 66–7; H. Mommsen, 'Zur Verschränkung traditioneller und faschistischer Führungsgruppen in Deutschland beim Übergang von der Bewegungs- zur Systemphase', in Schieder, p. 165; and H. Mommsen, 'Der Mythos des nationalen Aufbruchs und die Haltung der deutschen Intellektuellen und funktionalen Eliten', in *1933 in Gesellschaft und Wissenschaft*, ed. Pressestelle der Universität Hamburg, Hamburg, 1983, p. 134.

[11] See K.-J. Müller, 'Nationalkonservative Eliten zwischen Kooperation und Widerstand', in Schmädeke and Steinbach, pp. 25–6; R. Baum, *The Holocaust and the German Elite*, London, 1981, pp. 52–3, 178ff., 183ff.

[12] See Müller, 'Nationalkonservative Eliten', pp. 25–6.

However little 'charisma' had come into these considerations in 1933, there seems no doubt that the 'Hitler myth'—or significant elements of it—played an important role in shaping the behaviour of the conservative élites in the following years in at least two ways. Firstly, misplaced conceptions within the élites of Hitler as a man whom they could trust and 'work with', in contrast to the Party radicals, integrated the disparate sectors of the élites and mobilized their support behind the Nazi leadership in the critical early years at the same time that Hitler's popularity provided the mass base of legitimation for the presumed reassertion of their own spheres of domination. Important figures from within the 'national-conservative' élites who later played prominent roles in resistance to Nazism—such as Ernst von Weizsäcker in the bureaucracy, Carl Goerdeler in the economy, and Henning von Tresckow in the military—were all prepared to distance Hitler in the early years from their mounting criticism of the radicals in the Movement.[13] Their path into fundamental opposition was, partly for this reason, a hesitant one, and their objections to the regime for long less than fundamental.[14]

Secondly, their underrating of the 'caesaristic' elements of Hitler's mass charismatic base meant that, far from providing a new foundation for the power of the traditional élites, as they had hoped, the plebiscitary acclamation of the Führer enabled Hitler's own power to detach itself from its likely shackles and develop a high degree of relative autonomy, at the same time reducing former dominant groups like the army from 'power-élites' proper to merely 'functional élites',[15] unable to check Hitler himself and the 'wild men' of the Nazi Movement, even when wishing to do so. In cementing the basis of the Führer's pivotal position, the 'Hitler myth' had been instrumental in establishing a situation in which the traditional élites could become outflanked by the specifically Nazi élites. Unlike the position in classic 'Bonapartist' theory, therefore, the Dictator and his entourage could not be edged aside by the traditional 'ruling class' once the economy had been stabilized. The dynamic driving-force of the 'Hitler myth'

---

[13] Ibid., pp. 28–30.

[14] The ways in which conservative opposition groups, even when actively conspiring to destroy the regime, could accommodate—without, of course, identifying with them—central parts of Nazi ideology in their 'world view' has recently been shown with regard to the 'Jewish Question'. See C. Dipper, 'The German Resistance and the Jews', *Yad Vashem Studies*, xvi (1984), 51–93.

[15] See K.-J. Müller, *Armee, Politik und Gesellschaft in Deutschland 1933–1945*, Paderborn, 1979, pp. 39–47.

allowed, in fact, no stabilization or 'normalization', but rather conditioned circumstances in which the traditional 'ruling class' became ever more subsumed in and dependent upon the 'behemoth'[16] of the Nazi State which it was no longer able to control in its mad rush to destruction.

From the early 1920s onwards, Hitler had built up his power base in the Party above all on the strength of the bonds of personal loyalty with his 'paladins', the second-rank Nazi leaders and *Gauleiter*. Hitler's personal magnetism, his unique demagogic talents, his strength of will, apparent self-confidence and certainty of action, and his indispensability to the Movement (which had fractured without his leadership following the ill-fated Putsch of 1923), all provided the foundations of charismatic authority of extraordinary strength within his own entourage, resting upon bonds of personal loyalty. For his part, Hitler always felt most at home in the company of his closest group of 'fellow fighters' from the 'time of struggle'. He realized that their loyalty was the firmest basis of his own personal power, that he needed them as they needed him. His hatred for those who crossed him having once shared the bonds of mutual loyalty was unbounded, but equally he never forgot old services performed, and, apart from the 'Night of the Long Knives' in June 1934, he did not resort to purges within the Party.[17]

The institutionalization of Hitler's charismatic leadership, first of all within the Party during the 1920s and then within the State after 1933, served a crucial function in sealing the bonds between Hitler and the subordinate Party leadership. The integrative function was the decisive one here. The fragmentation of the Nazi 'élite' groupings had shown itself plainly in 1924, and the inner-Party factionalism and opposition in the early 1930s had been countered only through the strength of Hitler's personal position. After 1933, too, the ferocious personal enmities and political conflicts within the Nazi élite, which otherwise would have torn the system apart, were resolved only in Hitler's own charismatic authority—in his indisputable position as the base of Nazism's popular legitimacy and the embodiment of Nazism's 'idea'.

These Party leaders were of course closer to the real Hitler than were the mass of ordinary Germans or even the mass of Party activists.

---

[16] See F. Neumann, *Behemoth. The Structure and Practice of National Socialism*, London, 1942.

[17] See Kater, 'Hitler in a Social Context', pp. 257–60; Schweitzer, pp. 66 ff.

What is striking, therefore, and of importance for the drive and dynamism of the regime, is that the undiluted 'Hitler myth'—the fully-fledged cult of the 'superman' Leader in all its glorification— embraced the Nazi élite almost in its entirety, and was not simply regarded cynically as a functional propaganda manufacture. If the glorifying speeches and writings of subleaders during the Third Reich itself[18] are no proof of this, the behaviour of Nazi leaders arraigned at Nuremberg and post-war memoirs (for all their obvious apologetics) demonstrate it conclusively.[19]

Even after the war and the revelations of Nuremberg, Alfred Rosenberg called Hitler the 'driving force and untiring motor of the great achievements of the National Socialist State'.[20] For Hans Frank, the Führer had been 'a sort of superman' in whom he had believed 'without reservation' and whom he regarded as being right 'in all decisive matters'.[21] Albert Speer, the ambitious, calculating, and rational power technician who had climbed to the top of the ladder, and who distanced himself most clearly from Hitler at Nuremberg and in his memoirs, admitted that he had seen in the Führer something approaching 'a hero of an ancient saga' and, after the victory in France, as 'one of the greatest figures in German history'.[22] And the former head of the Hitler Youth, Baldur von Schirach, who retained even at Nuremberg a naïve attachment to Hitler, indicated in his memoirs the effect on Hitler himself of the constant toadying and sycophancy which surrounded him, shielding him from rational criticism or genuine debate, and bolstering his increasing detachment from reality. Von Schirach pointed out that 'this unlimited, almost religious veneration, to which I contributed as did Goebbels, Göring, Heß, Ley, and countless others, strengthened in Hitler himself the belief that he was in league with Providence'.[23]

As these memoirs (in which the element of self-defence based upon complete submission to the Führer does not contradict the apologists' genuine belief in his power and the extreme personal devotion to him)

[18] See Schweitzer, p. 82.

[19] See e.g. G. M. Gilbert, *Nuremberg Diary*, London, 1948, pp. 186–96; and D. Jahr, 'Die Einstellung der engeren NS-Elite zur Persönlichkeit und politischen Strategie Adolf Hitlers', Ruhr-Universität Bochum Magisterarbeit, 1984.

[20] A. Rosenberg, *Letzte Aufzeichnungen. Ideale und Idole der nationalsozialistischen Revolution*, Göttingen, 1955, p. 328.

[21] H. Frank, *Im Angesicht des Galgens*, Munich, 1953, pp. 139, 322.

[22] Speer, pp. 177, 184.

[23] B. von Schirach, *Ich glaubte an Hitler*, Hamburg, 1967, p. 160.

clearly suggest, Hitler's own person gradually became inseparable from the 'Führer myth'. Hitler had to live out more and more the constructed image of omnipotence and omniscience. And the more he succumbed to the allure of his own Führer cult and came to believe in his own myth, the more his judgement became impaired by faith in his own infallibility,[24] losing his grip on what could and could not be achieved solely through the strength of his 'will'. Hitler's capacity for self-deception had been profound ever since the mid-1920s, if not earlier, and was vital in order to carry conviction among his immediate entourage about the greatness of his cause and the righteousness of his path towards attaining it. But as his success within the Movement, within the German State, and on the international stage grew until it knew no bounds, so the self-deception of the 'conviction' ideologist magnified to the extent that it ultimately consumed all traces of the calculating and opportunist politician, leaving in its place only a voracious appetite for destruction—and ultimately self-destruction. In this sense, the 'Hitler myth' was a fundamental component of the underlying instability of the Nazi regime and its untrammelled dynamic of destruction.

It would have been expecting too much to imagine that the once-mighty 'Hitler myth' might disappear overnight in 1945, disintegrating along with the mortal remains of the Führer himself and being scattered with the ashes of the Third Reich. Not only had its hold been too strong for that among considerable sections of the population, but the conditions of the immediate post-war era were miserable enough for many to compare them unfavourably with the peacetime era under Nazism.

An early post-war opinion survey undertaken by the United States occupying forces in October 1945 among a representative sample of the population of Darmstadt suggested differences in attitudes towards Nazism among those under nineteen years of age and older Germans. As many as 42 per cent of the youth, compared with 22 per cent of the adults, thought the reconstruction of Germany could best be carried out by 'a strong new Führer'. According to the report, '. . . a

---

[24] According to Otto Dietrich, Hitler began around 1935–6 'to hate objections to his views and doubts in his infallibility', wanting 'to speak but not to listen'—Dietrich, pp. 44–5. And Fritz Wiedemann claimed it had been impossible to contradict a leader 'who immediately became aggressive if the facts did not fit into his conception'—Wiedemann, p. 90, and see also pp. 73–4, 89.

considerable difference appeared in the attitude towards Hitler, the majority of the youth offering an opinion being ready to excuse Hitler as a good man with bad advisers, while the majority of the older people condemned Hitler as an evil individual.'[25] The Nuremberg Trials lifted the scales from the eyes of many Germans, and later OMGUS surveys reported that only one in eight (12 per cent) of those questioned in the American Zone recalled trusting Hitler as Leader up to the end of the war, while 35 per cent claimed never to have trusted him and a further 16 per cent to have kept faith in him only until the outbreak of war.[26] Nevertheless, around one in two Germans in both the American and the British Zones—and a percentage on the increase—thought that National Socialism had basically been a good idea, badly carried out, and were far more favourably disposed to it than to communism.[27] Good social conditions, good living conditions, full employment, unified State and government, and order and security were the attributes, in that order, picked out as the best thing about National Socialism.[28] As late as 1950, 10 per cent of a nation-wide opinion survey sample in West Germany regarded Hitler as the statesman who had achieved most for Germany—second only to Bismarck.[29] In summer 1952, around a quarter of the population had a 'good opinion' of Hitler.[30] A tenth of those questioned thought that Hitler was the greatest statesman of the century, whose true greatness would only be recognized at a later date, and a further 22 per cent thought that, while he had made 'some mistakes' he had nevertheless been an excellent head of State.[31] Around a third of those questioned still opposed the attack on Hitler's life on 20 July 1944.[32] In 1953, some

[25] IfZ, OMGUS-Akten, 5/234–2/2, 13 oct. 1945.

[26] A. J. and R. L. Merritt (ed.), *Public Opinion in Occupied Germany. The OMGUS Surveys, 1945—1949*, Urbana, 1970, pp. 30–1.

[27] Ibid., pp. 32–3; A. J. and R. L. Merritt (ed.), *Public Opinion in Semisovereign Germany. The HICOG Surveys, 1949—1955*, Urbana, 1980, p. 7; IfZ, OMGUS-Akten, 5/233–3/2, reports from 11 June 1948, 5 Jan. 1949, 11 Feb. 1949 from the British Zone Public Opinion Research Office, Bielefeld.

[28] IfZ, OMGUS-Akten, 5/233–3/2, 11 Feb. 1949.

[29] *Jahrbuch der öffentlichen Meinung 1947—1955*, ed. E. Noelle and E. P. Neumann, Allensbach, 1956, p. 132. K. D. Bracher, *The German Dictatorship*, Harmondsworth, 1973 p. 589, states that as many as 32% of West Germans in 1953 though that Hitler had been possibly the greatest statesman of this century, but this seems to be a misreading of the figure in the opinion polls given for Bismarck, not Hitler.

[30] *Jahrbuch der öffentlichen Meinung 1947—1955*, p. 135.

[31] Ibid., p. 136.

[32] Ibid., p. 138.

14 per cent still voiced their willingness to vote again for a man such as Hitler.[33]

A sample of youth in north Germany interviewed in the late 1950s still revealed significant traces of the 'Hitler myth': he had done much good in abolishing unemployment, punishing sexual criminals, constructing the motorways, introducing cheap radio sets, establishing the Labour Service, and reinstating Germany in the esteem of the world. He had been an idealist with many good ideas at first, only later making errors, turning out to be basically evil, and becoming insane and a mass murderer.[34]

The decisive drop in the level of Hitler's posthumous popularity came during the era of the 'economic miracle' under Adenauer and Erhard. By the mid 1960s, only four per cent were reporting that they might be willing once again to vote for someone like Hitler.[35] By this date, only about two or three per cent thought Hitler had achieved more than any other leader for Germany. (Adenauer had, by now, far outstripped Bismarck as the favourite in these stakes.)[36] Even so, the number of those who believed that Hitler would have been one of the greatest German statesmen of all time had it not been for the war remained relatively high, though this figure too had fallen sharply (from 48 per cent in 1955 to 32 per cent by 1967).[37]

By the mid 1960s, admiration for Hitler was almost entirely confined to the residual extreme radical Right, the neo-Nazis. During the first years of the Federal Republic, from 1949 to 1953, when the Right was staging something of a recovery, attempts had been made to distinguish between 'insane Hitlerism' and the positive aspects of National Socialism.[38] But as this phase of radical Right optimism died away from 1953, it was replaced in the hard-core by professed adherence to the Nazi past and outright glorification of Hitler.[39] The basic tenor of the publications of the extreme Right has scarcely altered since that date. The short-lived revitalization of the neo-Nazi

[33] Merritt and Merritt, *Public Opinion in Occupied Germany*, p. 62 n. 17.

[34] W. Jaide, 'Not interested in Politics?' in W. Stahl (ed.), *The Politics of Postwar Germany*, New York, 1963, pp. 368– 9.

[35] Merritt and Merritt, *Public Opinion in Occupied Germany*, p. 62 n. 17.

[36] *Jahrbuch der öffentlichen Meinung 1965–1967*, ed. E. Noelle and E. P. Neumann, Allensbach, 1974, p. 201.

[37] *Jahrbuch der öffentlichen Meinung 1965–1967*, p. 144.

[38] H.-H. Knuetter, 'Ideologies of Extreme Rightists in Postwar Germany', in Stahl, p. 224.

[39] Ibid., pp. 224–6.

Right which saw the temporary rise to prominence of the NPD between 1966 and 1968 brought a very minor revival of positive views about Hitler and Nazism. In 1968, six per cent of the West German population (compared with four per cent in 1965 and 1967) reported their willingness to vote again for a man such as Hitler.[40] The 'Hitler Wave' of publications during the 1970s appears to have contributed to renewed and open glorification of Hitler on the extreme Right.[41] Hitler is still today regarded there in 'heroic' terms as a 'great statesman' and 'significant personality', whose foreign policy achieved German power and autonomy, while his failure and the loss of the war are put down to sabotage from within, and the war itself attributed not to Hitler but to the meddling of the western powers in a German–Polish conflict.[42] Systematic sampling of West German voters carred out in 1979–80 indicated that 13 per cent of all voters in the Federal Republic had a consolidated extreme rightist 'world view'; 14 per cent responded positively to the statement that 'we should again have a Leader who would rule Germany with a strong hand for the good of all'.[43]

Though these figures shock, they need to be put into perspective. Since 1945, West Germany has become a 'normal' liberal democracy, with close affinities to the political systems of other western countries. These countries, too, have their unreconstructed fascists and nazis, their residual lunatic right-wing fringe, and their broader bands of sympathizers with various aspects of rightist thinking. And apart from the pecularities of the relationship with the German Democratic Republic, the structural problems of the West German State are in the main those common to most (and less acute than in many) advanced capitalist industrial societies of the present: problems of social equality and distribution of wealth, and of maintaining in an era of world-wide recession the economic growth so central to the legitimacy of post-war liberal democracies; problems of the exploitation (and often ruination) of limited natural resources in the interests

[40] Merritt and Merritt, *Public Opinion in Occupied Germany*, p. 62. Presumably for mainly tactical reasons, only a third of the NPD adherents questioned admitted their readiness to vote again for a man such as Hitler.

[41] For the commercial 'marketing' of Hitler during the 1970s, see C. H. Meyer, 'Die Veredelung Hitlers. Das Dritte Reich als Markenartikel', in W. Benz (ed.), *Rechtsextremismus in der Bundesrepublik*, Frankfurt a.M., 1984, pp. 45–67.

[42] *5 Millionen Deutsche: 'Wir sollten wieder einen Führer haben. . .' Die SINUS-Studie über rechtsextremistische Einstellungen bei den Deutschen*, Reinbek bei Hamburg, 1981, pp. 54–5.

[43] Ibid., pp. 78–9.

of the economy; problems of national defence in a nuclear age; and the corresponding problems of containing and absorbing often justified social and political protest without destroying civil liberties and undermining the very essence of the liberal democratic state.

The socio-economic problems in West Germany as elsewhere have given rise to an inevitable resurgence of hostility towards ethnic and other minorities, and have put some pressure on the political system itself (reflected in the emergence of the part ecological, part anti-nuclear, part general social protest 'Green Party'). But the specific features and structural characteristics of the German socio-political culture in the short-lived and ill-fated nation-state, which conditioned the manufacture and appeal of the extraordinary 'Hitler myth', were largely swept away in the whirlpool of change arising from total defeat, and were completely banished in the process of long-term change deriving from post-war reconstruction. Unlike the 1920s and 1930s, the current socio-economic problems, acute though they are, have not seen a marked upswing in the political fortunes of the extreme Right. Crucially, they have not produced, nor do they appear likely to do so, a damaging crisis of legitimacy for the State.

Only such a crisis, of almost inconceivably devastating proportions—such as might follow a major war—could so undermine and destroy the existing pluralist political structures that a new form of fascist-style charismatic leadership might appear to sizeable proportions of the population to be a viable and attractive solution. Without wanting to appear too sanguine, and without trivializing the persistent phenomenon of right-wing extremism and the need to maintain vigilance against it, the full realization of the responsibility which Hitler bears for the untold agonies suffered by millions has so discredited everything he stood for in the eyes of sane persons everywhere that, except in circumstances beyond the scope of our realistic imagination, it is difficult to see that there could be a resurrection or a new variant of the once-mighty 'Hitler myth', with its power to capture the imagination of millions.

Old myths are, however, replaced by new as the combination of modern technology and advanced marketing techniques produce ever more elaborate and sophisticated examples of political image-building around minor personality cults, even in western democracies, aimed at obfuscating reality among the ignorant and gullible. The price for abdicating democratic responsibilities and placing uncritical trust in the 'firm leadership' of seemingly well-intentioned political authority was paid dearly by Germans between 1933 and 1945. Even if a collapse into new forms of fascism is inherently unlikely in any western democracy, the massive extension of the power of the modern State over its citizens is in itself more than sufficient cause to develop the highest level possible of educated cynicism and critical awareness as the only protection against the marketed images of present-day and future claimants to political 'leadership'.

LIST OF ABBREVIATIONS

AND GLOSSARY OF GERMAN TERMS AND NAMES
USED IN THE TEXT AND NOTES

AA	*Arbeitsamt* (Employment Office)
Abschnitt	SD regional administrative office, equivalent in status to the *Hauptaußenstelle*
AS	*Außenstelle* (local SD office)
ASD	Archiv der sozialen Demokratie, Bonn
BA	*Bezirksamt, Bezirksamtsvorstand*, District Office, Head of District Office, local government administrative unit, from 1939 *Landratsamt*
BAK	Bundesarchiv Koblenz
BA/MA	Bundesarchiv/Militärarchiv, Freiburg im Breisgau
Bayern I—VI	*Bayern in der NS-Zeit*, ed. M. Broszat *et al.*, 6 vols., Munich/Vienna, 1977–83
BDC	Berlin Document Centre
Blockleiter, Blockwart	Block Leader, Nazi Party functionary responsible for political control of a residential block
BPP	*Bayerische Politische Polizei* (Bavarian Political Police, after 1936 Gestapo)
DBS	*Deutschland-Berichte der Sozialdemokratischen Partei Deutschlands 1934—1940 (Germany Reports of the Social Democratic Party of Germany 1934—1940)*, 7 vols., Frankfurt am Main, 1980
ES	*Emigration Sopade* (name of the collection of files containing the reports of the *Sopade* Border Secretaries, in the Archiv der sozialen Demokratie, Bonn)
Gau	Nazi Party administrative region
Gauleiter	Head(s) of Party regional administration
GBF	*Gendarmerie-Bezirksführer* (head of district police)
Gendarmerie	Police constabulary in non-urban areas
GenStA	*Generalstaatsanwalt* (Chief State Attorney in an OLG region)
Gestapo	*Geheime Staatspolizei* (Secret State Police)
GHS	*Gendarmerie-Hauptstation* (District main police station)
GI	*Gendarmerie-Inspektion* (Police inspectorate of a district)

GKF	*Gendarmerie-Kreisführer* (head of district police, change of nomenclature from GBF in 1939)
GP	*Gendarmerie-Posten* (local police station, name changed from GS in 1939)
GS	*Gendarmerie-Station* (local police station, name changed to GP in 1939)
GStA	Bayerisches Hauptstaatsarchiv, Abteilung II, Geheimes Staatsarchiv, Munich
HAS	*Hauptaußenstelle* (main SD office of a region)
HICOG	United States High Commission for Germany
IfZ	Institut für Zeitgeschichte, Munich
IML/ZPA	Institut für Marxismus-Leninismus, Zentrales Parteiarchiv, East Berlin
IWM	Imperial War Museum, London
KL	*Die kirchliche Lage in Bayern nach den Regierungspräsidentenberichten 1933–1943*, 4 vols., ed. H. Witetschek and (vol. iv) W. Ziegler, Mainz, 1966, 1967, 1971, 1973
KL	*Kreisleiter* (Nazi Party District Leader)
KPD	*Kommunistische Partei Deutschlands* (German Communist Party)
Landrat	Head of state administration at district level (known before 1939 as *Bezirksamtsvorstand*)
LB	*Lagebericht* (situation report)
LK	*Landkreis* (government administrative district from 1939, formerly *Amtsbezirk*)
LR	*Landrat* (see above)
LRA	*Landsratsamt* (district government office, known before 1939 as *Bezirksamt*)
MadR	*Meldungen aus dem Reich. Die geheimen Lageberichte des Sicherheitsdienstes der SS 1938–45*, 17 vols., ed. H. Boberach, Herrsching, 1984
Meldungen	*Meldungen aus dem Reich*, ed. H. Boberach, Neuwied, 1965
MF	Mittelfranken (Central Franconia)
NB	Niederbayern (Lower Bavaria)
NS	*Nationalsozialismus, nationalsozialistisch* (Nazism, Nazi)
NSDAP	*Nationalsozialistische Deutsche Arbeiterpartei* (Nazi Party)
NSLB	*Nationalsozialistischer Lehrerbund* (Nazi Teachers' Association)
NSV	*Nationalsozialistische Volkswohlfahrt* (Nazi People's Welfare Association)
OB	Oberbayern (Upper Bavaria)
OF	Oberfranken (Upper Franconia)

OLG	*Oberlandesgericht* (Higher Regional Court)
OLGP	*Oberlandesgerichtspräsident* (President of a Higher Regional Court)
OMGUS	Office of Military Government of the United States for Germany
OP	Oberpfalz (Upper Palatinate)
Ortsgruppenleiter	Nazi Party Local Group Leader
Pd	*Polizeidirektion* (City police administration)
Pg	*Parteigenosse* (Nazi 'Party Comrade')
PLG	*Präsident des Landesgerichts* (President of regional court)
Reichskristallnacht	'Reich Crystal Night', sarcastic Nazi term, taken from the amount of broken glass from Jewish property damaged and destroyed in the nationwide pogrom of 9–10 November 1938
Reichssicherheits-hauptamt	Reich Security Head Office
RI	*Rüstungsinspektion* (Armaments Inspectorate)
RMdI	*Reichsministerium des Innern* (Reichs Ministry of the Interior)
RP	*Regierungspräsident* (Government President, head of state regional administration, controlling a governmental region (*Regierungsbezirk*))
RSHA	*Reichssicherheitshauptamt* (see above)
S	Schwaben (Swabia)
SA	*Sturmabteilung* (Nazi Storm Troop, paramilitary organization)
Schupo	*Schutzpolizei* (municipal police constabulary)
Schutzhaft	'Protective custody', a euphemism for summary arrest and internment, usually in a concentration camp
SD	*Sicherheitsdienst* (Security Service, part of the SS organization, responsible for internal surveillance and the monitoring of opinion)
SGM	*Sondergericht München* (Munich 'Special Court' dealing mainly with political offences)
Sopade	*Sozialdemokratische Partei Deutschlands* (exiled SPD executive based in Prague (1933–8), Paris (1938–40), and finally, from 1940, in London)
SPD	*Sozialdemokratische Partei Deutschlands* (German Social Democratic Party)
SS	*Schutzstaffeln* (police and security organization run by Himmler)
StAA	Staatsarchiv Amberg
StAB	Staatsarchiv Bamberg

StAL	Staatsarchiv Landshut
StAM	Staatsarchiv München
StANeu	Staatsarchiv Neuburg an der Donau
StAN	Staatsarchiv Nürnberg
Stapo	*Staatspolizei* (state police = Gestapo)
StAW	Staatsarchiv Würzburg
Stützpunktleiter	Nazi Party leader of local base
UF	Unterfranken (Lower Franconia)
USSBS	*United States Strategic Bombing Survey*, repr. New York/ London, 1976, vol. 4 ('The Effects of Strategic Bombing on German Morale')
VfZ	*Vierteljahreshefte für Zeitgeschichte*
Völkisch	racial-nationalist
Volksgemeinschaft	'People's Community'—Nazi social concept implying an ethnically pure and harmonious society free from class conflict and internal divisions
WL	Wiener Library, London (since removed to Tel Aviv, with microfilm copies of archival holdings retained in London)
WWI	*Wehrwirtschaftsinspektion* (Army Economic Inspectorate)
ZStA	Zentrales Staatsarchiv, Potsdam

ARCHIVAL SOURCES AND
NEWSPAPERS CONSULTED

1. *Archiv der sozialen Demokratie (Friedrich-Ebert-Stiftung), Bonn*
ES 31–4, 63–6, 147

2. *Bayerisches Hauptstaatsarchiv, Abt. II, Geheimes Staatsarchiv, Munich*

(i) *Government Presidents' and Police Reports*
MA 101241/1–2, MA 102138, MA 102141, MA 102144, MA 102149, MA 102151, MA 102154, MA 102155/3, MA 106670–4, MA 106677–91, MA 106693–7

(ii) *Other Files*
MA 102257, MA 106457, MA 106468, MA 106765, MA 106767, MA 107257, MA 107291; Reichsstatthalter 39–40, 112–13, 157, 694

3. *Berlin Document Centre*
Personal File of SS-Oberf. Hermann von Schade (re. Adolf Wagner)

4. *Bundesarchiv Koblenz*
NL118/62–6, 87, 102–3; NS6/129, 406–7; NS10/154–5, 157–60; NS29/71; R18/5038, 5350, 5355; R22/3355, 3379, 3381; R43II/315a, 318, 318a, 528, 533, 972, 991, 1263–4; R55/vorl. 443, vorl. 445, 571, 580, 583–4, 601–3, 612, 622–3, 1461; R58/81, 100, 144–94, 381, 386, 432, 535, 548, 552, 566–8, 570–1, 582, 584, 604, 656, 663–4, 666, 672, 681, 717, 1094–6, 1127–8, 1145; Zsg. 101/27–9, 33; Zsg. 102/1–3, 13; Zsg. 110/1–3

5. *Bundesarchiv/Militärarchiv, Freiburg im Breisgau*
RW19/9–34, 38, 41, 48, 57, 67–78; RW20/7/16–17; RW20/13/8–9

6. *Imperial War Museum, London*
'Aus deutschen Urkunden', unpublished documentation, n.d. (?*c.* 1945–6)

7. *Institut für Marxismus–Leninismus, Zentrales Parteiarchiv, East Berlin*
PSt.3/100, 152; St.3/38/I–IV, 39/I–III, 44/I–III, 47, 54–5, 64; St.3/936

8. *Institut für Zeitgeschichte, Munich*
MA 441/1–9, 731, 738, 1217, 1226; OMGUS-Akten, 5/233–3/2, 5/234–2/2

9. *Landratsamt Neumarkt in der Oberpfalz (Registratur)*
LRA Parsberg 939

10. *Landratsamt Obernburg am Main (Registratur)*
Sammelakt 'Kirche und Nationalsozialismus'

11. *Staatsarchiv Amberg*
BA Amberg 2397–9, 2859; BA Vohenstrauß 4674

12. *Staatsarchiv Bamberg*
K8/III, 18470–5; M33/153–5, 175, 410

13. *Staatsarchiv Landshut*
164/10, 5094–5; 164/14, 5731; 164/19, 3681

14. *Staatsarchiv München*
LRA 28340, 29130, 29654–6, 30676–8, 31933, 47140, 48235, 59595, 61611–20, 79887–8, 99497, 99532, 112209, 113813, 116116, 134055–60, 135112–17; NSDAP 126–7, 249, 256, 285, 318, 349, 375–8, 440, 447, 494, 654–5, 980, 983; OLG 127; SGM (holding of some 10,000 files of the *Sondergericht München*)

15. *Staatsarchiv Neuburg an der Donau*
NSDAP Mischbestand, Gau Schwaben: Sammlung Schumacher LO 47, 51–2, 60 Anhang Nr. 3; LO A5, 15, 18, 30/35, 53, 66

16. *Staatsarchiv Nürnberg*
212/1/III, 2145; 212/8/V, 4237, 4241, 4266, 4346; 212/11/VI, 1530, 1792; 212/12/V, 99; 212/13/II, 654; 212/17/III, 8444; 212/18/VIII, 661; 218/1/I, 357–9; 218/1/I, 431

17. *Staatsarchiv Würzburg*
Gauleitung Mainfranken II/5; IV/9; Sammlung Schumacher 29; SD-Hauptaußenstelle Würzburg 1–59; uncatalogued, provisional file nos. given: BA Alzenau 1936–40; BA Bad Neustadt 125/1–7

18. *Wiener Library, London*
'Deutsche Inlandsberichte', 1939–41

19. *Zentrales Staatsarchiv, Potsdam*
RMdI, 25721, 25732/1–2, 25736, 26058–60, 26186/1, 27079/28–71

20. *Newspapers*

Augsburger National-Zeitung; Bayerischer Kurier; Bayerische Volkszeitung; Fränkischer Kurier; Fränkische Tagespost; Miesbacher Anzeiger; Münchner Neueste Nachrichten; Münchner Post; Regensburger Anzeiger; Rheinisch-Westfälische Zeitung; Stürmer; Völkischer Beobachter

LIST OF WORKS CITED

Ake, C., 'Charismatic Legitimation and Political Integration', *Comparative Studies in Society and History*, ix (1966–7).

Allen, W. S., *The Nazi Seizure of Power. The Experience of a Single German Town, 1922–1945*, 2nd edn., New York, 1984.

——, 'The Appeal of Fascism and the Problem of National Disintegration', in H. A. Turner (ed.), *Reappraisals of Fascism*, New York, 1975.

——, 'Die deutsche Öffentlichkeit und die "Reichskristallnacht". Konflikte zwischen Werthierarchie und Propaganda im Dritten Reich', in Peukert and Reulecke (eds.), *Die Reihen fast geschlossen*.

Andreas-Friedrich, R., *Schauplatz Berlin. Ein deutsches Tagebuch*, Munich, 1962.

Aretin, E. von, *Krone und Ketten. Erinnerungen eines bayerischen Edelmannes*, Munich, 1955

Auerbach, H., 'Hitlers politische Lehrjahre und die Münchener Gesellschaft 1919–1923', *VfZ*, xxv (1977).

——, 'Volksstimmung und veröffentlichte Meinung in Deutschland zwischen März und November 1938', in F. Knipping and K.-J. Müller (eds.), *Machtbewußtsein in Deutschland am Vorabend des Zweiten Weltkrieges*, Paderborn, 1984.

Bahne, S., 'Die Kommunistische Partei Deutschlands', in Matthias and Morsey (eds.), *Das Ende der Parteien*.

Baird, J. W., *The Mythical World of Nazi War Propaganda 1939–1945*, Minneapolis, 1974.

Balfour, M., *Propaganda in War, 1939–1945*, London, 1979.

Bankier, D., 'German Society and National Socialist Antisemitism, 1933–1938', Hebrew University of Jerusalem Ph.D. thesis, 1983 (Engl. abstract of Hebrew text).

Bartov, O., 'The Barbarisation of Warfare. German Officers and Men on the Eastern Front, 1941–1945', *Jahrbuch des Instituts für Deutsche Geschichte, Tel Aviv*, xiii (1984).

Baum, R., *The Holocaust and the German Elite*, London, 1981.

Bayern in der NS-Zeit, ed. M. Broszat *et al.*, 6 vols., Munich/Vienna, 1977–83, (cited in the text as *Bayern I* etc.).

Berghahn, V., 'Meinungsforschung im "Dritten Reich": Die Mundpropaganda-Aktion der Wehrmacht im letzten Kriegshalbjahr', *Militärgeschichtliche Mitteilungen*, i (1967).

Berning, C., *Vom 'Abstammungsnachweis' zum 'Zuchtwart'. Vokabular des Nationalsozialismus*, Berlin, 1964.

Bessel, R., 'The Rise of the NSDAP and the Myth of Nazi Propaganda', *Wiener Library Bulletin*, xxxiii (1980).

——, *Political Violence and the Rise of Nazism*, New Haven/London, 1984.

Beuth, W., *Der deutsche Hitler-Frühling. Die Wiederaufrichtung Deutschlands durch den Volkskanzler des Deutschen Reiches Adolf Hitler*, Frankfurt am Main, 1933.

Binion, R., *Hitler among the Germans*, New York, 1976.

Blessing, W. K., 'The Cult of Monarchy, Political Loyalty, and the Workers' Movement in Imperial Germany', *Journal of Contemporary History*, xiii (1978).

Bohrer, K. H. (ed.), *Mythos und Moderne*, Frankfurt am Main, 1983.

Bracher, K. D.., *The German Dictatorship*, Harmondsworth, 1973.

——, Schultz, G., and Sauer, W., *Die nationalsozialistische Machtergreifung*, Ullstein edn., 3 vols., Frankfurt am Main, 1974.

Bramsted, E. K., *Goebbels and National Socialist Propaganda 1925–1945*, Michigan, 1965.

Bretschneider, H., *Der Widerstand gegen den Nationalsozialismus in München 1933 bis 1945*, Munich, 1968.

Broszat, M., *The Hitler State*, London, 1981.

——, 'Soziale Motivation und Führer-Bindung des Nationalsozialismus', *VfZ*, xviii (1970).

——, 'Politische Denunziationen in der NS-Zeit', *Archivalische Zeitschrift*, lxxiii (1977).

——, 'Hitler and the Genesis of the "Final Solution" ', *Yad Vashem Studies*, xiii (1979).

Bullock, A., *Hitler. A Study in Tyranny.* Pelican edn., Harmondsworth, 1962; (rev. edn., London, 1964).

Carr, W., *Hitler. A Study in Personality and Politics*, London, 1978.

Chickering, R., *We Men Who Feel Most German. A Cultural Study of the Pan German League, 1886–1914*, London, 1984.

Childers, T., *The Nazi Voter. The Social Foundations of Fascism in Germany, 1919–1933*, Chapel Hill/London, 1983.

——, 'Interest and Ideology: Anti-System Politics in the Era of Stabilization 1924–1928', in G. Feldman (ed.), *Die Nachwirkungen der Inflation auf die deutsche Geschichte*, Munich, 1985.

Conway, J., *The Nazi Persecution of the Churches, 1933–1945*, London, 1968.

——, 'National Socialism and the Churches during the Weimar Republic', in Stachura (ed.), *The Nazi Machtergreifung*.

Das andere Gesicht des Krieges. Deutsche Feldpostbriefe 1939–1945, ed. O. Buchbender and R. Sterz, Munich, 1982.

Der italienische Faschismus. Probleme und Forschungstendenzen, Kolloquien des Instituts für Zeitgeschichte, Munich, 1983.

Der Nationalsozialismus. Dokumente 1933–1945, ed. W. Hofer, Frankfurt am Main, 1957.

Deuerlein, E. (ed.), *Der Aufstieg der NSDAP in Augenzeugenberichten*, Düsseldorf, 1968.

Deutschkron, I., *Ich trug den gelben Stern*, 4th edn., Cologne, 1983.

Deutschland-Berichte der Sozialdemokratischen Partei Deutschlands 1934—1940, 7 vols., Frankfurt am Main, 1980 (cited in the text as *DBS*).

Diels, R., *Lucifer ante Portas. Zwischen Severing und Heydrich*, Zurich, n.d. (1949).

Diephouse, D. J., 'The Triumph of Hitler's Will', in J. Held (ed.), *The Cult of Power. Dictators in the Twentieth Century*, New York, 1983.

Dietrich, O., *Zwölf Jahre mit Hitler*, Cologne/Munich, n.d. (1955).

Dipper, C., 'The German Resistance and the Jews', *Yad Vashem Studies*, xvi (1984).

Domarus, M. (ed.), *Hitler. Reden und Proklamationen 1932—1945*, Wiesbaden, 1973. (Cited as Domarus.)

Domarus, W., *Nationalsozialismus, Krieg und Bevölkerung*, Munich, 1977.

Eiber, L., *Arbeiter unter der NS-Herrschaft. Textil- und Porzellanarbeiter im nordöstlichen Oberfranken 1933—1939*, Munich, 1979.

Eley, G., *Reshaping the German Right*, New Haven/London, 1980.

Ericksen, R. P., *Theologians under Hitler*, New Haven/London, 1985.

Eschenburg, T., 'Streiflichter zur Geschichte der Wahlen im Dritten Reich', *VfZ*, iii (1955).

Fabry, P., *Mutmaßungen über Hitler. Urteile von Zeitgenossen*, Düsseldorf, 1969.

Fehrenbach, E., *Wandlungen des deutschen Kaisergedankens 1871—1918*, Munich/Vienna, 1969.

——, 'Images of Kaiserdom: German attitudes to Kaiser Wilhelm II', in J. C. G. Röhl and N. Sombart (eds.), *Kaiser Wilhelm II. New Interpretations*, Cambridge, 1982.

Fest, J. C., *Hitler. Eine Biographie*, Frankfurt am Main, 1973.

Flechtheim, O., *Die KPD in der Weimarer Republik*, Frankfurt am Main, 1969.

Frank, H., *Im Angesicht des Galgens*, Munich, 1953.

Friedrich, C. J., 'Political Leadership and the Problem of Charismatic Power', *Journal of Politics*, xxiii (1961).

Fröhlich, E., 'Die Partei auf lokaler Ebene. Zwischen gesellschaftlicher Assimilation und Veränderungsdynamik', in Hirschfeld and Kettenacker (eds.), *Der 'Führerstaat'*.

—— and Broszat, M., 'Politische und soziale Macht auf dem Lande. Die Durchsetzung der NSDAP im Kreis Memmingen', *VfZ*, xxv (1977).

Fryman, D. (= Class, H.), *Wenn ich der Kaiser wär*, 5th edn., Leipzig, 1914.

Fünf Millionen Deutsche: 'Wir sollten wieder einen Führer haben . . .' Die SINUS-Studie über rechtsextremistische Einstellungen bei den Deutschen, Reinbek bei Hamburg, 1981.

Funke, M., '7. März 1936. Fallstudie zum außenpolitischen Führungsstil Hitlers', in W. Michalka (ed.), *Nationalsozialistische Außenpolitik*, Darmstadt, 1978.

Gilbert, G. M., *Nuremberg Diary*, London, 1948.

Goebbels, J., *Vom Kaiserhof zur Reichskanzlei*, 21st edn., Munich, 1937.

——, *Tagebücher 1945. Die letzten Aufzeichnungen*, Hamburg, 1977.

Goebbels-Reden, ed. H. Heiber, 2 vols., Düsseldorf, 1972.

Gordon, S., *Hitler, Germans, and the 'Jewish Question'*, Princeton, 1984.

Gorz, A., *Farewell to the Working Class*, London, 1982.

Gottschling, E., 'Der faschistische Staat', in D. Eichholtz and K. Gossweiler (eds.), *Faschismusforschung. Positionen, Probleme, Polemik*, East Berlin, 1980.

Graml, H., 'Probleme einer Hitler-Biographie. Kritische Bemerkungen zu Joachim C. Fest', *VfZ*, xxii (1974).

Gross, L., *The Last Jews in Berlin*, London, 1983.

Gruchmann, L., *Der Zweite Weltkrieg*, Munich, 4th edn., 1975.

——, 'Jugendopposition und Justiz im Dritten Reich', in W. Benz (ed.), *Miscellanea. Festschrift für Helmut Krausnick*, Stuttgart, 1980.

Grunfeld, F. V., *The Hitler File*, London, 1974.

Gurfein, I. M. and Janowitz, M., 'Trends in Wehrmacht Morale', *Public Opinion Quarterly*, x (1946).

Haffner, S., *Anmerkungen zu Hitler*, Munich, 1978.

Hagmann, M., *Der Weg ins Verhängnis*, Munich, 1946.

Hahn, F., *Lieber Stürmer. Leserbriefe an das NS-Kampfblatt 1924 bis 1945*, Stuttgart, 1978.

Hambrecht, R., *Der Aufstieg der NSDAP in Mittel- und Oberfranken, 1925–1933*, Nuremberg, 1976.

Hamilton, R., *Who voted for Hitler?*, Princeton, 1982.

Hassell, U. von, *The von Hassell Diaries 1938–1944*, London, 1948.

Heer, F., *Der Glaube des Adolf Hitler. Anatomie einer politischen Religiosität*, Munich, 1966.

Hehl, U. von, *Priester unter Hitlers Terror. Eine biographische und statistische Erhebung*, Mainz, 1984.

Heimann, H., 'Die Entwicklung des Automobils zum Massenkonsumartikel in Deutschland', Ruhr-Universität Bochum, Magisterarbeit, Bochum, 1985.

Hellfeld, M. von, *Edelweißpiraten in Köln*, Cologne, 1981.

Henderson, N., *Failure of a Mission*, London, 1940.

Heyen, F. J. (ed.), *Nationalsozialismus im Alltag*, Boppard am Rhein, 1967.

Hirschfeld, G. and Kettenacker, L. (eds.), *Der 'Führerstaat': Mythos und Realität*, Stuttgart, 1981.

Hoffman, H., ' "Victory of Faith" (1933) by Leni Riefenstahl', unpubl. paper (1986).

Horn, W., *Führerideologie und Parteiorganisation in der NSDAP, 1919–1933*, Düsseldorf, 1972.

Huber, H., and Müller, A. (eds.), *Das Dritte Reich. Seine Geschichte in Texten, Bildern und Dokumenten*, 2 vols., Munich/Vienna/Basle, 1964.

Irving, D., *Hitler's War*, London, 1977.

Jäckel, E., *Hitler in History*, Hanover/London, 1984.

——, 'Hitler und der Mord an europäischen Juden', in P. Märthesheimer and I. Frenzel (eds.), *Im Kreuzfeuer: Der Fernsehfilm 'Holocaust'*, Frankfurt am Main, 1979.

——, and Kuhn, A. (eds.), *Hitler. Sämtliche Aufzeichnungen 1905–1924*, Stuttgart, 1980.

Jahr, D., 'Die Einstellung der engeren NS-Elite zur Persönlichkeit und politischen Strategie Adolf Hitlers', Ruhr-Universität Bochum Magisterarbeit, 1984.

Jahrbuch der öffentlichen Meinung 1947–1955, ed. E. Noelle and E. P. Neumann, Allensbach, 1956.

Jahrbuch der öffentlichen Meinung 1965–1967, ed. E. Noelle and E. P. Neumann, Allensbach, 1967.

Jahrbuch der öffentlichen Meinung 1968–1973, ed. E. Noelle and E. P. Neumann, Allensbach, 1974.

Jaide, W., 'Not interested in Politics?', in Stahl (ed.), *The Politics of Postwar Germany*.

Jamin, M., *Zwischen den Klassen. Zur Sozialstruktur der SA-Führerschaft*, Wuppertal, 1984.

——, 'Zur Rolle der SA im nationalsozialistischen Herrschaftssystem', in Hirschfeld and Kettenacker, *Der 'Führerstaat'*.

Kater, M., *The Nazi Party. A Social Profile of Members and Leaders, 1919–1945*, Oxford, 1983.

——, 'Sozialer Wandel in der NSDAP im Zuge der NS-Machtergreifung', in Schieder (ed.), *Faschismus als soziale Bewegung*.

——, 'Hitler in a Social Context', *Central European History*, xiv (1981).

Keim, A. M. (ed.), *Yad Vashem. Die Judenretter aus Deutschland*, Mainz/Munich, 1983.

Kershaw, I., *Popular Opinion and Political Dissent in the Third Reich*, Oxford, 1983.

——, *The Nazi Dictatorship. Problems and Perspectives of Interpretation*, London, 1985.

——, 'The Persecution of the Jews and German Popular Opinion in the Third Reich', *Yearbook of the Leo Baeck Institute*, xxvi (1981).

——, 'Ideology, Propaganda, and the Rise of the Nazi Party', in Stachura (ed.), *The Nazi Machtergreifung*.

——, 'Alltägliches und Außeralltägliches: ihre Bedeutung für die Volksmeinung 1933–1939', in Peukert and Reulecke (eds.), *Die Reihen fast geschlossen*.

Kettenacker, L., 'Sozialpsychologische Aspekte der Führer-Herrschaft', in Hirschfeld and Kettenacker, *Der 'Führerstaat'*.

——, 'Hitler's Impact on the Lower Middle Class', in D. Welch (ed.), *Nazi Propaganda: the Power and the Limitations*, London, 1983.

282   *List of Works Cited*

Kettenacker, L., 'Der Mythos vom Reich', in Bohrer, *Mythos und Moderne.*

King, C., *The Nazi State and the New Religions*, New York/Toronto, 1983.

Kirchliche Lage in Bayern nach den Regierungspräsidentenberichten 1933–1943, ed. H. Witetschek und (vol. iv) W. Ziegler, 4 vols., Mainz, 1966, 1967, 1971, 1973 (cited in the text as *KL*, i, etc.).

Kirwan, G., 'Waiting for Retaliation. A Study in Nazi Propaganda Behaviour and German Civilian Morale', *Journal of Contemporary History*, xvi (1981).

—, 'Allied Bombing and Nazi Domestic Propaganda', *European History Quarterly*, xv (1985).

Klee, E., *'Euthanasie' im NS-Staat. Die 'Vernichtung lebensunwerten Lebens'*, Frankfurt am Main, 1983.

Klönne, A., *Jugend im Dritten Reich. Die Hitler-Jugend und ihre Gegner*, Düsseldorf, 1982.

Klotzbücher, A., *Der politische Weg des Stahlhelm, Bund der Frontsoldaten, in der Weimarer Republik*, Erlangen, 1965.

Knox, M., 'Conquest, Foreign and Domestic, in Fascist Italy and Nazi Germany', *Journal of Modern History*, lvi (1984).

Knuetter, H.-H., 'Ideologies of Extreme Rightists in Postwar Germany', in Stahl (ed.), *The Politics of Postwar Germany.*

Kotze, H. von, and Krausnick, H., *'Es spricht der Führer'. 7 exemplarische Hitler-Reden*, Gütersloh, 1966.

Krausnick, H., and Wilhelm, H.-H., *Die Truppe des Weltanschauungskrieges*, Stuttgart, 1981.

Kulka, O. D., 'Die Nürnberger Rassengesetze und die deutsche Bevölkerung', *VfZ*, xxxii (1984).

—, ' "Public Opinion" in Nazi Germany and the "Jewish Question" ', *Jerusalem Quarterly*, xxv (1982).

—, ' "Public Opinion" in Nazi Germany: the Final Solution', *Jerusalem Quarterly*, xxvi (1983).

—, and Rodrigue, A., 'The German Population and the Jews in the Third Reich', *Yad Vashem Studies*, xvi (1984).

Kwiet, K., and Eschwege, H., *Selbstbehauptung und Widerstand. Deutsche Juden im Kampf um Existenz und Menschenwürde 1933–1945*, Hamburg, 1984.

Lagebesprechungen im Führerhauptquartier, ed. H. Heiber, Berlin, 1962.

Laqueur, W., *The Terrible Secret*, London, 1980.

Lepsius, M. R., 'From Fragmented Party Democracy to Government by Emergency Decree and National Socialist Takeover: Germany', in J. J. Linz and A. Stepan (eds.), *The Breakdown of Democratic Regimes*, Baltimore/London, 1978.

Leuner, H. D., *When Compassion was a Crime*, London, 1966.

Lewy, G., *The Catholic Church and Nazi Germany*, London, 1964.

Mann, G., *The History of Germany since 1789*, Harmondsworth, 1974.

Mann, R., 'Politische Penetration und gesellschaftliche Reaktion. Anzeigen zur Gestapo im nationalsozialistischen Deutschland', in R. Mackensen and F. Sagebiel (eds.), *Soziologische Analysen. Referate aus den Veranstaltungen der Sektionen der Deutschen Gesellschaft für Soziologie beim 19. Deutschen Soziologentag*, Berlin, 1979.

Maser, W., *Der Sturm auf die Republik. Frühgeschichte der NSDAP*, Stuttgart, 1973.

Mason, T. W., *Arbeiterklasse und Volksgemeinschaft*, Opladen, 1975.

——, 'The Legacy of 1918 for National Socialism', in A. Nicholls and E. Matthias (eds.), *German Democracy and the Triumph of Hitler*, London, 1971.

——, 'Intention and Explanation: A Current Controversy about the Interpretation of National Socialism', in Hirschfeld and Kettenacker (eds.), *Der 'Führerstaat'*.

——, 'Open Questions on Nazism', in R. Samuel (ed.), *People's History and Socialist Theory*, London, 1981.

Matthias, E., and Morsey, R. (eds.), *Das Ende der Parteien*, Düsseldorf, 1979.

Mayer, M., *They Thought They Were Free. The Germans 1933–1945*, Chicago, 1955.

McKee, I., *Tomorrow the World*, London, 1960.

Meldungen aus dem Reich, ed. H. Boberach, Neuwied, 1965 (cited in the text as *Meldungen*).

Meldungen aus dem Reich. Die geheimen Lageberichte des Sicherheitsdienstes der SS 1938–1945, ed. H. Boberach, 17 vols., Herrsching, 1984 (cited in the text as *MadR*).

Melograni, P., 'The Cult of the Duce in Mussolini's Italy', *Journal of Contemporary History*, xi (1976).

Merkl, P., *Political Violence under the Swastika*, Princeton, 1975.

Merritt, A. J., and Merritt, R. L. (eds.), *Public Opinion in Occupied Germany. The OMGUS Surveys, 1945–1949*, Urbana, 1970.

—— and —— (eds.), *Public Opinion in Semisovereign Germany. The HICOG Surveys, 1949–1955*, Urbana, 1980.

Meyer, C. H., 'Die Veredelung Hitlers. Das Dritte Reich als Markenartikel', in W. Benz (ed.), *Rechtsextremismus in der Bundesrepublik*, Frankfurt am Main, 1984.

Moltmann, G., 'Goebbels' Speech on Total War, February 18, 1943', in H. Holborn (ed.), *Republic to Reich*, Vintage Books edn., New York, 1972.

Mommsen, H., 'Social Views and Constitutional Plans of the Resistance', in H. Graml *et al.*, *The German Resistance to Hitler*, London, 1970.

——, 'Zur Verschränkung traditioneller und faschistischer Führungsgruppen in Deutschland beim Übergang von der Bewegungs- zur Systemphase', in Schieder (ed.), *Faschismus als soziale Bewegung*.

——, 'Der Mythos des nationalen Aufbruchs und die Haltung der deutschen

Intellektuellen und funktionalen Eliten', in *1933 in Gesellschaft und Wissenschaft*, ed. Pressestelle der Universität Hamburg, Hamburg, 1983.

——, 'Die Realisierung des Utopischen: Die "Endlösung der Judenfrage" im "Dritten Reich" ', *Geschichte und Gesellschaft*, ix (1983).

Morsey, R., 'Die Deutsche Zentrumspartei', in Matthias and Morsey (eds.), *Das Ende der Parteien*.

Mosse, G. L., *The Nationalization of the Masses*, New York, 1975.

Müller, K.-J., *Armee, Politik und Gesellschaft in Deutschland 1933–1945*, Paderborn, 1979.

——, 'Nationalkonservative Eliten zwischen Kooperation und Widerstand', in Schmädeke and Steinbach, *Der Widerstand*.

Müller-Claudius, M., *Der Antisemitismus und das deutsche Verhängnis*, Frankfurt am Main, 1948.

Muth, H., 'Jugendopposition im Dritten Reich', *VfZ*, xxx (1982).

Nadler, F., *Ich sah wie Nürnberg unterging*, 2nd edn., Nuremberg, 1959.

——, *Eine Stadt im Schatten Streichers*, Nuremberg, 1969.

Neumann, F., *Behemoth. The Structure and Practice of National Socialism*, London, 1942.

Neumann, S., *Die Parteien der Weimarer Republik*, Stuttgart, new edn. 1965.

Nipperdey, T., 'Nationalidee und Nationaldenkmal in Deutschland im 19. Jahrhundert', *Historische Zeitschrift*, ccvi (1968).

Noakes, J., *The Nazi Party in Lower Saxony*, Oxford, 1971.

——, and Pridham, G. (eds.), *Documents on Nazism*, London, 1974.

Nyomarkay, J., *Charisma and Factionalism within the Nazi Party*, Minneapolis, 1967.

Obenaus, H., 'Haben sie wirklich nichts gewußt? Ein Tagebuch zum Alltag von 1933–1945 gibt eine deutliche Antwort', *Journal für Geschichte*, ii (1980).

——, and Obenaus, S., *'Schreiben, wie es wirklich war!' Aufzeichnungen Karl Dürkefäldens aus den Jahren 1933–1945*, Hanover, 1985.

Orlow, D., *The History of the Nazi Party, 1919–1933*, Pittsburgh, 1969.

——, *The History of the Nazi Party, 1933–1945*, Pittsburgh, 1973.

O'Sullivan, N., *Fascism*, London, 1983.

Parteistatistik, ed. Reichsorganisationsleiter der NSDAP, 3 vols., Munich, 1935.

Parteitag der Freiheit vom 10.–16. September 1935. Offizieller Bericht über den Verlauf des Reichsparteitages mit sämtlichen Kongreßreden, Munich, 1935.

Parteitag der Ehre vom 8. bis 14. September 1936, Munich, 1936.

Petersen, J., 'Mussolini. Wirklichkeit und Mythos eines Diktators', in Bohrer (ed.), *Mythos und Moderne*.

Peterson, E. N., *The Limits of Hitler's Power*, Princeton, 1969.

Petzold, J., *Die Demagogie des Hitlerfaschismus*, East Berlin, 1982.

Peukert, D., *Die KPD im Widerstand*, Wuppertal, 1980.

——, 'Edelweißpiraten, Meuten, Swing. Jugendsubkulturen im Dritten Reich', in G. Huck (ed.), *Sozialgeschichte der Freizeit*, Wuppertal, 1980.

——, and Reulecke, J. (eds.), *Die Reihen fast geschlossen. Beiträge zur Geschichte des Alltags unterm Nationalsozialismus*, Wuppertal, 1981.

Picker, H., *Hitlers Tischgespräche im Führerhauptquartier 1941 bis 1942*, Stuttgart, 1963.

Pridham, G., *Hitler's Rise to Power. The Nazi Movement in Bavaria, 1923—1933*, London, 1973.

Reck-Malleczewen, F. P., *Tagebuch eines Verzweifelten*, Frankfurt am Main/Hamburg, 1971.

Rosenberg, A., *Letzte Aufzeichnungen. Ideale und Idole der nationalsozialistischen Revolution*, Göttingen, 1955.

Rothfels, H., 'Zerrspiegel des 20. Juli', *VfZ*, x (1962).

Ruge, W., *Das Ende von Weimar. Monopolkapital und Hitler*, East Berlin, 1983.

Schieder, W., *Faschismus als soziale Bewegung*, Hamburg, 1976.

Schirach, B. von, *Ich glaubte an Hitler*, Hamburg, 1967.

Schmädeke, J., and Steinbach, P. (eds), *Der Widerstand gegen den Nationalsozialismus*, Munich, 1985.

Schmidt, C., 'Zu den Motiven "alter Kämpfer" in der NSDAP', in Peukert and Reulecke (eds.), *Die Reihen fast geschlossen.*

Schmidt, P., *Statist auf diplomatischer Bühne 1923—45*, Bonn, 1953.

Schnatz, H., *Der Luftkrieg im Raum Koblenz 1944/45*, Boppard am Rhein, 1981.

Schörken, R., *Luftwaffenhelfer und Drittes Reich. Die Entstehung eines politischen Bewußtseins*, Stuttgart, 1984.

Schreiber, G., *Hitler. Interpretationen 1923—1983. Ergebnisse, Methoden und Probleme der Forschung*, Darmstadt, 1984.

Schweitzer, A., *The Age of Charisma*, Chicago, 1984.

Semmler, R., *Goebbels. The Man Next to Hitler*, London, 1947.

Shirer, W., *Berlin Diary 1934—1941*, Sphere Books edn., London, 1970.

Sington, D., and Weidenfeld, A., *The Goebbels Experiment*, London, 1942.

Smith, C. A. A., 'The National Socialist Organisation NSV: "NS-People's Welfare", propaganda and influence, 1933–1945', Univ. of Edinburgh Ph.D. thesis 1986.

Sontheimer, K., *Antidemokratisches Denken in der Weimarer Republik*, 4th edn., Munich, 1962.

Speer, A., *Erinnerungen*, Frankfurt am Main/Berlin, 1969.

Spiegelbild einer Verschwörung, ed. Archiv Peter, Stuttgart, 1961.

Stachura, P. D. (ed.), *The Shaping of the Nazi State*, London, 1978.

——, *The German Youth Movement 1900—1945. An Interpretative and Documentary History*, London, 1981.

—— (ed.), *The Nazi Machtergreifung*, London, 1983.

——, *Gregor Strasser and the Rise of Nazism*, London, 1983.

Stachura, P. D., 'German Youth, the Youth Movement, and National Socialism in the Weimar Republic', in Stachura (ed.), *The Nazi Machtergreifung*.

Stahl, W. (ed.), *The Politics of Postwar Germany*, New York, 1963.

Statistisches Jahrbuch für das Deutsche Reich, ed. Statistisches Reichsamt, 1933–1942.

Steinbach, L., *Ein Volk, ein Reich, ein Glaube?*, Berlin/Bonn, 1983.

Steinert, M. G., *Hitlers Krieg und die Deutschen*, Düsseldorf, 1970.

Stern, J. P., *Hitler. The Führer and the People*, London, 1975.

Stoakes, G., 'The Evolution of Hitler's Ideas on Foreign Policy 1919–1925', in Stachura, *The Shaping of the Nazi State*.

Stokes, L. D., 'The *Sicherheitsdienst (SD)* of the *Reichsführer SS* and German Public Opinion, September 1939–June 1941', Johns Hopkins University Ph.D. thesis, Baltimore, 1972.

Streit, C., *Keine Kameraden. Die Wehrmacht und die sowjetischen Kriegsgefangenen*, Stuttgart, 1978.

Struve, W., *Elites against Democracy. Leadership Ideals in Bourgeois Political Thought in Germany, 1890–1933*, Princeton, 1973.

Taylor, S., *Prelude to Genocide*, London, 1985.

Terveen, F., 'Der Filmbericht über Hitlers 50. Geburtstag. Ein Beispiel nationalsozialistischer Selbstdarstellung und Propaganda', *VfZ*, vii (1959).

Toland, J., *Adolf Hitler*, New York, 1976.

Totalitarismus und Faschismus. Kolloquien des Instituts für Zeitgeschichte, Munich, 1980.

Treue, W., 'Rede Hitlers vor der deutschen Presse (10. Nov. 1938)', *VfZ*, vi (1958).

True to Type. A Selection of Letters and Diaries of German Soldiers and Civilians collected on the Soviet–German Front, London, n.d. (?1944).

Turner, H. A. (ed.), *Hitler aus nächster Nähe*, Frankfurt am Main/Berlin/Vienna, 1978.

Tyrell, A., *Führer befiel . . . Selbstzeugnisse aus der 'Kampfzeit' der NSDAP. Dokumentation und Analyse*, Düsseldorf, 1969.

—, *Vom 'Trommler' zum 'Führer'*, Munich, 1975.

—, *III. Reichsparteitag der NSDAP, 19.–21. August 1927*, Filmedition G122 des Instituts für den wissenschaftlichen Film, Ser. 4, No. 4/G122, Göttingen, 1976.

Unger, A. H., *The Totalitarian Party*, Cambridge, 1974.

United States Strategic Bombing Survey, repr. New York/London, 1976, vol. 4 ('The Effects of Strategic Bombing on German Morale'), (cited in the text as *USSBS*).

Vierhaus, R., 'Faschistisches Führertum', *Historische Zeitschrift*, clxxxviii (1964).

Voges, M., 'Klassenkampf in der "Betriebsgemeinschaft" ' *Archiv für Sozialgeschichte*, xxi (1981).

Volk, L., 'Kardinal Faulhabers Stellung zur Weimarer Republik und zum NS-Staat', *Stimmen der Zeit*, clxxvii (1966).

Volksopposition im Polizeistaat. Gestapo- und Regierungsberichte 1934–1936, ed. B. Vollmer, Stuttgart, 1957.

Vondung, K., *Magie und Manipulation*, Göttingen, 1971.

Wagner, J. V., *Hakenkreuz über Bochum*, Bochum, 1983.

Waite, R. G. L., *Vanguard of Nazism. The Free Corps Movement in Postwar Germany 1918–1923*, Cambridge, Mass., 1952.

——, *The Psychopathic God—Adolf Hitler*, New York, 1977.

Weber, M., *Economy and Society*, ed. G. Roth and C. Wittich, Berkeley, 1978.

Wehler, H.-U., '30. Januar 1933—Ein halbes Jahrhundert danach', *Aus Politik und Zeitgeschichte*, 29 Jan. 1983.

Weinstein, F., *The Dynamics of Nazism. Leadership, Ideology, and the Holocaust*, New York, 1980.

Weißbecker, M., 'Zur Herausbildung des Führerkults in der NSDAP', in K. Drechsler *et al.* (eds.), *Monopole und Staat in Deutschland 1917–1945*, East Berlin, 1966.

Welch, D., *Propaganda and the German Cinema 1933–1945*, Oxford, 1983.

—— (ed.), *Nazi Propaganda: The Power and the Limitations*, London, 1983.

Wiedemann, F., *Der Mann, der Feldherr werden wollte*, Velbert/Kettwig, 1964.

Wilhelm, H.-H., 'The Holocaust in National Socialist Rhetoric and Writings', *Yad Vashem Studies*, xvi (1984).

'Wollt ihr den totalen Krieg?' Die geheimen Goebbels-Konferenzen 1939–1943, ed. W. A. Boelcke, Deutscher Taschenbuch Verlag edn., Munich, 1969.

Zeman, Z. A. B., *Nazi Propaganda*, Oxford, 1964.

Zofka, Z., *Die Ausbreitung des Nationalsozialismus auf dem Lande*, Munich, 1979.

——, 'Dorfeliten und NSDAP', in *Bayern IV*.

INDEX

OXFORD

MORE OXFORD PAPERBACKS

This book is just one of nearly 1000 Oxford Paperbacks currently in print. If you would like details of other Oxford Paperbacks, including titles in the World's Classics, Oxford Reference, Oxford Books, OPUS, Past Masters, Oxford Authors, and Oxford Shakespeare series, please write to:

UK and Europe: Oxford Paperbacks Publicity Manager, Arts and Reference Publicity Department, Oxford University Press, Walton Street, Oxford OX2 6DP.

Customers in UK and Europe will find Oxford Paperbacks available in all good bookshops. But in case of difficulty please send orders to the Cash-with-Order Department, Oxford University Press Distribution Services, Saxon Way West, Corby, Northants NN18 9ES. Tel: 01536 741519; Fax: 01536 746337. Please send a cheque for the total cost of the books, plus £1.75 postage and packing for orders under £20; £2.75 for orders over £20. Customers outside the UK should add 10% of the cost of the books for postage and packing.

USA: Oxford Paperbacks Marketing Manager, Oxford University Press, Inc., 200 Madison Avenue, New York, N.Y. 10016.

Canada: Trade Department, Oxford University Press, 70 Wynford Drive, Don Mills, Ontario M3C 1J9.

Australia: Trade Marketing Manager, Oxford University Press, G.P.O. Box 2784Y, Melbourne 3001, Victoria.

South Africa: Oxford University Press, P.O. Box 1141, Cape Town 8000.

HISTORY IN OXFORD PAPERBACKS
TUDOR ENGLAND
John Guy

Tudor England is a compelling account of political and religious developments from the advent of the Tudors in the 1460s to the death of Elizabeth I in 1603.

Following Henry VII's capture of the Crown at Bosworth in 1485, Tudor England witnessed far-reaching changes in government and the Reformation of the Church under Henry VIII, Edward VI, Mary, and Elizabeth; that story is enriched here with character studies of the monarchs and politicians that bring to life their personalities as well as their policies.

Authoritative, clearly argued, and crisply written, this comprehensive book will be indispensable to anyone interested in the Tudor Age.

'lucid, scholarly, remarkably accomplished . . . an excellent overview' *Sunday Times*

'the first comprehensive history of Tudor England for more than thirty years' Patrick Collinson, *Observer*

THE STRUGGLE FOR THE MASTERY OF EUROPE 1848–1918

A. J. P. Taylor

The fall of Metternich in the revolutions of 1848 heralded an era of unprecedented nationalism in Europe, culminating in the collapse of the Hapsburg, Romanov, and Hohenzollern dynasties at the end of the First World War. In the intervening seventy years the boundaries of Europe changed dramatically from those established at Vienna in 1815. Cavour championed the cause of *Risorgimento* in Italy; Bismarck's three wars brought about the unification of Germany; Serbia and Bulgaria gained their independence courtesy of the decline of Turkey—'the sick man of Europe'; while the great powers scrambled for places in the sun in Africa. However, with America's entry into the war and President Wilson's adherence to idealistic internationalist principles, Europe ceased to be the centre of the world, although its problems, still primarily revolving around nationalist aspirations, were to smash the Treaty of Versailles and plunge the world into war once more.

A. J. P. Taylor has drawn the material for his account of this turbulent period from the many volumes of diplomatic documents which have been published in the five major European languages. By using vivid language and forceful characterization, he has produced a book that is as much a work of literature as a contribution to scientific history.

'One of the glories of twentieth-century writing.'
Observer

PAST MASTERS

A wide range of unique, short, clear introductions to the lives and work of the world's most influential thinkers. Written by experts, they cover the history of ideas from Aristotle to Wittgenstein. Readers need no previous knowledge of the subject, so they are ideal for students and general readers alike.

Each book takes as its main focus the thought and work of its subject. There is a short section on the life and a final chapter on the legacy and influence of the thinker. A section of further reading helps in further research.

The series continues to grow, and future Past Masters will include **Owen Gingerich** on *Copernicus*, **R G Frey** on *Joseph Butler*, **Bhiku Parekh** on *Gandhi*, **Christopher Taylor** on *Socrates*, **Michael Inwood** on *Heidegger*, and **Peter Ghosh** on *Weber*.

MASTERS

RUSSELL

A. C. Grayling

Bertrand Russell (1872–1970) is one of the most famous and important philosophers of the twentieth century. In this account of his life and work A. C. Grayling introduces both his technical contributions to logic and philosophy, and his wide-ranging views on education, politics, war, and sexual morality. Russell is credited with being one of the prime movers of Analytic Philosophy, and with having played a part in the revolution in social attitudes witnessed throughout the twentieth-century world. This introduction gives a clear survey of Russell's achievements across their whole range.

OXFORD

FOUR ESSAYS ON LIBERTY

Isaiah Berlin

'those who value liberty for its own sake believe that to be free to choose, and not to be chosen for, is an inalienable ingredient in what makes human beings human'
Introduction to *Four Essays On Liberty*

Political Ideas in the Twentieth Century
Historical Inevitability
Two Concepts of Liberty
John Stuart Mill and the Ends of Life

These four essays deal with the various aspects of individual liberty, including the distinction between positive and negative liberty and the necessity of rejecting determinism if we wish to keep hold of the notions of human responsibility and freedom.

'practically every paragraph introduces us to half a dozen new ideas and as many thinkers—the landscape flashes past, peopled with familiar and unfamiliar people, all arguing incessantly'
New Society

OXFORD

RETHINKING LIFE AND DEATH
THE COLLAPSE OF OUR TRADITIONAL ETHICS

Peter Singer

A victim of the Hillsborough Disaster in 1989, Anthony Bland lay in hospital in a coma being fed liquid food by a pump, via a tube passing through his nose and into his stomach. On 4 February 1993 Britain's highest court ruled that doctors attending him could lawfully act to end his life.

Our traditional ways of thinking about life and death are collapsing. In a world of respirators and embryos stored for years in liquid nitrogen, we can no longer take the sanctity of human life as the cornerstone of our ethical outlook.

In this controversial book Peter Singer argues that we cannot deal with the crucial issues of death, abortion, euthanasia and the rights of nonhuman animals unless we sweep away the old ethic and build something new in its place.

Singer outlines a new set of commandments, based on compassion and commonsense, for the decisions everyone must make about life and death.

OPUS

A HISTORICAL INTRODUCTION TO THE PHILOSOPHY OF SCIENCE

John Losee

This challenging introduction, designed for readers without an extensive knowledge of formal logic or of the history of science, looks at the long-argued questions raised by philosophers and scientists about the proper evaluation of scientific interpretations. It offers an historical exposition of differing views on issues such as the merits of competing theories; the interdependence of observation and theory; and the nature of scientific progress. The author looks at explanations given by Plato, Aristotle, and Pythagoras, and through to Bacon and Descartes, to Nagel, Kuhn, and Laudan.

This edition incorporates an extended discussion of contemporary developments and changes within the history of science, and examines recent controversies and the search for a non-prescriptive philosophy of science.

'a challenging interdisciplinary work'
New Scientist

Oxford
Paperback
Reference

OXFORD PAPERBACK REFERENCE

From *Art and Artists* to *Zoology*, the Oxford Paperback Reference series offers the very best subject reference books at the most affordable prices.

Authoritative, accessible, and up to date, the series features dictionaries in key student areas, as well as a range of fascinating books for a general readership. Included are such well-established titles as Fowler's *Modern English Usage*, Margaret Drabble's *Concise Companion to English Literature*, and the bestselling science and medical dictionaries.

The series has now been relaunched in handsome new covers. Highlights include new editions of some of the most popular titles, as well as brand new paperback reference books on *Politics*, *Philosophy*, and *Twentieth-Century Poetry*.

With new titles being constantly added, and existing titles regularly updated, Oxford Paperback Reference is unrivalled in its breadth of coverage and expansive publishing programme. New dictionaries of *Film*, *Economics*, *Linguistics*, *Architecture*, *Archaeology*, *Astronomy*, and *The Bible* are just a few of those coming in the future.

Oxford
Paperback
Reference

THE CONCISE OXFORD COMPANION
TO ENGLISH LITERATURE

*Edited by Margaret Drabble and
Jenny Stringer*

Derived from the acclaimed *Oxford Companion to English Literature*, the concise maintains the wide coverage of its parent volume. It is an indispensable, compact guide to all aspects of English literature. For this revised edition, existing entries have been fully updated and revised with 60 new entries added on contemporary writers.

* Over 5,000 entries on the lives and works of authors, poets and playwrights

* The most comprehensive and authoritative paperback guide to English literature

* New entries include Peter Ackroyd, Martin Amis, Toni Morrison, and Jeanette Winterson

* New appendices list major literary prize-winners

From the reviews of its parent volume:

'It earns its place at the head of the best sellers: every home should have one'
Sunday Times